PARIS

FODOR'S
TRAVEL PUBLICATIONS

NEW YORK • TORONTO
LONDON • SYDNEY • AUCKLAND

WWW.FODORS.COM

CONTENTS

157

92

234

124

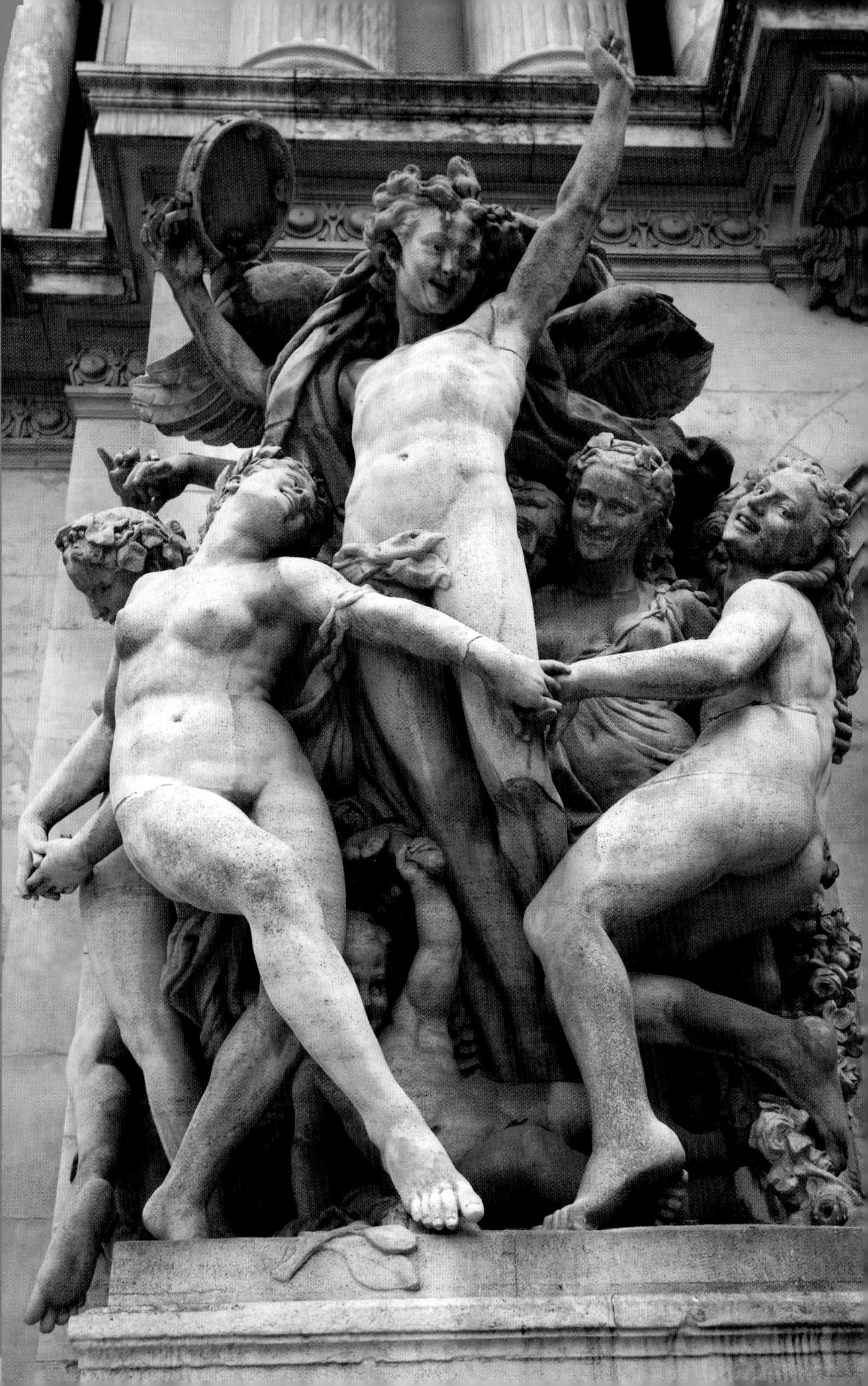

UNDERSTANDING PARIS

Understanding Paris is an introduction to the city, its geography, economy, history and its people. Living Paris gets under the skin of Paris today, while The Story of Paris takes you through the city's past.

Paris is a seductive capital city, legendary for its cuisine, fashion, art collections and architectural beauty. It is a vibrant international city and the heart of France's political, economic, social and cultural life. Although it is thoroughly modern, reminders of the past are vital to the tourism economy, and the government strictly enforces building codes and protects historic monuments. So change comes in smaller ways — in fashions, food styles and shop facades. Parisians are still as willing to take to the streets in protest as they were during the Revolution, although they can also demonstrate a strong conservative, conformist streak. The city is making a concerted effort to help visitors feel welcome and Parisians are friendlier and more helpful than they are sometimes reputed to be.

FINDING YOUR WAY AROUND

Paris has no shortage of must-see sights, but if you spend your visit dashing between them you'll miss out on the essence of the city. The secret to glimpsing Paris's heart is to enjoy the humble pleasures as well as the world-famous landmarks. Make time to people-watch in a café in St-Germain-des-Prés or in the increasingly fashionable Marais district, relax in the peaceful Jardin du Palais Royal or shop for cheese at one of the local markets.

The Métro is a good way of getting around, with stops by all the key sights, but to really get to know the layout of the city, you can't beat walking between the *quartiers* (districts). Try wandering from St-Germain-des-Prés, through the Latin Quarter, to the Île de la Cité, or from Bastille to Le Marais and then across to the Centre Georges Pompidou. In addition to its *quartiers*, identified by name, Paris is broken into *arrondissements*, numbered 1 to 20. These spiral out in a clockwise direction from the Louvre. You can usually tell which *arrondissement* your destination is in by looking at the last two digits of the postal code.

Paris is split in two by the curving river Seine, with the northern section called the Right Bank and the smaller southern part called the Left Bank. Thirty-seven bridges connect the two sides. Northeast of the Latin Quarter, two islands sit in the middle of the Seine: the historic Île de la Cité and the tiny Île St-Louis.

THE ECONOMY

Paris and the rest of the Île-de-France region are the economic powerhouse of France, accounting for 30 per cent of French GDP. The Île de France has a population of 11 million and is home to more than 650,000 companies, while Paris has almost 2.25 million residents and 300,000 companies.

Tourism is one of its major economic strengths — Paris attracted 28 million visitors in 2010. Other key sectors are financial services, information technology, digital imaging, fashion, design and creative industries. In 2010, the Economic Intelligence Unit also placed Paris at the top of its list of the 132 most expensive cities in the world to live in. As in many other European countries, France's economic growth is currently sluggish, although less than it was in 2006, and reform of state employment and pension laws has been high on the agenda during the first decade of the new millennium. Trade unions and worker's groups have been staging stiff opposition to any loss of privileges.

POLITICS

Paris is the undisputed heart of national power, although the government has been making some moves to decentralize and devolve power to the regions. The 2007 national elections were the most keenly contested in recent history, with two charismatic candidates— Ségolène Royal on the left, the first woman to stand, and Nicolas Sarkozy on the right. Sarkozy was the victor, and by a larger majority than the pundits had predicted.

Paris is run by the popular Socialist mayor Bertrand Delanoë, who is working on making the city greener. He angered motorists by closing the highway running along the Seine's Right Bank to traffic in the summer, turning part of it into Paris Plage, an urban beach and pleasure park, complete with sand and deck chairs. As it turned out, the new beach has become highly popular—but so, too, has Mayor Delanoë, who is openly gay. The citizens have bestowed on him an affectionate nickname, 'Notre Dame de Paris' (our lady of Paris).

LANGUAGE AND SOCIETY

French is spoken by the entire population of France, although the country has some regional dialects. Most children study English, and many Parisians make the effort to speak it to visitors. The French are extremely proud of their language, however, and make a concerted effort to protect it from anglicization by coining French replacements for such words as Walkman *(balladeur)* and email *(mèl)*.

Paris is a multicultural city, with large communities of people of North African, African, Vietnamese, Chinese and other origins. Like most major cities, it is undergoing gentrification, with families and people on lower incomes pushed out to the suburbs as property prices rise in the central districts.

Crime rates are still on the increase, but Paris remains a fairly safe city for visitors, as long as they take reasonable precautions to protect their belongings from pickpockets.

PARIS'S DISTRICTS AT A GLANCE

Latin Quarter (Left Bank, east): Paris's heart of learning since the Middle Ages, packed with churches, medieval alleyways and the beautiful Jardin du Luxembourg.
St-Germain-des-Prés (Left Bank, central): Bordering the Latin Quarter and packed with cafés and bookshops.
Montparnasse (Left Bank, south): Dominated by the giant Tour Montparnasse.
Chaillot (Right Bank, west): Its focal point is the Palais de Chaillot, with its wonderful views across the Seine to the Eiffel Tower.

Champs-Élysées (Right Bank, west-central): Paris's most famous avenue is packed with shops, cinemas and cafés, and crowned by the Arc de Triomphe.
Faubourg St-Honoré (Right Bank, north of Champs-Élysées): The place to head for haute couture.
Les Halles (Right Bank, central): Once the hub of market life, Les Halles now comprises a vast modern shopping complex, together with what is probably Paris's most confusing Métro station.
Le Marais (Right Bank, east-central): Trendy cafés, shops and avant-garde art galleries. The Centre Georges Pompidou sits on its western border.
Bastille (Right Bank, east): Once the launch pad of the Revolution, Bastille is now a fashionable nightspot, close to Le Marais.
Île de la Cité (on the Seine): This hectic island is the birthplace of Paris, and home to Notre-Dame, the Conciergerie and Sainte-Chapelle.
Île St-Louis (on the Seine): Smaller and quieter than its more famous cousin, the Île de la Cité.
Pigalle (Right Bank, south of Montmartre): The infamous red-light district.
Montmartre (Right Bank, far north): This former village, on a hill overlooking the city, has two of Paris's most famous landmarks—Sacré-Cœur and, on the Pigalle border, the Moulin Rouge.

Opposite Paris is famed for its high fashion and elegant shops, particularly on the Right Bank of the Seine
Below *Distinctive Parisian street signs*

AROUND THE TOUR EIFFEL

Hôtel Duc de St-Simon (▷ 103) This hotel occupies a beautifully decorated 18th-century mansion near the boulevard St-Germain.

Hôtel Square (▷ 103) An urban-chic 4-star hotel, Square is close to the Eiffel Tower.

Musée d'Orsay (▷ 80–83) This former train station hosts a stunning collection of Impressionist paintings and a lot more.

Musée du Quai Branly (▷ 84) The city's most innovative museum celebrates the equal dignities of the world's cultures, with more than 300,000 non-European artefacts showcased.

Musée Rodin (▷ 85) This wins a mention as much for its idyllic surroundings as its art. Auguste Rodin's mesmerizing sculptures are situated around a soothing garden.

Palais de Chaillot—La Cité de l'Architecture et du Patrimoine (▷ 86–87) This is the world's largest architectural museum, spanning 12 centuries of French architecture. Its central terrace has wonderful views of the Eiffel Tower.

Tour Eiffel (▷ 90–95) Test your nerves on the third level, 280m (918ft) above ground.

Above The Eiffel Tower, Paris's most famous landmark
Opposite left The Ritz—luxury accommodation in the heart of the city
Opposite right Fauchon is a gourmet's paradise

Tour Montparnasse (▷ 89) Take the elevator for the 59th-floor terrace for vertigo-inducing views of the city.

LATIN QUARTER, ST-GERMAIN AND ISLANDS

Café de Flore (▷ 141) Follow in the footsteps of Jean-Paul Sartre.

La Coupole (▷ 143) This art deco brasserie was once frequented by Pablo Picasso.

Les Deux Magots (▷ 141) Hemingway was a frequent visitor to this café-bar in St-Germain-des-Prés.

L'Hôtel (▷ 144) Oscar Wilde spent his last days at this deluxe 4-star hotel.

Musée National du Moyen Âge—Thermes de Cluny (▷ 122–123) This 15th-century mansion is home to a fascinating collection of medieval art, religious items and day-to-day objects.

Notre-Dame (▷ 124–127) France's most visited religious building has wonderful views from its towers.

Panthéon (▷ 128) You can see the Eiffel Tower from the front steps, but for the best panoramas, climb the 206 steps to the circular colonnade.

Pont des Arts (▷ 120) The breathtaking view downriver takes in the length of the Louvre along the Right Bank.

Shakespeare and Company (▷ 140) This famous American bookshop is alongside the Seine.

La Tour d'Argent (▷ 143) Exquisite French cuisine is served in a chic interior with great views.

MARAIS AND BASTILLE

Antik Batik (▷ 174) For ethnic chic visit this shop.

Café Beaubourg (▷ 175) This trendy café is near the Centre Georges Pompidou.

Centre Georges Pompidou (▷ 156–161) It's not to everyone's taste, but this eye-catching venue is a must for students and admirers of modern art.

Musée Carnavalet (▷ 164–165) Paris's history is brought to life with lavish re-creations of period rooms, memorabilia from the Revolution and prehistoric finds.

Musée Picasso (▷ 167) Paintings, sculptures and drawings by the great 20th-century artist are displayed in the beautiful Hôtel Salé.

Pavillon de la Reine (▷ 179) Louis XIII's wife once lived in this 17th-century residence, now a hotel, on the place des Vosges.

LOUVRE AND CHAMPS-ÉLYSÉES

L'Arc (▷ 213) The beautiful and the moneyed flock to this popular club.

Arc de Triomphe (▷ 187–189) The arch is the focal point for some of France's most famous celebrations.

Fauchon (▷ 212) The best of French food shopping can be found here—at a price.

Galeries Lafayette (▷ 212) Shop in an opulent setting of stained glass and gilt in this vast department store.

Grande Arche (▷ 254) It's not yet as famous as the other landmarks mentioned here, but this colossal marble-clad arch symbolizes Paris's eye to the future.

Guy Savoy (▷ 215) This gastronomic temple is close to the Champs-Élysées.

Market (▷ 215) In this contemporary venue you will find a raw bar and fusion food.

Musée du Louvre (▷ 199–203) This is one of the world's most famous art galleries—but you'll have to fight your way through crowds to see the *Mona Lisa*.

Place de la Concorde (▷ 206) From here, look northwest along the Champs-Élysées to the Arc de Triomphe, southeast through the Jardin des Tuileries, and southwest across the Seine to the Palais Bourbon.

Ritz (▷ 217) Former guests of this elegant and luxurious hotel include Coco Chanel and Ernest Hemingway.

Spring (▷ 215) At this wacky, madcap restaurant, which is truly unmissable, a set four-course dinner is served on the dot at 8.30pm.

MONTMARTRE

Fourmi (▷ 239) This bar, with its retro interior, is popular with arty types.

Hôtel Amour (▷ 242) An uncluttered hotel in the up-and-coming area known these days as SoPi (for South Pigalle), the Amour is owned by a group of local artists. Some of its rooms have been decorated by their friends.

Marché aux Puces de St-Ouen (▷ 225) Browse in this vast flea market and you may find an antique or two.

Mercure Montmartre (▷ 243) There are stunning views from the rooms at this modern 4-star hotel in the heart of Montmartre.

Le Moulin de la Galette (▷ 241) A restaurant named after the nearby Galette windmill, this has been the subject of many paintings by great artists including Van Gogh and Toulouse-Lautrec.

Moulin Rouge (▷ 225) A Parisian institution, the Red Windmill has been a saucy cabaret venue since 1889.

Parc de la Turlure (▷ 237) Small and out of the way, this park in Montmartre has lovely views over Paris and an unusual view of the northern side of Sacré-Cœur.

Sacré-Cœur (▷ 233–235) This glistening basilica crowns Montmartre.

TOP EXPERIENCES

Get a bird's-eye view of Paris at night by climbing the Eiffel Tower (▷ 90–95) or the Arc de Triomphe (▷ 186–189).

Sit in a café in St-Germain-des-Prés and watch the world go by, or find a bench in the animated Jardin du Luxembourg or Jardin des Tuileries.

Take a boat trip along the Seine—it's a cliché but it really is a great way to appreciate the city's major landmarks (▷ 210–211).

Visit place des Vosges (▷ 169) on a Sunday afternoon, when the cafés are packed with Parisians relaxing to the sounds of street musicians.

Take advantage of late-opening nights at the Louvre (Wednesdays and Fridays; ▷ 199–203) and Musée d'Orsay (Thursdays; ▷ 80–83), when it is quieter.

Stroll around the Marais to soak up the Parisian atmosphere. It easily rivals the Latin Quarter and, unlike much of Paris, it's still buzzing on Sundays.

Stroll along the Champs-Élysées, Paris's most famous tree-lined avenue.

Take the Métro up to Montmartre for a taste of village life and wonderful views of the city.

Visit Notre-Dame cathedral just before a service.

Haggle at one of the city's markets (▷ 225 and Shopping listings), where you can buy anything from cheese and olives to furniture and chandeliers.

Leave your Métro *carnet* behind for an afternoon and take a wander—it's the best way to get to know the layout of the city.

Enjoy a cruise on the Canal Saint-Martin between Port de l'Arsenal and Parc de la Villette, past chestnut trees, squares and delightfully retro bistros and cafés.

See a performance at the prestigious Opéra Palais Garnier or the striking Opéra Bastille, or experience the glitz of a show at the famous Moulin Rouge.

Escape the city and enjoy some fresher air in the leafy Bois de Vincennes or Bois de Boulogne (▷ 250–251).

Stroll through the elegant 19th-century shopping arcades known as Les Galeries (▷ 191).

Below Galerie Vivienne, the most fashionable of the Galeries

LIVING PARIS

Since Paris no longer has a monarchy, it would be easy to assume the class system is dead and buried. Wrong. In this city, one is defined by the table one chooses. No one eats for mere sustenance—food is a lifestyle statement, an evening's entertainment and a way of life. At the sharp end, new chefs flit in and out of vogue with the changing of the seasons. Each September's newspaper reviews can determine the fortunes of a fashionable restaurant as surely as a drama critic's pen assures the life or death of a new musical on Broadway. However, the chic eateries are but the tip of a gastronomic iceberg. Regional restaurants reflect the diversity of French cuisine, with special dishes from Auvergne and Alsace, the Loire and Provence, offering French out-of-towners a taste of home and Parisians a hint of what lies beyond the city. Café culture has an equally wide following, with the smart crowd sipping designer coffees on terraces outside the more fashionable museums and blue-collar Parisians chatting in slang at the zinc counters of their local bars.

LE TRAIN BLEU

High above the 21st-century fleet of TGV high-speed trains at Gare de Lyon nestles a relic from travel's golden age. Le Train Bleu is a belle-époque station brasserie of the type that has been demolished elsewhere on Europe's flagship railway system to make room for high-tech efficiency and cutting-edge design. The restaurant was featured in the 1972 film *Travels with My Aunt* and on news broadcasts when President Mitterrand famously entertained Margaret Thatcher there. Ornate mirrors, chandeliers and paintings have been lovingly restored to match the moustachioed waiters, with their starched ankle-length aprons. Service is as unhurried as ever, and it would not be unusual to spend longer over lunch than on the three-hour journey to the south of France.

Clockwise from above *Berthillon, on the Île St-Louis, draws the crowds to sample its wonderful ice cream; fine dining is synonymous with Paris—Le Train Bleu restaurant in the Gare de Lyon epitomizes elegance and style; the Jules Verne restaurant on level two of the Eiffel Tower is literally haute cuisine*

BISTRONOMIE

'Bistronomie' is the welcome re-emergence of little bistros run by well-known chefs. Some are owned by stars of show business who offer gourmet meals in their own image. Actors Gérard Depardieu and Carole Bouquet own Fontaine Gaillon (1 place Gaillon, 75002; tel 01 47 42 63 22; www.la-fontaine-gaillon. com) and the nearby oyster and seafood bar L'Ecaille de la Fontaine (15 de la rue Gaillon, 75002; tel 01 47 42 02 99). Catherine Deneuve's restaurant-tea room is in the historic Panthéon cinema (Le Salon du Panthéon, 13 rue Victor-Cousin, 75005; tel 01 56 24 88 80; www. whynotproductions.fr/ pantheon) and rocker Eddy Mitchell has chosen Thai restaurant Oth Sombath (184 rue du Faubourg-St-Honoré, 75008; tel 01 42 56 55 55; www.othsombath.com).

LE FAST FOOD

After decades of barely concealed hostility to anything other than a leisurely meal, Paris is learning to love *le fast food*, or at any rate *le Marks & Spencer sandwich*. When the Paris branch of this British institution closed in 2001 (to prime ministerial protest), a concerted campaign began to bring back M&S. When Marks and Spencer had a change of heart in April 2011 and announced they would be opening a new store on the Champs-Élysée, there was unbridled enthusiasm from the French press. Fans of *le fast food* also have an unlikely ally in France's most decorated chef, Alain Ducasse, who reinvented the deli sandwich bar with the opening of BE Boulangépicier, his stylish interpretation of the deli. Here, eat-in customers enjoy their meals standing up.

NEW TRENDS

World cuisine is on the menu in Paris where dishes from every continent make a melting pot of flavours and dining experiences. Japanese cooking is sweeping through the capital and chef Alain Ducasse has taken up the trend with 'bento dej' (bento lunch) which he offers at his restaurant Spoon (▷ 215). There is also a devoted following of molecular cooking where terms such as liquid nitrogen and spherification appear on the menu. Renowned chef Pierre Gagnaire is famous for his culinary wizardry at his eponymous restaurant (6 rue Balzac, 75008; tel 01 58 36 12 50; www. pierre-gagnaire.com) in collaboration with the chemist Hervé This.

THE STAR OF STARS

In France the only measure of culinary success is the Michelin star. There are currently 10 restaurants in Paris that hold the highest accolade of three stars; 17 have two stars and 70 more have one star. Entry into this exclusive club guarantees success. The current 'King of the Kitchen' has to be Alain Ducasse. The only chef to have been awarded three Michelin stars for restaurants in three countries, he received his first star at La Terrasse restaurant in Juan-les-Pins in 1984. He is executive chef at Plaza Athénée restaurant on avenue Montaigne, and in 2007 he took the helm of the Jules Verne restaurant in the Eiffel Tower, where the cuisine is as spectacular as the views.

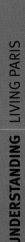

hybris hybris hybris h

Parisian style takes a lot of effort or none at all. It is the expensively coutured mannequin walking her identically attired and tinted dog along the Champs-Élysées. Then again, it is also the scruffy unshaven student with his upturned collar and dangling cigarette, flirting with the pretty girl outside a Métro station.

Paris loves style, in that it celebrates those who are happy with and proud of their own image. Parisian style is as much about lifestyle as the packaging. It is not enough simply to wear the right clothes, you must wear them in the right places, be it a sophisticated bar in the 8th *arrondissement* or a hang-out for poets in the Bastille district. Just as new designers emerge with each fashion week, so up-and-coming streets stake their claim on the consumer map: People shopping for traditional art and antiques choose the galleries by the Louvre and Musée d'Orsay; those on the cutting edge prefer the racier art showrooms around the quai d'Austerlitz; and the truly self-confident set their own trends with finds from the flea markets.

HAUTE COUTURE FOR LESS

Every well-tailored Parisian knows the avenue Matignon, but they may not be so ready to admit familiarity with the rue de la Pompe. After all, it would be folly to confess to having spent a mere fraction of the showroom price on a genuine Moschino or Versace original. Nevertheless, canny good dressers will brave the hordes picking their paths through the racks at the seven Réciproque stores on this street in order to snatch up Lacroix and Dior. Since celebrities rarely wear an outfit again after it has been photographed by the paparazzi, Réciproque buys them to resell. To deter potential thieves, Chanel suits have their prized buttons removed, to be sewn back on once the transaction is complete!

Clockwise from above *Parisians seem to have an innate sense of style in every aspect of life; a Jean Paul Gaultier haute couture design is modelled on the catwalk; chocolatiers collaborate with couturiers at the* Salon du Chocolat

OPEN SECRETS OF THE LEFT BANK

The nearest the art and antiques dealers of the Left Bank get to shouting about their wares is during the Cinq Jours de l'Objet Extraordinaire, in late spring. The Carré Rive Gauche is an association of galleries located along the tributaries of the rue du Bac and rue de Lille. For five days, the dealers choose to flaunt their prize possessions. Each shop selects one special item to promote. To celebrate this uncharacteristic sharing of buried treasure, red carpets appear outside and abundant floral displays grace the doorways. In recent years, visitors have been invited to admire Venetian chandeliers that were long hidden away in a Sicilian palazzo, Egyptian textiles and rare Beauvais tapestries.

IT'S A GIRL THING

No matter how expensive the hotel or how hard you push the credit card, as a casual visitor to Paris you can usually just look on in envy at the assurance of true society *Parisienne*. But now female visitors have the opportunity to join, albeit temporarily, the ladies who lunch, women who shop and glamorous patrons of the arts. For a price, women staying at the Le Meurice hotel, which overlooks the Jardin des Tuileries in rue de Rivoli, are paired with a chic local girlfriend for the day and taken out on the town. They can visit Left Bank artists' studios for a private viewing, stop off for a bite to eat and a gossip at the latest see-and-be-seen restaurant, or go shopping with the girls, touring the boutiques of up-and-coming fashion designers.

CHOCCY COUTURE

Since the opening of the Carrousel du Louvre, the catwalk has rarely been free from the popping of flashbulbs and the scrutiny of the fickle arbiters of style. But between the prêt-à-porter shows and Paris Fashion Week, there is one event where critics agree that every item of clothing is good enough to eat. Edible couture is the highlight of the autumn *Salon du Chocolat* (www. salonduchocolat.fr), with a catwalk show combining the skills of the finest chocolatiers with the city's daring designers. Despite the irony of painting supermodels in calorie-laden treats, the event appeals to those who like their style off the shoulder as much as on the tip of the tongue.

IN THE FAST LANE

The Champs-Élysées is packed with traffic even in the small hours, but once a month the famous avenue closes to cars. To benefit from this, be sure to pack your in-line skates. Pari-Roller is the social event of the week, as tens of thousands gather near Montparnasse station on Friday evening. Skaters start to gather at 9.30pm and at 10pm the crowd becomes a parade and sets off to explore the city. Strictly for experienced skaters, the route varies each week. Itineraries are posted on the website (www.pari-roller. com) before the event. Once a month, the skaters finish the two-hour event with a high-speed descent down the Champs-Élysées from place Charles-de-Gaulle.

There are few parts of Paris that don't invoke the memory of the lives of the artists or of the city's great literary heritage. Some are marked indelibly on tourist maps; others are less obvious: A visitor taking a child to play in Le Jardin de Champs-Élysées would be recreating moments in the life of Marcel Proust retold in his *À la Recherche du Temps Perdu* (translated as either *In Search of Lost Times* or *Remembrance of Things Past)*. There are also the cafés where both Rousseau and Sartre drank coffee, though not at the same time, and restaurants where Thomas Jefferson and Benjamin Franklin no doubt discussed the American Declaration of Independence. In a dozen or more generations, Paris's contribution to art and literature has been staggering. The city itself has bred some of the greatest artistic and literary figures in the world, from Voltaire to Jean-Paul Sartre, while its cultural vibrancy has attracted the cream of the world's most artistically gifted people, including Dutch painters of the High Renaissance, Pablo Picasso, and great writers of the 19th and 20th centuries. Paris has also played a starring role as the setting of works of art—by painters like Van Gogh and writers like Victor Hugo—and as the stunning backdrop to motion pictures.

Clockwise from above *Three of Claude Monet's Impressionist paintings on display in the Musée d'Orsay; Salvador Dalí lived and worked in Paris for several years, joining the Surrealist group of artists in Montparnasse; the art deco tomb of Oscar Wilde in Père Lachaise cemetery*

SLEEPLESS IN AUTEUIL

Marcel Proust (1871–1922) was born in Auteuil, a western suburb just across the river from the Latin Quarter, and lived his entire life in that corner of Paris. Here he wrote one of the world's most respected—and most challenging—pieces of literature, comprising a series of novels in six volumes.

Early parts of *À la Recherche du Temps Perdu* appeared in *Le Figaro* in 1912, but it was not easy getting it published. It was turned down by André Gide (1869–1951) when Gide was editor of the *Nouvelle Revue Française*, and then by a less notable publisher who confessed: 'I may be dense. But I just don't understand why a man should take 30 pages to describe how he rolls around in bed before sleep. It made my head swim'.

QUI EST-CE QUI?

Any list of great names associated with Paris would read like a Who's Who. In a single year in the city (1875–76), writer Henry James met Ivan Turgenev, Gustave Flaubert, Émile Zola, Edmond de Goncourt, Guy de Maupassant and Alphonse Daudet. Paris-born Claude Monet was brought up in Normandy but returned to the city which features in many of his paintings. His friend Edouard Manet started his career in 1858 with a painting of a man in a shadowy Paris backstreet, called *The Absinthe Drinker*. In Les Deux Magots and Café de Flore in Paris, Sartre and Simone de Beauvoir thrashed out their caffeine-fuelled existentialist philosophy. And the friendship between F. Scott Fitzgerald and his great American contemporary Ernest Hemingway was forged in Paris in 1925.

IN DEATH AS IN LIFE

'Who-did-what-where' tours around Paris are available in various forms although, typically, the haunts of the visual artists are around Montmartre while those of the writers are in the Latin Quarter. Other options include tours taking in the homes associated with various arts celebrities, viewing sights that figure in great paintings — like Van Gogh's Montmartre windmill, or a view of the Seine from a Monet painting — or in novels like Victor Hugo's *Hunchback of Notre-Dame*, or following the trail of the films *Amélie* and *The Da Vinci Code*. One trail that is surprisingly popular is of the graveyards of Paris — Montparnasse (▷ 73) and Père Lachaise (▷ 155) where a surprising number of the great, the good, the talented and the tragic keep each other company in death as they did in life.

AVIDA DOLLARS

It was in Paris that Salvador Dalí (1904–89) helped to create the 'marriage' of painting with motion pictures. He came to the French capital in 1926 to meet his compatriot hero Pablo Picasso. During his stay, Dalí teamed up with the Paris-based Spanish filmmaker, Luis Buñuel, and added his scary surrealism to a film called *Un Chien Andalou* which wowed the artistic community. He met and married his lifelong muse, Gala, in Paris, and mixed with many intellectuals including master-surrealist André Breton (1896–1966). Breton and Dalí worked together but later fell out over Dalí's suspected fascist sympathies and later his commercialism. After Dalí's move to the USA, where he worked in Hollywood, Breton nicknamed him Avida Dollars — an anagram of his name which translates as 'hungry for dollars'.

DYING BEYOND HIS MEANS

It was in Paris that Oscar Wilde famously and prophetically proclaimed: 'I am dying beyond my means'. Sure enough, he did die — in a hotel on rue des Beaux Arts, (now simply called L'Hôtel, ▷ 144), having fled to Paris after his disgrace and imprisonment in Britain. The management of the hotel insist that the great Irish playwright and author of *The Picture of Dorian Gray* died in one of the downstairs rooms. However, respected biographies of Wilde, based on eye-witness accounts, describe him as being in his room with a close friend at his bedside. Predictably, he died leaving his hotel bill unpaid. He was buried in the Cimetière de Bagneux outside Paris but his body was later moved to Père Lachaise cemetery (▷ 155) in the east of the city, marked by an art deco monument designed by Jacob Epstein.

For a city that is so proud of its artistic and architectural heritage, Paris is surprisingly open to new and challenging ideas. Somehow, the integration of the classic and the avant-garde is irresistibly successful. One of the most controversial encounters between old and new was I.M. Pei's Pyramid in the courtyard of the Louvre. Some people were appalled at the idea of setting such an uncompromisingly modern structure within the arms of the palace. Yet the brilliant play of light and water not only revived the museum, but focused attention on the beauty of the original building. Likewise, the 1970s Centre Georges Pompidou stands next to the 16th-century church of St-Merri, on the Left Bank, the shadows of the 1980s Institut du Monde Arabe mingle with those of Notre-Dame, on the Île de la Cité, and the recently opened Cité de l'Architecture et du Patrimoine is a splendid monument to design in the elegant Palais de Chaillot. The same refreshing attitude marks out the city's cultural life. Where else are you as likely to see a classic Katharine Hepburn film as a contemporary Eddie Murphy flick? As varied a crowd will pack a church to enjoy an evening of Vivaldi as will join a jazz or blues jam session by street musicians.

THE FILM THAT SAVED THE STATION

When Orson Welles came to Europe to film Franz Kafka's *The Trial* (1962), he saved a Paris landmark from demolition. Having just learned that the production had run out of money and could no longer afford Yugoslav locations, he looked across the river from his room in the Hôtel Meurice and saw two full moons— the twin rose windows of the abandoned Gare d'Orsay. He was inspired to film the rest of the movie inside the imposing railway station, so Orsay became a cathedral and a court of law. The station had a happier ending than the movie, since filming delayed demolition and gave protesters time to lobby the Ministry of Culture to convert it into a building that became one of the world's great museums.

Clockwise from above *The Pyramid designed by I.M. Pei was a controversial addition to the Louvre; Richard Rogers and Renzo Piano's 'inside out' Centre Georges Pompidou; the former Gare d'Orsay, saved from demolition by Orson Welles, is now a principal museum of modern art*

BIGGER THAN THE BIG SCREEN

No matter how huge the blockbuster, there is one cinema in Paris that can always be relied upon to upstage the action on screen. Le Grand Rex, on the boulevard Poissonnière, is the last of the world's extravagant picture palaces of the 1930s still operating as a mainstream cinema. A depiction of a fabulous Mediterranean night sky adorns the interior of the spectacular domed building, and there is an arched art deco stage that once hosted lavish shows. You can rent an audioguide for a fabulous high-tech walk backstage, through and above the screen, where you'll face a life-size King Kong that escapes its tethers and terrorizes chorus girls waiting in the wings. Eventually, you'll become the unsuspecting star of a film premiere, performing on the big screen alongside some of the world's most famous movie greats.

MONSIEUR SHAKESPEARE'S FIRST NIGHT

Shakespeare is big in Paris. His plays pack commercial theatres and the Bois de Boulogne has a garden planted with flowers, herbs and trees mentioned in his works. But one play had to wait until 1999 before receiving its Parisian premiere—the jingoistic *Henry V*, in which English bowmen decimate the French army at the Battle of Agincourt. In fact, outside the village itself, Agincourt remains relatively unknown in France. Director Jean-Louis Benoît risked opening his Avignon festival production in the capital, managing to blame the defeat of the French army on an inept and weak monarchy. The choice of venue was laden with ironies—La Cartoucherie, a former French army arsenal, is in the grounds of the Château de Vincennes, where the victorious Henry V died in 1422.

REDESIGNING PARIS

He was the man who changed the face of café society, with the influential and much missed Café Costes. Philippe Starck first came to the public's attention when he was commissioned to strip François Mitterrand's presidential apartments at the Élysée Palace of their stuffy imperial furnishings and replace them with the bare minimum.

Today, Starck's designs are the sign that you have arrived in a city where style is more important than budget. The completely renovated Royal Monceau Raffles hotel is Starck's latest luxury hospitality project in the city. Nightclubs and bars that have undergone the Philippe Starck treatment are strictly reserved for the beautiful people. Weekenders coming by train from London can imbibe the Starck chic before reaching town, in Eurostar trains revitalized by the designer.

SUMMER CINEMA

Summer is the season of cinema in the open air—and in the most unlikely places. From mid-July until the end of August huge screens are erected on the lawns of the Parc de la Villette for the annual Cinéma en Plein Air festival. Specializing in original-language movies with French subtitles, this is the big event of the Parisian picnic season. For the last fortnight of the event, the entire city takes part in Cinéma au Clair de Lune, a series of moonlight screenings in appropriate locations. Previous festival audiences have delighted in *Le Fabuleux Destin d'Amélie Poulain* shown in the streets of Montmartre and the 1947 version of *Les Misérables* screened outside Victor Hugo's former home on place des Vosges. Other venues include the canal banks where seafaring yarns were shown and the outlying parks featuring major pastoral idylls.

ENTERTAINMENT IN PARIS

Paris comes with a musical soundtrack. Any place that has inspired so many classic love songs is bound to lure musicians from all corners. On the Métro at all hours, outside packed restaurants at noon and in shop doorways by night, itinerant musicians play popular tunes. The music reaches its crescendo at the *Fête de la Musique* on 21 June, with live bands and orchestras in the main railway stations and huge stages erected in public squares for a night of free concerts. Music cuts across society, no more so than at the end of the Gay Pride celebrations in June, when party animals of all persuasions dance on the banks of the Seine as the celebrations end with the several-thousand strong dawn chorus of *La Vie en Rose*. Indoor entertainment ranges from productions at the concert halls and the two opera houses to feathered and sequinned showgirl performances. Between the two extremes is a drama scene as varied as that in the West End or on Broadway. Many English-language productions are also staged.

THE FABULOUS PARIS OF AMÉLIE

Jean-Pierre Jeunet's cinematic vision *Le Fabuleux Destin d'Amélie Poulain* (2001) re-established Paris as a city for smooching. Keen to capture for themselves a hint of the romance, visitors to the city eagerly scout locations from the film's most memorable moments.

Much of the movie was shot around Montmartre, where the Métro station and streets are just as bustling and picturesque in real life as on screen. The actual café and shops featured in the film are on rue des Trois Frères.

Other key scenes took place at the Gare de l'Est and Gare du Nord, behind which lies Amélie's hideaway, the Canal St-Martin. The funfair, where actress Audrey Tautou and actor Mathieu Kassowitz ride the ghost train, is the Foire du Trône, in the Bois de Vincennes, a fair which takes place every April and May.

Clockwise from above The Moulin Rouge has been entertaining Parisians and visitors with saucy shows since 1889; Pont Neuf has been the backdrop to many well-loved films; the cancan and its dancers were popular subjects for 19th-century painters

DANCING BY THE BRIDGE OF SONGS

Films sell Paris as a place where lovers burst into song and dance at the drop of a shoulder strap. The bridge in the city most danced under, over and on is le Pont Neuf. This was the backdrop for Gene Kelly to sweep Leslie Caron off her feet to the strains of George Gershwin's 'Our Love is Here to Stay' in *An American in Paris* (1951). Woody Allen paid homage to that scene when he re-created the moment, with the help of Goldie Hawn in *Everyone Says I Love You* (1996).

The location shared top billing in *Les Amants du Pont Neuf* (1991) and was the spot where Jeanne Moreau dived into the Seine in François Truffaut's *Jules et Jim* (1962). Romance also blossomed here for the characters played by Audrey Hepburn and Fred Astaire in *Funny Face* (1957).

OF PETTICOATS AND SAFETY PINS

These days the whirl and blur of bright petticoats of the cancan are as much a part of Paris sightseeing as the Eiffel Tower and Louvre. But it was not always socially acceptable. Banned as licentious, the cancan was performed, without underwear, beyond the city limits by prostitutes when it arrived in Paris in the first half of the 19th century. When dance halls gained respectability, performers were obliged to wear suitable undergarments onstage. Some performers continued to indulge in a little private enterprise by tearing holes in opportune places, and so, at the Moulin Rouge, Monsieur Durocher sat in the wings to check that the girls were properly dressed before going on stage. If he discovered a tear, he would repair it with safety pins.

CABARET ON THE HILL

Just as Baz Luhrmann's sensational 2001 film *Moulin Rouge* dazzled audiences, so the sails of the famous red windmill still dominate the entertainment strip between Pigalle and Clichy, at the foot of Montmartre's hill. Yet beyond the glitz of today's touristy Moulin lie many less lavish, but still authentic, cabaret shows. Rue des Martyrs is home to rumbustuous musical entertainment every night. Michou, with his outrageous glasses and sharp suits, still presents Paris's most famous drag revue. Across the road is the rival drag show at Madame Arthur, while more conventional cancan can be seen at the fabulously brash La Nouvelle Eve, at 25 rue Fontaine. For a glimpse of the former haunt of penniless artists such as Toulouse-Lautrec, climb Montmartre's hill to Au Lapin Agile, at 22 rue des Saules.

STARS IN THEIR NATURAL HABITAT

The gossip columns will have you believe that movie stars always hang out at trendy, stylish places such as the Buddha Bar, just off the place de la Concorde. In truth, celluloid legends who call Paris home tend to be seen more usually in the streets around their houses and apartments. Icon Catherine Deneuve likes to shop and sip on the Left Bank—not around the postcard vendors of St-Michel, but in the quieter streets beyond the boulevard St-Germain. Le Bon Marché is the department store where you are most likely to bump into a French film star doing their weekly shop. Opposite the shop is the Hotel Lutétia, where Miss Deneuve may be seen granting an interview to journalists from publications such as *Madame Figaro* or *Marie Claire*.

THE RIVER SEINE

To say that a river runs through Paris is to do the Seine a disservice. It would be fairer to acknowledge that Paris runs along the river. Originally the entire city was surrounded by the Seine, when the Romans founded Lutetia on the Île de la Cité. Indeed, Paris owes its motto to the Seine, *Fluctuat Nec Mergitur*, which translates as: 'It is buffeted by the waves but does not sink.' Principal sites are strung along the riverbanks. From early February to early January, a water shuttle—the Batobus—stops at many of them, from the Eiffel Tower in the west, to the Bibliothèque Nationale de France–Site François Mitterrand in the east. Year round, *bateaux mouches* dinner cruises glide past the illuminated buildings and bridges for those who prefer to sightsee from their table. But to discover the true spirit of the riverside and all its contrasts, try to explore the *quais* on foot. There are floating nightclubs by quai François Mauriac on Saturday nights, families strolling along quai de Montebello on Sunday afternoons and the St-Michel *bouquinistes* selling old books and vintage postcards.

KINDNESS IS ITS OWN REWARD
There is a sign above the door of the rickety American bookstore across the water from Notre-Dame, that reads 'Be not inhospitable to strangers, lest they be angels in disguise'. Shakespeare and Company, established by George Whitman in 1951, is a strange and delightful sanctuary, where new and second-hand volumes stacked on the floor or arranged on shelves are pushed aside to store a blanket here and a sleeping bag there. Visiting writers and artists are welcome to sleep among the paperbacks. When fire ravaged part of the old building some years ago, many such strangers worked tirelessly to repay the hospitality.

Clockwise from above *Spectacular vistas are revealed beyond the bridges that cross the Seine; the quais of the Seine are inviting if you want to get away from the bustle of the city; the shelves of bookstore Shakespeare and Company are laden with second-hand volumes*

BRIDGING THE DIVIDE

Thirty-seven bridges cross the Seine in Paris, carrying rail and metro trains, vehicles and those on foot and bicycle. There's been a bridge on the site of the Petit Pont since before Roman times but the oldest bridge still in original condition is Pont Neuf (▷ 120), which dates from 1604.

The Seine's newest crossing is the Passerelle Simone de Beauvoir, named after the French philosopher and essayist who was born in Paris in 1908 and died in 1986. The bridge opened in 2006 to offer a foot/bicycle crossing between the 12th and 13th *arrondissements*. The central span of the bridge was fitted as one piece, more than 100m (110 yards) long. It had to be floated down the Seine on a barge, causing logistical problems at several locks.

STAYING ALIVE

Thanks to a programme of improvement in the river's water quality, fish and aquatic flora are returning to the Seine (and the city's Canal St-Martin) in significant numbers. They include some 20 different species of fish, including chub, gudgeon, pike, bream and roach. They have been joined by more black-headed gulls, grey wagtails and kingfishers, along with mallard ducks and coots. Another relatively new feature of the river is on the Left Bank between Pont de Sully and Pont d'Austerlitz where the Saint-Bernard quayside has been turned into a pleasant garden featuring works by contemporary artists. By day it attracts walkers and joggers and on spring and summer evenings it's an open-air dance floor.

WHEN THE POOL FLOATS AGAIN

Long before the Paris Plage idea, citizens of the capital would cool off at Piscine Deligny, a floating swimming pool moored at quai Voltaire. Constructed from the timbers of the *Dorade*, the ship that brought Napoléon's ashes to Paris, the lido welcomed the beautiful people to flaunt perfect tans by day and hosted fabulous soirées for the 'in' crowd until one day in 1993 when one of the pontoons moved and the legendary pool was swallowed up by the Seine in less than an hour. Parisians were in mourning, but not for long. In July 2006 the Piscine Joséphine Baker was opened on the river in front of the Bibliothèque Nationale de France–Site François Mitterrand. The complex, built on a huge barge, has more luxuries than its predecessor, including a sauna, whirlpool and solarium.

DOWN BY THE RIVERSIDE

An eclectic collection of boats is moored along the eastern section of the Seine. In the shadow of the Bibliothèque Nationale de France, the Chinese junk and light-boats become Paris's floating nightclub district, where the young and charmed take to the decks to dance until dawn. Waterside partying is the latest thing. Or is it? Farther along the quaysides, just beyond the Bois de Vincennes, is Joinville-le-Pont, where the Seine meets the River Marne. Here blue-collar Parisians have been dancing at the water's edge for generations. Real *guinguette* bars, where the grandparents of today's party animals romanced by the light of the moon, still feature accordionists who play the songs of Edith Piaf and you can dance to the strains of java, tango and the waltz.

ROMANCE IN PARIS

If there is a monument to romance in Paris, it sits in rue de Varenne, where *The Kiss* takes pride of place in the Rodin Museum. But less specific romantic locations abound, from the Pont des Arts footbridge across the Seine (good for watching sunsets) to the temple of love perched on top of a cliff in the Parc des Buttes-Chaumont. This is accentuated by the sheer range of restaurants designed for 'sweet nothings' to be whispered across a candlelit table. A literary heritage illuminated by tragic lovers and grand passions also helps to fuel present-day relationships. But Parisian romance is not just about candlelit dinners and sunset-watching on bridges: There is little to match the magic of breakfasting on onion soup in a Les Halles bistro after a night on the town, then walking home hand-in-hand through the flower market.

Above *Paris has long been considered by many to be the world capital of romance*

JE T'AIME

Incurable romantic Frédéric Baron asked visitors to Montmartre to write down 'I love you' in their own language in the 1990s. He collected more than a thousand *billets-doux* (love letters), which were transcribed by calligrapher Claire Kito and transformed into a mural of tiles and broken hearts by artist Daniel Boulogne.

This wall, Le Mur des Je t'Aime, stands in the Jean Rictus garden on place des Abbesses. Here, holiday romances are sealed by young lovers sharing their innermost thoughts in languages such as Esperanto, Basque and Navajo. The garden has cult status among lovers and serial wooers alike, and the wall has a website (www. lesjetaime.com), where lovers can perfect their pronunciation in order to melt hearts in situ at dusk.

KISSING STORY

Kissing on the street is part of Paris's romantic liberality—which up until the mid-20th century made other nationalities blush. It has its roots in a past when well-heeled men openly escorted mistresses who were little more than high-class ladies of the night. The Parisians have a variety of names for *Les Belles de nuit*. As well as courtesans, there were *amazons, cocottes* and, peculiar to Paris—because they frequented the area of Notre-Dame de Lorette—the *lorettes*. One such *lorette* became the self-styled Comtesse Valtesse de la Bigne whom the artist Henri Gervex painted in a tableau which became his painting *Le Mariage Civil*. It hangs in the wedding chamber of the Marais Town Hall and, in spite of its history, the picture looks perfectly in place when couples pledge their love and fidelity.

THE STORY OF PARIS

UNDERSTANDING THE STORY OF PARIS

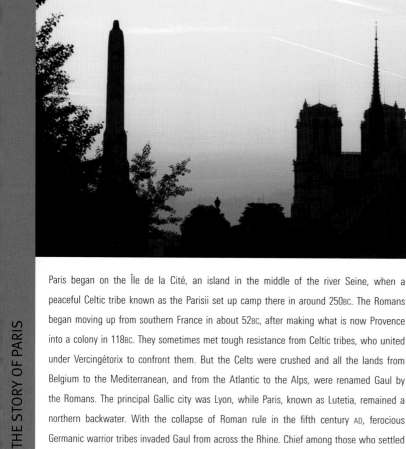

Paris began on the Île de la Cité, an island in the middle of the river Seine, when a peaceful Celtic tribe known as the Parisii set up camp there in around 250BC. The Romans began moving up from southern France in about 52BC, after making what is now Provence into a colony in 118BC. They sometimes met tough resistance from Celtic tribes, who united under Vercingétorix to confront them. But the Celts were crushed and all the lands from Belgium to the Mediterranean, and from the Atlantic to the Alps, were renamed Gaul by the Romans. The principal Gallic city was Lyon, while Paris, known as Lutetia, remained a northern backwater. With the collapse of Roman rule in the fifth century AD, ferocious Germanic warrior tribes invaded Gaul from across the Rhine. Chief among those who settled in northern Gaul were the Franks, who based themselves at Paris. They grew immensely powerful and extended the Frankish empire until, under Charlemagne in the eighth century AD, the Franks controlled all of Roman Gaul. In AD987, Hugues Capet, the Count of Paris, was crowned king of France and made Paris his capital.

LUTETIA

Vercingétorix was and is a national hero. After his resistance was crushed, the Roman settlement of Lutetia grew, spreading onto the Left Bank of the Seine. It had a theatre, a forum (public square) and a 10,000-seat arena for circuses and entertainments such as pitting humans against animals. The Romans built public baths, where people met to wash, have a massage, gossip and wrestle. On the island, still occupied mainly by Parisii, the Romans built a temple to Jupiter. Then disaster struck in the third century AD. Warrior tribes from Germany attacked and destroyed the town before being defeated themselves. It was triumphantly rebuilt and renamed Paris. The barbarians became the entertainment in the arena.

Clockwise from above *A statue of St. Geneviève stands near the cathedral of Notre-Dame; Denis and his companions arrive at Lutetia; Charlemagne the Frank became the first Holy Roman Emperor*

ST. DENIS

St. Denis, the patron saint of France, was born in Italy and was one of seven bishops sent by the Pope to convert Gaul to Catholicism in AD250. Denis became the first bishop of Paris and was so good at converting the populace that the Romans had him killed. He was beheaded at Montmartre (Martyr's Hill) and, according to legend, the indefatigable Denis picked up his own head and kept walking. It is more likely that, in reality, his body was thrown into the Seine and later rescued by his followers, who built the Basilica of St-Denis on the spot to commemorate him. Where did the legend come from? St. Denis was always depicted with his head in his hands and in the medieval mind image and reality became one.

ST. GENEVIÈVE

St. Geneviève, patroness of Paris, was a forceful woman who won through despite the misogyny of the times. She even saved Paris from Attila the Hun. Born in Nanterre in AD422, it is said that St. Germain of Auxerre caught the look in her eye when she was seven and suggested she dedicate her life to God. She did so, eating only twice a week and having frequent visions. The Bishop of Paris appointed Geneviève Mother Superior to the nuns of Paris and her inspiration and energy helped the Parisians when Attila's armies approached the city in AD451. She told the citizens to trust in God and to repent of their sins. When they did, the Huns turned away and galloped onwards to Châlons-en-Champagne.

CLOVIS, CHIEF OF THE FRANKS

Geneviève's spiritual powers did not work against the next wave of invaders. With Roman power collapsing, it was impossible for the inhabitants of Paris to fight off warrior tribes like the Franks. With their powerful leader Clovis at their head, the Franks swept into Paris and took control. Clovis based himself in the offices of the expelled Roman governor on the Île de la Cité, and commanded his troops as they fought other tribes for more territory. Geneviève visited Clovis, preached to him, and eventually converted the warrior king to Christianity. A changed man, Clovis built an abbey where in death he and his queen Clotilde could be buried alongside the saintly Geneviève.

CHARLEMAGNE

The power of the Franks culminated in the rise of a majestic yet simple leader, Charlemagne, or Carolus Magnus (Charles the Great). He was a hero of poetry, song and legend and grandson of Carolus Martel (Charles The Hammer), who had triumphed over the Moorish forces invading from the south. Charlemagne directed an indomitable army into every corner of Gaul and from there across much of Germany and Italy, thus carving out a vast kingdom. Throughout his dominion, he imposed a devout Christianity and the pursuit of learning. In AD800, the Pope crowned Charlemagne the first Holy Roman Emperor. Charlemagne the Frank had proved beyond doubt that Gaul was now France.

The growing importance of Paris in medieval times had much to do with the city's position on the river Seine. The institutions of Church and Government stood on the Île de la Cité, while much of the population lived in simple homes on the Left Bank. Many were skilled craftsmen, while others continued to farm the land. Important religious sites, notably at St-Denis and St-Germain, attracted large commercial fairs that brought in thousands of traders and visitors. Everything was dominated by the Church—its beliefs and authority were beyond question. Those who did disagree with the Church risked their lives and at the end of the 12th century, Jews all over France were rounded up and slaughtered. However, the Church was also the chief provider of education and medical care to the poor and was the guiding hand behind the greatest engineering project in medieval Paris: the draining of the marshes of the islands and the Right Bank. When this was done, the city really began to grow.

NOTRE-DAME
One of the greatest European cathedrals, Notre-Dame dates from 1163 and took almost 200 years to complete. It is a symbol of Paris but was not always treated respectfully. The revolutionaries desecrated it in the 18th century and turned it into a Temple of Reason, even decapitating the statues in the Gallery of Kings. Victor Hugo, romantic creator of a mythic Paris, restored it to the public imagination in 1831 with his novel *Notre-Dame de Paris*. Rebuilding soon followed and, like Quasimodo, the Parisians discovered that 'the cathedral was not only company [for them]…it was the universe, nay, more, it was Nature itself'.

Clockwise from above *Beautiful Sainte-Chapelle was built to house the Crown of Thorns holy relic; Abélard and Héloïse were tragic lovers in medieval Paris; Notre-Dame cathedral dates from the middle of the 12th century*

ABÉLARD AND HÉLOÏSE

Peter Abélard, a much-admired 12th-century scholar, taught philosophy at the university in Paris. Héloïse, the niece of Canon Fulbert of Notre-Dame, was one of his students. The two fell madly in love and would meet secretly in Héloïse's uncle's house. Eventually Héloïse became pregnant, then she fled to Abélard's family home in Brittany and he pledged to marry her. But the enraged Fulbert had Abélard castrated. Héloïse became a nun and Abélard entered a monastery, yet their letters show a torment of love that continued until Abélard's death in 1142. Héloïse lived for another 21 years, and was buried in Abélard's grave. The tragic lovers were moved to Père Lachaise cemetery in the 19th century.

LOUIS IX AND THE CROWN OF THORNS

Louis IX was an enthusiastic buyer of holy relics, acquiring the staff of Moses, a portion of the True Cross and Jesus's swaddling clothes. His greatest prize was the Crown of Thorns, which he bought from the Emperor of Constantinople in the 13th century.

The Emperor was anxious for French aid, and Louis was eager for the prestige this crown would give his own claim to the throne of France. The crown cost more than three times as much as Sainte-Chapelle, the chapel Louis built to house the holy relic. Sainte-Chapelle is famed for its beauty, particularly its vibrant and towering stained-glass windows. The Crown of Thorns is still in Paris, housed in Notre-Dame.

THE SORBONNE

Robert de Sorbon founded this college of the University of Paris in 1257. The fellows gave free lectures and lived in a closed community, although without religious vows. Robert de Sorbon was a respected professor and preacher, but also a natural administrator. He drew up a list of regulations for the fellows, which included a dress code (no scandalous clothing) and guidelines for returning library books. Even eating and drinking in private rooms were frowned upon. Robert didn't care to have secrets bandied about, so guests, especially women, were discouraged. Robert seemed to know what caused real trouble, however, when he decided that 'No fellow shall have a key to the kitchen'.

HUNDRED YEARS' WAR

Between 1337 and 1453 two royal houses (Valois and Plantagenet) fought over the French crown. On 14 December 1431, the Plantagenet 10-year-old Henry VI of England was crowned King of France in Notre-Dame. Joan of Arc wrote a wonderfully rude letter to Henry, warning 'go home…or beware of the Maid and all the damage you will suffer'. She had attempted to expel the English from France in 1429 and to help the Valois Charles VII be crowned king. He did not support Joan in her attack on Paris, although she might have taken it if he had. Henry VI did not enjoy his crown for long—by 1453 the French had driven the English from country except the northern port of Calais.

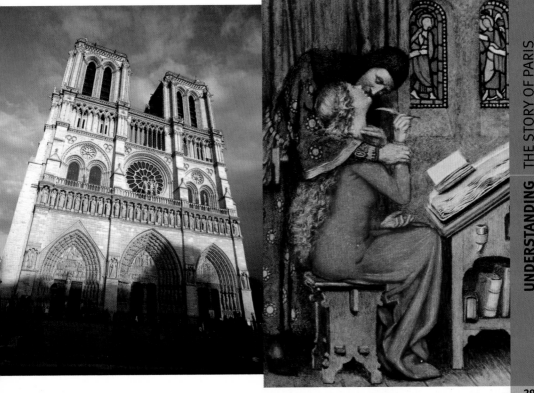

Paris took several decades to recover from the Hundred Years' War (mid-14th to mid-15th century), and also from the Black Death (1348) and the decadence of the royal court. But by the end of the 15th century, the city eagerly embraced the ideas of the Italian Renaissance, giving French character to the new architecture, and was proud of its role as the capital of the reunited French nation. King François I (reigned 1515–1547) most embodied the French Renaissance. A devotee of Italian art, he invited Leonardo da Vinci to live at the royal palace in Amboise. The king used the artist's *Mona Lisa* as the cornerstone of his art collection. In 1528, François commissioned significant rebuilding of the Louvre palace. More fine buildings followed under the Protestant Henri IV, crowned king in 1589. He converted to Catholicism in 1593 in a bid to stop the Wars of Religion that swept through France in the latter half of the 16th century. He was assassinated in 1610 and was succeeded by his son, Louis XIII.

Clockwise from above *Leonardo da Vinci lived in the palace of Amboise under the patronage of art-lover François I; former President Valéry Giscard d'Estaing was received into the Académie Française in 2004; Charles IX, urged by Catherine de Médicis, orders the massacre of Protestants*

FRANÇOIS VILLON

François Villon, born in 1431, was one of the greatest of French poets, but he has a bitter connection to Paris. He graduated from the University of Paris and was destined for a career in law or the Church, but he became restless and spent time in taverns mixing with thieves. In 1455 he killed a priest in a drunken quarrel. After this, he wandered the country, spending time in and out of prison until he was banished in 1463 and was never heard of again. Villon's poetry is vigorous and haunting, but without self-pity. It is fashionable to view him as the country's first cultural rebel, although he is actually a mystery.

FIT FOR A KING

Even for a king, François I was larger than life. He adored Renaissance style—he grew up at the Loire chateau of Amboise, probably the first French building redesigned on Italianate lines—and on becoming king he invited Leonardo da Vinci to live at Amboise. François moved ceaselessly from chateau to chateau, and had two more magnificent palaces built, at Fontainebleau and Chambord. Eventually, he decided to move to the Louvre, taking his art collection with him. He ordered the palace to be completely rebuilt, but died soon after work began. He left his mark on many buildings in Paris in the form of the salamander and the letter F, his way of saying 'François was here'.

THE MASSACRE OF ST. BARTHOLOMEW'S DAY

The brutal murder of thousands of Protestants in Paris on 24 August 1572 is one of the most shocking events in French history. France was riven by wars between Protestants and Catholics but the marriage of King Charles IX's sister, the Catholic Marguerite de Valois, to the Protestant Henri de Navarre (the future Henri IV) was meant to bring the two sides together. The opposite occurred when the king, pressed by his mother, Catherine de Médicis, ordered the massacre of Protestant nobles gathered at the Louvre to celebrate the wedding. Three thousand people died in Paris and many more throughout France. Civil war raged throughout the country for more than 20 years.

THE MÉDICIS CYCLE

Between 1622 and 1625, Rubens painted 21 murals on the life of Marie de Médicis, Louis XIII's mother, for her palace in Paris. Marie, second wife of Henri IV, was bad-tempered, ugly and dangerous, so Rubens needed all his diplomatic skills to deal with her. The paintings, he explained carefully, are allegories of how one should look rather than how one does look. In immense baroque extravaganzas, a beautiful Marie is shown arriving in France, getting married and governing the country accompanied by a flock of gods. This propaganda has little to do with reality, as even her husband said she was the biggest troublemaker he had ever known, and her son banished her from France. Ironically, she died in Cologne in a house once occupied by Rubens.

L'ACADÉMIE FRANÇAISE

Cardinal Richelieu, chief minister to Louis XIII, formed the Académie Française in 1635—and it still exists today. The academy consists of 40 members and only the death of a member creates a vacancy. Each member is presented with a richly decorated sword and is addressed as *monsieur*, which rankles with the women academicians. Richelieu, busy creating a centralized government, wanted the Académie to act as a ministry to legislate on the use and development of the French language. In 1638 the academicians began work on their dictionary—it took them a long time. One wit, on hearing they had reached the letter F, loudly hoped to live until they got to G. In 1694, a mere 58 years after starting, their dictionary was published and has been updated regularly ever since.

When Louis XIII built a hunting lodge near Versailles, a hamlet just over 16km (10 miles) southwest Paris, he had little idea that he was laying the foundation stone of an institution that was to become a byword for the elegant tyranny which would ultimately be responsible for the downfall of the monarchy in France. When Louis XIII died in 1643 his son was under five years old. The new king's mother, Anne of Austria, governed with Cardinal Mazarin as regents until 1661 when, on the death of Mazarin, Louis XIV shocked the Court by announcing he would rule on his own even though he was not yet 25. His authority was absolute and his egotism and extravagance dominated every aspect of life in Paris and the rest of France. He ordered the building of a palace at Versailles and moved the Court and parliament there. In this period, Louis XIV adopted a golden sun as his symbol because, in his opinion, he radiated light over the whole nation. While the Sun King's reign represents the apotheosis of the French monarchy, his lavish lifestyle and ceaseless wars led to the political isolation of France, financial problems and extreme social injustice. Much of the vitality of the great King's reign was extinguished long before his death in 1715.

IN THE BEGINNING...
Versailles effectively became the capital of France in two important periods—under Louis XIV and later under Louis XV. Of course, the nominal capital was always Paris and the royal residence was always officially the Louvre, but the location of the politically pivotal palace at Versailles built up the settlement from a tiny hamlet of barely 100 residents on the outskirts of a medieval castle to a city power base. The village had emerged from the feudal age ravaged by the plague and the Hundred Years' War. By the start of the 16th century it had a population of 500 and its seigneur was a Florentine cohort of the powerful Italian Médicis, called Gondi, whose heirs often invited Louis XIII to hunt in the forest of Versailles. So the king had a hunting lodge built there, and the rest is history...

Clockwise from above *Detail of* View of the Chateau, Gardens and Park of Versailles from the Avenue de Paris *(1668) oil on canvas by Pierre Patel (1605–1676); one of the opulent bedrooms in the palace of Versailles; an equestrian statue of the Sun King, Louis XIV, in place des Victoires, Paris*

UNDERSTANDING THE STORY OF PARIS

BEHIND THE THRONE

Great minds were at work behind the Sun King. At first, Louis XIV's affairs of state were run by Chief Minister Cardinal Mazarin, who closely followed the footsteps of his predecessor, Cardinal Richelieu. After Mazarin's death in 1661, the King sought advice on all matters of state from Jean-Baptiste Colbert, a brilliant but unassuming politician, son of a cloth merchant. Colbert arranged the downfall of the Superintendant of Finance and took over as finance minister himself. He increased tax revenues, imposed tariffs to protect French commerce, built new canals, revived ailing industries and enabled the navy to protect French merchant shipping. But Colbert's efforts were undermined by the king's search for personal glory.

LADY OF LETTERS

With the Court tucked away at Versailles, intellectual life in Paris flourished—and women presided over it. In 1676 the writer Madame de Sévigné spent a day at Versailles, gambling, lolling about in boats on the canal and having supper at midnight. But it was not for her. She decided to stay away and wrote the great series of letters to her daughter that give a picture of life in 17th-century Paris. In the 18th century other ladies held literary salons where writers Voltaire and Diderot could discuss the *Encyclopédie*, the great intellectual work of the century. This freedom provided the background to the Revolution, as 'the Church, the Law and the Government' were questioned. Versailles was blissfully unaware of any of this dissent.

THE ASCENT OF THE SUN KING

As a boy of about 10 until well into his teens Louis XIV lived through a five-year French civil war known as the Fronde (1648–1653) in which Parisian mobs armed only with slings *(les frondes)* smashed the windows of houses belonging to supporters of Cardinal Mazarin. It is thought that this experience explains Louis' disposition towards moving the Court and seat of government out of Paris and into the country. Versailles already had family connections and in 1661 Louis conceived the idea of transforming the existing castle into a palace and of developing the surrounding landscape into a sumptuous parkland garden. Though it was virtually his first royal decree, the concept was not realized until some 17 years later.

THE BUILDING OF VERSAILLES

To build Versailles 30,000 workers were hired. Leading architect Louis Le Vau, interior designer Charles Le Brun and landscape architect André Le Nôtre were commissioned to provide a royal home of unprecedented grandeur, in classical style. The king required vast formal gardens full of statuary and fountains and a sumptuous interior adorned with Europe's finest craftsmanship. Work continued up to Louis XIV's death in 1715, with no expense spared. While draining the grounds, thousands of workers died from marsh fever, but were quickly replaced. Mature trees from all over France were replanted here and a whole new town was built alongside the palace. The Royal Court moved into Versailles in 1671.

Universally admired for its architecture and design, Versailles had grown into a city of 30,000 inhabitants by the time of the death of Louis XIV, and its stylish influence spread all over Europe. However, at the same time, Paris enjoyed a renewal of its fortunes with the removal of the five-year-old Louis XV (reigned 1715–1774) to the Tuileries Palace by the regent, Philippe d'Orléans. The Court and nobility moved to Paris to throw themselves into a life devoted to pleasure. Paris regained its status as the focus of French life, despite the Court's return to Versailles in 1724. Some of its self-respect was restored, too, at the expense of the welfare of the ordinary citizenry. Whether ignorant, negligent or indifferent to this, the king had other things to think about. Between 1730 and 1770 there wasn't a decade without war and, in spite of his nickname, 'the Well-Beloved', Louis XV had become hugely unpopular. Although he attempted to institute some regal reforms, at the time of his death the monarchy was much weakened. And when Louis XVI (reigned 1774–1793) with his beautiful and frivolous queen Marie-Antoinette took over the reins, the polite mood of reformism had turned into a flood of sedition. Political resentment consumed the populace who were scandalized by the Court's behaviour, extravagance and frivolity.

SCENTS OF DESPAIR AND DISSENT

In contrast to the virility, elegance and youth of Versailles, Paris during this time had become a victim of rot and decay. The film of Patrick Süskind's novel, *Perfume*, graphically depicted the reality of pre-Revolutionary Paris as a veritable cesspit. Although fictional, the tale rang many historical bells when its author wrote of 'a stench barely conceivable to us modern men and women'. It went on: 'The streets stank of manure, the courtyards of urine, the stairwells stank of mouldering wood and rat droppings...

'The stench of sulphur rose from the chimneys, the stench of caustic lyes from the tanneries, and from the slaughterhouses came the stench of congealed blood.' But there was more than just bacteria feeding off this despair and squalor; the seeds of dissent were about to germinate.

Clockwise from above *Portrait of Marie-Antoinette (1788) by Elisabeth Louise Vigee-Lebrun (1755–1842); portrait of Madame de Pompadour by François-Hubert Drouais (1727–1775); contemporary illustration of the Queen's Boudoir at the Petit Trianon*

CE PAYS ÇI

Courtiers called Versailles *ce pays çi* (this country). They walked differently, developed their own *argot* (slang) and lived by hundreds of meaningless rules (dukes kneeled on crooked cushions in church, the royal princes on straight ones). It was said that the king encouraged these rules of etiquette and added a few of his own as a way of keeping his courtiers dancing attendance upon him and, perhaps more importantly, having to pay so much attention to maintaining the rules meant they had less time for plots and intrigues. There were codes for politeness, for dress—and even for knocking on the king's door, which was not allowed. When anyone wanted an audience with the king or just to pass on a message, the king's etiquette ruled that they had to scratch on the door with the nail of the little finger of their left hand.

QUEEN OF THE BOURGEOISIE

The Parisian bourgeoisie visited Versailles but could never be a part of it. So when Jeanne-Antoinette Poisson, a beautiful Parisian *bourgeoise*, first caught Louis XV's eye, subsequent direct contact with the king was not officially allowed. One story claims they met at a masked ball; others are more prosaic. Either way the problem was resolved when she was made Marquise de Pompadour. She became the royal mistress in 1745 and, by all accounts, his most trusted adviser—and ultimately the most powerful woman in 18th-century France. She managed to get her brother, the Marquis de Marigny, appointed director of the king's buildings and together with the king the three designed and built the École Militaire and place de la Concorde in Paris, and the Petit Trianon in the grounds at Versailles.

THE WOMEN OF PARIS SPEAK

The working-class women of Paris were a tough breed, and members of the Court never knew how they would be received when they ventured from Versailles. Madame de Pompadour, a Parisienne herself, found her carriage splattered in mud, while Louis XV was forced to build a road round the city to avoid the insults of the market women and fishwives, delivered in the slang known as *poissard*. Meaning simply 'vulgar', this was an anarchic mix of fractured words and chaotic grammar, ideal for ridicule. Indeed, *poissard* featured a great deal in the comedies, parodies, comic operas and verse of the day—most notably in the work of the composer, librettist and poet Jean-Joseph Vadé (1720–1757) who created a theatrical genre based on the market women's slang.

FOR HER MAJESTY'S AMUSEMENT

Marie-Antoinette invited the fishwives of Paris to Versailles in 1777 to teach her friends *poissard* for the dramatics they performed for their and the Court's amusement, and much later the women sang a *poissard* song inviting the Court to choke on molten gold since they loved it so much.

In fact, one of Marie-Antoinette's passions was for privacy, for herself and her coterie. She found it in the Petit Trianon, a chateau with surrounding parkland which her husband Louis XVI gave to her on his accession. It afforded Marie-Antoinette and her closest friends, who included the Princess de Lamballe, an escape from the excessive formality of Court life. No one—not even the king himself—might enter the château without the express permission of the queen.

The Fronde rebellion (1648–1652) had given just a hint of what was to come and anger simmered beneath the surface of life in Paris. The power of the monarchy and the decadent privileges of the aristocracy contrasted sharply with the poverty of working people, and the growing industrial middle class, resentful at their lack of political voice, demanded a proper constitution. The Royal Court continued to enjoy an exceptionally pampered life. The arts flourished, and craftsmen catering to the aristocracy did well. All over Europe, Paris became a byword for luxury and the good life. At the same time, the state sank further into debt and ordinary people further into poverty. To offset the state's huge debts, repressive taxes were imposed. On 14 July 1789, spontaneous crowds (there had been rumblings of something afoot the previous day) converged on Les Invalides to grab the weapons stored there. From there, to the Bastille. The Revolution had started, and would lead France through many years of savage brutality and instability towards a new Republic.

Clockwise from above *Revolutionaries storm the Bastille on 14 July 1789; the condemned are carried in a tumbril to the place of execution; the Colonne de Juillet stands as the centrepiece of place de la Bastille, once the site of the infamous prison*

THE GUILLOTINE

Dr. Joseph-Ignace Guillotin was a physician and deputy of the National Assembly. In 1789 he proposed decapitation as the most democratic means of death. A committee was formed to design a suitable machine which was set up in the place du Carrousel, and on 21 August 1792 was used for the execution of a Royalist general. As the Revolution progressed so did the executions and by 1794, during the *Grande Terreur*, 26 people a day were being guillotined. Those accused of crimes against the state were despatched on an industrial scale. This brought problems of disposal, with blood flowing in the city's gutters and bodies being thrown into mass graves.

THE CUSTOMS WALL

The attack on the Bastille on 14 July 1789 was preceded on 12 July by an attack on something less well known: the Customs Wall around Paris, built on the order of the Controller-General, Callone. In a desperate effort to raise money for the huge national debt (60 per cent of the budget went to pay the interest), Callone imposed a duty on goods entering and leaving the city. This was collected by private tax collectors who took a large cut for themselves, and were hated by the citizens of Paris for their brutal tactics. The wall was rather beautiful, the work of the chemist Antoine Lavoisier, who was also a tax collector. These well-fed gentlemen had, for once, miscalculated — after the wall came down, they were swiftly executed.

14 JULY 1789

The Revolution made a slow start. A bread shortage had caused months of angry revolt in Paris and on 12 and 13 July thousands of rioters surged through the city. On the morning of 14 July a group tricked its way into Les Invalides, seized its huge store of weapons and marched to the Bastille, the fortress-prison. The mob liberated the prisoners (all seven of them), decapitated the governor and paraded his head on a pole. This attack heralded a summer of violence and on 5 October thousands of women marched on Versailles to ask King Louis XVI for bread, which he gave them. Joined by their menfolk, they rampaged through the palace and took the King and Queen Marie-Antoinette to house arrest in Paris.

THE MARRIAGE OF FIGARO

Beaumarchais' play *The Marriage of Figaro* was due to open in Paris in 1783, in a theatre owned by Queen Marie-Antoinette. She was looking forward to seeing the production, but Louis XVI, realizing that its unprecedented attacks on the aristocracy were dangerous, stopped the performance and had the play banned, which led to riots in Paris. After some changes the play finally opened in another Paris venue the following year. When Figaro tells his master, 'You only took the trouble to be born… you're an ordinary person' the people of Paris roared with delight, as did the watching nobles, including Marie-Antoinette. An observer noted with amazement how the aristocracy slapped its own face while laughing at the same time.

FESTIVAL OF THE SUPREME BEING

On 8 June 1794 (20 Prairial Year II by the Revolutionary calendar), the Revolution reached a pitch of insanity, and Paris witnessed the Festival of the Supreme Being, as artificial and ridiculous as any royal pageant. Deputies from the Convention marched along clutching wheat sheaves, girls in white distributed flowers, oxen pulled a printing press and a plough on a chariot and blind children sang inspiring songs. In the Champ de Mars, Maximilien Robespierre, one of the Revolution's leaders, set fire to a statue of Atheism, then descended from the top of a cardboard mountain to enthusiastic applause. 'Did the day of Creation…' he asked, 'shine with a light more agreeable?' Seven weeks later Robespierre was guillotined.

Following the bloody days of The Terror, France was ruled by an intermediary government known as the *Directoire* (1795–1799). Problems arose at once — the war against surrounding countries threatened to turn against France and a violent royalism arose that sought to revive the *ancien régime*. An ambitious young Corsican army general emerged who felt able to deal with both issues — Napoléon Bonaparte (1769–1821). Given command of the army in Italy by the *Directoire* in 1796, he rapidly achieved victory. His next step, the invasion of Egypt, proved a mistake, but nevertheless his rise to power was now unstoppable. He became First Consul of the Republic after the 1799 *coup d'état* that overthrew the Directoire. To begin with, things looked good and the French border expanded. But in 1812 Napoléon made the fatal error of invading Russia during winter. Ice and snow killed thousands of his soldiers. In 1814 the Russians invaded Paris and Napoléon was exiled to the island of Elba. He made a brief return in 1815, before meeting his final defeat at Waterloo a few months later. He was expelled to the island of St-Helena, where he died in 1821.

A REPUBLICAN CORONATION

Napoléon Bonaparte went through swift changes in under 10 years–from extreme anti-royalist Jacobin supporter to army general serving the *Directoire*, to crowned head of state. His military successes, ability to restore order and sweeping vision of a modern France inspired the nation. Despite impeccable Republican credentials, in 1804 the military dictator decided he deserved to wear a crown. In an opulent ceremony fit for a king, Napoléon was crowned Emperor in Notre-Dame. The Pope, summoned to Paris for the purpose, gave his blessing. Since no one had authority to place the crown on Napoléon's head, in an act fraught with symbolism he did the job himself, after having first chivalrously crowned his wife Empress Josephine.

Clockwise from above *The Arc de Triomphe was ordered by Napoléon to commemorate his victories; Les Invalides house the tomb of Napoléon; Napoléon leaves for the island of St-Helena*

ARC DE TRIOMPHE

Military triumph was the essence of Napoléon's right to wear a crown. The Emperor kept France in a constant state of belligerency against the rest of Europe, distributing conquered lands among friends and family. In 1805, only a year after his coronation, the greatest moment of glory for Napoléon came at Austerlitz, where French troops defeated the might of Austria. At the height of his power, in 1806, Napoléon ordered a huge Roman-style triumphal arch to be built to commemorate his victories. The Arc de Triomphe was to stand in pride of place at the end of the Champs-Élysées. Construction had barely started, however, when Napoléon's bubble burst. Work on the arch stopped until after his death; it was completed in 1836.

NAPOLÉON'S ELEPHANT

To obliterate memories of the Revolution, Napoléon commissioned an enormous bronze elephant, 10m (33ft) high, for the site of the demolished Bastille prison. When the elephant was finally built in 1814, the Empire could afford only a plaster version, which soon started to disintegrate into a bizarre, broken-down mess. No one seemed to know why it was there, or even why it was an elephant. A concierge was employed to look after the construction, but that didn't help. The elephant appears in the book *Les Misérables* as the home of the young Gavroche. Author Victor Hugo calls it a mysterious and mighty phantom. In 1846 the wretched beast was finally demolished, seemingly vanishing from the place de la Bastille as mysteriously as it had appeared.

BISTRO! BISTRO!

When Russian soldiers occupied Paris in 1814 they liked to visit the small cafés in the city. Unsurprisingly, they got the cold shoulder from their French waiters. *'Bystro! Bystro!'* (Quickly!) shouted the unhappy Cossacks and legend has it that this is the origin of this uniquely French type of restaurant. However, the word didn't enter the language until 1884 and there are other, less attractive, explanations for it. The term bistro might equally have derived from the word *bistre* (dull yellowy brown), describing a smoky, gloomy place.

The Russians haven't made many notable contributions to French cuisine, so it's nicer to think they've sneaked in a term known for simple, but excellent, food.

FUNERAL OF NAPOLÉON

Napoléon's remains were returned to France in 1840. His state funeral at Les Invalides on 15 December 1840 was not a jolly affair. Inside, kings, princes and ancient heroes sat for hours in pious boredom. They were surrounded by black and purple drapes fringed with silver, hundreds of glowing candles, military decorations and the Imperial Crown itself. Outside, it was a different story. The day was bitterly cold and so the waiting crowd and the soldiers lining the route had to keep themselves warm. A few people in the stands started to dance, which then spread to the crowds on the streets and then to the soldiers themselves, until a vast, happy round-dance snaked along the funeral route, only to stop when the coffin finally went by.

The turbulence of the Napoleonic period, its war-making patriotism, far-reaching social changes and violent politics, continued through the rest of the 19th century. The people of Paris, marked out in the Revolution as more passionately radical than their provincial compatriots, continued to call for equality, democracy and workers' protection. The 1830 Uprising brought the 'citizen king' Louis-Philippe of Orléans to the throne. Yet Parisians seemed to hanker for grandiose, dictatorial leadership along the lines of a Sun King or a Bonaparte. Following the 1848 Revolution that finally did away with the French monarchy, a brief Second Republic gave way to yet another authoritarian, egotistical ruler: Napoléon's nephew, Napoléon III. He used his power to enhance Paris, especially during the transformation overseen by Baron Haussmann, when much of the city was rebuilt. Constant themes of Parisian life still remained, such as the poverty of workers, the lavish hedonism of the rich, and war. During the bloody episode of the Commune, in 1871, Paris even waged war against the rest of France. The century began with war against the Prussians, later saw the Prussians bombard Paris, and ended with another war looming. But for those with money, the mood was increasingly festive in *gay Paris*.

HAUSSMANN'S GRAND DESIGN

Napoléon III adored luxury and prestige as much as his uncle had done. He and Empress Eugénie mixed with the crowned heads of Europe and came to exemplify the aristocratic style that Paris had suffered so much in trying to abolish. At the same time, the Emperor, like Bonaparte, had grand plans to improve the look of his capital city and so he commissioned Baron Haussmann to undertake massive urban improvement. Haussmann demolished large areas of the city, including almost everything on the historic Île de la Cité, sweeping away overcrowded and rebellious workers' districts. In their place he constructed wide, straight boulevards radiating from the riverside. The workers were rehoused in new suburbs away from the heart of the city.

Clockwise from above *Baron Haussmann's design for grand boulevards swept aside crowded workers' districts; cancan dancer La Goulue was immortalized by Toulouse-Lautrec; Communards patrol the streets of Paris*

THE SIEGE OF PARIS

Thanks to the Emperor and Baron Haussmann, Paris had become the world's most beautiful and modern city. The Emperor had even agreed to improving workers' rights and an enjoyment of life permeated the city. But Napoléon III's pre-emptive declaration of war against Prussia in 1870 came as a blow to the city.

Confronting the Prussians, the French suffered an immediate defeat and the country called for Napoléon III to abdicate. Later that year, Prussians surrounded the city and the siege of Paris began. For six winter weeks, nothing was allowed in or out and freezing Paris began to starve, resorting to eating rats, cats and even zoo animals. In January 1871, the bombardment began and France accepted defeat rather than see their city destroyed.

THE COMMUNE

The Prussian war infuriated Parisians, who felt that monarchist elements were to blame. To get away from the Paris mob, the government of the new, conservative National Assembly left the city for Versailles. In Paris, the people took the law into their own hands, establishing an anarchist-socialist Commune to run the city in March 1871, which planned to re-establish the gains of the Revolution.

The Communards (fédérés) seized National Guard weapons and fought pitched battles in the streets against government troops. During the Semaine Sanglante (Bloody Week) of 21 to 28 May, the army ruthlessly regained control. Leading fédérés were executed in Père Lachaise cemetery. Around 10,000 Parisians were killed and a further 40,000 arrested.

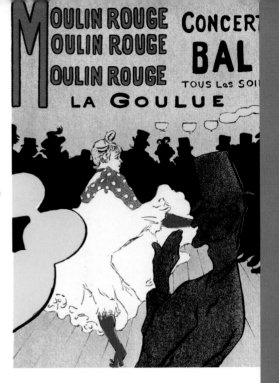

A SAINT IN THE RUE DU BAC

In 1830, while revolution rocked Paris, Catherine Laboure, a nun in the convent of the Sisters of Charity on the rue du Bac, experienced three visions of the Virgin Mary. Standing on a globe and emanating rays of light that shone out over the globe, Mary commanded that a medal be struck that would give grace to anyone who wore it. Church authorities eventually approved and the first medal was struck in 1832. But illiterate Catherine, who had been a waitress before taking her vows, continued to live out her drab existence at the convent, where she looked after the poultry and was a gatekeeper. She was strangely uninterested in her visions, and her superiors branded her insignificant, cold and apathetic. Catherine died in 1876.

THE CANCAN

Paris was the city of pleasure in the 1890s, with performers dancing the wildly daring cancan at the Moulin Rouge (immortalized in Henri de Toulouse-Lautrec's lithographs). The dance may have started in Brittany in the 16th century, when women performed a similar dance by lifting their dresses and kicking their legs to the ceiling, although the version that came to Paris in the 1820s is probably a bawdy version of the quadrille.

Two well-known dancers were Jane Avril and La Goulue. Avril was willowy and elegant, while La Goulue, big and earthy, was known as The Glutton due to her penchant for finishing off the customers' drinks. They both came to a melancholy end, drunk, poor and forgotten, with La Goulue selling matches in a Paris park.

A savage century came to an end, but a worse one was to come, despite the *fin-de-siècle* atmosphere of frivolity and avant-garde art. The two world wars were the great disaster of the 20th century. In post-war years, the population of Paris grew rapidly, as did its prosperity, and the city itself expanded into new suburbs. Once more the preoccupations of Paris returned to luxury and fashion, sophisticated entertainment, good food and wine, avant-garde art, literature and also the increasingly popular medium of film. A brief interlude of disorder in 1968 was a forceful reminder that Paris had not lost its capacity or appetite for revolutionary politics. Nor had it lost its flair for stunning, cutting-edge architecture and development on a Napoleonic scale—magnificent modern buildings and immense rebuilding schemes, like François Mitterrand's *Grands Projets*, continue to help to maintain Paris's reputation as one of the world's greatest and most popular cities.

Clockwise from above *The Mémorial de la Shoah commemorates the 76,000 members of the Jewish community who were deported from France in World War II; in May 1968 demonstrators occupied the Sorbonne; the Louvre glass pyramid was one of President Mitterrand's Grands Projets*

THE RITE OF SPRING

The premiere of the ballet *The Rite of Spring* in May 1913 was a genuine Parisian scandal. Stravinsky's wild music and Nijinsky's even wilder choreography were matched by a riot in the audience. The crowd made so much noise booing that Nijinsky had to stand in the wings shouting out the rhythms for his deafened dancers. The poor aesthetes in the stalls turned on the aristocrats in their boxes. The Comtesse de Pourtalès, tiara askew, shouted that no one had ever dared to make fun of her, when threatened by excitable young men who loved new art. The owner of the venue, Gabriel Astruc, leaned out of his box and screamed at the audience, 'First listen! Then boo!'

MAY 1968

Paris was caught up in the mood of anti-authoritarianism and liberty that swept the world in 1968. It started as a student sit-in against the regime at the out-of-town University of Nanterre, but a heavy-handed police response changed the mood to anger and confrontation. Action spread to the Sorbonne university, with demonstrators' demands expanding to include sweeping away all that was outdated and repressive in society. A heady air of revolution took hold as millions of discontented factory workers joined the fray. The army was called in but at first could not contain the situation. Yet by mid-June, less than a month later, order had been restored. Although workers were unwilling to see the state toppled, far-reaching liberalization and reforms began to take place.

MITTERRAND'S *GRANDS PROJETS*

On becoming the first Socialist President of the Fifth Republic, François Mitterrand indulged grandiose ambitions to enhance the capital. One of these was the construction of the gigantic Grande Arche, in the business district of La Défense, which marks the western end of an imaginary line across the city joining the Arc de Triomphe and the Louvre. The Louvre was enhanced by the glass pyramid erected in the main courtyard, and the Opéra Bastille, a gigantic cultural venue, was built as a focal point in the working-class district of Bastille.

Other grand Mitterrand projects include the transformation of the former river port at Bercy, and the construction of the Institut du Monde Arabe and the new Bibliothèque Nationale on the Left Bank of the river Seine.

CITY OF ART AND LITERATURE

Le Consulat bar, on a street corner in Montmartre, together with À La Bonne Franquette across the road, were haunts of the large crowd of young artists gathering in the city. Such was Paris's reputation in the early years of the century that artists such as Pablo Picasso, Georges Braque and Marc Chagall came to stay or live in the city. Picasso, who moved to Paris in 1904, was one of few who did not derive his inspiration from the people, streets and bars of Montmartre, concentrating on more imaginative imagery and, with Braque, the development of Cubism. Between the wars, many French and foreign writers came to immerse themselves in Paris, among them Gertrude Stein, Ernest Hemingway, Ezra Pound and Henry Miller.

OCCUPATION AND LIBERATION

Nazi Germany invaded France in May 1940, and a month later entered Paris. German troops and tanks marched proudly down the Champs-Élysées. Many Parisians fled, and the Government left for Vichy. There was staunch resistance to the Germans, but also collaboration.

In July 1942, some 13,000 members of the Jewish community were rounded up and deported east to concentration camps. This was the turning point, and the silent majority began to form an underground resistance movement.

The liberation of Paris in August 1944 saw thousands of people throng the Champs-Élysées in celebration. Resistance politician and leader of the Free French Forces Charles de Gaulle swept to power as provisional president.

Paris is one of the world's most-loved cities, welcoming more than 28 million foreign visitors each year. The capital has a resident population of just over 2.2 million people, including students and temporary workers from elsewhere in France and other countries. In 2002 four per cent of French citizens were Parisian. Around 11 million people live in the suburbs and satellite towns of the Île de France, and fast, inexpensive and relatively pleasant rail services bring these out-of-town Parisians into the city to work, shop, dine and be entertained.

SUMMER HEAT

Summer 2003 took a tragic turn when hundreds of elderly Paris residents died of hyperthermia and dehydration, as temperatures soared to above 40°C (104°F). In July, the heatwave was assumed to be nothing more than part of a national hot spell and television news reports advised people leaving town to take plenty of cold drinks and keep children cool. But by mid-August the crisis in Paris had escalated, with nine-day waits for funerals. The government added heatwaves to the list of national emergencies covered by the White Plan which grants special powers to hospital chiefs and local authorities in the event of terrorist attacks and nuclear accidents.

PARIS PLAGE

Paris Plage, the beach by the Seine, has become a summer must-see in Paris. From mid-July to mid-August, when most Parisians desert the city, part of the Right Bank is transformed into a seaside.

Palm trees (Parisian-style, in a chic row) sway over 1,350 tonnes of imported sand, along with 300 deck chairs, 150 parasols (umbrellas) and striped changing tents. Paris Plage was introduced in summer 2002. In 2011 the 'plage' also included free concerts and exhibitions and a volleyball tournament.

CITY OF PROTEST

Parisians seem to feel it a matter of pride to pour into the streets to express their grievances by rallying, marching and putting up barricades. But while the Left demonstrates on the streets, when it is time to step into the polling booths it is the Right that has consistently won control of Paris. The election of Socialist mayor Bertrand Delanoë in 2001 meant that for the first time in almost 100 years Paris was ruled by the Left. He was re-elected in 2008. Meanwhile, the Paris-based national government is dominated by the Right under the charismatic and internationally popular Nicolas Sarkozy.

Clockwise from above *Paris Plage brings the seaside to the city every year at the height of summer; Parisians rally in place du Trocadéro to mark World Poverty Day on 17 October 2007*

ON THE MOVE

On the Move gives you detailed advice and information about the various options for travelling to Paris before explaining the best ways to get around the city once you are there. Handy tips help you with everything from buying tickets to renting a car.

ON THE MOVE | PARIS

ARRIVING BY AIR

You can get flights to Paris from most major European cities and direct from many other destinations worldwide. Major international carriers are served by the larger Roissy-Charles de Gaulle Airport, 23km (14 miles) northeast of central Paris. There are good rail and bus links between the airport and the city centre. Orly Airport has domestic flights and some international flights. It is 14km (8.5 miles) south of the city's heart, with bus but no direct rail links.

TIPS

» The tourist office on the arrivals level of Orly Ouest is open from 7.15am to 9.45pm. The office in T1 of Roissy-Charles de Gaulle is open from 7am to 8.30pm and the T2 office is open 8am to 10.30pm.
» Terminals 1 and 2 at Roissy-Charles de Gaulle airport are a fair distance apart. When departing make sure you know which terminal you are leaving from.
» When departing from any of the airports, you should allow plenty of time for extra security checks.

ROISSY-CHARLES DE GAULLE

Paris's busiest airport has three terminals: T1, T2 and T3 (formerly T9). Terminal 2 is subdivided into 2A, 2B, 2C, 2D, 2E, 2F and 2G. Airlines operating out of T1 include Aer Lingus, bmi, United Airlines and US Airways. T2 serves Air France, American Airlines, British Airways, KLM and others. Airlines using T3 include the low-cost Jet2. Airlines change terminals from time to time so check with the airport before setting off. You'll find information desks, shops, restaurants, banks,

GETTING TO PARIS FROM THE AIRPORT

AIRPORT	TAXI	RER
Roissy-Charles de Gaulle (CDG)	Cost: €50–€60. From 8pm–7am taxi fares are 40 per cent higher. N.B. For heavy luggage there is an additional charge of €0.90. Journey time: 30 min–1 hour	RER line B takes you into the heart of Paris (Gare du Nord, Châtelet or St-Michel). Trains leave every 5–15 min, 5am–0.15am. Cost: €10. Journey time: 40 min
Orly (ORY)	Cost: around €40–€50. Journey time: 15–30 min	The Orlyval train (Mon–Sat 6am–11pm, Sun 7am–11pm) takes you two stops to Antony, where you pick up RER line B. Cost: €11. Journey time: 35 min
Beauvais Tillé (BVA)	Cost: around €140–€180. Journey time: 1 hour 20 min	From Beauvais train station, take the TER train (Train Express Régional) to the Gare du Nord in Paris (Gare du Nord, Magenta). Departures daily 6.30am–8pm, every 30–90 min. Cost: €13 for a single fare. Journey time: around 1 hour 15 min

bureaux de change, car rental companies and first-aid facilities in T1 and T2. Left luggage (luggage storage) facilities are available at T2 TGV-RER station level. T3 has shops, cafés, a bureau de change and car rental outlets. The airport has two RER stations—CDG1 for T1 and T3 and CDG2 for T2. Shuttle buses run from the terminals to both stations. From there you can then take RER line B into Paris. Buses also run to the city (see the chart below).

ORLY

Orly Airport has two terminals—Orly Sud and Orly Ouest. Shuttle buses or the Orlyval train link the two. The airport has shops, restaurants, bureaux de change, car rental firms and medical facilities. There are no direct rail links into Paris, but the Orlyval train takes you two stops to Antony, where you can change to RER line B. The Orlybus runs from the airport to Denfert-Rochereau Métro station; the Air France bus will take you farther into the city, to Les Invalides. Alternatively, take a shuttle bus to Pont de Rungis RER station then RER line C to Gare d'Austerlitz, St-Michel-Notre-Dame or Les Invalides.

BEAUVAIS TILLÉ

Beauvais Tillé is a small airport in Beauvais, north of Paris, in the Oise *département*. It is currently used by low-cost airlines. Facilities include a news vendor, restaurant, tourist information desk and car rental desks. A bus connects with incoming flights and takes you to Porte Maillot, on the northwestern edge of Paris. It is also possible to take a taxi, although this is an expensive option.

USEFUL TELEPHONE NUMBERS AND WEBSITES

ROISSY-CHARLES DE GAULLE
www.adp.fr
Information: 01 70 36 39 50 (€0.34 per min)
Police: 01 48 62 31 22
Air France: 36 45 (€0.34 per min)
Air France bus to Paris: 0892 350 820 (€0.34 per min); www.cars-airfrance.com
RATP (RER): 32 46; www.ratp.fr

ORLY
www.adp.fr
Information: 39 50 (€0.34 per min) or +33 1 70 36 39 50 from outside Paris
Police: 01 49 75 43 04
Air France bus to Paris: 0892 35 08 20; (€0.34 per min); www.cars-airfrance.com
Orlybus information: 0892 68 77 14
RATP information (Orlyval train and RERB): 32 46; www.ratp.fr
SNCF information and ticket sales (RERC): 36 35 (€0.34 per min) or 0892 335 335

BEAUVAIS TILLÉ
www.aeroportbeauvais.com
Information: 0892 682 066 (8am–10.30pm; €0.37 per min)
Transfer bus information: 0892 682 064 (€0.37 per min)

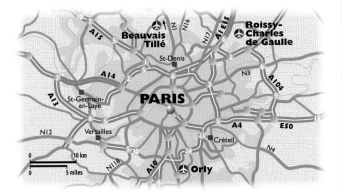

MÉTRO	BUS	CAR
None	The Air France bus runs from Terminals 1 and 2 to Montparnasse and Gare de Lyon every 30 min, 6am–10pm. Cost: €17. Journey time: 45 min–1 hour. Another Air France bus runs to the Arc de Triomphe every 20–30 min, 6am–11pm. Cost: €15. Journey time: 45 min–1 hour. The Roissybus runs every 15 min from Terminals 1, 2 and 3 to Opéra, 6am–11pm. Cost: €10. Journey time: 60 min	Take the A1 south to Paris. Journey time: 30 min–1 hour, depending on traffic
None	The Air France bus runs from Orly Sud and Ouest to Les Invalides and Gare Montparnasse every 20 min, 6am–10.20pm. Cost: €12. Journey time: 30 min. The Orlybus runs from Orly Sud and Ouest to Denfert-Rochereau Métro station every 15–20 min, 6am–11.30pm. Cost: €7. Journey time: 30 min. Bus 285 links terminal Sud with Louis Aragon Métro station in Villejuif for onward connection to central Paris services. Runs every 25–30 min, 4.30am–1am. Cost €1.90	Take the A6, then A6A or A6B into Paris. Journey time: 15–40 min, depending on traffic
None	Bus to Porte Maillot. Cost: €15 (available exclusively for passengers holding a valid flight ticket). Journey time: around 1 hour 15 min	Take the N1, A16, N1 then A1. Journey time: 1 hour 20 min

ARRIVING BY TRAIN

The Channel Tunnel rail link has revolutionized travel between London and Paris, allowing you to reach France's capital from Britain's in less than three hours, without leaving the ground or boarding a boat. The Queen and François Mitterrand, France's president at the time, opened the tunnel in 1994, almost 200 years after the first designs were submitted for an undersea link between England and France. It is the longest undersea tunnel in the world, with 39km (24 miles) of its 50km (31-mile) length under the English Channel.

BOARDING EUROSTAR

» Up to 19 trains per day travel to Paris from London; some stop en route at Ashford International and Ebbsfleet International (UK) and Calais (France). There are also direct trains to Disneyland® Resort Paris. The journey time to Paris is 2 hours 15 minutes.
» Trains leave from special platforms at St. Pancras International Station, which has connections to underground services for central London locations and mainland train services.
» The terminal is a combination of fully refurbished Victorian architecture and a 21st-century glass edifice, incorporating a shopping mall, eateries and the longest champagne bar in Europe.
» Automatic check-in facilities are available for passengers with suitable tickets, otherwise check in at the desks. You must do this at least 30 minutes before your train is due to leave.
» Before you reach the departure lounge you must go through airport-style security checks and passport control. French passport control is actually carried out at St. Pancras.
» Once in the departure lounge there are newspaper and gift shops, cafés, toilets, internet points and a post box.
» Boarding begins around 20 minutes before departure. Information screens in the lounge tell you where and when to board.
» Each train has 18 carriages (cars) so you could face a long walk along the platform. Trolleys (carts) are available, but you'll need a £1 coin as a deposit.
» Once on board, large cases must be stored on the luggage racks at the end of each carriage (car), although you can put smaller bags in the racks above your seat.

THE JOURNEY

» A buffet car serves drinks, snacks and light meals. There are toilets and baby-changing facilities on board. The journey through the tunnel itself takes around 20 minutes and an announcement is made just before you enter.

ARRIVING

» When you arrive at Paris's Gare du Nord station you don't need to go through passport control again. Watch for pickpockets at the station.
» The covered taxi stand is well signposted. Don't be too depressed by the long queue—it moves fairly quickly. A taxi into the heart of Paris usually costs €10 to €15. There are extra charges for luggage and for travel after 7pm and on Sundays.

» Gare du Nord is on Métro lines 4 (purple) and 5 (orange). Line 4 (direction Porte d'Orléans) will take you across the river to the Left Bank. If your hotel is on the Right Bank, you can change lines at Gare de l'Est, Strasbourg St-Denis, Réaumur Sébastopol or Châtelet. Line 5 (direction place d'Italie) is handy if you're heading to the Bastille area.

» Gare du Nord is also on three RER lines: D (green), E (mauve) and B (blue). Line B takes you to Châtelet, then on to the Left Bank (St-Michel-Notre-Dame and Luxembourg). The RER can be a confusing rail system to the uninitiated (▷ 59) so if it's your first time in Paris it may be better to take the Métro or a taxi.

RETURN JOURNEY

» The Eurostar terminal is on the first floor of the Gare du Nord. There are a few gift shops and coffee bars, but facilities are not as comprehensive as in London. There is no post box, so rid yourself of any last-minute postcards before you get to the terminal. British officials check passports at the Gare du Nord, immediately after check-in.

» Electronic screens will tell you which of the two boarding points to use and when to board.

FACTS AND FIGURES

» Construction work on the tunnel began in 1987, completed in 1991.

» The tunnel is 40m (131ft) below the seabed.

» Trains travel at up to 300kph (186mph).

» Each train is 400m (1,312ft) long.

» There are two main tunnels and a service tunnel. This doubles as a safety tunnel and is designed to stay smoke-free in the event of a fire.

» Trains have a driver's carriage (car) at either end, so they can quickly change direction and exit the tunnel if an emergency arises ahead.

» Celebrated French designer Philippe Starck has designed staff

Opposite *TGV high-speed trains serve France and parts of Spain*
Right *Gare du Nord station in Paris*

uniforms, business lounges and train interiors.

» As a result of the Tread Lightly campaign, a cut of 31 per cent in carbon dioxide emissions per passenger journey has been achieved compared with 2007. Eurostar now aims to cut all their emissions by 25 per cent by 2015.

TIPS

» You'll usually pay less for your ticket if you reserve it in advance.

Return (round-trip) fares are from £69. This is highly recommended as non-reserved seats are limited.

» The train is split into Premium, First and Standard classes. Premium and First class give you a meal, extra legroom, a reclining seat and free newspapers. Certain tickets allow admission to the business lounges in London and at Gare du Nord.

» You need your passport to travel between Britain and France (see Passports and Visas, ▷ 267).

» The official luggage allowance is two suitcases and one piece of hand luggage, labelled with your name and seat number.

» Luggage trolleys (carts) are available on the platforms in London and at Gare du Nord, but you need a £1 or €1 coin (refundable). If you have a heavy case, a trolley is a good idea as the walk along the platform can be long if your carriage (car) happens to be the last of 18.

ARRIVING BY CAR OR LONG-DISTANCE BUS

If you want to drive from the UK to France you can take either the Eurotunnel or a ferry, both of which run to Calais. From here it should take around 3 hours 15 minutes to drive to Paris. Driving to France from countries on mainland Europe is straightforward.

EUROTUNNEL

If you are driving from the UK, you can load your car onto the Shuttle train at Folkestone for the 35-minute journey under the English Channel to Calais. There are up to four departures per hour, 24 hours a day. Reserve ahead.

To reach the Folkestone terminal take the M20 to junction 11A, then follow signs to the Channel Tunnel. Border controls take place in the UK. You stay with your vehicle during the journey, although you can go to the toilet or walk about within the carriage (car). Staff are available if you need assistance. To reach Paris from Calais you can take the A16 (E40) in the direction of Dunkerque, then join the A26 (E15). At the junction with the A1, head south on the A1 (E15), which takes you to Paris. You will have to pay autoroute tolls. For more driving information, ▷ 62–63.

Eurotunnel Contact Details

08705 353 535 (UK number);
www.eurotunnel.com

BY SEA

The cost of crossing to France from England by ferry varies widely according to the time, day and month of travel. Most companies require you to check in at least 30 minutes before departure, although you may need to arrive earlier.

P&O Ferries sail from Dover to Calais (journey time: 70 to 90 minutes). Facilities on board the ferries include shops, cafés, bureaux de change and lounges. From Calais, it takes around 3 hours 15 minutes to drive to Paris—for directions, see Eurotunnel.

Brittany Ferries sail from Portsmouth to Caen (journey time: 4 hours). The drive to Paris takes around 2 hours 40 minutes. The company also operates services from Portsmouth to Cherbourg (3 hours), Portsmouth St-Malo (11 hours), Poole to Cherbourg (2.5 hours) and Plymouth to Roscoff (6–8 hours). Transfers to Paris are longer for these routes.

DFDS ferries operate a service between Dover and Dunkerque. Crossing time is two hours.

P&O Ferries sail from Portsmouth to Le Havre (journey time: 5 hours 30 minutes). The drive to Paris takes around 2 hours 25 minutes.

Ferry Contact Details

Brittany Ferries: 0871 244 0744 (UK); www.brittany-ferries.co.uk
DFDS: 0871 574 7235 (UK); www.dfds.com
P&O Ferries: 08716 642 121 (UK); www.poferries.com

BY LONG-DISTANCE BUS

Taking the bus from the UK can be a useful option if you're on a tight budget, although the journey from London takes almost eight hours. Eurolines runs from Victoria coach station to Paris up to five times a day, with pick-up points at Canterbury and Dover, in Kent. The Channel crossing is made either by Eurotunnel or ferry. You arrive at the bus terminal in avenue du Général de Gaulle, in Bagnolet, on the eastern edge of Paris.

Try to reserve your ticket at least 30 days in advance to get the best prices.

Eurolines Contact Details

08717 818 179;
www.eurolines.co.uk

TIPS

» It is often less expensive to reserve Eurotunnel tickets online than by telephone.
» Vehicles running on Liquid Petroleum Gas cannot use the Eurotunnel.
» Look for low-cost ferry deals in British newspapers.
» The phone numbers given on this page are UK-based. To call from the US, dial 011 44, then omit the initial zero from the number. To call from mainland Europe, dial 00 44, then omit the zero.

Below *Car ferries operate between Dover in the UK and Calais in northern France*

Paris has a comprehensive, efficient and relatively inexpensive transportation network and you should have few problems finding your way around the city. The Métro (underground/subway) is the backbone of the network. Other useful options include buses, riverboats and the suburban RER trains. Finally, don't forget your own two feet—central Paris is compact and walking is a great way to get your bearings.

The Métro is often the quickest way of getting from A to B, and with around 300 stations you're rarely more than five minutes' walk from a line. Trains vary from ultra modern to past-their-best, depending on the line, but services usually run with minimum delays (barring strike action). Once in the station, be prepared for long walks to reach the platform—especially at Châtelet—although you won't need to go deep underground. During rush hour the trains can become uncomfortably crowded and you're unlikely to find a seat. Lines that connect key visitor attractions (such as Line 1) can be crowded all day.

Buses give you the chance to see the city as you travel and their routes are clearly marked at the stops and on the buses. But they are slower than the Métro and can become crowded in rush hour.

The Métro, some RER lines and most buses are operated by RATP.

Taxis are useful if you have lots of baggage or if you don't want to use the Métro at night.

TRAVEL INFORMATION
» You can pick up free Métro maps at every station.
» For 24-hour recorded information in English, Italian, Spanish and German, call 0892 68 41 14.
» To speak to an advisor (in French only) call 32 46.
» The major stations have information desks, although communication can sometimes be limited if you don't speak French.
» The website www.ratp.fr has lots of helpful information, in French and English. Click on Paris Visite for advice for visitors.

» There are travel information points at the airports.

ON THE MOVE WITH CHILDREN
» Children under the age of four travel free on the Métro, buses and RER.
» Children under the age of 10 receive a 50 per cent reduction on ticket prices.
» Some buses have ramps for pushchairs (strollers) and wheelchairs at the central doors.
» Taking a pushchair (stroller) on the Métro can be tricky, owing to ticket barriers and steps to platforms.

TICKETS
» The Métro and buses use the same tickets and travel cards (▷ 52). These can also be used on the RER within central Paris.
» The city is divided into fare zones. Most of the key sights are in Zone 1, although the Grande Arche is in Zone 3, Roissy-Charles de Gaulle airport is in Zone 5 and Orly airport is in Zone 4.
» Buy tickets at Métro stations, on buses (single tickets only) and at some news-stands.
» To save time, use the ticket machines in station concourses. Instructions are given in a choice of languages.
» Most stations have ticket offices, generally open from 5.30am to midnight. If you don't speak French, take a copy of the RER or Métro map with you so you can point to where you want to go if necessary.
» Major credit and debit cards are accepted at stations, although cash is more convenient.
» A single ticket costs €1.70 and covers all Métro stations, RER

stations within the heart of Paris and most buses (▷ 52).
» If you are planning to make good use of the Métro and buses during your visit, a *carnet* (book) of 10 tickets or a travelcard could be a better option.
» For more information on tickets and travelcards, ▷ 52.

TIPS
» Try to avoid using buses and the Métro during rush hour (roughly 7.30am–9.30am and 4.30pm–7pm).
» Smoking is banned on buses, the Métro and the RER.
» Buying a *carnet* of 10 tickets is better value than buying tickets separately for each bus or Métro journey, and also saves time waiting at the ticket office.
» If you are on your own, you may feel uncomfortable using the Métro late at night.
» It is now possible to travel on the Métro until 2.15am on Friday and Saturday.

Below *Ticket machines display instructions in a choice of languages*

TICKETS

TYPE	PRICE	VALID	EXTRA INFORMATION
Single ticket	€1.70 (€1.90 if bought on the bus)	Tickets are valid on the Métro, the RER (within central Paris) and most buses. You don't have to use them on the day of purchase, but once you have stamped a ticket (by inserting it into the automatic barrier at Métro stations or in the machine on buses) it is valid for 90 minutes	You can change Métro and RER lines within one journey on the same ticket, but you can't change from the Métro to a bus on the same ticket. t+ tickets (▷ 58), sold by RATP, are valid for bus to bus and bus to tram transfers, but not, currently, tickets sold by bus drivers on vehicles
Carnet	€12.50 for 10 single tickets	As single tickets, see above	This is cost-effective if you are planning eight journeys or more
Mobilis	Zones 1–2: €6.50 Zones 1–3: €8.50 Zones 1–4: €10.50 Zones 1–5: €14	Valid for one day, within the relevant zones, on the Métro, buses, RER and Transilien services, except airport shuttles Roissybus, Orlybus and Orlyval	A less expensive option than the one-day Paris Visite card (see below)
Paris Visite, Zones 1–3	1 day: €9.50 2 days: €15.50 3 days: €21 5 days: €30 Children's passes (4- to 11-year-olds) are roughly half-price	Valid for an unlimited number of journeys on the Métro, bus, RER and Transilien services, within Zones 1–3. The ticket is valid from the first occasion you use it	If you need to travel for one day only or if you are staying within Zone 1, the Mobilis pass (see above) is a less expensive option. But with the Paris Visite card you also receive special offers for various sights. Buy the ticket at Paris tourist offices or at stations
Paris Visite, Zones 1–6	1 day: €20 2 days: €30 3 days: €42 5 days: €52	Valid for an unlimited number of journeys on the Métro, bus, RER and Transilien services, within Zones 1–5 (including Versailles, Disneyland Resort Paris, and Orly and Roissy–Charles de Gaulle airports)	An expensive option
Navigo Mois et Semaine	Zones 1–2: €19 Zones 1–3: €25 Zones 1–4: €30 Zones 1–5: €34	Valid for a week on the Métro, buses and RER	The card is officially intended for residents of the Île de France and runs from Monday to Sunday. So the earlier in the week you purchase it, the better the value. You'll need a passport-size photo
La Carte Orange-Coupon Mensuel	Zones 1–2: €62 Zones 1–3: €81 Zones 1–4: €99	Valid for a month on the Métro, buses and RER	See the Navigo Mois et Semaine pass above

PARIS MÉTRO

Paris's Métro (Métropolitain) system is the lifeblood of the city, carrying around four million passengers each day. The first trains ran in 1900, during the belle-époque era. The network has since grown to 16 lines and 211km (131 miles) of track. The Métro system is efficient, inexpensive and relatively clean. It is the quickest way to travel for most journeys within the city.

Each line is colour-coded and numbered (1–14, 3b and 7b). Stations are identified either by a large M or by the famous art nouveau Métro signs. Steps, or occasionally escalators, lead down into a lobby, where you can buy tickets from either a manned booth or a machine. Larger stations have shops and cafés.

To reach the platforms, validate (composter) your ticket by inserting it into the machine at the automatic barrier, then collect it and keep

UNDERSTANDING THE MÉTRO MAP

The information below will help you understand the Métro map on pages 56–57 and on the inside back cover. Symbols used on the map in this book may differ slightly from the symbols found on the maps posted up at Métro stations.

MÉTRO STATION

A small triangle indicates a station with no interchanges.

LINES

Each line is colour-coded and is marked at each end with its number and final destination.

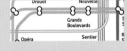

STATION WITH INTERCHANGE

Stations used by more than one line are marked with a white circle.

END OF THE LINE

Terminus stations are placed in a white box.

ROUTE MAPS

Route maps are posted up inside each train, allowing you to follow your journey.

INTERCHANGING LINES

On route maps, any connecting lines are marked underneath the station.

it with you—inspectors make random checks. You'll often have a fairly long walk to the platform, so follow direction signs carefully. Signs will show the line number and colour. You also need to know the final destination of the train in the direction you wish to travel. Trains are frequent but get crowded during rush hour. An orange *Correspondance* sign on the platform gives directions to connecting lines. Blue signs marked *Sortie* indicate the exits.

DID YOU KNOW?

» Hector Guimard's famous art nouveau Métro entrances are at Abbesses and Porte Dauphine.
» Fittingly for a city known for its perfume, Paris's Métro stations are freshened up with a specially created musk and vanilla scent, known as *Madeleine*.
» Look out for Métro stations whose decoration reflects the location. Examples include Bastille, with murals depicting the uprising, and Louvre-Rivoli, with its museum-style displays.
» The newest line, number 14, has glass doors separating the platform and the tracks. On the trains, a PA system announces the station you are approaching.

USEFUL LINES FOR REACHING THE SIGHTS

Line 1 (yellow) runs from east to west across the city, starting at Château de Vincennes and finishing at Grande Arche de la Défense. Key stops include Gare de Lyon, Bastille, Louvre-Rivoli and Concorde. It also runs up the Champs-Élysées—stopping at Champs-Élysées-Clemenceau, Franklin D. Roosevelt, George V and Charles de Gaulle-Étoile—allowing you to hop from one end of the avenue to the other.

Line 4 (light purple) connects the St-Germain-des-Prés district with the Right Bank. It also stops at Gare du Nord, location of the Eurostar terminal.

Line 9 (light green) takes you from the outskirts of the Bois de Boulogne, in the west of the city, up to the popular shopping areas of the Right Bank (Havre-Caumartin for Printemps and Chaussée d'Antin for Galeries Lafayette). It then continues eastwards through République and Nation.

Line 12 (dark green) is useful if you're heading to Montmartre (use the Abbesses stop). It runs from the Left Bank. Useful stations en route include Solférino (for the Musée d'Orsay), Concorde and Madeleine.

Line 14 (purple) is handy if you are staying on the eastern side of the city, within walking distance of the Gare de Lyon. This ultramodern line is the quickest way to reach the heart of the city, taking you straight to Châtelet with no stops, then on to Pyramides and Madeleine. In the other direction, it runs to

HOW TO USE THE MÉTRO

• Trains run from 5.30am to around 12.30am.
• When waiting for the train, stand away from the edge of the platform.

• To open train doors press the button (on newer trains) or lift the handle (on older trains). Most trains on Line 1 have doors that open automatically.
• Let passengers leave the train before you enter.

• A signal sounds when the automatic doors are about to close. Stand clear of the doors.

• Keep your bags close to you and watch out for pickpockets. Don't carry valuables in back pockets or rucksacks.

• Keep hold of your ticket, in case an inspector asks to see it.
• Watch for the gap between the train and the platform as you step onto and off the train.

• If you need to change lines, don't leave the interchange station or you will invalidate your ticket.
• If you find you're going in the wrong direction, come off at the next station and double-back. Follow directions to the correct platform, but stay within the automatic barriers or you'll invalidate your ticket.
• Once you have finished your journey, signs in the station indicate which exit leads to which road.
• As with many large cities, you'll probably come across people begging in Paris's Métro stations.

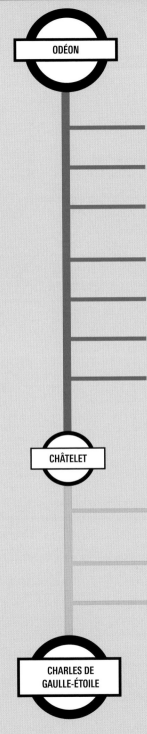

ODÉON

CHÂTELET

CHARLES DE GAULLE-ÉTOILE

Below is a typical Métro journey from Odéon to Charles de Gaulle-Étoile (the Arc de Triomphe).

● Find a map and note the colours and numbers of the lines you'll need.

● Purchase a single ticket or use one of your *carnet* tickets or a travel pass (▷ 52).

● To reach the platforms, insert your ticket into the automatic barrier and pick it up when it re-emerges.

● Follow signs for Line 4 (light purple) in the direction of Porte de Clignancourt.

● Once at the platform, you shouldn't have too long to wait for a train.

● A route map on board the train allows you to follow your journey.

● Get off at Châtelet and follow the orange *Correspondance* signs for Line 1 (yellow), in the direction of La Défense.

● Bear in mind that Châtelet is one of the largest Métro stations, with a long walk between some platforms.

● Board the train, then get off at Charles de Gaulle-Étoile.

● Follow the blue Sortie (exit) signs and look for the street exit that you require.

Bercy then across the river to the Bibliothèque François Mitterrand.

TIPS

» When planning your route, don't confuse Métro lines with the suburban RER lines—both are usually shown on Métro maps. RER lines have letters rather than numbers and will usually flow off the map.

» The RATP website (www.ratp.fr) has a helpful route planner and also gives up-to-date traffic and travel information.

» To estimate your journey time, allow two minutes between each station. Remember that it could take five minutes to walk to the platform (especially in stations such as Châtelet).

» For recorded information in various languages call 0892 68 41 14.

» To speak to a travel advisor (in French only) call 32 46.

» Cash is more useful than credit cards when paying for tickets.

» Keep hold of your ticket until you have left the station, as you may come across an inspector.

» Street maps of the local areas are posted up in most station lobbies.

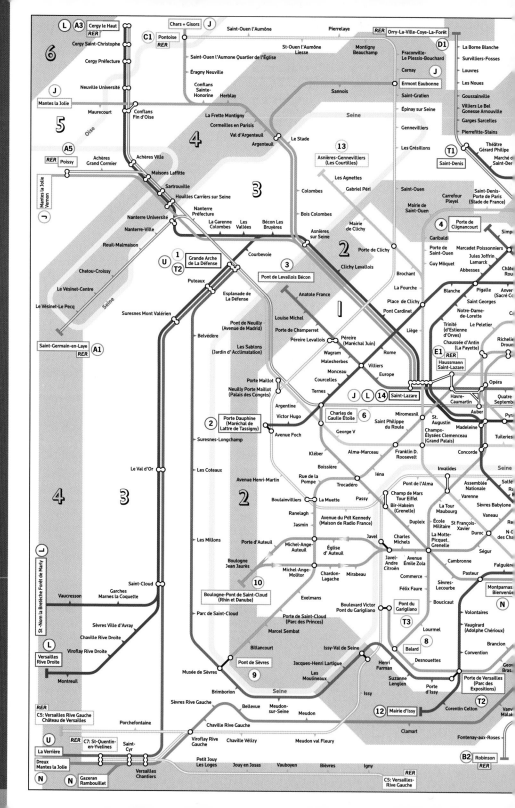

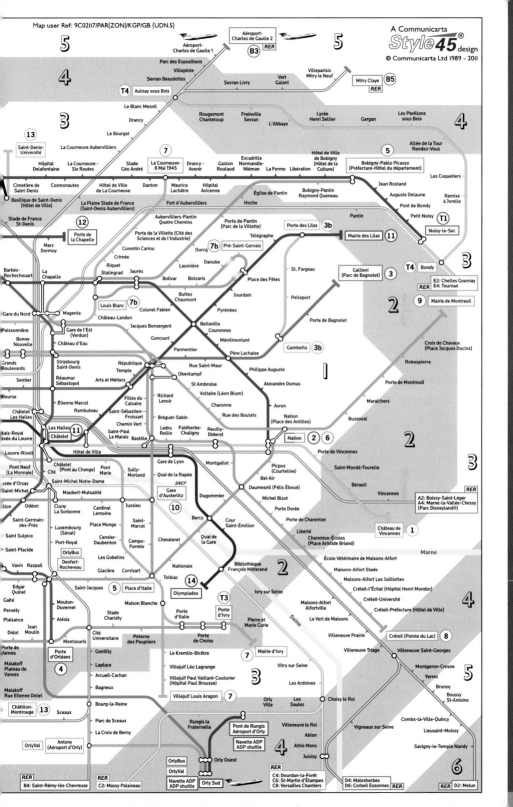

A Communicarta
Style45® design
© Communicarta Ltd 1989 - 2011

ON THE MOVE GETTING AROUND

Paris has a good network of buses, with more than 1,300 vehicles negotiating the city's traffic. Taking the bus is a good idea if you want to see the streets and sights rather than simply passing under them on the Métro, but don't expect to get anywhere quickly—the average speed is less than 13kph (8mph)!

GETTING AROUND BY BUS

» Most buses are painted easy-to-see turquoise and run from 7am to 8.30pm, although some continue until around 12.30am. You're unlikely to have to wait more than 5 or 10 minutes from Monday to Saturday, but services are reduced or, on some routes, non-existent on Sunday.

» The route number is displayed on the front of the bus, along with the final destination.

» Hold out your hand as a signal for the driver to stop the bus.

» If you need to buy a ticket, have the exact money ready as drivers do not carry much change. You can buy only single tickets on board. For information on travelcards, ▷ 52.

» Enter at the front of the bus and show your travelcard or *carnet* ticket (▷ 52) to the driver. *Carnet* tickets or single tickets must be stamped in the machine next to the driver.

» In rush hour you're unlikely to get a seat. Be prepared for a long and uncomfortable stand.

» If you are unsure of the route, you can track your journey on the route map in the bus.

» Just before your stop, press the red button to alert the driver that you want to get off. You'll see the *arrêt demandé* (stop requested) sign light up.

» Leave by the central doors.

UNDERSTANDING BUS STOPS

Bus Numbers

Bus numbers are marked on the stop in the colour in which they appear on the route map. The number is also shown on the front of the bus.

Routes

The route is displayed on a large-scale map and every stop is marked. The stop you are standing at will be highlighted.

Timetables

Information is available about the hours and days each route operates.

Bus Stop Types

» Major bus stops are covered and have a small seat. Minor stops are marked by a pillar showing the bus numbers and routes.

» All bus stops are a distinctive turquoise.

» Major stops will also display a helpful map of the area, as well as the ubiquitous advertising posters.

» When planning your return journey, note that buses do not necessarily follow the same route in both directions, so you may have to find a different bus to take you back.

TICKET OPTIONS

» Buses use the same tickets as the Métro. A t+ ticket allows you to change buses within a 90-minute period, but these must be bought from an RATP kiosk.

» You can buy single tickets on board, but not travelcards or *carnets* of 10 tickets. Be sure to have the exact change ready.

» Always stamp single tickets (including *carnet* tickets) in the machine near the driver, but not *Paris Visite, Mobilis* or *Carte Orange* passes. Keep your ticket until you have left the bus.

FINDING INFORMATION

» The *Grand Plan Lignes et Rues*, available from Métro stations, has a useful bus map.

» www.ratp.fr has bus information in French and English, as well as a handy route planner.

» Call 0892 68 41 14 for a recorded message in various languages or 32 46 to speak to an advisor (in French).

OTHER SERVICES

Airport buses: ▷ 46–47.

Balabus: The Balabus runs between La Grande Arche and Gare de Lyon, taking in the Right Bank on its eastward journey and the Left Bank on its westward journey. It operates only on Sundays (afternoon to early evening), April to September.

Montmartrobus and funicular: ▷ 226–227.

Noctilien: Night buses link Châtelet with the suburbs from 1am to 5am. Buses are identified by a letter and tickets cost €1.70 for Zones 1 and 2 plus €1.70 per extra zone. With waits of up to one hour, you may prefer to take a taxi.

USEFUL ROUTES (OR SECTIONS OF ROUTES) FOR SIGHTSEEING

27 (southbound)	• Opéra Palais Garnier • Musée du Louvre • Pont Neuf • Pont St-Michel • Jardin du Luxembourg
29 (eastbound)	• Opéra Palais Garnier • Bourse • Place des Victoires • Centre Georges Pompidou • Musée Carnavalet • Place des Vosges • Bastille
42 (northbound)	• Tour Eiffel • Rond-Point des Champs-Élysées • Place de la Concorde • Place de la Madeleine
69 (westbound)	• Bastille • Musée du Louvre • Musée d'Orsay • Les Invalides • Champ de Mars
73 (eastbound)	• Arc de Triomphe • Champs-Élysées • Place de la Concorde • Assemblée Nationale • Musée d'Orsay

The RER train network travels through the city en route to the suburbs and can be a good time-saver if you are going from one side of town to the other. For trips farther afield, the Transilien network covers the Île de France region.

RER

The RER (Réseau Express Régional) dates from 1969 and is operated by RATP and SNCF. It serves Disneyland® Resort Paris to the east, Roissy-Charles de Gaulle Airport to the north, Versailles to the west and the Orly Airport train link to the south. Trains run underground in central Paris and overground in the suburbs. For a short trip you're usually better off using the Métro.

Tickets

» A single Métro ticket is valid for RER journeys in central Paris and you can change lines (including Métro lines) on the same ticket. For journeys farther afield, you'll need to buy a separate ticket valid for the particular destination.
» Travelcards (▷ 52) must cover all the zones you travel through.

Using the RER

» Trains run from around 5.30am to 12.30am.
» The RER has five lines, named A to E. Each line breaks into offshoots, which bear a number after the letter.
» Pick up a *Grand Plan Touristique* or another RER map from the station to identify the line and offshoot you need. The RER lines in central Paris are on the Métro map (▷ 56–57).

» Information screens in the foyer tell you which platform you need; or you could ask at the ticket desk.
» Insert your ticket into the automatic barrier and remember to retrieve it when it emerges.
» An increasing number of platforms have screens with information on arrival times for the next five trains.
» When leaving the train, follow blue *Sortie* signs if it is the end of your journey, or orange *Correspondance* signs if you need to change lines.
» Slot your ticket into the automatic barrier to leave the station.

TRANSILIEN TRAINS

The Transilien network, operated by SNCF, covers stations all over the Île de France. You are most likely to use these trains if you are taking an excursion to places such as Fontainebleau (▷ 258–259). Trains leave from mainline stations.

Using Transilien Trains

» Buy tickets from the ticket desk or the machine. Prices vary according to destination. Travelcards are valid if they cover all the zones you travel through.
» Stamp your ticket before boarding, either in the automatic barrier if you pass through one or in the orange machine near the platform entrance.

» Timetables are available at the station. Platform numbers are shown on the information boards in the station concourse.
» Check there is a suitably timed train to bring you back into Paris.

TIPS

» The RATP website (www.ratp.fr) has a helpful route planner, as well as other travel information.
» To speak to an advisor (in French only), call 32 46. Remember that the French pronounce RER *'air-eu-air'*.
» Few visitors use the RER outside central Paris (unless they are going to Versailles, Disneyland or the airport) so you may feel conspicuous. Be aware that some of the suburbs the RER passes through may be run down, and the trains tend to have more graffiti than on the Métro. Trains may be quite empty outside peak times.
» Trains run frequently in central Paris, but less so in outlying areas.
» SNCF's website (www.sncf.fr) has a useful route planner.
» For information over the phone, call 36 36 or 0892 33 53 35.
» If you are leaving from a mainline station, give yourself plenty of time to buy a ticket and find the platform.
» Keep hold of your ticket in case an inspector boards the train.

WHERE TO GO

DESTINATION	LINE	STOP	TIME	ZONE	NOTES
Disneyland Resort Paris	A4	Marne-la-Vallée Chessy (Parc Disneyland)	35 min	Zone 5	You can buy passes for Disneyland Resort Paris from some RATP ticket offices, to save time later, although the passes do not include travel
Versailles	C5	Versailles-Rive Gauche	35 min	Zone 4	Versailles-Rive Gauche is the closest station to the chateau, but you can also travel to Versailles-Chantiers on C7 and C8. Tickets covering train travel and entrance are available (▷ 261)
Roissy-Charles de Gaulle Airport	B3	Aéroport Charles de Gaulle 1 or 2	35 min	Zone 5	Use Charles de Gaulle 1 for Terminal 1 and Terminal 3. Use Charles de Gaulle 2 for Terminal 2
Orly Airport	B4	Antony	30 min to Antony	Zone 3 (Antony)	From Antony, take the Orlyval train to the airport, which is in Zone 4
Chantilly	SNCF (Gare du Nord)	Chantilly-Gouvieux	30 min	Outside the zones	The chateau is a 30-min walk from the station

Taxis are not exorbitantly expensive and can be a relatively stress-free way of getting around. Paris's 16,000 taxis are operated by a variety of companies, but all adhere to the same pricing structure.

USING A TAXI

» The best way to find a taxi is to head to one of the city's 470 taxi stands, marked by a blue Taxis sign. You can phone for a taxi but this is more expensive as the meter starts running as soon as the taxi sets off to collect you.

» You can hail a taxi in the street, if you can find one that is free. A white light on the roof indicates the taxi is available. When the light is off, the taxi is busy.

» All taxis are non-smoking.

» Taxi drivers are permitted to refuse a journey if there are more than three people, if you have animals with you or if it involves taking you outside Paris.

» If you want a receipt, ask for *un reçu*.

» If you have a complaint, contact the Préfecture de Police, Service des Taxis, 36 rue des Morillons, 75015; tel 01 55 76 20 05. Quote the taxi's registration number.

CHARGES

» Prices are regulated and tariffs should be displayed in each taxi. Always check the meter is reset when you enter the taxi. Daytime trips within central Paris should cost under €15.

» Some taxis accept bank cards but it is best to have cash available. It is usual to tip 10 per cent.

» The three tariffs (A, B and C) are set out in the prices chart (below).

TAXI COMPANIES

Taxi companies include:
Abeille Radio Taxi: tel 01 45 83 59 33
Alpha Taxis: tel 01 45 85 85 85; www.alphataxis.fr

Taxis Bleus: tel 0891 70 10 10; www.taxis-bleus.com
Taxis G7: tel 36 07; www.taxisg7.fr
Dedicated phone number for all taxi firms: 01 45 30 30 30.

THE BATOBUS

The Batobus is a relaxing way to get around the city, allowing you to hop on and off at eight stops along the Seine. It runs from early February to early January. From June to the end of August it runs 10–9.30; April to end May and end August to early November 10–7; early November–early January and early February–March 10.30–4.30. Boats leave every 15–30 minutes, stopping at *quais* near the Eiffel Tower, Champs-Élysées, Musée d'Orsay, Louvre, St-Germain-des-Prés, Notre-Dame, Hôtel de Ville and Jardin des Plantes. A one-day pass costs €14, a two-day pass €18 and a five-day pass €21 (half-price for children under 12). You can buy passes at the stops or the tourist office, tel 0825 05 01 01; www.batobus.com.

TAXI PRICES		
Pickup charge	€2.30 (or €3.10 at mainline stations)	
Tarif A	€0.92 per km	Central Paris Mon–Sat, 10am–5pm
Tarif B	€1.17 per km	Suburbs Mon–Sat, 7am–7pm. Central Paris 5pm–10am and all day Sun and public hols. Daytime journeys to and from the airports
Tarif C	€1.42 per km	Suburbs 7pm–7am and all day Sun and public hols. All day, every day outside the suburbs. Night journeys to and from the airports
Surcharges	You will be charged €3 for a fourth passenger and €1 for each piece of luggage over 5kg (11lb). There is a minimum fare of €6.20	
Note: When the taxi waits for you or runs slowly, the hourly tariff applies: Tarif A €30; Tarif B €34; Tarif C €31		

ON THE MOVE · GETTING AROUND

WALKING, BICYCLING, IN-LINE SKATING

Paris is gradually accepting more eco-friendly ways of getting about. An increasing number of people travel by foot or bicycle — you may well find that some sights can be reached more quickly by either of these methods than by the Métro, with its labyrinthine corridors. Bicyclists need to keep their wits about them, but may find their journeys are quicker than by car or bus. In-line skating is also popular, with up to 12,000 people turning out to the special rides on Friday nights. On Sundays and public holidays some of the Seine expressways and canal roads are reserved exclusively for pedestrians, bicyclists and rollerbladers.

WALKING
Métro stations are everywhere and this can make it tempting to hop on a train even for short journeys. But if the weather is good try going on foot instead — it's a great way to get to know the layout of the city. You can easily walk from one district to another and it is far more enjoyable than the Métro.

The downside is the amount of traffic on the busier streets, especially place de la Concorde, Pont Neuf and the roads running alongside the Seine.

BICYCLING
Paris has more than 371km (230 miles) of bicycle tracks and plenty of rental outlets. In 2007 city authorities launched the Velib bike rental initiative (www.velib.paris.fr) to encourage greener transport options. In excess of 20,000 bikes are available to pick up and drop off at more than 1,000 locations around the city.

Fees are paid in the form of an access card (current charges are €1.70 per day, €8 per week or €29 per year) which entitles riders to 30 minutes free use per journey, after which costs are €1 for an additional 30 minutes, €2 for a further 30 minutes and €4 for each additional 30 minutes.

One- and seven-day cards can be bought at rental sites around the city or online and fees due at the end of the rental period can be paid at automatic machines.

Transfers between many major museums and monuments are possible within the initial 30-minute period. The Paris à Vélo map, available from the tourist office,

town hall or bicycle rental shops, gives details of bicycle routes.

Remember that if a bicycle lane is available, you must use it. You must also wear a helmet and have bicycle lights and a bell. Lock your bicycle well. Bicycles are not allowed on the Métro but are permitted on certain RER lines outside rush hour. A good option if you're keen to bicycle is to take a tour run by Paris à Vélo C'est Sympa or Paris Bike Tour.

TIPS
» Be aware that a green-man signal or a striped pedestrian crossing do not necessarily mean cars will stop.
» When crossing roads, British and Australian visitors need to remember that traffic drives on the right in France.
» Avoid walking in deserted areas at night.

USEFUL CONTACTS
Paris Bike Tour
www.parisbiketour.net
Bicycle rental and guided tours.
✉ 38 rue de Saintonge, 75003
☎ 01 42 74 22 14

Paris à Vélo C'est Sympa
www.parisvelosympa.com
Bicycle tours during the day and night and bicycle rental. Tours leave from the address below, and reservation is compulsory.
✉ 22 rue Alphonse Baudin, 75011
☎ 01 48 87 60 01

IN-LINE SKATING
In-line skating is popular in Paris, helped by the Pari-Roller (www.pari-roller.com) rides on Friday evening, which can attract up to 12,000 participants. You need

to be an experienced skater to take part in this three-hour ride and you must check your insurance cover. The skate departs from outside the Gare Montparnasse (place Raoul Dautry) at 10pm (in good weather only).

An easier ride, run by Rollers et Coquillages (tel 01 44 54 94 42; www.rollers-coquillages.org), leaves from Nomades roller store (37 boulevard Bourdon, tel 01 44 54 07 44; www.nomadeshop.com), Bastille, on Sunday just after 2pm.

If you want to skate on your own, remember that by law you must stay off the roads. You are not allowed to skate along the Champs-Élysées walkways or wear skates on the Métro, buses or RER.

Opposite *Taxis are operated by different companies, but use the same prices*
Below *On Sundays some expressways are reserved for rollerbladers and bicyclists*

DRIVING IN PARIS

The best advice for driving in Paris is to avoid it if at all possible. You'll face heavy traffic, tricky and expensive parking and confusing one-way systems. In addition, petrol (gas) stations can be hard to find. It is far better to use the Métro or buses, or take a taxi. However, if you do decide to drive, here are some tips.

TIPS

» The speed limit in central Paris is 50kph (31mph). On the ring road (périphérique) the limit is 80kph (49mph).
» Don't park or stop on any of the axes rouges (key routes through the city).
» In built-up areas, give way to traffic approaching from the right (priorité à droite), unless signs advise you otherwise.
» Don't use the bus lanes.
» Try to avoid driving during rush hour: weekdays from around 7am to 9.30am and 4.30pm to 7.30pm.
» The city's roads are least congested in August, when many Parisians escape to the coast. But August is also when most road repairs take place.

FINDING YOUR WAY

» Paris's complex network of frequently narrow streets can be very confusing. Always plan your route in advance.
» Useful maps include Plan de Paris par Arrondissement, published by Grafocarte, and Paris par Arrondissement, by Editions L'Indispensable.

LOCAL DRIVING CUSTOMS

» You may find the concept of lanes is not taken too seriously, nor are red traffic lights—but don't be tempted to follow suit as you can be fined €90 for ignoring a red light or stop sign.
» Parisian drivers can be aggressive.
» Cars move fast when they can.
» Watch for delivery vehicles that may block you in by double parking.

PARKING
On-Street Parking

» Charges usually apply from 9am to 7pm, Monday to Saturday. Sundays and holidays are generally free, but always check before parking your car on the street.
» You can park for up to two hours.
» Parking meters accept special cards (buy these from some cafés or tobacconists).
» Hourly rates vary from under €1 to more than €2.

Parking Areas

» You'll usually find underground parking areas in shopping complexes, near large department stores, in business districts and in certain tourist areas. Look for the 'P' sign.
» Prices vary, and charges can be by the hour, day, weekend, month or year.
» For more information on parking areas for cars or motorcycles, buy the 288-page guide Parkings de Paris, which lists more than 200 parking areas, above and below ground, and gives prices. It also contains street maps, and maps of the Métro, RER and bus routes. It costs €15 and can be bought at the Paris Tourist Office, bookshops or from Editions Com 3000, 21 rue Lamartine, 75009 (tel 01 45 26 59 74; www.parkingsdeparis. com). Visitors can book and pay for suitable parking through the website before arriving in the city.

Parking on the Outskirts

» To save parking charges, some people park in the suburbs and take the Métro, RER or bus into central Paris.
» Stick to one of the safer areas like Maison-Lafitte, Neuilly, St-Cloud or Levallois-Perret (for advice on visiting areas outside the périphérique, ▷ 274).
» It is possible to park for free at some supermarkets—but don't stay overnight.

Towing Away

» If your car isn't where you left it, contact the local police station or the police headquarters (tel 01 53 71 53 71) for details of the car pound.

Left The Champs-Élysées is busy with traffic at all times of the day and night

GENERAL DRIVING HINTS

A car is useful if you want to take an excursion out of cental Paris, or move on to stay at a second destination within France. A good system of *autoroutes* links Paris with the main cities: The A1 leads to the north, the A13 to Normandy and the northwest, the A4 to the east, the A10 to the west and southwest, and the A6 to the Alps and the Riviera. Note that most autoroutes charge a toll. The French drive on the right.

PLANNING

» You must have at least third-party motor insurance to drive in France. Fully comprehensive cover is strongly advised.

» If driving your own car, display an international sticker near the rear registration (licence) plate.

» Adjust headlights of left-hand drive vehicles for driving on the right in France.

RENTING A CAR

▷ 273.

ROADS

» The *autoroute* is the French counterpart of the British motorway or American expressway and is marked by an 'A' on maps and road signs. A few sections around key cities are free of charge, but tolls are charged on the rest *(autoroutes à péage)*. Always have cash available as foreign credit cards may not be accepted.

» In France, a highway or trunk road is called a *Route Nationale* (N).

» The next level down is the *Route Départementale* (D), although these roads can still be wide and fast. There are also quieter country roads.

THE LAW

» Always carry a passport or national ID card, a valid driving licence, the vehicle's registration document and a certificate of motor insurance.

» The minimum age to drive in France is 18.

» In built-up areas, vehicles should give way to traffic coming from the right *(Priorité à droite)*, unless signs advise otherwise. At roundabouts (traffic circles) with signs saying *Cédez le passage* or *Vous n'avez pas la priorité*, traffic already on the roundabout has priority. On roundabouts without these signs, traffic entering has priority. A priority road can also be shown by a white diamond-shaped sign with a yellow diamond within it. A black line through the diamond indicates the end of priority. A red-bordered triangle with a black cross on a white background, with the words *passage protégé*, also shows right-of-way.

» You must wear a seatbelt. Children under 10 must travel in the back, sitting on an approved type of booster seat, except for babies under nine months with a specially adapted rear-facing front seat (but not in cars with air bags).

» Do not overtake (pass) where there is a solid single central line.

» Don't drive after drinking alcohol. There are harsh penalties in place for offenders.

» Always stop at stop signs.

ROAD SIGNS

Allumez vos phares Switch on your lights
Cédez le passage Give way (yield)
Péage Toll
Priorité à droite/gauche Priority (right-of-way) to the right/left
Rappel Reminder (continue with the previous instruction)
Route barrée Road closed
Sens interdit No entry
Sens unique One way
Serrez à droite/gauche Keep to the right/left
Stationnement interdit No parking
Travaux Roadworks

EQUIPMENT

» Carry a red warning triangle and reflective safety vest in case of breakdown.

» Have a spare-bulb kit available.

FUEL

» Fuel is generally available as unleaded *(sans plomb*, 95 and 98 octane), lead replacement petrol *(LRP* or *supercarburant)*, diesel *(gasoil* or *gazole)* and Liquid Petroleum Gas.

» Many petrol (gas) stations close all day on Sundays and at 6pm during the rest of the week.

» Prices are high at filling stations on *autoroutes*.

» Filling stations can be situated far apart in rural areas, so make sure you never let the level of fuel in your tank get too low.

CAR BREAKDOWN

» Make sure you have adequate breakdown coverage.

» If you break down on an *autoroute* or the Paris *périphérique*, you must call the police or the official breakdown service for that area. There are emergency telephones on the roadside.

SPEED LIMITS	
Urban roads	50kph (31mph)
Outside built-up areas	90kph (56mph); 80kph (49mph) in wet weather
Dual carriageways (divided highways) and non-toll autoroutes	110kph (68mph); 100kph (62mph) in wet weather
Toll autoroutes	130kph (80mph); 110kph (68mph) in wet weather

Visiting drivers who have held a licence for fewer than two years are not allowed to exceed the wet-weather limits, even in good weather.

Train	n°	Heure	Destination	Particularités
TGV	6131	20h16	TOULON	1ERE ET 2EME CLASSE
iDTGV	7905	20h16	TOULON	ACCUEIL A L'EMBARQU
TGV	6221	20h20	MONTPELLIER	1ERE ET 2EME CLASS
ter	891169	20h20	AUXERRE	DEPART DE PARIS-BE
ter	891047	20h35	LAROCHE-MIGENNES	
TGV	6929	20h38	GRENOBLE	1ERE ET 2EME CLAS
Transilien	151845	21h05	MONTARGIS	2EME CLASSE
TGV	6137	21h16	MARSEILLE-ST-CHARLES	1ERE ET 2EME CLA
TGV	6225	21h20	MONTPELLIER	1ERE ET 2EME CL
Transilien	152889	21h35	MONTEREAU	2EME CLASSE
TGV	6637	21h54	LYON-PERRACHE	1ERE ET 2EME C
	22h00	TRAIN SUPPRIME		TRAIN SUPPRIME
				2EME CLASSE

France has a comprehensive rail network and moving between cities and other European countries is simple. The network, run by SNCF, is made up of *Grandes Lignes* (long-distance lines) and *Lignes Régionales* (regional lines). The *Grandes Lignes* have the regular Corail trains and the faster TGV trains, which can travel at speeds of up to 357kph (221mph). The *Lignes Régionales* have TER trains *(Trains Express Régionaux)*, called Transilien trains in Paris. Paris has six mainline stations, each serving different regions in France and the rest of Europe. There are good connections with the Métro and buses (and RER in some cases).

TICKETS

» Most trains have first and second classes, both of which are perfectly acceptable.

» Fares are split into blue and white (Corail) or normal and peak (TGV). Reduced-rate fares are generally available for normal travel on mainline routes, excluding couchette services.

» Ticket prices vary according to the level of comfort (first or second class; called Comfort Level 1 and Comfort Level 2 on Thalys) and departure time.

» First-class fares are roughly 50 per cent more expensive than second class.

FASTEST JOURNEY TIMES FROM PARIS (APPROXIMATE)

Amsterdam	4 hours 10 min
Bordeaux	3 hours
Brussels	1 hour 20 min
Lille	1 hour
Marseille	3 hours

» You can buy tickets at the stations, at SNCF offices around the city and through some travel agents.

» Tickets for TGV trains must be reserved. You can do this up to a few minutes before departure, although in peak season it is best to book well in advance. Sleeping cars must be booked at least 75 minutes before the train leaves its first station.

» Make sure you stamp your ticket in one of the orange machines on the platforms before you start your journey. You'll risk a fine if you forget to do this.

» If you are under 26, you can get a 25 per cent discount (called *Carte 12–25*) on train travel. Seniors also receive discounts (called *Carte Senior*).

» Other discounts include *Carte Familles Nombreuses* and *Carte Enfent Famille* (for families with children) and *Prem's* fares (second class only; available online); special conditions apply to all three.

» A variety of rail passes are available, which allow travel either within France only, or within France and certain other countries, or within the whole of Europe. You should buy these before you enter France, either through travel agents or Rail Europe (▷ 65).

CATERING SERVICE

» Catering facilities—ranging from simple sandwiches and salads to hot meals—are available on most TGV and Corail services, but they are expensive.

» A benefit of first class is that you can have food served at your seat during meal times on most TGV trains. You'll need to reserve in advance, except on TGV *Méditerranée* trains.

» You can reserve meals when you purchase your train ticket. Ticket machines dispense meal vouchers.

Above *Trains from Gare de Lyon serve southeast France, Italy and Switzerland*

MAINLINE STATION INFORMATION

STATION	MAJOR DESTINATIONS	MAJOR TRAIN OPERATOR	CONNECTIONS: MÉTRO	RER	TOURIST DESTINATIONS INCLUDE
Gare d'Austerlitz	Central and southwest France, Spain, Portugal	Corail Trainhôtel Elipsos	Lines 5, 10	Line C	Poitiers, Limoges, Madrid, Barcelona, the Alps
Gare de l'Est	Eastern France, Germany, Luxembourg, Switzerland, Austria, Eastern Europe	Corail	Lines 4, 5, 7	None	Strasbourg
Gare de Lyon	Southeast France, Switzerland, Italy	TGV	Lines 1, 14	Lines A, D	Lyon, Nice, Grenoble, Milan, Florence, Geneva, Marseille
Gare Montparnasse	Western and southern France, Spain	TGV	Lines 4, 6, 12, 13	None	Brest, Quimper, Nantes, Toulouse, Bordeaux, Biarritz
Gare du Nord	Northern France, UK, Germany, Holland, Belgium, Scandinavia	TGV, Thalys, Eurostar	Lines 4, 5	Lines B, D, E	Brussels, London, Amsterdam, Lille
Gare St-Lazare	Northwest France	Corail	Lines 3, 12, 13	Line E	Normandy

TGV services also leave from Aéroport Charles-de-Gaulle TGV and Marne-La-Vallée Disneyland® Resort Paris.

» Hot and cold drinks, sandwiches and other snacks are served on most trains.

» Overnight trains (and some day services) have vending machines dispensing hot and cold drinks and sweets (candy).

OVERNIGHT TRAINS

» Most overnight trains offer either reclining seats, couchette berths or a sleeper car.

» Reclining seats are available only in second class. You can adjust the head and foot rests.

» In first class, couchettes are in four-berth compartments; in second class they are in six-berth compartments.

» Sleeper car compartments are for up to two people in first class and up to three people in second class.

» Trains travel to cities in France and to other European countries.

STATION ASSISTANCE

» Larger stations have an information kiosk, which is usually easy to find.

» If you need assistance, look for a member of the station staff, identifiable by their red waistcoats.

» You'll need a €1 deposit to use the luggage trolleys (carts).

» Porters are on hand to help with your luggage in main stations. They wear red jackets and black or navy caps.

LEFT LUGGAGE STORAGE

» Some stations have a left-luggage office or coin-operated lockers. Electronic locks issue a printed ticket with a code number. You'll need to keep this ticket for when you return to collect your items.

» Don't store valuables in lockers.

» Security concerns mean that left-luggage facilities are not always available.

UNDERSTANDING RAILWAY TIMETABLES

» You can pick up free timetables (horaires) at stations.

» SNCF timetables are usually published twice a year—the summer one lasts from mid-June/early July to mid-December and the winter one from mid-December to mid-June/early July.

» There are two styles of timetable: one for the Grandes Lignes, covering high-speed TGV and other mainline services, and another for the regional TER trains.

» Be prepared to decipher French railway terminology. On Grandes Lignes timetables, two rows of boxed numbers at the top refer to the numéro de train (train number) and to the notes à consulter (footnotes). In TER timetables, the train number is not listed.

» Footnotes at the bottom of the timetable explain when a particular train runs (circule). Tous les jours means it runs every day; sauf dimanche et fêtes means it doesn't run on Sundays and public holidays. Jusqu'au, followed by a date, indicates the service runs only up until that date.

USEFUL CONTACTS
Rail Europe
www.raileurope.com (for US visitors)
www.raileurope.co.uk (for UK visitors)
Sells a variety of European rail passes.

SNCF
www.sncf.com
☎ 36 35
www.voyages-sncf.com
www.tgv.com
☎ 0033 892 35 35 35 (from outside France)

Thalys
www.thalys.com
Trains to cities in northern Europe.
☎ 0892 35 35 36

Facilities are gradually improving for visitors travelling with a disability to Paris. All renovated and newly constructed buildings are now well equipped. Some buses and certain RER stations are accessible to wheelchair users and often announce their stops. However, if you have reduced mobility you're still likely to encounter challenges in getting around Paris—kerbs (curbs) can be high, ramps are few and elevators are sometimes too small.

ARRIVING

By Air Both Roissy-Charles de Gaulle and Orly airports are well equipped for people with disabilities. Shuttle buses between terminals have ramps for wheelchair users, as well as voice announcements for the visually impaired. The terminals have adapted toilets, low-level telephones and reserved parking spaces. For more information, download the *Guide Pratique Roissy* or the *Guide Pratique Orly Sud et Ouest* from the Aéroports de Paris website, www.adp.fr, or order a copy online.

Operators that offer specialist transport from the airports into Paris include ATAGH (tel 01 40 05 12 15); in addition, G7 HORIZON (tel 01 47 39 00 91; www.taxi-g7.fr) has a fleet of specially adapted taxis. Reserve them in advance. The Orlyval train (▷ 46–47) is accessible to wheelchairs.

By Train The modern design of the Eurostar trains and terminals makes them wheelchair-friendly. Passengers using a wheelchair can also benefit from discounted tickets.

GETTING AROUND

The Métro is virtually inaccessible to wheelchair users because of its steps, passageways and automatic barriers. The exception is Line 14, which also has voice announcements.

Ninety percent of RER stations on lines A and B have elevators, although some can be operated only by a member of staff (press the *Appel* button for assistance).

RATP's Mission Accessibilité (tel 01 49 28 18 84) publishes a *Guide Pratique* listing the accessible RER stations. Even when a station is listed as accessible, wheelchair users are still likely to need help to board the train. Most ticket offices have induction loops for the hard of hearing.

Buses can be a useful way of getting around as virtually all vehicles are wheelchair accessible. All routes in Île-de-France are to be accessible by 2015. The 29, 31, 43, 54, 63, 64, 81, PC1, PC2, PC3 and NOI buses, including routes 26, 63, 80, 84, 91, 92, 94 and 96, are fitted with voice announcements of the next stop. For information on the accessibility of the public transport system, look up the website of the operator RATP (www.ratp.fr) or pick up the map *Grand Plan Lignes et Rues*—2 from stations.

RATP runs an accompaniment service (Les Compagnons du Voyage) to assist people with reduced mobility. You have to reserve in advance and a fee is charged (tel 01 58 76 08 33).

The UK-based Access Project (see below) publishes a helpful book about travel, accommodation, sights and getting around (£10 donation).

USEFUL ORGANIZATIONS

A2 Paris Île de France
Guided tours adapted for visitors with disabilities.
☎ 0950 14 10 28

Access Project
www.accessproject-phsp.org
✉ 39 Bradley Gardens, West Ealing, London, W13 8HE, UK ☎ No phone

Les Compagnons du Voyage
www.compagnons.com
✉ 34 rue Championnet, 75018
☎ 01 58 76 08 33

Infomobi
www.infomobi.com
Information about buses, the Métro and RER trains in the Île de France.
☎ 0810 64 64 64

Mobile en Ville
www.mobile-en-ville.asso.fr
Information on disability access. Also offers sightseeing tours.
☎ 09 52 29 60 51 or 0682 917 216

Mobility International USA
www.miusa.org
Promotes international travel and exchange programmes.
☎ 541/343-1284

Paris Tourist Office
www.parisinfo.com
Information about access under the 'Tourisme & Handicaps' sign.
☎ 01 49 52 42 63 or 0892 683 000

RATP Mission Accessibilité
www.ratp.fr
✉ 163 bis avenue du Clichy, 19 place Lachambaudie ☎ 0810 64 64 64

Society for Accessible Travel and Hospitality (SATH)
www.sath.org
A US organization offering advice and promoting awareness.
☎ 212/447-7284

Tourism for All
www.tourismforall.org.uk
General information and guidance for travelling in the UK and abroad.
☎ 0845 124 9971 (UK)

Tourisme & Handicaps
A blue, white and yellow sign is awarded to sites that provide special facilities for people with disabilities.

REGIONS

This chapter is divided into five regions of Paris (▷ 8–9). Region names are for the purposes of this book only and places of interest are listed alphabetically in each region.

REGIONS PARIS

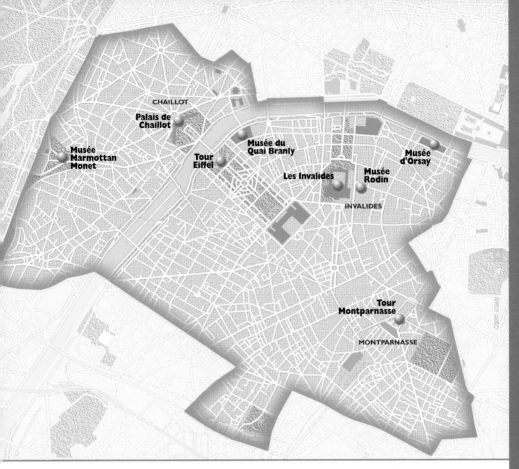

CHAILLOT

Palais de
Chaillot

Musée du
Quai Branly

Musée
Marmottan
Monet

Tour
Eiffel

Les Invalides

Musée
Rodin

Musée
d'Orsay

INVALIDES

Tour
Montparnasse

MONTPARNASSE

AROUND THE TOUR EIFFEL

With the Eiffel Tower as its big attraction, this region plays a starring role in the success story of Paris tourism. Occupying the southwest of the city, the area is the location of some of Paris's best-loved places of interest. Curiously, some attractions here are far from sky-high: subterranean tours of Les Catacombes and Les Égouts are on many itineraries. The Catacombes, once a Roman quarry, are the resting place of the bones of more than six million Parisians, and Les Égouts is the network of sewers, more than 1,600km (1,000 miles) built in the late 19th century by Baron Haussmann. The district of Montparnasse was once popular with the artistic community, many of whom are buried at the Cimetière. The area is also distinguished by Paris's other tower, Tour Montparnasse, which has a restaurant, Le Ciel de Paris, on the 56th floor, offering superb views from a different aspect.

The area is also home to some of the best museums in Paris. Foremost among these is the Musée d'Orsay, formerly a great railway station, which houses a huge collection of mid-19th to early 20th-century art. However, the largest collection of Monet's works is to be found at the Musée Marmottan Monet, in an elegant town house which was bequeathed to the nation in 1932 by the artist Paul Marmottan. There are also museums celebrating the work of Honoré de Balzac (Maison de Balzac), Auguste Rodin (Musée Rodin), the non-European world (Musée du Quai Branly) and the military and Napoléon (Les Invalides), along with the sea and anthropology (both in the Palais de Chaillot). The colonnaded Palais de Chaillot affords wonderful views of the Eiffel Tower and the Champ de Mars, and it is now also home to the world's largest architectural museum, the Cité de l'Architecture et du Patrimoine.

Musée Baccarat

Musée Galliéra

Musée National des Arts Asiatiques-Guimet

CHAILLOT

Musée d'Art Moderne de la Ville de Paris

Palais de Tokyo

Place du Trocadéro et du 11 Novembre

Palais de Chaillot

Jardins du Trocadéro

Musée du Quai Branly

Tour Eiffel

Musée Marmottan Monet

Maison de Balzac

Pont de Bir-Hakeim

Seine

ASSEMBLÉE NATIONALE (PALAIS BOURBON)

www.assemblee-nationale.fr

The 18th-century Palais Bourbon sits on the banks of the Seine and is home to the French National Assembly, the lower house of the French Parliament. Its 577 members debate in the Chamber and have offices nearby. The palace, with its imposing neoclassical facade, was built for Louis XIV's daughter, Louise-Françoise de Bourbon. Its political role began in 1798, when the Council of the Five Hundred met there. The library ceiling (1838–1847), by Eugène Delacroix, depicts the history of civilization.

🕀 71 J6 ✉ Palais Bourbon, 33 quai d'Orsay, 75007 ☎ 01 40 63 60 00 🕙 Guided tours (must show passport/identity card) by invitation of a deputy, booked at least three months in advance and confirmed a month in advance. Telephone and ask for the member of parliament in charge of relations between France and your country. Admission to public debates is also by prior appointment 🖐 Free 🚇 Assemblée Nationale 🚌 24, 63, 73, 83, 84, 94 🚉 RER line C, Invalides

CHAMP DE MARS AND ÉCOLE MILITAIRE

The green lawns of the Parc du Champ de Mars stretch out in a rectangular design between the Eiffel Tower and the imposing 18th-century École Militaire. It was on this site that Roman invaders battled it out with the Parisii in 52BC to win supremacy over the area, and the Parisians later beat off the Vikings. The Champ de Mars was laid out in 1765 as an army parade ground. Its name, Field of Mars, refers to the Roman god of war. Over the years it has witnessed national celebrations, parades, international exhibitions, horse races and early balloon experiments conducted by Jacques Charles and the Robert brothers. Today it is popular with families, joggers and strolling visitors.

The colonnaded and domed École Militaire dominates the opposite end of the Champ de Mars. It was commissioned in 1751 by Louis XV and his mistress, Madame de Pompadour, who wanted somewhere to train impoverished young gentlemen. Architect Jacques-Ange Gabriel, who also worked on the place de la Concorde and Versailles's Petit Trianon, was responsible for the design. Work finished in 1773 and a new tax on gambling financed the grooming of France's military cadets, including Napoléon Bonaparte.

Champ de Mars

🕀 71 H8 ✉ Champ de Mars, 75007 ☎ Mairie de Paris information: 39 75 🕙 Always open 🖐 Free 🚇 Bir-Hakeim 🚌 42, 69, 80, 82, 87 🚉 RER line C, Champ de Mars-Tour Eiffel

École Militaire

🕀 71 H8 ✉ 21 place Joffre, 75007 🕙 Visits by written application only 🚇 École Militaire 🚌 28, 49, 80, 82, 87, 92

LES CATACOMBES

This labyrinth of tunnels—the world's largest repository of human bones—is the resting place of more than six million Parisians. This is the entrance to the tunnels (3,000 km/1,900 miles) that run under the city. The inscription above the entrance reads 'Stop! Here is the empire of death!' Skulls and bones are arranged along the walls of these recesses, 20m (65ft) beneath the city. The tunnels were created in Roman times as quarries. Bones were transferred here from overcrowded cemeteries in 1786. During World War II the catacombs were used by the Resistance as a meeting place. Be prepared for lots of stairs and take a torch (flashlight).

🕀 71 L11 ✉ 1 avenue du Colonel Henri Rol-Tanguy, 75014 ☎ 01 43 22 47 63 🕙 Tue–Sun 10–5 🖐 Adult €8, under 14 free 🚇 Denfert-Rochereau 🚌 38, 68 ❓ Not recommended for young children (or the faint-hearted!)

CIMETIÈRE DU MONTPARNASSE

Montparnasse Cemetery opened in 1824 and is the final resting place of many notable former residents of the area. Here you can pay homage to an array of illustrious writers, composers, musicians, artists and sculptors, including Jean-Paul Sartre, Simone de Beauvoir, Charles Baudelaire, Guy de Maupassant, Constantin Brancusi, Camille Saint-Saëns, Ossip Zadkine and Auguste Bartholdi, father of the Statue of Liberty. Also buried here are car manufacturer André Citroën and Prime Minister Pierre Laval, who was executed for treason after World War II following his open collaboration with the Germans.

Adorning a tomb in the northeastern corner of the cemetery is Brancusi's charmingly childlike sculpture *The Kiss*—supposedly a response to Rodin's famous work.

🕀 71 K10 ✉ 3 boulevard Edgar Quinet, 75014 ☎ 01 44 10 86 50 🕙 Mid-Mar to early Nov Mon–Fri 8–6, Sat 8.30–6, Sun 9–6; early Nov to mid-Mar Mon–Fri 8–5.30, Sat 8.30–5.30, Sun 9–5.30 🖐 Free 🚇 Edgar Quinet, Raspail, Montparnasse-Bienvenüe 🚌 28, 68

Opposite *The Champ de Mars offers a stunning view of the Eiffel Tower*
Below *Ornament in Montparnasse Cemetery*

INFORMATION

www.invalides.org

✚ 71 J7 ✉ Hôtel National des Invalides, 129 rue de Grenelle, 75007 ☎ 01 44 42 38 77 or local calls 08 10 11 33 99 🕐 Apr–Sep daily 10–6 (Église du Dôme mid-Jun to mid-Sep also 6–7pm); Oct–Mar 10–5. Closed 1st Mon of each month 💷 Adult €9 (with audioguide), under 18 free 🚇 La Tour-Maubourg, Invalides, Varenne 🚌 28, 63, 69, 82, 83, 93 🚉 RER line C, Invalides 👥 Guided tours available 🎧 €8.50 🍴 Selling salads, pizza and sandwiches 🎁 Gift shop/bookshop

INTRODUCTION

On entering the stately grounds of Les Invalides you'll be following in the footsteps of many a military hero, including General de Gaulle and Winston Churchill. The building started life as a hospital for wounded soldiers but now houses an army museum. The adjacent Église du Dôme shelters Napoléon's tomb. Unless you are a particular devotee of war history, you may be tempted to skip the Army Museum and head straight to Napoléon's tomb. Don't. The museum is one of the largest of its kind in the world and among the extensive collections of weapons, armour, flags, uniforms and paintings are some real gems. The museum is split into three wings—east, south and west. For the poignant World War II exhibition head to the south wing; to see the Musée des Plans-Reliefs, with its huge scale models of French towns, go to the fourth floor of the east wing. The entrance to the Église du Dôme is at the front of the church, on the south side of the complex.

Pompous, severe and authoritarian, Les Invalides was built to house wounded and elderly soldiers. Louis XIV was thinking of others for once when he commissioned Libéral Bruant to design the imposing building, with its 195m (640ft) facade. The first soldiers arrived in 1674 and were welcomed by the king himself. It took another 32 years before the gold-encrusted Église du Dôme was completed. Bruant's design for the church never got off the ground and in 1676 the king approved new plans by Versailles architect Jules Hardouin-Mansart. The church was finally completed in 1706.

WHAT TO SEE

REMINDERS OF NAPOLÉON

As you would expect, Napoléon Bonaparte features prominently in the Musée de l'Armée and you can see his frock coat, hat, coronation saddle and even his actual horse, Vizir (not for the squeamish). There is a re-creation of the room where he died in exile on the island of St-Helena and a variety of paintings, including Paul Delaroche's portrait of the Emperor looking unusually undignified just before his abdication in Fontainebleau in 1814.

WORLD WAR II EXHIBITION

Don't miss the World War II exhibition, which moves chronologically through the war years over three floors of the south wing. The evocative, sometimes chilling, displays use a combination of film footage, photos and

Above *Les Invalides houses a superb military museum*
Opposite *A cannon in the Cour d'Honneur*

day-to-day objects to convey the horrors of the war and the bravery of those who fought against Hitler. Exhibits include a BBC microphone and French Resistance equipment.

THE COUR D'HONNEUR

It is worth spending a few minutes admiring the architecture of this central courtyard. The arcades that surround it were thriving thoroughfares during Les Invalides's heyday in the late 17th and early 18th centuries. During this time the site was a mini-town, home to around 1,500 soldiers. At times demand for places was so high that only soldiers with 20 years' service were admitted. On arrival they were measured for their blue uniform and black hat, and issued with a comb, knife and wooden spoon. They were not allowed tobacco or to leave the site without permission, and punishments included being placed on a water-only diet. There was a hospital on site, staffed by almost 40 nurses. From the courtyard, look up to the first floor and you'll see the small grey doors that led to the dormitories. Today Les Invalides is still home to around 100 war veterans.

ÉGLISE DU DÔME

The golden dome of this church rises 107m (350ft) above the ground, a glistening monument to two of France's most influential and charismatic rulers: Louis XIV and Napoléon. The Emperor's tomb sits in a grandiose crypt directly below the dome. He died in exile on the island of St-Helena in 1821 but his remains were brought back to France in 1840. It took another 21 years to create his mausoleum and the task was not without controversy as it involved excavating part of the church. Napoléon's remains are encased in six coffins, inside a red porphyry sarcophagus, set on an immense granite base. The 12 statues guarding the tomb represent his military campaigns. Behind the Église du Dôme stands the Soldier's Church, reached from the Cour d'Honneur. It was originally designed by Jules Hardouin-Mansart as part of a vast church with two separate entrances, one for the king and one for soldiers. In time, the two churches became separate entities, known respectively as the Église du Dôme and St-Louis-des-Invalides.

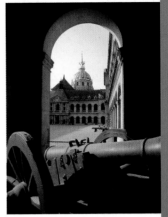

TIPS

» The best way to appreciate the grandeur of Les Invalides is to approach the site from the Pont Alexandre III (▷ 88).

» The Army Museum is busiest between 11am and 1pm.

» As an antidote to Les Invalides's war focus, unwind in the nearby gardens of the Musée Rodin (▷ 85).

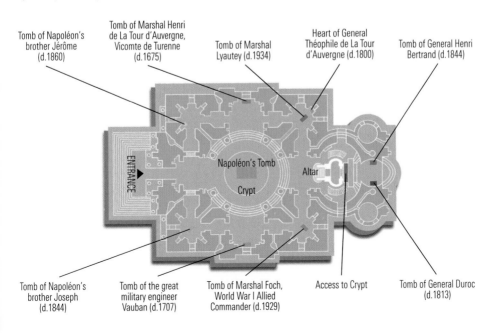

Tomb of Napoléon's brother Jérôme (d.1860)

Tomb of Marshal Henri de La Tour d'Auvergne, Vicomte de Turenne (d.1675)

Tomb of Marshal Lyautey (d.1934)

Heart of General Théophile de La Tour d'Auvergne (d.1800)

Tomb of General Henri Bertrand (d.1844)

ENTRANCE ▶

Napoléon's Tomb

Altar

Crypt

Tomb of Napoléon's brother Joseph (d.1844)

Tomb of the great military engineer Vauban (d.1707)

Tomb of Marshal Foch, World War I Allied Commander (d.1929)

Access to Crypt

Tomb of General Duroc (d.1813)

LES ÉGOUTS

www.paris.fr

Paris's sewers are a surprisingly popular visitor attraction. A worker guides you through part of the city's 2,100km (1,302-mile) subterranean network and shows an audiovisual presentation. The sewers were built by Baron Haussmann in the latter part of the 19th century, and during World War II the Germans used sections as offices. They have even made it onto the stage, featuring in the musicals *Les Misérables* and *Phantom of the Opera*.

🟥 71 H6 ✉ place de la Résistance (Pont de l'Alma). Entrance opposite 93 quai d'Orsay, 75007 ☎ 01 53 68 27 81 🕓 May–Sep Sat–Wed 11–5; Oct–Apr Sat–Wed 11–4. Closed 2 weeks in mid-Jan ✋ Adult €4.30, child (6–12) €3.50, under 6 free 🚇 Alma-Marceau 🚌 42, 63, 80, 92 🚆 RER line C, Pont-de-l'Alma

LES INVALIDES

▷ 74–75.

MAISON DE BALZAC

www.paris.fr

The writer Honoré de Balzac (1799–1850) lived in this pretty house on the Passy hillside from 1840 until 1847. Pursued by debtors, he lay low here assuming a false identity. It was also here, in a creative flow that often lasted all night, that Balzac penned some of the works now considered masterpieces of *La Comédie Humaine, La Cousine Bette* and *Le Cousin Pons*. The house is now an intimate museum dedicated to his life and works. Many original editions, illustrations and manuscripts are on show and there is a library devoted to his works. You can also visit temporary exhibitions.

🟥 70 F7 ✉ 47 rue Raynouard, 75016 ☎ 01 55 74 41 80 🕓 Tue–Sun 10–6 ✋ Free (except temporary exhibitions) 🚇 Passy, La Muette 🚌 32, 50, 70, 72

MONTPARNASSE

Montparnasse was a popular district with artists and writers in the early 20th century, attracting the likes of Amedeo Modigliani, Marc Chagall and Ernest Hemingway. Legendary meeting places (including the brasserie La Coupole, ▷ 143) still exist, haunted by shadows of literary and artistic giants from the 1920s and 1930s. Although Montparnasse's main boulevards have lost some of their charm, sacrificed to the whims of consumerism, the area's many theatres, cafés, cinemas and cabarets remain lively. Tour Montparnasse (▷ 89) looms over the district and you get wonderful views from the public gallery on the 56th floor. The tower, 209m (685ft) high, was built in the early 1970s as part of a huge urban development project. Across a windy esplanade is the Gare Montparnasse, one of the most confusing stations in Paris. Years of hectic redevelopment in Montparnasse have replaced atmospheric narrow streets with uninspiring apartment blocks. Some corners are worth seeking out, however, such as 18 rue Antoine Bourdelle, where you can visit the Musée Bourdelle (Tue–Sun 10–6). The museum focuses on the sculptor Émile-Antoine Bourdelle (1861–1929), a former pupil of Auguste Rodin, who once lived and worked in this picturesque house. Also worth a visit is the Cimetière du Montparnasse (▷ 73) where many notable former residents are buried, including Jean-Paul Sartre, Simone de Beauvoir and writer Guy de Maupassant.

🟥 71 K10 🚇 Montparnasse-Bienvenüe, Vavin, Edgar Quinet 🚌 28, 58, 82, 88, 89, 91, 92, 94, 95, 96

MUSÉE D'ART MODERNE DE LA VILLE DE PARIS

www.mam.paris.fr

Quality temporary exhibitions help keep this modern-art museum within an international sphere. The collection covers Fauvism, Cubism, Surrealism, Abstraction and Nouveau Réalisme. Raoul Dufy's 1937 mural *La Fée Electricité* is a staggering 60m (197ft) by 10m (33ft). *La Danse* (1931–33), a mural

Below *The sewers beneath the streets of Paris, Les Égouts, are a popular attraction*

Above *The Musée Galliéra stages temporary exhibitions of urban fashion*

by Henri Matisse, hangs in a room devoted to him.

✚ 70 G6 ✉ 11 avenue du Président Wilson, 75016 ☎ 01 53 67 40 00 🕓 Tue–Sun 10–6 (also Thu 6–10); temporary exhibitions also Fri–Sat 6–8 ✋ Free. Temporary exhibitions: adult €5, under 13 free, but variable according to exhibitions 🚇 Iéna, Alma-Marceau 🚌 32, 42, 72, 80, 82, 92

MUSÉE BACCARAT
www.baccarat.fr
Baccarat began making mirrors, window-panes and goblets in the village of Baccarat, in Lorraine, in 1764. The company fired up its first crystal kiln in 1816, and since then prestigious clients have included Louis XVIII, Tsar Nicholas II of Russia and Napoléon III. The operation moved to Paris in 1832. Baccarat crystal figures and vases are among the popular designs. The museum displays around 5,000 examples of Baccarat's work. Look for items made for World's Fairs.
✚ 70 G6 ✉ 11 place des États-Unis, 75016 ☎ 01 40 22 11 00 🕓 Mon and Wed–Sat 10–6.30 ✋ Adult €5, under 18 free 🚇 Iéna, Kléber 🚌 22, 30, 32, 82 🎧 Guided tours available in French, English, German and Japanese 🎁 Gift shop

MUSÉE GALLIÉRA–MUSÉE DE LA MODE DE LA VILLE DE PARIS
www.galliera.paris.fr
Urban fashion from the 18th century to the present day is the theme of the temporary exhibitions held here, which draw from a collection of 80,000 objects, such as dresses by Jean Paul Gaultier, outfits worn by Marlene Dietrich and ball gowns.
✚ 70 G6 ✉ Palais Galliéra, 10 avenue Pierre 1er de Serbie, 75016 ☎ 01 56 52 86 00 🎧 The Musée Galliéra is closed for renovations until 2013. Temporary exhibitions of the collections are being organized in other locations until the reopening.

MUSÉE MARMOTTAN MONET
▷ 78–79.

MUSÉE NATIONAL DES ARTS ASIATIQUES-GUIMET
www.museeguimet.fr
This museum, which opened in 1889, has a remarkable display of Oriental antiquities, built up by industrialist Émile Guimet (1836–1918). Around 45,000 items are on display, including sculptures, carvings, paintings and other objects from Korea, China, Japan, Tibet, Afghanistan, Thailand, Pakistan and India. The stunning collection of Khmer art (sixth to nineteenth centuries) includes serene stone buddhas and Hindu gods. The museum also has richly painted Tibetan and Nepalese *tankas* (portable paintings). The Indian department includes bronze deities, and Moghul and Rajput miniatures. The rich Chinese department has a vast ceramics collection. Japanese religious art is represented in the museum annexe, the Buddhist Pantheon at 19 avenue d'Iéna (open Wed–Mon 9.45–5.45).
✚ 70 G6 ✉ 6 place d'Iéna, 75016 ☎ 01 56 52 53 00 🕓 Wed–Mon 10–6 (ticket office closes 30 min earlier) ✋ Permanent collection: adult €7.50. Temporary exhibitions: adult €8, under 18 free. Combined ticket: adult €9.50, under 18 free. Free to all on 1st Sun of month 🚇 Iéna, Boissière, Trocadéro 🚌 22, 30, 32, 63, 82 🎧 Free audioguides (lasting around 90 min) are available in several languages. For information about guided tours, see the schedule at the entrance

MUSÉE D'ORSAY
▷ 80–83.

MUSÉE DU QUAI BRANLY
▷ 84.

MUSÉE RODIN
▷ 85.

PALAIS DE CHAILLOT
▷ 86–87.

PALAIS DE TOKYO
www.palaisdetokyo.com
This showcase for contemporary art opened in 2002, in an art nouveau palace opposite the Eiffel Tower. There is no permanent collection, but exhibitions, shows and performances have earned it the reputation of being daringly avant-garde. It has a splendid terrace with views of the Eiffel Tower, a self-service café, and funky Tokyo Eat.
✚ 70 G6 ✉ 13 avenue du Président-Wilson, 75016 ☎ 01 47 23 54 01 🕓 Tue–Sun 12–12 ✋ Adult €6, under 18 free 🚇 Iéna, Alma-Marceau 🚌 32, 42, 72, 80, 82, 92

INFORMATION

www.marmottan.com

✠ 70 D7 ✉ 2 rue Louis-Boilly, 75016
☎ 01 44 96 50 33 ⊘ Tue–Sun 10–6
(last entry 5), also Thu 10–8. Closed Mon
✋ Adult €10, child €5, under 7 free
Ⓜ La Muette (then a 10-min walk; follow
signs from the station) 🚌 22, 32, 52, 63
🚆 RER line C, Boulainvilliers 📖 €7.50
🏛 Gift shop/bookshop

INTRODUCTION

It's a bit of a trek out to this museum in the leafy 16th *arrondissement* but you'll be rewarded with a feast of famous paintings by Monet and his contemporaries. The intimate setting in a discreetly elegant 19th-century town house makes a pleasant change from Paris's larger, more impersonal museums. And if the Impressionist works fail to satisfy your appetite, there are also paintings and furniture from the Napoleonic period, as well as more than 300 illustrated pages from medieval and Renaissance manuscripts. It's a curious but compelling combination.

The walk to the museum from La Muette Métro station is well signed and takes you through the pleasant Jardins du Ranelagh. There is no café at the museum, so you may wish to bring your own refreshments to have in the park on the way back.

The Marmottan Museum did not start life as a showcase for Monet's work. It takes its name from art historian Paul Marmottan, who left his house and collection of Empire paintings and furniture to the nation in 1932. The collection, built up by both Paul and his father Jules, also includes paintings from the Flemish, Italian and German primitives. It wasn't until later that various donors added the Impressionist works that have now become the museum's main attraction of which there are more than 300 works (including paintings and sculptures).

Monet was born in Paris in 1840 and died in Giverny 86 years later. During his life he drew inspiration from his travels around France, as well as those to London, Norway, Holland and Italy. But it was in the gardens of Giverny, his home from 1883 until his death, that he produced some of his most famous works. You can see family portraits near the steps to the basement gallery.

WHAT TO SEE
MONET

Without a doubt, the main draw for visitors is the Monet collection, built up over the last 50 years through donations from the artist's son, Michel, and various other collectors. Many of the 60 paintings on display are in the purpose-built basement gallery—remarkably light and airy considering its underground location. Clouds of irises, wisteria and water lilies fill many of the frames, inspired by the artist's 43 years at Giverny.

Above Impression: Sunrise, *1872, oil on canvas by Claude Monet (1840–1926)*

Various views of the Thames are also on display, including *Londres: Le Parlement, Reflets sur la Tamise* (1899–1901). Monet worked on almost 100 paintings of the river during a visit to London at the turn of the 20th century.

The gallery has a selection of works from the *Rouen Cathedral* series, created during two visits to Rouen in 1892 and 1893. Don't miss the influential *Impressions—soleil levant* (c.1873), which gave the Impressionist movement its name. The masterpiece depicts the port at Le Havre and focuses on one of Monet's preferred themes—the play of light on water. It is the only painting behind glass, installed after it was stolen in 1985 and recovered five years later in Corsica.

OTHER IMPRESSIONISTS

The Impressionist collection, on the upper floor, includes works by Edgar Degas, Gustave Caillebotte, Camille Pissarro, Berthe Morisot and Pierre-Auguste Renoir. Look for Renoir's beguiling *Claude Monet lisant (Claude Monet reading;* 1872). Monet was particularly fond of this portrait, painted by his friend, and kept it until his death.

THE EMPIRE COLLECTION

Highlights from the Empire period in the collection include the Geographical Clock (1813) on the ground floor, originally made for Napoléon and later altered by Louis XVIII.

THE ILLUMINATIONS

The Musée Marmottan Monet has around 300 medieval and Renaissance illustrated pages, collectively known as the Illuminations. These were amassed by art dealer Georges Wildenstein and were donated to the museum by his son in 1980.

Many of the pages come from French and Italian religious manuscripts and are vividly illustrated with saints and biblical characters. Others are from Books of Hours, compilations of prayers and religious sayings. Some show scenes from feudal life in the 15th century. The illuminations are now displayed in a dedicated room on the first floor.

TIPS

» Look for the amusing *Le Havre* caricatures *(c.* 1858), on the first floor, markedly different in style to Monet's later, more famous paintings.

» The museum lets you see some of Monet's most famous works in a refreshingly tranquil setting. But if you are in Paris for only a few days you may find it easier to see the Impressionist collection in the more central Musée d'Orsay (▷ 80–83).

» If you have time, you may like to combine a trip to the Musée Marmottan Monet with a visit to the Musée National des Arts Asiatiques-Guimet (▷ 77) or the Musée Galliéra (▷ 77), a few stops back on Métro Line 9, at Iéna.

GALLERY GUIDE
LOWER FLOOR
Monet collection and Impressionist works.

GROUND FLOOR
Impressionist works, the Empire Collection and bookshop.

UPPER FLOOR
The Illuminations and the Primitives.

Below Sasso Valley. Sun Effect, *1884 oil on canvas by Claude Monet*

INFORMATION

www.musee-orsay.fr

✚ 71 K7 ✉ 62 rue de Lille, 75007.
Entrance on the square in front of the
building, 1 rue de la Légion d'Honneur
☎ 01 40 49 48 14 🕐 Tue–Wed, Fri–Sun
9.30–6, Thu 9am–9.45pm; last ticket
45 min before closing 👆 Adult €8,
under 18 free, free to all on 1st Sun of
month. Temporary exhibitions cost extra
🚇 Solférino, Assemblée Nationale
🚌 24, 63, 68, 69, 73, 83, 84, 94 🚆 RER
line C, Musée d'Orsay 🎫 Guided tours,
including 'Masterpieces of the Musée
d'Orsay' (€6, 90 min), Jul–Sep Tue–Sat
11.30, 2.30, also Thu 6.30; Oct–Jun
Wed–Sat 11.30, Tue 11.30, 2.30, Thu
6.30. Audioguides (€5) in English, French,
Italian, Spanish, Japanese, German 📖 A
wide selection of books, including Guide
to the Musée d'Orsay 🍴 On the middle
level (11.45–5.45; dinner 7:30–9.30 on
Thu). Lunch €16.50, dinner €55 (excluding
drinks) ☕ Café Campana on upper level,
with wonderful view of the old station
clock; self-service café just above it (open
Fri–Mon 10–5, Thu 10–9) (€14.50) 🎁 Gift
shop and bookshop

Above The former Orsay train station
makes an imposing gallery on the left
bank of the Seine

INTRODUCTION

The Musée d'Orsay's collection spans 1848 to 1914, a crucial period in
Western art that witnessed such giants as Claude Monet, Pierre-Auguste
Renoir and Paul Cézanne. Chronologically, the museum fits neatly between
the Louvre and the Centre Georges Pompidou. Most people come to see
the breathtaking Impressionist collection, which includes Monet's *Houses of
Parliament*, Vincent van Gogh's *The Church at Auvers-sur-Oise* and Renoir's
Ball at the Moulin de la Galette. But Impressionism forms less than a third
of the vast display, which also includes sculpture, Symbolist and historical
paintings, photography and art nouveau furniture. The building is an attraction
in itself, with its vast main hall, lavish ballroom and wonderful station clocks.

The imposing Orsay station and its accompanying hotel were constructed
along the banks of the Seine in just two years, in time for the Exposition
Universelle in 1900. Victor Laloux designed the soaring glass and iron roof,
together with the wildly ornate belle époque restaurant and ballroom; all
still intact. The station had all modern facilities, including elevators and
underground tracks. But in 1939 the advent of longer electric trains forced it
to close for long-distance travel (it was still used for suburban trains). During
the war it became a mail depot, then a reception venue for freed prisoners
of war. Later, various films were shot here, including Orson Welles' *The Trial*.
Public protest saved the station from demolition, and final approval was given
to turn it into a museum in 1977. Italian architect Gae Aulenti masterminded
the conversion of the interior, encasing both the walls and floors with stone,
and President François Mitterrand opened the museum in December 1986.

The museum has benefited from a major reorganization and renovation
programme. Impressionist works are now displayed on the fifth floor with
post-Impressionists on the middle level. Foreign artists and the Nabi works
can be found in the multi-storey Pavillon Amont, and the 'columns gallery' will
be devoted to temporary exhibitions.

The Musée d'Orsay continues to expand its collection. One recent addition
is *Le Cercle de la rue Royale* (1868) by James Tissot, classed as a national
treasure by the French government. The work is both artistically and socially
important, depicting a group of high-ranking men of the time. One of these is
Baron Hottinger whose family owned the painting until its acquisition.

WHAT TO SEE

The Impressionist and post-Impressionist collections (upper level) are a real treat, with airy galleries filled with row upon row of legendary works by Pierre-Auguste Renoir, Edgar Degas, Claude Monet, Edouard Manet, Vincent Van Gogh and others.

EDGAR DEGAS

Founding father of Impressionism, Degas brought scenes of everyday life to his canvases and is particularly known for Paris street scenes and people such as flower sellers or dancers going about their daily lives. One of almost 200 works by this French artist held by the museum, *La Classe de Danse* (1873–1876) is a fine example of his work.

EDOUARD MANET

Related to the Swedish Royal family through his mother's line, Manet did not fit the image of the penniless and starving artist but he looked to the street for his early inspiration, painting gypsies and beggars. His *Olympia* (1863) caused uproar when it was first displayed in Paris for the provocative and self-assured pose of the prostitute subject.

CLAUDE MONET

Monet, one of the father figures of Impressionism, is well represented, with works such as *Régate à Argenteuil* (c. 1872), *Nymphéas Bleus* (c. 1916–19) and *La Gare St-Lazare* (1877). There are five paintings from the 28-strong *Cathédrales de Rouen* series, painted between 1892 and 1894. Monet rented a studio opposite the cathedral to allow him to paint the building in different lights and weather conditions. More paintings from the series can be seen at the Musée Marmottan Monet (▷ 78–79).

PIERRE-AUGUSTE RENOIR

Renoir's cheerful *Le Bal du Moulin de la Galette* (1876) portrays Montmartre at a time when it was the focus of Paris's nightlife. Renoir painted it while actually at the open-air dance hall, on the site of the Galette windmill (▷ 227). Notice the play of light and shade on the dancers, and the way the

TIPS

» A Paris Museum Pass (▷ 279) gives you free entrance and allows you to skip the queues.
» Tuesday, Saturday and Sunday are the museum's busiest days. Thursday evening is the quietest time to visit.
» To see Monet's paintings in a more tranquil setting, visit the Musée Marmottan Monet (▷ 78–79).
» The Musée d'Orsay is closed on Monday, unlike the Louvre and Centre Georges Pompidou, which close on Tuesday.
» Entrance is free to teachers, art students and professional artists.
» The café on the upper floor gives you a stunning view of Paris through the glass of the huge station clock. An open-air terrace is open from May to October, weather permitting. There is a self-service cafeteria just above it, and a lavish restaurant on the middle level.
» From Wednesday to Sunday a cumulative passport ticket is available for the Musée d'Orsay and Musée de l'Orangerie for €13.
» A day ticket covering both the Orsay and Musée Rodin costs €12.
» In the week following your visit to the Musée d'Orsay, keep your ticket to allow you to take advantage of reduced rates for the Gustave Moreau museum and the Palais Garnier (Paris National Opera).

Left *Three paintings from the collection*
Below *Montmartre framed by the face of the station clock*

dancers seem to merge with their surroundings. Like many artists of the time, Renoir had studios in Montmartre and was a regular at the Moulin de la Galette.

VINCENT VAN GOGH

Van Gogh is among the most prominently displayed post-Impressionists, with masterpieces including the vivid *La Chambre à Arles* (1889), the sinisterly swirling *L'Église d'Auvers-sur-Oise* (1890) and the relaxed *La Sieste* (1889–90). His turquoise self-portrait of 1889 was painted in the same year he admitted himself to a psychiatric hospital in St-Rémy-de-Provence. It is one of the last of the artist's 40 self-portraits and shows him as pale and gaunt. Van Gogh suffered from severe depression and hallucinations and a year after painting this portrait he killed himself.

SCULPTURE ON THE LOWER LEVEL

Even if your sole reason for visiting the museum is the Impressionist collection on the upper level, don't leave without wandering through the central aisle on the lower floor. This is the best place to catch the atmosphere of the building—part museum, part belle époque train station—with its ornate clock, magnificent glass roof and contrastingly solid stone-clad floor and walls. In addition to allowing you to admire the building, the central aisle is also a gallery for 19th-century neoclassical sculpture. Near the eastern end, look out for Jean-Baptiste Carpeaux's *La Danse* (1869), formerly part of the facade of the Opéra Palais Garnier (▷ 204) and controversial when it was first unveiled because of the detail in the nude figures. Also worth spotting, in the entrance hall, is François Rude's ferocious bust *Génie de la Patrie* (1836), moulded from a larger bas-relief on the Arc de Triomphe.

THE BALLROOM

Don't miss the lavish Salles des Fêtes (room 51), tucked away at the end of the middle level. The extravagantly chandeliered and mirrored room was originally part of the station's hotel and served both as a reception room and venue for special events. In 1958 General de Gaulle declared his return to government here to a gathering of reporters.

Below *Light streams through the soaring glass roof to highlight the sculptures on the lower level*

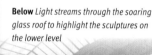

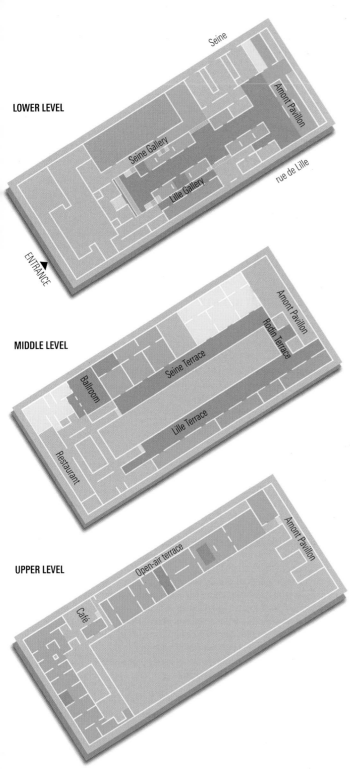

LOWER LEVEL

Seine

Amont Pavillon

Seine Gallery

Lille Gallery

rue de Lille

ENTRANCE ▼

MIDDLE LEVEL

Amont Pavillon

Rodin Terrace

Seine Terrace

Ballroom

Lille Terrace

Restaurant

UPPER LEVEL

Amont Pavillon

Open-air terrace

Café

MUSÉE D'ORSAY FLOORPLAN GALLERY GUIDE

If you opt for a chronological visit, look at the sculpture and paintings on the lower level then take the escalator at the end of the hall straight to the upper level, leaving the middle level for the end (rooms are numbered accordingly).

LOWER LEVEL
Central Aisle: Sculpture, including Carpeaux's *Ugolin* (1860) and Louis-Antoine Barye's *Seated Lion* (1874)
Lille Gallery: Second Empire Collection
Seine Gallery: Exhibition space

MIDDLE LEVEL
Ballroom
Seine Terrace (mezzanine): Sculpture, including Camille Claudel's *Middle Age* (1899–1903)
Rodin Terrace: Sculpture by Rodin, including *Gates of Hell* (1880–1917) and *Balzac* (1897)
Lille Terrace (mezzanine): Post-Impressionists up to 1900
Amont Pavillon: Nabis school
Restaurant

UPPER LEVEL
Galleries: Impressionists and Impressionism
Amont Pavillon: Decorative Arts from foreign schools
Café Campana

INFORMATION

www.quaibranly.fr

⊞ 70 G7 ✉ 29–37 quai Branly, 75007 (east of avenue de la Bourdonnais) ☎ 01 56 61 70 00 🕐 Tue–Wed, Sun 11–7, Thu–Sat 11–9 💷 Adult €8.50, under 18 free 🚇 Pont de l'Alma, Alma-Marceau 🚌 42, 63, 72, 80, 92 🚃 Champ de Mars-Tour Eiffel 🎧 Audioguide €5

TIPS

» Look for the museum's logo — a *chupicuaro* from the southeastern central Mexican state, Guanajuato. These pot-bellied figurines are typical of this ancient Mexican culture which flourished in Pre-Conquest times.

» Follow the floor colourings which designate the different regions: red is Oceania, blue is the Americas, brown is Africa, yellow is Asia.

» Try to catch the forum of questions and answers (Central Mezzanine; every Sunday at 3pm; free, first come first served) when there's an opportunity to discuss individual objects and your personal experience of the museum (in French only).

» Café Branly in the garden serves refreshments all day or Les Ombres restaurant on the roof terrace, has lovely views (reservations essential: tel 01 47 53 68 00; www.lesombres-restaurant.com).

Above *The glass palisade and plant wall of the Musée du Quai Branly*

MUSÉE DU QUAI BRANLY

'A sacred wood — a sanctuary without walls' is how the architect of the Musée du Quai Branly, Jean Nouvel, describes his creation. Built on five levels, crowned by a wide terrace with fine views of the Eiffel Tower, it is hailed as an architectural masterpiece. The buildings are hidden from view by trees and thick vegetation in a 2.4ha (6-acre) site, protected from the noise of the quays by a glass palisade. *Le mur végétal* (plant wall) festoons the facade of the administrative building with 15,000 plants representing 150 species from all over the world. Curved, fluid lines mimic the undulating Seine and inside glass walls replace windows.

EGALITÉ, FRATERNITÉ

The equal dignity of the cultures of the world is the ethos of this museum. The cultures of Africa, Asia, the Americas and Oceania are showcased, supplemented by themed exhibitions. Of 300,000 works in the museum, 3,500 are exhibited in the permanent collections and 10 temporary exhibitions are staged annually. A swooping white ramp leads through a dark tunnel before reaching the display area, where you are greeted by a 10th-century anthropomorphic Dogon wood statue from Mali.

This sets the tone for the rest of the treasures, including many formerly hidden away in the dismantled Musée des Arts d'Afrique et d'Océanie and the ethnology collections of the Musée de l'Homme. Highlights include a glass tower of 9,000 musical instruments, a huge totem pole from Canada, Vietnamese costumes, Gabonese masks, Aztec statues, aboriginal art decorating ceilings and facades, rare frescoes from Ethiopia, feather headdresses and painted animal hides from the Americas, and the Harter bequest of masks and sculptures from Cameroon.

A DIALOGUE BETWEEN CULTURES

There's a programme of live entertainment in the theatre creating a non-European cultural city of art. The Quai Branly's Open University, which is accessible to everyone, organizes debates on historic and contemporary issues and encourages dialogue through its series of lectures. It is also a research centre, a meeting place for the university and museum worlds, enabling the public, researchers and curators to work together. Additionally, it carries out in-the-field operations designed to protect cultural heritage.

MUSÉE RODIN

The Musée Rodin's open-air gallery, spread over 3ha (7 acres) of beautiful garden hidden in the heart of the city, makes a great escape from more strenuous sightseeing. After a stroll through the grounds, you can see more of Rodin's works in the Hôtel Biron, the airy 18th-century mansion where he once lived.

THE GARDEN

Don't miss the brooding bronze *Le Penseur (The Thinker;* 1880–1904), thought to represent the Italian poet Dante and originally placed outside the Panthéon, or the gruesome doorway *La Porte de l'Enfer (The Gates of Hell;* 1880–1917), inspired by Dante's *Divine Comedy. Les Bourgeois de Calais (The Burghers of Calais;* 1884–1889) depicts six burghers who gave up their lives to save their townsfolk during a siege by the English in the 14th century, while *Balzac* (1891–1898) is a rather unflattering portrayal of the famous writer in his dressing gown.

THE HÔTEL BIRON

Inside the elegant mansion, you can follow Rodin's artistic evolution chronologically, from his early academic sketches and paintings to his vigorous watercolours. The highlight is the intensely passionate white marble *Le Baiser (The Kiss;* 1882–1898), one of Rodin's best-known pieces. There are also works by the artist's contemporaries, including sculptor and graphic artist Camille Claudel, and the Impressionists Pierre-Auguste Renoir, Vincent Van Gogh and Claude Monet.

THE ARTIST

Rodin was born in Paris in 1840 and showed an early aptitude for drawing. In 1857 he applied to study sculpture at the École des Beaux-Arts but was rejected because tutors felt his style was old-fashioned. Most of his famous pieces date from the latter half of his life.

In 1908 Rodin moved into the ground floor of the rococo Hôtel Biron (1730), where other residents included Surrealist Jean Cocteau, artist Henri Matisse and dancer Isadora Duncan. In 1916 Rodin welcomed a decision to turn the mansion into a museum of his work, but he died in 1917, two years before the plans became reality.

INFORMATION

www.musee-rodin.fr

✚ 71 J7 ✉ 77 rue de Varenne, 75007 ☎ 01 44 18 61 10 🕐 Apr–Sep Tue–Sun 10–5.45 (gardens until 6); Oct–Mar 9.30–4.45 (gardens until 5) 🖐 Adult €6, under 18 free, free to all on 1st Sun of month. Museum, exhibition and gardens €10. Exhibition: €7. Garden only: €1 🚇 Varenne 🚌 69, 82, 87, 92 🚉 RER line C, Invalides 🎧 Audioguides €4. Guided tours available 📖 €15 ☕ Garden café 🛍 Bookshop/gift shop

TIPS

» The garden-only ticket lets you view some of Rodin's most important works for only €1; children should enjoy the play area.
» If the Rodin Museum whets your appetite for open-air sculpture, try the Musée de la Sculpture en Plein Air, on quai St-Bernard, which has around 40 avant-garde works. (Visit during the day only.)
» There are few information boards in the garden, so rent an audioguide or pick up a free leaflet from the Hôtel Biron.
» There is a day passport for the Musée Rodin and Musée d'Orsay, which costs €12 for both museums.

Above *Detail of Rodin's* Les Bourgeois de Calais *in the museum garden*

INFORMATION

➕ 70 F6 ✉ 17 place du Trocadéro et du 11 Novembre, 75016 🚇 Trocadéro

🚌 22, 30, 32, 63, 72, 82

Musée National de la Marine

www.musee-marine.fr

☎ 01 53 65 69 69 🕐 Mon, Wed–Thu 11–6, Fri 11–9.30, Sat, Sun 11–7 (last entry 45 min before closing) 💷 Adult (museum + exhibition + audioguide) €9, under 18 free. Museum only adult €7, child €5 🎧 Audioguides (French, English; included in the entrance fee) 📖 Bookshop/gift shop

Musée de l'Homme

www.mnhn.fr

☎ 01 44 05 72 72 🕐 Mon, Wed–Fri 10–5, Sat–Sun 10–6 (last entry 30 min before closing) 💷 Adult €7, child €5 🍴 Café-restaurant place du Trocadéro 📖 Bookshop/gift shop ❓ Museum closed until late 2012 for renovations

Above *The Palais de Chaillot overlooks the Jardins du Trocadéro*

INTRODUCTION

The colonnaded Palais de Chaillot was built for the *Exposition Universelle* of 1937 and offers stunning views of the Eiffel Tower, and the Champ de Mars beyond. Its curved wings are dotted with gleaming bronze statues and the wide terraces, overlooking the fountains of the Jardins du Trocadéro, bustle with street artists, souvenir sellers, food kiosks and visitors admiring the Eiffel Tower. The palace currently houses two museums and the Théâtre National de Chaillot (tel 01 53 65 30 00; www.theatre-chaillot.fr), which sits beneath the terrace, between the two wings.

WHAT TO SEE

MUSEUMS

The Musée National de la Marine and the Musée de l'Homme are in the palace's west wing. The Musée National de la Marine is one of the largest maritime museums in the world and was founded by Charles X in 1827. It focuses on French naval history from the 18th century to the present day and displays paintings, naval instruments and a vast array of model ships. There is also a workshop where you can watch the models being restored. The Musée de l'Homme has collections of anthropology and prehistory illustrating the evolution of the human species, the growth of the world's population and the similarities and diversity of mankind. The ethnological collections were transferred to the Musée du Quai Branly, which opened in 2006 (▷ 84).

CITÉ DE L'ARCHITECTURE ET DU PATRIMOINE

www.citechaillot.fr

The east wing of the *palais* was renovated following a fire in 1997 and forms part of the Cité de l'Architecture et du Patrimoine, the national repository of architectural excellence and the École de Chaillot restoration school. It is the world's largest architectural museum, spanning 12 centuries of French architecture. There is everything here from cathedrals and abbeys to private mansions and from railway stations to skyscrapers—all testimony to the main developments in French architecture throughout the centuries. On the ground floor the Galerie des Moulages displays 350 larger than life-size plaster casts and 60 maquettes of architecture, including entire portals of churches and cathedrals such as Chartres. The first floor is devoted to the Bibliothèque (library), the leading national centre for information on contemporary architecture, with free public access.

On the second level you come first to the Galerie des Peintures Murales et des Vitraux where there is a splendid collection of more than 100 mural copies from the 11th to 16th centuries. Perhaps even more dazzling are the reproductions of the stained-glass windows: the first of these in the collection was The Crucifixion (St-Pierre Cathedral, Poitiers 1163–1173). There are 13 in total nowadays, including replicas from the cathedrals of Rouen, Châteauroux and Chartres. On the same level, the Galerie d'Architecture Moderne et Contemporaine charts developments from the 1850s to the present day. Highlights include a reconstructed, walk-in apartment from the Cité Radieuse in Marseille designed by Le Corbusier in the mid-20th century.

✉ 1 place du Trocadéro, 75116 ☎ 01 58 51 52 00 🕐 Mon, Wed, Fri–Sun 11–7, Thu 11–9. Last entrance 30 min before closing ✋ Permanent collections: adult €8, child free. Permanent collections and temporary exhibitions: adult €10. Free on 1st Sun of month 🎫 Guided tours €7

TIPS
» The Café Carlu is housed in the Pavillon de Tête. The café has been fitted with touch screens where you can access the museum collection. They provide a useful way to prepare for your visit or to learn more about items that interest you.
» The Cité hosts important temporary exhibitions throughout the year, organized in consultation with cutting-edge architects and urban planners, including such luminaries as Jean Nouvel, Roland Castro and Sir Richard Rogers.

MORE TO SEE

CINÉAQUA
www.cineaqua.com

Cinéaqua reopened its doors in 2006 after a closure of 21 years. Created originally for the Universal Exhibition in 1878, this is now both aquarium and cinema complex and is especially popular with children. The visit slowly takes you down to 19m (62ft) underground, as you watch the fish swim by. There are 9,000 sea creatures including 25 sharks—feeding time (usually around 4pm) is always a highlight. The futuristic cinema complex shows cartoons and animal documentaries and there is a good, albeit expensive, Japanese restaurant overlooking the largest tank. At night (after 8pm) the Aqualounge becomes an adult venue, backed by a huge aquarium.

✉ 5 avenue Albert de Mun, 75016 ☎ 01 40 69 23 23 🕐 Daily 10–7 (last entry 60 min before closing) ✋ Adult €19.50, child (3–12) €12.50, 13–17 €15.50, under 3 free

Below *French architecture from the eighth century to the present day is celebrated at the Cité de l'Architecture et du Patrimoine*

PLACE DU TROCADÉRO ET DU 11 NOVEMBRE

Semicircular place du Trocadéro et du 11 Novembre faces the monumental wings of the Palais de Chaillot (▷ 86–87), the fountains of the Jardins du Trocadéro and, across the Seine, the Eiffel Tower. Six avenues radiate from it and an equestrian statue of World War I Allied Commander Marshal Foch stands at its heart. The square was named after an Andalusian fort occupied by the French in 1823 and was given its present shape in 1858, when a first palace was built. This palace was replaced with the Palais de Chaillot, built for the 1937 Universal Exhibition. There are plenty of cafés and restaurants in the area.

✚ 70 F6 ✉ place du Trocadéro et du 11 Novembre, 75016 Ⓜ Trocadéro 🚌 22, 30, 32, 63

PONT ALEXANDRE III

Four gilded bronze Pegasus figures watch over this wildly ornate bridge, which sparkles in the setting sun. The bridge forms a link between Les Invalides (▷ 74–75) on the Left Bank and the Grand Palais and Petit Palais (▷ 192) on the Right, its glory marred only by the stream of traffic.

Symbolic of the optimism of the belle époque, it was built for the 1900 *Exposition Universelle* and dedicated to a new alliance between Russia and France. The foundation stone was laid by Tsar Nicholas II, and the facade bears the coats of arms of both Paris and Russia. The bridge is crammed with elaborate decoration by more than 15 artists.

✚ 71 J6 ✉ cours La Reine/quai d'Orsay Ⓜ Invalides, Champs-Élysées-Clémenceau 🚌 63, 83, 93 🚊 RER line C, Invalides

PONT DE L'ALMA

The first Pont de l'Alma was built in 1856 to commemorate a victory over the Russians by the Franco-British alliance in the Crimean War. The bridge developed subsidence and was replaced in 1974. The underpass running along the Seine here is where the fatal car

Above *Golden statues in front of the Palais de Chaillot line place du Trocadéro*

crash involving Diana, Princess of Wales, happened in August 1997. The Liberty Flame, placed near the entrance in 1987 by the *International Herald Tribune* as a symbol of American and French friendship, has become a memorial to the People's Princess. A statue of a Zouave soldier from the original bridge is now a high-water marker.

✚ 71 H6 ✉ place de l'Alma/place de la Résistance Ⓜ Alma-Marceau 🚌 42, 63, 72, 80, 92 🚊 RER line C, Pont de l'Alma

PONT DE BIR-HAKEIM

The Pont de Bir-Hakeim was built between 1903 and 1905, replacing a 19th-century footbridge. The two-tiered art nouveau bridge has a walkway, roadway and a viaduct for the Métro. It is made up of two unequal metal structures on either side of the allée des Cygnes. Trains rattle across the top level, which is supported by cast-iron pillars. Originally called the Passy Viaduct, the bridge was renamed in 1949,

to commemorate of the victory of General Koenig in Libya in 1942.

✚ 70 F7 ✉ quai Branly Ⓜ Bir-Hakeim, Passy 🚌 72

PONT ROYAL

The Pont Royal was a gift from Louis XIV, replacing a wooden bridge that had been destroyed by fire. The king chose one of his most prized architects, Jules Hardouin-Mansart, to design the graceful stone structure, and the bridge was in place by 1689. Nobles used it to travel from the exclusive Faubourg St-Germain district to the Tuileries Palace. In the 18th century, the bridge became the site of major Parisian festivities and fireworks. The hydrographic scales on each end pillar show high-water levels.

✚ 71 L7 ✉ quai des Tuileries/quai Voltaire Ⓜ Palais Royal 🚌 24, 68, 69, 72 🚊 RER line C, Musée d'Orsay

TOUR EIFFEL

▷ 90–95.

TOUR MONTPARNASSE

The Tour Montparnasse dominates the Paris skyline, rising 210m (689ft) over the Montparnasse district. For awe-inspiring views of the city let the ear-popping elevator whizz you up to the enclosed, air-conditioned viewing gallery on the 56th floor, in just 38 seconds. From here you can spot many of Paris's major attractions, including the Eiffel Tower, Les Invalides, the Arc de Triomphe, Sacré-Cœur, the Louvre, Musée d'Orsay, Centre Georges Pompidou, St-Germain-des-Prés, Église St-Sulpice, Notre-Dame and the Panthéon. A mini-cinema projects a short film by Albert Lamorisse showing aerial views of Paris. There are also temporary exhibitions and displays. Farther up, the 59th-floor open-air terrace is the highest in Paris—and not for the faint-hearted. You can see up to 40km (25 miles) on a clear day.

OFFICE BLOCK

The tower has 58 floors, each covering an area of almost 2,000sq m (21,500sq ft). Offices occupy 53 floors, with a workforce of around 5,000 people. Only two floors are open to the public—the 56th floor and the 59th-floor terrace. The tower is 50m (164ft) long, 32m (105ft) wide and weighs 150,000 tonnes. Its foundations reach a depth of 70m (230ft). It has a concrete core with a steel structure. The facades are predominantly glass, aluminium and bronze.

AN EYESORE?

The Tour Montparnasse was built between 1969 and 1973, as part of a huge urban development project to modernize the Montparnasse district. It was designed by architects Beaudouin, Cassan, De Marien and Saubot and stands on the site of the old Gare Montparnasse railway station—the Métro runs directly underneath it. The tower has always been highly controversial. President Georges Pompidou, who authorized its construction, took a helicopter tour to observe the completed job and is reported to have said to his urban planners, 'That's enough, we stop right there'. It is still considered an eyesore by many Parisians, and remains one of the capital's least-liked buildings, despite the spectacular views it offers.

INFORMATION

www.tourmontparnasse56.com

✚ 71 K9 ✉ 33 avenue du Maine, 75015 ☎ 01 45 38 52 56 🕐 Apr–Sep daily 9.30am–11.30pm; Oct–Mar Sun–Thu 9.30am–10.30pm, Fri, Sat 9.30am–11pm; last elevator up 30 min before closing ✋ Adult €11.50, child (7–14) €4.70, under 7 free 🚇 Montparnasse-Bienvenüe 🚌 28, 82, 89, 92, 94, 95, 96 🚉 Gare Montparnasse 📖 €2.50 🍴 Bar on the 56th floor 🍽 360 Café offers light snacks

TIPS

» The 59th-floor open-air terrace is closed on very windy days.

» If you're short on time, don't stop to watch the film—enjoy the amazing views instead.

» Interactive information screens on floor 56 give added information about a range of topics relating to Paris and views from the tower.

Below *Pont Alexandre III offers a clear view of Tour Montparnasse*

INTRODUCTION

Whether you see it as a 'hollow candlestick' or an elegant emblem of Paris, you can't ignore the Eiffel Tower. Its sleek iron silhouette, rising up 324m (1,063ft), finds its way into many of the city's best views.

Around 7 million people visit the Iron Lady each year, so be prepared for a long wait (and the indefatigable attentions of trinket salesmen). Before you buy a ticket, you'll need to decide whether you want to go as far as level one (57m/187ft), level two (120m/394ft) or level three (280m/918ft), and whether you'll take the elevator or brave the stairs (to levels one and two only). The price will vary accordingly. The stairs are at the south pillar. The two-level elevators, with room for 80 people, are in the north, west and east pillars, although only one or two are operational at any one time. These take you as far as levels one and two, then you face another wait for a second, smaller elevator that takes you on the three-minute journey to level three. The plush Jules Verne restaurant, on level two, has a separate elevator at the south pillar.

CONTROVERSIAL BEGINNINGS

Slammed as a 'hollow chandelier' and 'tower of Babel' when it was built in 1889, the Eiffel Tower went on to become the emblem of Paris. Gustave Eiffel took only two years to complete the unconventional monument, finishing just in time for the 1889 Universal Exhibition. At the peak of the construction work, the tower grew 30m (98ft) a month. Despite this breakneck operation, when the opening day came, Gustave Eiffel and a gaggle of officials still had to walk up the 1,665 steps to the top because the elevators weren't working. The tower is a feat of engineering, weighing more than 10,000 tons and made up of 18,000 iron parts. No one knew then that it would become the symbol of Paris—it was due to be demolished after 20 years. By the time its allotted two decades were up it had as many fans as opponents. It was eventually saved simply for its broadcasting antennae. Its growing popularity vindicated the opinions of literary and artistic allies such as Guillaume Apollinaire, Raoul Dufy, Maurice Utrillo and Camille Pissarro. The objections of Paul Verlaine, Émile Zola and Guy de Maupassant were relegated to history. For 40 years the tower basked in the glory of being the highest structure in the world until New York's Chrysler Building usurped the title. It gained another 20m (66ft) in 1957 when television antennae were added. Famous visitors have included Thomas Edison, King George VI and his wife Queen Elizabeth, and the Shah of Persia.

INFORMATION

www.tour-eiffel.fr

✚ 70 G7 ✉ quai Branly, Champ de Mars, 75007 ☎ 0892 70 12 39 (€0.33 per min) 🕐 Mid-Jun to late Aug daily 9am–12.45am; late Aug to mid-Jun 9.30am–11.45pm; last entry 45 min before closing ✋ **By elevator:** Adult €8.20 (levels one and two), €13.40 (level three); student (12–24) €6.60 (levels one and two), €11.80 (level three); child (4–11) €4.10 (levels one and two), €9.30 (level three). **By stairs to levels one and two:** Adult €4.70, student (12–24) €3.70, child (4–11) €3.20 🚇 Bir-Hakeim, Trocadéro, École Militaire 🚌 42, 69, 82, 87 🚆 RER line C, Champ de Mars-Tour Eiffel 🖝 Centre des Monuments Nationaux leads occasional guided tours (tel 0825 05 44 05, €0.15 per min) 🍴 58 Tour Eiffel brasserie on level one; Jules Verne on level two—Alain Ducasse's restaurant is popular and expensive (lunch €100, dinner €200). Reservations essential: online at www. restaurants-toureiffel.com 🍹 Snack bars on ground floor, level one and level two 📖 In a variety of languages 🎁 Gift shops on levels one and two ♿ Wheelchair access to first and second levels only. Classical music concerts are organized by the Association Musique et Patrimoine (tel 01 42 50 96 18; www.ampconcerts.com)

Opposite and below *The spectacular and iconic Tour Eiffel*

TIPS

» To skip the wait for the elevators, walk up the stairs to level one, then catch the elevator to level two. The climb isn't too daunting. Note that you can only buy tickets for either the stairs or the elevator from the ground to the second floor (▷ 91). If you buy a stairs ticket, you will have to buy an additional ticket at the first floor for the elevator.

» The wait for the elevator is generally shorter at night.

» Pushchairs (strollers) are allowed up the tower only if they are collapsible.

» If you want to dine at the elegant Jules Verne restaurant book well ahead.

» For security reasons large bags are not allowed. Other bags may be searched.

» Book tickets online through the website to save time queuing at the tower.

Below and right *Spotlights illuminate the ironwork to great effect at night*

TOWERING FIGURE

Gustave Eiffel beat more than 100 other entrants in the competition to design a focal point, 300m (984ft) high, for the 1889 Universal Exhibition. The resulting magnificent tower is the ultimate symbol of Eiffel's considerable skill and imagination, but the 'magician of iron' has left hundreds of other constructions all over the world.

Born in 1832 in Burgundy, he was already working on Bordeaux bridge at the age of 26. Bridges soon became his particular area of expertise: Iron and the hydraulic methods he used for installing their supports helped to build his reputation, first throughout France and later across many countries of the world. Factories, churches, a synagogue (rue des Tournelles), shops (Le Bon Marché), banks and, over a period of 18 years, 31 railway viaducts and 17 major bridges all came within his creative sphere. Egypt, Peru, Portugal, Hungary and Bolivia all have their Eiffel monuments. He even designed the frame for New York's Statue of Liberty.

Eiffel kept an office in his most famous tower until his death. You can see a reconstruction of the room, complete with waxwork figures, on level 3. A bust of the engineer, by Bourdelle, stands near the north pillar. Gustave Eiffel died in 1923, at the age of 91.

WHAT TO SEE

THE VIEW

The view is the reason you climb the Eiffel Tower, whether it's for the magnificent sweep across the city or to test your nerves peering down 115m (377ft) through the glass window on the floor of level two. The tower was the world's tallest building for 40 years, and from the gallery on level three you can see up to 75km (45 miles) on a clear day. If you can't face the vertigo-inducing top level, the views are just as impressive on level two, where you can see the city in more detail. There is also a viewing gallery on level one, with information boards. Sights to look out for include the Arc de Triomphe (north), the Palais de Chaillot (northwest), the gardens of the Champ de Mars (southeast), with the Tour Montparnasse farther back, and the golden dome of Les Invalides (east). The views are often at their best in the run up to sunset, when the light is kinder to cameras. At night a totally different picture unfolds, as hundreds of thousands of lights sketch out the city.

Above *Visitors can choose to climb the stairs in the south pillar to level one and two or take one of the elevators*

FLOOR GUIDE
LEVEL ONE
Cineiffel, Observatory, Feroscope, gift shop, post office, viewing gallery, Altitude 95 restaurant, snack bar, hydraulic elevator pump, part of the original spiral staircase.

LEVEL TWO
Jules Verne restaurant, glass-floor viewing window, gift shops, viewing gallery, snack bar.

LEVEL THREE
Viewing gallery, panoramic photo, reconstruction of Gustave Eiffel's office, Champagne Bar.

THE LIGHTS
Make sure you catch a glimpse of the tower at night, even if you want to reserve your actual visit for daylight. A staggering 10,000 light bulbs contribute to the glittering spectacle. More than 350 spotlights illuminate the latticework, topped by a rotating beacon that can be seen up to 80km (50 miles) away. One of the best ways to appreciate the shimmering display is on a boat trip (▷ 210–211), when the tower takes you by surprise as you turn the corner at the Pont de l'Alma. On foot, the views from the Palais de Chaillot (▷ 86–87) are memorable.

The tower was originally lit by gas, before electricity was introduced in time for the Universal Exhibition in 1900. In 1925, car manufacturer André Citroën bankrolled a dramatic display of lights advertising his company. The current 350,000-watt system was inaugurated on New Year's Eve 1985. It replaced an unpopular system that beamed light onto the tower from more than 1,000 spotlights on the Champ de Mars, dazzling visitors inside. The rotating beacon was added in 1999. Special displays were staged for the centenary of the tower in 1989 and for the countdown to 2000. Now, for five minutes every hour from nightfall to 1am, 20,000 extra bulbs add a magical shimmer to the golden lighting of the tower.

THE ANTICS
The Eiffel Tower has inspired more than its fair share of eccentric behaviour. In 1912 a would-be Icarus plunged to his death when his cape failed to act as wings as he had hoped. In 1928 a watchmaker tried out an innovative new design for a parachute but, once again, it failed to open and he rapidly met his maker. A bicyclist who pedalled down the steps to win a bet in 1923 was more successful, although he was arrested when he reached the bottom.

Below *The entrance to the elevator in the north pillar*

Mountaineers have scaled the tower, pilots have tried to fly through its pillars and in 1909 the Comte de Lambert circled 100m (330ft) above it in a flying machine. More recently, in 1984 a British couple survived an unofficial parachute jump from level three and in 1989 Philippe Petit walked a tightrope strung up between the tower and the Palais de Chaillot.

Humans are not the only creatures involved in antics at the tower. While animals are usually banned, in 1948 a circus elephant was allowed to walk up the stairs to the first floor!

OTHER ATTRACTIONS

On level three, a panoramic photo helps you to identify monuments on the skyline. You can also discover the distance from the tower of various capital cities (none of them within sight!).

Once you have soaked up the spectacular view, you can learn more about the fascinating history of the tower from the short film shown at Cineiffel (level one). Other attractions on the first floor include the Observatory, where you can monitor the tower's sway (during the storms of 1999, the sway at the top of the tower measured 13cm/5in), and the Feroscope, focusing on all things iron. You can also see the original hydraulic elevator pump—the elevators cover the equivalent of 100,000km (62,000 miles) each year—and a piece of the original spiral staircase that linked the second and third levels, as used by Monsieur Eiffel himself. If you want to boast of your lofty whereabouts to your friends back home, you can have your postcards franked with Tour Eiffel at the tower's own post office (open 10–7).

FACTS AND FIGURES

» The tower weighs 10,100 tonnes. It has 18,000 metal sections and two and a half million rivets.

» In hot weather it expands by up to 15cm (6in).

» 370 people committed suicide by jumping from the tower, until protective shields were installed in 1971.

» More than 200 million people have visited the tower since its opening.

» There are 1,665 steps to the top.

» It takes 60 tonnes of paint to spruce up the tower. It is completely repainted every seven years, taking 18 months. The colour has varied from yellow/orange (1899) to reddish brown in the 1950s, but since 1968 the specially created brown colour, 'brun Tour Eiffel' has been used.

Above *The intricate iron framework took two years to complete, utilizing 18,000 sections and two and a half million rivets*

AROUND THE TOUR EIFFEL

Not one but two towers dominate the skyline in this area, which holds many of Paris's best-loved monuments and lesser-known, but equally fascinating, sights on the Left Bank.

THE WALK

Distance: 4.2km (2.6 miles)
Time: 3 hours
Start at: Cimetière du Montparnasse
End at: École Militaire

HOW TO GET THERE

Take the Métro to Raspail/Place de Clichy/Blanche, or bus 30, 54, 74, 80 or 95.

★Begin in the boulevard Edgar Quinet in the lively Montparnasse district. The Raspail Métro brings you out into boulevard Edgar Quinet where you will find the Cimetière du Montparnasse (▷ 73).

❶ Between the two world wars Montparnasse was the heartland of artists, writers, intellectuals and bons vivants from all over the world. The inflated rents of Montmartre resulted in an exodus to 'Mount Parnassus' and all the famous and infamous of the era are buried here in the tree-lined cemetery. Literary

luminaries include Jean-Paul Sartre, Simone de Beauvoir and Charles Baudelaire (whose tomb is always surrounded by 'little poems in prose' left by admirers), and famous artists include Man Ray and Frédéric Bartholdi (the Statue of Liberty sculptor) and, more recently, the singer Serge Gainsbourg. Brancusi placed a cubist statue, *Kiss,* in the northeast corner and Niki de Saint Phalle a cat in mosaic on the grave of a friend.

Turn left and head north on the boulevard Edgar Quinet where on Wednesday and Saturday mornings there is a vibrant market specializing in *gourmandises* such as wild mushrooms in season, *charcuterie,* cheeses and wines. Look in on the café La Liberté near the Edgar-Quinet Métro. This is where Sartre spent many hours writing his longest novel, *Les Chemins de la Liberté*. Cross rue du Départ to Tour Montparnasse (▷ 89).

❷ When it was constructed in 1973, the tower's 59 floors of smoked glass and steel provoked cries of indignation. Since then it has become a familiar landmark, visible from all over Paris and spectacular by night when hundreds of windows light up the sky. An elevator whizzes you up to the 56th floor in just 38 seconds for fabulous views over the city. Three floors higher bring you to the highest open-air terrace in Paris from where you can see literally for miles—25 (40km) on a clear day.

Cross rue de l'Arrivée and then turn left into rue Antoine-Bourdelle, where you will find the Musée Bourdelle (▷ 76) at No. 18.

❸ The sculptor Émile-Antoine Bourdelle, Auguste Rodin's star pupil, lived here from 1885 until his death in 1929. His sculpted works, canvases and watercolours are on display in his former studio

and apartments. Some of his greatest works include the *Centaure Mourant, Hercules the Archer* and 21 studies of Beethoven. The works continue in a winter garden of ivy and acacias where, according to Bourdelle, 'spring laughs, summer burns and time dreams'.

Turn left onto rue Falguière, then right onto rue Dulac. At the beginning of the 20th century, artists' studios filled this area. Then turn left into rue de Vaugirard and right into boulevard Pasteur to the crossroads and the beginning of the avenue de Breteuil. Designed by Jules Hardouin-Mansart in 1680, this is one of Paris's most elegant streets and leads directly up to Les Invalides (▷ 74–75).

4 In 1671 Louis XIV decided to build 'a royal hostel that would be large and spacious enough to house all officers, crippled, old and retired alike'. The magnificent ensemble of Les Invalides with long green lawns today houses the Ministry of Defence and the Musée de l'Ordre de la Libération, Musée des Plans et Reliefs and the Musée de l'Armée. Beneath the dome of the Eglise du Dôme, redecorated with 12kg (26 pounds) of gold in 1989, lies the tomb of Napoléon Bonaparte.

Walk along the right-hand side of Les Invalides on the boulevard des

Opposite *Tour Eiffel viewed through* Wall for Peace, *conceived by Clare Halter, in Champ de Mars*

Invalides and turn right into the rue de Varenne where, at number 79, you will find the Musée Rodin (▷ 85).

5 The great sculptor Auguste Rodin took up residence here in 1908 surrounded by a park teeming with rabbits. Nowadays, the gardens are speckled with treasures and roses and statues have replaced the rabbits. The symbolic figure, *Le Penseur,* is the focal point of the rose garden where 700 bushes of the specially created purple-hued Rodin rose were planted in 2005. Elsewhere in the gardens are his monumental *Porte d'Enfer* inspired by Dante, *Les Bourgeois de Calais* and many bronze sculptures of nudes, copied from Roman or Greek originals, gloriously displayed in this natural setting.

Retrace your steps and in front of the Invalides Dome, turn left along the Jardin de l'Intendant and follow

avenue de Tourville up to the corner with the École Militaire (▷ 73).

6 Designed by Jacques-Ange Gabriel, architect of the Petit Trianon at Versailles and place de la Concorde, the École Militaire was completed in 1773. The Corinthian pillars, quadrangular dome and central pavilion are a superb example of the French Classical style. At the age of 15, a young Corsican who was an excellent sailor—none other than Napoléon Bonaparte—entered the school in 1784. From here there are spectacular views of the Eiffel Tower (▷ 90–95). The symbol of Paris was originally intended to be a temporary monument for the 1889 Universal Exhibition to celebrate the centenary of the French Revolution. After sunset, on the hour, the entire structure sparkles with thousands of tiny flashbulbs (until 1am).

WHEN TO GO
The best time to do this walk is in the afternoon as virtually all the sights are open till late and the Eiffel Tower glitters in all its glory after dark.

WHERE TO EAT
For a drink or something more substantial, Montparnasse's La Coupole is the famous art deco brasserie, the literary haunt of luminaries and perfect for people-watching (▷ 143). For haute cuisine with a view to match, try Le Ciel de Paris on the 56th floor of the Tour Montparnasse (▷ 100).

SHOPPING

BARTHÉLÉMY (STÉ)

Established in 1904, this is a cheese-lover's paradise, selling Brie, Mont d'Or (from Jura), Roquefort and Vacherin (in winter), and accompanying *gourmandises* such as chutneys, biscuits and wine. The old-fashioned shop supplies both the Élysée Palace and Matignon, home to France's president and prime minister respectively.

✚ 105 K7 ✉ 51 rue de Grenelle, 75007 ☎ 01 42 22 82 24 ⊙ Tue–Sat 7–1, 3.30–7.30 Ⓜ Rue du Bac

LE BON MARCHÉ

www.lebonmarche.fr

You'll find the classiest brands and goods in this Left Bank store. Don't miss the beauty centre, appropriately named 'Théâtre de la Beauté', on the ground floor, and the food hall, La Grande Epicerie (38 rue de Sèvres; open Mon–Sat 8.30am–9pm), in an adjoining building.

✚ 105 K8 ✉ 24 rue de Sèvres, 75007 ☎ 01 44 39 80 00 ⊙ Mon–Wed 10–7.30, Thu 10–9, Fri 10–8, Sat 9.30–8 Ⓜ Sèvres-Babylone, Vaneau

THE CONRAN SHOP

www.conran.com

English designer Sir Terence Conran is a hit with the Parisian crowd. Top quality materials, a post-1970s influence, and sometimes an ethnic twist give Conran's furniture a modern elegance. Bathroom, kitchen and garden accessories complete the range.

✚ 105 K8 ✉ 117 rue du Bac, 75007 ☎ 01 42 84 10 01 ⊙ Mon–Fri 10–7, Sat 10–7.30 Ⓜ Sèvres-Babylone

MARCHÉ DE LA CRÉATION

www.marchecreation.com

Some 100 artists and craftsmen exhibit and sell their creations in this Sunday market—paintings, engravings, sculpture, ceramics and painted silks—in this open-air gallery traditionally popular with artists. There is a similar event near Bastille (Sat 9–7).

✚ 105 K9 ✉ boulevard Edgar Quinet, 75014 ☎ 01 53 57 42 60 ⊙ Sun 10am–nightfall (in summer the market closes around 9pm; in winter around 5pm) Ⓜ Edgar-Quinet

MARITHÉ + FRANÇOIS GIRBAUD

www.girbaud.com

Come here for designer streetwear in innovative fabrics and lines for men and women. The jeans collection is particularly futuristic and the store design is striking and Modernist.

✚ 105 K8 ✉ 8 rue Babylone, 75007 ☎ 01 45 48 78 86 ⊙ Tue–Sat 10–7, Mon 11–7 Ⓜ Sèvres-Babylone

L'OCCITANE

www.loccitane.fr

The essence of Provence is captured in bath oils, shower gels, shampoos, olive-oil based creams for the face and body, and fragrances. There are perfumes for the home, scented candles and herbal incenses such as fig tree and sandalwood.

✚ 104 G8 ✉ 27 rue du Commerce, 75015 ☎ 01 45 75 59 81 ⊙ Mon–Sat 10.30–7.30 Ⓜ Grenelle

SALLE RASPAIL

This second-hand shop stocks antiques from the 18th, 19th and 20th centuries. The selection is wide enough to have some funky 1970s pieces sitting next to a chest of drawers from the 19th century. It's likely that everyone will be tempted by something, all the more because only quality pieces are displayed.

✚ 105 L10 ✉ 224 boulevard Raspail, 75014 ☎ 01 56 54 11 90 ⊙ Tue–Fri 11–8, Sat 11–7 Ⓜ Raspail

ENTERTAINMENT AND NIGHTLIFE

CAFÉ D'EDGAR–THÉÂTRE D'EDGAR

www.edgar.fr

This was a pioneer of the café-theatre style launched in the 1970s.

Above *A dragon decorates the garden of La Pagode cinema*

It offers small-production comedy acts that appeal to a wide audience, and is a springboard for new talent.
✚ 105 K9 ✉ 58 boulevard Edgar Quinet, 75014 ☎ 01 43 22 11 02 🚇 Edgar Quinet

LE DOKHAN'S BAR
www.radissonblu.fr
The first champagne bar in Paris, this elegant room features three different *cuvées* per week but has a choice of over 60 labels to choose from. There's regular live music.
✚ 104 F6 ✉ Hotel Radisson Blu, 117 rue de Lauriston, 75016 ☎ 01 53 65 66 99 🕐 Daily 6pm–12.15am 🚇 Trocadéro, Victor Hugo

L'ENTREPÔT
www.lentrepot.fr
A cinema that film buffs dream of: Cult movies and art films, from all periods and parts of the world, are screened in their original language. There is a bar-restaurant on site. L'Entrepôt also holds artistic and cultural exhibitions and concerts.
✚ 105 J11 ✉ 7–9 rue Francis de Pressensé, 75014 ☎ 01 45 40 07 50 🕐 Daily 9am–midnight 🖐 Adult €7.50, child €4 🚇 Pernety, Plaisance

LOUNGE BAR DU ZEBRA SQUARE
The intimate surroundings suit the somewhat older clientele (35-plus), comfortably seated on Chesterfield sofas, listening to the music. This is part of a complex that includes the Hôtel Square (▷ 103) and the Zebra Square restaurant.
✚ 104 E8 ✉ 3 place Clément-Ader, 75016 ☎ 01 44 14 91 91 🕐 Mon–Sat 8pm–4am 🖐 Free 🚇 Passy, Ranelagh

MAISON DE LA CULTURE DU JAPON À PARIS
www.mcjp.asso.fr
This open-plan, glass and steel building showcases Japanese culture. Dance performances, both modern and traditional, are staged. The centre holds regular demonstrations of Japanese arts, crafts and cuisine including the traditional tea ceremony. The auditorium can hold 300 people.

✚ 104 G7 ✉ 101 bis quai Branly, 75015 ☎ 01 44 37 95 01 🕐 Tue–Wed, Fri–Sat noon–7, Thu noon–8 🚇 Bir-Hakeim

MAISON DE RADIO FRANCE
www.radiofrance.fr
Top-notch symphony orchestras, jazz concerts and operas are all presented here, either as live broadcasts or pre-recorded for subsequent broadcasts.
✚ 104 F8 ✉ 116 avenue du Président-Kennedy, 75016 ☎ 32 30 (€0.34 per min) 🖐 €5–€55, occasional free events 🚇 Kennedy Radio France

MUSÉE DU QUAI BRANLY
▷ 84.

LA PAGODE
www.etoile-cinema.com
Housed in a 19th-century French replica of a Chinese pagoda, this cinema has two screens. Cult classics and recent arty releases fill the schedule. Films are shown in their original language.
✚ 105 J8 ✉ 57 bis rue de Babylone, 75007 ☎ 01 45 55 48 48 🕐 Daily 2–10 🖐 Adult €8, child €7.50 🚇 St-François-Xavier

PALAIS DE TOKYO
▷ 77.

LE PETIT JOURNAL MONTPARNASSE
www.petitjournalmontparnasse.com
This club, offering quality jazz and cuisine, has hosted some of France's best-loved jazz musicians. It is sister venue to the Petit Journal on the Latin Quarter's boulevard St-Michel.
✚ 105 K10 ✉ 13 rue du Commandant-Mouchotte, 75014 ☎ 01 43 21 56 70 🕐 Mon–Sat 8pm–2am, concerts start 10pm 🖐 €25 (includes one drink) 🚇 Montparnasse-Bienvenüe

THÉÂTRE NATIONAL DE CHAILLOT
www.theatre-chaillot.fr
This theatre, in the imposing Palais de Chaillot with views of the Eiffel Tower, stages productions of all kinds, from top-quality

contemporary works to classics, dance and music.
✚ 104 G6 ✉ 1 place du Trocadéro, 75016 ☎ 01 53 65 30 00 🕐 Performances: Tue–Fri 8.30pm, Sat–Sun 3:30pm 🖐 €25–€40 🚇 Trocadéro

THÉÂTRE LE RANELAGH
www.theatre-ranelagh.com
This 340-seat venue, built in 1890, has a rococo interior. The schedule includes classics, contemporary plays and opera. Most performances are in French.
✚ 104 E7 ✉ 5 rue des Vignes, 75016 ☎ 01 42 88 64 44 🕐 Performances: Tue–Sat evening, Sun afternoon 🖐 €25–€30 🚇 La Muette

SPORTS AND ACTIVITIES
BOWLING DE MONTPARNASSE
This venue has 16 bowling lanes. Every Friday and Saturday night only the lanes are illuminated.
✚ 105 K10 ✉ 25 rue du Commandant-Mouchotte, 75014 ☎ 01 43 21 61 32 🕐 Sun–Thu 10am–2am, Fri 10am–4am, Sat 10am–5am 🖐 €4.50–€6 per game, per person 🚇 Montparnasse-Bienvenüe

HEALTH AND BEAUTY
AQUARELLE INSTITUT
www.aquarelle-institut.com
Face and body treatments (including reflexology and shiatsu) are offered in a relaxing atmosphere.
✚ 104 F6 ✉ 9 rue St-Didier, 75016 ☎ 01 45 53 09 09 🕐 Tue–Wed, Fri 10–7, Thu 10–9, Sat 10–1, Mon 2–7 🖐 Face treatments €50–€76, body treatments €55, manicure €20–€50, massages €65–€75, face and body treatment + manicure + make-up €181 🚇 Boissière

SPA VILLA THALGO
www.villathalgo.com
An exceptional day spa that offers well-being treatments based on sea minerals. There's a mineral pool, face and body massages, anti-aging programmes, plus a standard fitness centre so you can build up a sweat.
✚ 104 F6 ✉ 8 avenue Raymond Poincaré, 75016 ☎ 01 45 62 00 20 🕐 Mon, Wed 8.30–9, Tue, Thu–Fri 8.30–8, Sat 9.30–8, Sun 10.30–6. Closed 3 weeks in Aug. 🖐 Treatments €55–€120 🚇 Trocadéro

PRICES AND SYMBOLS

The prices given are the average for a two-course lunch (L) and a three-course dinner (D) for one person, without drinks. The wine price is for the least expensive bottle.

For a key to the symbols, ▷ 2.

L'AFFRIOLÉ

Classical French dishes, like ham hock croquettes, pork ribs in wine, and cream of fennel soup with mussels and parmesan, are available at this popular nouvelle bistro which is within walking distance of the Eiffel Tower. Apart from classic favourites, and a noticeable Mediterranean influence, the menu is local and varies according to the markets day by day. It's also re-planned on a monthly basis. The surroundings are atmospheric rather than chic, but L'Affriolé offers great value and broad appeal.

✚ 105 H7 ✉ 17 rue Malar, 75007, Invalides ☎ 01 44 18 31 33 🕒 Tue–Wed, Sat 7.30–10; Thu–Fri 12–11 ✋ L €22, D €25, Wine €20 🚇 Pont de l'Alma

L'AMI JEAN

www.amijean.eu
The well-established reputation of this bistro-style regional restaurant was enhanced a few years ago by the arrival of Stéphane Jugo. The chef's regularly renewed menu includes delicious classical French dishes as well as Basque specialities such as Axoa: thin slices of veal in a spicy tomato, onion and pimento sauce. The fixed-price menu is available for both lunch and dinner.

✚ 105 H7 ✉ 27 rue Malar, 75007, Grenelle ☎ 01 47 05 86 89 🕒 Tue–Sat 12–2, 7–12 ✋ L €29, D €45 (à la carte), Wine €16 🚇 La Tour-Maubourg

L'ARPÈGE

www.alain-passard.com
This temple to gastronomy is overseen by the Michelin-starred chef Alain Passard. Expect exquisite cuisine and expert service where inventive specialities such as *avocat soufflé au chocolat noir* (avocado soufflé with dark chocolate) feature alongside more basic dishes such as free-range chicken served with roasted shallots. This is among the city's top starred restaurants for which both reservations and deep pockets are necessary.

✚ 105 J7 ✉ 84 rue de Varenne, 75007 ☎ 01 47 05 09 06 🕒 Mon–Fri 12–2.30, 8–10.30 ✋ L €140, D €350, Wine €30 🚇 Varenne

L'AUBERGE DU MOUTON BLANC

www.auberge-mouton-blanc.com
Molière, Jean Racine and Jean de La Fontaine were some of the famous 17th-century writers who came here for discussions over a glass of wine. More than three centuries later, the place still has plenty of charm. Inside there are wooden panels, exposed bricks and elegantly laid tables. The menu is traditional, regional cuisine, including leg of lamb, calf's head and steak tartare.

✚ 104 D9 ✉ 40 rue d'Auteuil, 75016, Auteuil ☎ 01 42 88 02 21 🕒 Daily 12–3, 7–11 ✋ L €23, D €35, Wine €14 🚇 Michel-Ange Auteuil

LE CIEL DE PARIS

www.cieldeparis.com
This restaurant, on the 56th floor of the Tour Montparnasse, claims to be the highest restaurant in Europe and gives stunning views over the whole city. The sleek, contemporary dining room has dark tones and Tulip Knoll armchairs, and chef Jean-François Oyon's creations are rich and impressive. The menu changes with the season—

Above *The entrance to Thoumieux brasserie*

examples of dishes include pan-sautéed fillet of beef with a truffle sauce, lobster risotto, crab with poached quails' eggs, and fried scallops accompanied by a parsley purée.

✚ 105 K9 ✉ Tour Montparnasse, 33 avenue du Maine, 75015, Montparnasse ☎ 01 40 64 77 64 🕐 Daily 12–2.30, 7–11 🍴 L €35, D €75, Wine €26 Ⓜ Montparnasse–Bienvenüe

FAKHR EL DINE
www.fakhreldine.com

This restaurant has been popular with both Parisian and Lebanese diners for more than 25 years. The menu includes *warak enab* (stuffed vine leaves with rice and parsley) and *kharouf mehchi* (stuffed lamb with rice). Try the traditional *meze*, a selection of up to 20 hot and cold hors d'œuvres. The extra-sweet desserts are just as tempting, and the baklava is a must.

✚ 104 G6 ✉ 30 rue de Longchamp, 75016, Trocadéro ☎ 01 47 27 90 00 🕐 Daily 12–3, 7.30–12 🍴 L €25, D €32, Wine €15 Ⓜ Trocadéro

LA FERME ST-SIMON
www.fermestsimon.com

Decorated to resemble an elegant country house, with exposed beams, elaborate candelabra and flowery curtains, this 'farm' is in reality surrounded by embassies and government ministries. The cuisine could be described as refined-rustic, with dishes such as tuna carpaccio with thyme and olive oil, and pan-sautéed sea bream with grilled Provençal vegetables. The menu changes weekly.

✚ 105 K7 ✉ 6 rue de St-Simon, 75007, Invalides ☎ 01 45 48 35 74 🕐 Mon–Fri 12–2.30, 7.30–10.30, Sat 7.30–10 🍴 L €36, D €53, Wine €16 Ⓜ Rue-du-Bac

LA FONTAINE DE MARS
www.fontainedemars.com

Excellent Parisian bistro with a host of local fans, and you'll love the country decor. The limited menu changes with the seasons, but favours regional classics from the southwest of France such as

escargots, cassoulet and *boudin noir* (black pudding).

✚ 105 H7 ✉ 127 rue St-Dominique, 75007, Invalides ☎ 01 47 05 46 44 🕐 Daily 12–11. Closed late Jul–late Aug 🍴 L €30, D €50, Wine €16 Ⓜ École Militaire

HIRAMATSU
www.hiramatsu.co.jp

When Hiramatsu opened its Paris branch in 2001, the chef became the first Japanese national to be awarded a Michelin star. The menu here is inventive, based on French ingredients and dishes transformed by the lightness of touch of Japanese food preparation. The restaurant interior is a suitably grand setting for the masterpieces that adorn the plate.

✚ 104 F6 ✉ 52 rue de Longchamp, 75016, Ternes ☎ 01 56 81 08 80 🕐 Mon–Fri 12.30–1.30, 7.30–9.30 🍴 L €48, D €115, Wine €25 Ⓜ Trocadéro

JULES VERNE
www.lejulesverne-paris.com

Paris has many fine restaurants and wonderful views, but only in a few places do these two come together. Le Jules Verne does not disappoint. A gastronomic menu from top chef Alain Ducasse is about as 'haute' as you can get and the views of the city from the top of the Eiffel Tower are breathtaking.

✚ 105 G7 ✉ quai Branly, Champ de Mars, 75007 ☎ 01 45 55 61 44 🕐 Daily 12.15–1.30, 7–9.30 🍴 L €100, D €220, Wine €39 Ⓜ Bir-Hakiem, Trocadéro, École Militaire

LA MARÉE PASSY
www.lamareepassy.com

This is an excellent seafood restaurant with a jaunty rustic atmosphere. The smart detail in the glassware and decor is anchored by red flashes in the furnishings. The menu reflects what is caught each season and includes excellent fresh oysters and mussels, plus more complex fish dishes.

✚ 104 E7 ✉ 71 avenue Paul Doumer, 75016 ☎ 01 45 04 12 81 🕐 Daily 12–2.30, 7.30–9.30 🍴 L €35, D €45, Wine €19 Ⓜ La Muette

PAUL CHÊNE
www.paulchene.com

This restaurant opened in 1959 by Paul Chêne has been managed with aplomb by succeeding teams. The menu concentrates on French bistro classics including excellent foie gras, tasty truffles, confit d'oie and crêpe Suzette. The dining room is also comfortably city bistro with velour banquettes and wall lights.

✚ 104 F6 ✉ 123 rue Lauriston, 75016 ☎ 01 47 27 63 17 🕐 Mon–Fri 12–2.30, 7.30–10.30, Sat 7.30–10.30. Closed Aug 🍴 L €35, D €55, Wine €22 Ⓜ Boissiere

THOUMIEUX
www.thoumieux.fr

Named after the Thoumieux family who ran the establishment from 1923 until the 2000s, this famed brasserie just minutes away from the Eiffel Tower has been taken over by two younger culinary guns Thierry Costes and Jean-François Piège who have revamped the decor and taken a new broom to the menu. Still popular with Parisians, it's worth giving the new owners a visit.

✚ 105 J7 ✉ 79 rue St-Dominique, 75007, Invalides ☎ 01 47 05 79 00 🕐 Mon–Fri 12–12 🍴 L €35, D €50, Wine €18 Ⓜ Invalides, La Tour-Maubourg

LE VIOLON D'INGRES
www.maisonconstant.com

This favourite locale has received a make-over, but the cuisine remains reassuringly top quality. The open kitchen concept is unusual in Paris, giving the restaurant a bustling atmosphere. Chef Christian Constant has worked at the Ritz and at the Michelin-starred Les Ambassadeurs, but has run the Violon since 1988 and has added two more restaurants to his portfolio. The menu looks to market freshness with signature dishes, including wood pigeon in season.

✚ 105 H7 ✉ 135 rue St-Dominique, 75007, Champ du Mars ☎ 01 45 55 15 05 🕐 Daily 12–2.30, 7–10.30 🍴 L €34, D €45, Wine €19 Ⓜ École Militaire

PRICES AND SYMBOLS

Prices are the lowest and highest for a double room for one night. Breakfast is included unless noted otherwise. All the hotels listed accept credit cards unless otherwise stated. Note that rates vary widely throughout the year.

For a key to the symbols, ▷ 2.

GRAND HÔTEL LÉVÊQUE

www.hotel-leveque.com
The bedrooms at this 2-star hotel have WiFi, satellite TV, safe, fan and hairdryer, and have been soundproofed to avoid disturbance from the lively fruit and vegetable market outside in the pedestrian-only street. Inside, the hotel is simple yet bright, with some nice pictures, and most rooms have been upgraded since 2008.
✚ 105 H7 ✉ 29 rue Cler, 75007, Eiffel Tower ☎ 01 47 05 49 15 ✋ €89–€150, excluding breakfast ❶ 50 ◈
▣ École Militaire

HAMEAU DE PASSY

www.paris-hotel-hameaudepassy.com
In a chic residential district, this 2-star hotel offers peace and quiet in a leafy cul-de-sac. The modern interior is tasteful and the bedrooms

face the garden. They have a direct dial phone with modem connection and cable TV. The hotel has a fax service, free WiFi, individual safes at reception, and parking is available at the nearby garage.
✚ 104 F7 ✉ 48 rue Passy, 75016, Passy ☎ 01 42 88 47 55 ✋ €87–€98 ❶ 32 ▣ Passy, La Muette

HÔTEL 7 EIFFEL

www.hotel-7eiffel-paris.com
One of the city's newest designer hotels within a couple of minutes of the Eiffel Tower and Les Invalides, the rooms at this 4-star establishment are spacious (though they do vary in size and price), chic and airy, decorated with subtle hues. There's a compact roof terrace for relaxing, a bar and a business centre.
✚ 105 H7 ✉ 17 bis rue Amélie, 75007, Invalides ☎ 01 45 55 10 01 ✋ €165–€395, excluding breakfast ❶ 32 ◈ ▣ La Tour-Maubourg

HÔTEL DE L'AVRE

www.hoteldelavre.com
Attention has been paid to every detail at this 2-star hotel. Bedrooms are decorated in a floral design, and there is satellite TV and WiFi

internet access. In spring and summer you can have breakfast in the garden.
✚ 104 G9 ✉ 21 rue de l'Avre, 75015, Champ de Mars ☎ 01 45 75 31 03 ✋ €87–€98 ❶ 25 ▣ La-Motte-Picquet-Grenelle

HÔTEL LA BOURDONNAIS

www.hotellabourdonnais.com
This elegant 3-star hotel, resembling a comfortable home, is close to the Eiffel Tower. The suites and bedrooms with four beds are perfect for families; all bedrooms have satellite TV, a safe, telephone, internet access and a hairdryer. No restaurant, but cookery courses and wine tastings can be pre-booked on site. Breakfast is served in the hotel's attractive winter garden.
✚ 105 H7 ✉ 111–113 avenue de la Bourdonnais, 75007, Tour Eiffel ☎ 01 47 05 45 42 ✋ €165, excluding breakfast ❶ 57 rooms, 3 suites ◈ ▣ École Militaire

HÔTEL DELAMBRE

www.delambre-paris-hotel.com
Close to Tour Montparnasse, this 3-star hotel has a beautiful interior,

Above *A strong emphasis is placed on service in the hotels of this region*

with warm tones, wrought-iron work and period furniture covered in modern fabrics. Bedrooms have a telephone, satellite TV and WiFi, safe and laundry service. There are two parking areas nearby.

✚ 105 K10 ✉ 35 rue Delambre, 75014, Montparnasse ☎ 01 43 20 66 31 ✋ €99–€160, excluding breakfast ⒤ 31 🚇 Vavin, Edgar-Quinet, Montparnasse

HÔTEL DUC DE ST-SIMON
www.hotelducdesaintsimon.com
Beautiful antiques and fine furniture decorate this elegant 3-star hotel, in an 18th-century mansion. Although close to the animated boulevard St-Germain, rue de St-Simon is very quiet. The hotel has a bar and terrace, offers room service, and a garage with entrance on boulevard Raspail.

✚ 105 K7 ✉ 14 rue de St-Simon, 75007, Invalides ☎ 01 44 39 20 20 ✋ €210–€295, excluding breakfast ⒤ 29 rooms, 5 suites 🆂 In some rooms 🚇 Rue-du-Bac

HÔTEL À L'EIFFEL RIVE GAUCHE
www.hotel-eiffel.com
This small hotel dates back to the beginning of the 20th century and is situated in a charming, quiet street at the heart of the Eiffel–Champs-Élysées–Invalides 'golden triangle'. Comfortable rooms decorated in Provençal style have authentic touches such as 1930s black and white floor tiles and themes reminiscent of the French Empire style but rooms benefit from WiFi and flat-screen TVs.

✚ 105 H7 ✉ 6 rue du Gros Caillou, 75007 ☎ 01 45 51 51 51 ✋ €75–€180, excluding breakfast ⒤ 29 🚇 École Militaire

HÔTEL LATOUR-MAUBOURG
www.hoteltourmaubourgparis.com
Set in an elegant and beautifully renovated Napoléon III-era mansion, the Latour-Maubourg is named after the Marquis de la Tour Maubourg, who commissioned and lived in the building. The 2006 renovation brought 21st-century luxuries, yet the hotel still harks back to

the historical heyday in its design features. All rooms are fitted out to a high standard with safe, mini-bar and WiFi access, though they do vary in size. There's a buffet breakfast every morning. The hotel has a garden.

✚ 105 J7 ✉ 150 rue de Grenelle, 75007, Invalides ☎ 01 47 05 16 16 ✋ €125–€260, excluding breakfast. ⒤ 17 🆂 🚇 La Tour-Maubourg

HÔTEL LENOX ST-GERMAIN
www.lenoxsaintgermain.com
The Lenox Club Bar at this 3-star hotel has comfortable armchairs and a collection of 1930s jazz musical instruments on display. In the hotel itself, the elegant bedrooms have beautiful wall lamps and pictures, as well as a safe, telephone, modem and satellite TV. There are also some duplex suites. Breakfast is served in a vaulted cellar.

✚ 105 L7 ✉ 9 rue de l'Université, 75007, St-Germain-des-Prés ☎ 01 42 96 10 95 ✋ €132–€260, excluding breakfast ⒤ 34 🆂 🚇 Rue-du-Bac, St-Germain-des-Prés

HÔTEL DE LONDRES EIFFEL
www.londres-eiffel.com
Comfort is a priority at this 3-star hotel, with soft armchairs in the salon and king-size beds in the bedrooms. Warm yellow and raspberry tones predominate in the classic interior. Interconnecting rooms are available for families.

✚ 105 H7 ✉ 1 rue Augereau, 75007, Eiffel Tower ☎ 01 45 51 63 02 ✋ €140–€220, excluding breakfast ⒤ 30 🆂 🚇 École Militaire

HÔTEL SAINT-DOMINIQUE
www.hotelstdominique.com
Floral motifs abound in this pleasant, small hotel very close to the Eiffel Tower. An open-air courtyard is the centrepiece around which the three buildings forming the hotel cluster, one of which was a convent in the 18th century.

✚ 105 J7 ✉ 62 rue St-Dominique, 75007 ☎ 01 47 05 51 44 ✋ €101–€158, excluding breakfast ⒤ 37 🚇 Invalides, La Tour-Maubourg

HÔTEL SQUARE
www.hotelsquare.com
This 4-star hotel close to the banks of the Seine is part of a larger complex including a conference room, a reading room and a restaurant, the Zebra Square. There's also an elegant lounge bar with music most evenings and an art gallery. Sleek lines, subtle lighting, designer furniture and ethnic objets d'art create a warm, contemporary atmosphere. A new luxury spa, Nuxe is part of the hotel complex and has five rooms for treatments.

✚ 104 E8 ✉ 3 rue de Boulainvilliers, 75016, Passy ☎ 01 44 14 91 90 ✋ €300–€580, excluding breakfast ⒤ 22 🆂 🏊 Indoor 🈺 🚇 RER Kennedy-Radio-France, Trocadéro

HÔTEL VALADON COLORS
www.hotelvaladon.com
This intimate hotel set on a quiet street in the 7th *arrondissement* was family run for many years but has been given a very contemporary makeover, reopening in 2011 under new management. Each of the 12 comfortable rooms sleep three and are minimalist and chic, with signature bedding. All have WiFi, a flat-screen TV and hip en-suite bathrooms. There's a small bar and breakfast room.

✚ 105 H7 ✉ 16 rue Valadon, 75007, Invalides ☎ 01 47 53 89 85 ✋ €161–€250 ⒤ 12 🆂 🚇 École Militaire

RELAIS BOSQUET
www.relaisbosquet.com
Space, elegance and comfort characterize this 3-star hotel, close to the Invalides and a 10-minute walk from the Eiffel Tower. Directoire-style furniture and soft hues set the tone. The bedrooms have cable TV, a phone, safe, WiFi, iPod docking station, and minibar, as well as an iron and ironing board. The breakfast room looks out onto a pleasant terrace filled with flowers.

✚ 105 H7 ✉ 19 rue du Champ de Mars, 75007, Eiffel Tower ☎ 01 47 05 25 45 ✋ €145–€285, excluding breakfast ⒤ 40 🆂 🚇 École Militaire

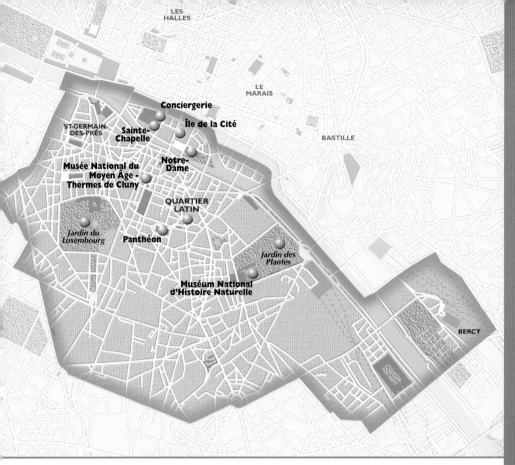

LATIN QUARTER, ST-GERMAIN AND ISLANDS

This section of the Left Bank remains quintessentially Parisian, set around the city's oldest church, St-Germain-des-Prés. The artistic institutions, café culture, ancient churches, *bouquinistes* and boutiques are what make the area around this quarter a symbol of the city's life. It was named the Latin Quarter as this was the language spoken by students of the Sorbonne until the Revolution.

People play boules at Arènes de Lutèce, once a Roman arena whose environs were originally meadows where sheep grazed. Centuries later, students from the nearby monasteries established a centre of learning that was to become the Sorbonne. Over the years the area has attracted intellectuals, philosophers, artists and venerable institutions, like the Institut de France and the Bibliothèque Nationale de France–site François Mitterrand. Today, much of the Latin Quarter is a warren that escaped the Rive Droite's 19th-century urban rationalization, though it does have thundering boulevards and beautiful open spaces. These include the Jardin du Luxembourg with its boating ponds and floral displays, and the Muséum National d'Histoire Naturelle and Jardin des Plantes. Special buildings include the Panthéon, a former basilica, where great Parisian figures, including Voltaire, are entombed, and the Musée National du Moyen Âge–Thermes de Cluny, a splendid celebration of feudal life.

Île de la Cité is dominated by Notre-Dame, though the less conspicuous, but beautiful, Conciergerie still echoes with the horrors of the Revolution. As well as Notre-Dame, there are some remarkable churches around the Latin Quarter. Don't miss the 15th-century St-Étienne-du-Mont, with its mixture of architectural styles. The church of St-Germain-des-Prés dates from 1163, and is the resting place of philosopher René Descartes *('Cogito ergo sum')* who fell into his eternal reverie in 1650 no longer thinking, but still embodying the spirit of the Enlightenment.

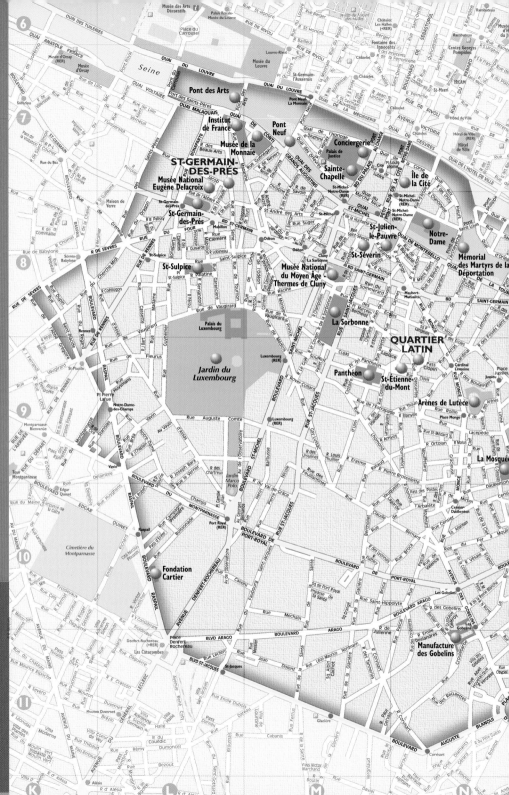

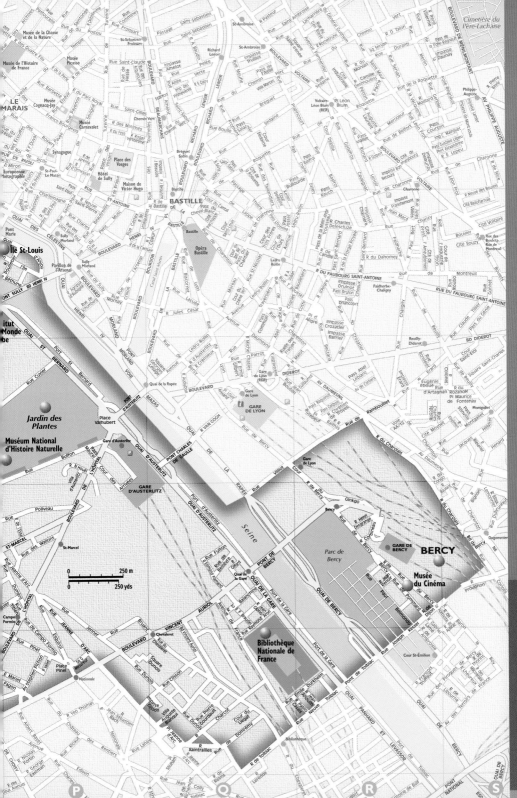

ARÈNES DE LUTÈCE

This Gallo-Roman arena dates from the end of the second century AD and takes its name from the Roman name for Paris, Lutetia. It was destroyed in AD280, rediscovered in 1869, and restored in the early 20th century. Today, the ruins and the gardens are popular with students, boules-players and walkers.

🔲 108 N9 ✉ Entrances at rue des Arènes, rue de Navarre and 49 rue Monge, 75005 🕐 May–Sep daily 8am–9.30pm; Oct–Apr 9–5.30 💷 Free 🚇 Cardinal Lemoine, Jussieu 🚌 47, 67, 89 ❓ Best avoided after dark

BERCY

Bercy spreads east from Gare de Lyon through a maze of new apartment and office blocks. Once known for its wine warehouses, it is undergoing intensive development. The most likely reason you'll come here is to see a rock concert or sporting event in the grass-walled Palais Omnisports (8 boulevard de Bercy; tel 0892 39 04 90; www.bercy.fr). Also of interest is the curvilinear former American Cultural Center, designed by Frank Gehry and recently relaunched as the

Musée du Cinéma (▷ 120). The Parc de Bercy provides welcome relief to the concrete jungle. At the far end, wine warehouses have been converted into the boutiques, bars and restaurants of Bercy Village (www.bercyvillage.com).

🔲 109 R10 ✉ Bercy, 75012 🚇 Bercy 🚌 24, 87

BIBLIOTHÈQUE NATIONALE DE FRANCE—SITE FRANÇOIS MITTERRAND

www.bnf.fr

Around 12 million books and innumerable documents belong to the national library, so it's not surprising that it was forced to find additional premises towards the end of the 20th century. The new library, with its glass corner towers designed like four open books, stands on the eastern edge of the Left Bank. The public has access to books, the internet and an excellent audiovisual section.

🔲 109 Q11 ✉ quai François-Mauriac, 75013 ☎ 01 53 79 59 59; guided visits 01 53 79 49 49 🕐 Upper Garden reading rooms: Tue–Sat 10–7, Sun 1–7. Closed 2 weeks in early Sep 💷 Adult 1-day pass: €3.50; under 16 not admitted to reading

room 🚇 Quai-de-la-Gare 🚌 62, 64, 89, 132 🚇 Bibliothèque François-Mitterrand 🔲 📖 Bookshop/gift shop

CONCIERGERIE

▷ 112–113.

FONDATION CARTIER

www.fondation.cartier.fr

The Fondation Cartier has been an avid promoter of contemporary art since it was founded in 1984. In 1994 it moved to central Paris, to the striking steel and glass building designed by Jean Nouvel. The building's light, spacious interior is the perfect setting for permanent and temporary exhibitions of French and international art. Vast glass windows open onto a garden and the small amphitheatre created by artist Lothar Baumgarten.

🔲 108 L10 ✉ 261 boulevard Raspail, 75014 ☎ 01 42 18 56 50 🕐 Wed–Sun 11–8, Tue 11–10 💷 Adult €9.50, child (11–24) €6.50, under 10 free 🚇 Raspail 🚌 38, 68, 88, 91 ❓ Nomadic Nights held on certain Thursdays at 8.30pm (advance booking necessary)

Opposite *Jean Nouvel's Fondation Cartier*
Below *Shops in Bercy Village*

CONCIERGERIE

INFORMATION

www.monuments-nationaux.fr
✚ 108 M7 ✉ 2 boulevard du Palais, Île
de la Cité, 75001 ☎ 01 53 40 60 80
◷ Mar–Oct daily 9.30–6; Nov–Feb
9–5 ✋ Adult €7 (€11 for combined
ticket with Sainte-Chapelle), under
18 free (bring passport to prove age),
Nov–Mar 1st Sun of month free Ⓜ Cité,
Châtelet 🚌 21, 24, 27, 38, 58, 81, 85
Ⓡ RER line B, C, St-Michel-Notre-Dame
🎧 Daily guided tours in French, English,
Italian (prebooking necessary for English
and Italian). No audioguides 📖 €7
📙 Bookshop

Above *Illuminated at night, the
Conciergerie resembles a fairytale castle
rather than a prison*

INTRODUCTION

Sailing past the Conciergerie's floodlit towers on an evening boat cruise, it is
hard to imagine the fear that lurked within its walls during the five centuries
it served as a prison. But step inside the gloomy main hall and the sense of
oppression is palpable.

The entrance is on the boulevard du Palais, near the gateway to the Palais
de Justice. If you also want to visit Sainte-Chapelle (▷ 132–133) you can buy
a joint ticket. Pick up a plan at the entrance as signage inside isn't particularly
clear. The first three rooms on your tour—the Salle des Gens d'Armes, the
medieval kitchens and the Salle des Gardes—date from the Middle Ages,
when the Conciergerie was a royal palace. To learn more about its gruesome
role during the Revolution head for the Galerie des Prisonniers, off the
southwestern corner of the main hall. Here you'll also find a reconstruction of
Marie-Antoinette's cell.

The Conciergerie is notorious for its role as a prison, but it began as a
palace, part of a royal complex including Sainte-Chapelle and the Palais de
Justice. The oldest parts of the Conciergerie date from the early 14th century,
although a fortress probably stood on the western part of the Île de la Cité
as far back as Roman times. In the late 14th century, Charles V chose to live
elsewhere and its role changed to a law court and prison, with occasional
use for royal functions. It was at this time that it gained its name, from the
concierge who oversaw the site. During the Revolution, the prison housed
more than 4,000 inmates, up to 600 at a time. Conditions were crowded and
disease was rife. Prisoners had nothing to do but wait in the dungeon-like
interior for the often inevitable death sentence and the terrifying journey
through the city to the guillotine. After the Revolution, the Conciergerie
continued as a prison until 1914. It now offers visitors a chilling reminder of
the darker side of Paris's history.

WHAT TO SEE

GOTHIC HALLS

On entry you are immediately plunged into semi-darkness in a vast Gothic chamber said to be Europe's oldest surviving medieval hall. Subtle uplighting adds to the eerie atmosphere of the Salle des Gens d'Armes, 63m (206ft) long and 8.5m (28ft) high. The hall dates from the 14th century, when it formed the lower floor of the Grand'Salle. The king's staff ate here, up to 2,000 at a time, while royal banquets and marriage celebrations were held upstairs. Later, the hall was divided into separate storerooms, but was restored in the 19th century by Viollet-le-Duc. A spiral staircase leads up to the kitchens, where four walk-in fireplaces, each big enough to roast a couple of sheep, indicate the scale of medieval appetites. From the kitchens walk back into the Salles des Gens d'Armes and up to the Salle des Gardes, in the northeastern corner. This Gothic hall sat underneath the Grand'Chambre, where the Revolutionary Court delivered death sentences like parking tickets to its unfortunate victims.

RE-CREATIONS OF THE REVOLUTION

The Galerie des Prisonniers was once the prison's most animated crossroads, where lawyers, visitors and inmates met. Here you'll find re-creations of the clerk's and concierge's offices, as well as the Salle de Toilette, where barbers cut off prisoners' hair before execution. There is also a reconstruction of Marie-Antoinette's cell. The spartan furnishings (not original), torn wallpaper and stifling gaze of the prison guard paint a sorry picture of the queen's last days. Upstairs in the Room of the Sentenced, wall panels list the 2,780 people guillotined between March 1793 and May 1795. Farther along the upstairs corridor, re-created cells give you a glimpse of the prisoners' harsh living conditions. The first cell, with no beds or lamp, was for the poorest prisoners, the *pailleux* (*paille* means straw). Prisoners with money shared a *chambre à la pistole*, with the relative luxury of beds and chairs. The famous or wealthy were granted their own cell, complete with a desk, bed, lamp and books.

THE CHAPEL

At the end of the upper corridor, stairs take you down to the Chapelle des Girondins, named after the 21 condemned Girondins (left-wing members of the 1791 Legislative Assembly) who sat around a banqueting table here on the night before their execution. Leading off this room, the Chapelle Expiatoire stands on the site of Marie-Antoinette's actual cell. The chapel was commissioned by Louis XVIII to commemorate members of the royal family killed during the Revolution. The silver pattern on the walls represents tears.

TIPS

» If you intend to visit Sainte-Chapelle as well, go to the Conciergerie first and buy a joint ticket, to avoid the long queues at Sainte-Chapelle. However, try to get to Sainte-Chapelle before lunchtime, as it is generally more crowded in the afternoon.

» The Conciergerie's main halls are empty of furniture, making it harder to imagine the events that once took place here. Come prepared to work your imagination.

» On the Seine side of the building, take a look at the Tour de l'Horloge, site of Paris's first public clock, commissioned in 1370. The present clock dates from the 16th century and has sculptures of Law and Justice.

Below *The Salle des Gens d'Armes served as the staff dining room in the 14th century*

INFORMATION

✚ 108 N7 ✉ Île de la Cité, 75001 and 75004 🚇 Cité (also Pont Neuf, St-Michel, Châtelet, Hôtel de Ville) 🚌 21, 24, 27, 38, 47, 58, 70, 85, 96 🚈 RER line B, C, St-Michel-Notre-Dame 🚢 On Île de la Cité, the nearby Île St-Louis and in the Latin Quarter 🍽 A selection

Above *Vibrant blooms for sale at the flower market in place Louis Lépine*

INTRODUCTION

The Paris story began on the Île de la Cité more than 2,000 years ago. Today it is still a key part of the city, packed with visitors, traffic and fabulous architecture. Despite the fact that both the Île de la Cité and Île St-Louis are the birthplace of Paris, these two neighbouring islands are very different in character. The first is a historical parade amid a flurry of uniforms and lawyers' paraphernalia and is still the headquarters of the French legal system. The little Île St-Louis is more like a village in character and a tranquil refuge for poets and artists, set among handsome historic buildings.

The Île de la Cité sits in the middle of the Seine like a tug, towing the smaller Île St-Louis behind it. One of the best ways to appreciate its beautiful architecture is by boat, taking one of the trips that start from below the Pont Neuf, Paris's oldest bridge. From the water you'll see the elegant Notre-Dame rising high above the banks, and the stern facade of the Conciergerie, once Paris's most notorious prison (▷ 112–113). In the evening, lighting gives the island an almost magical glow.

On foot, the Île de la Cité's charms may be harder to appreciate at first, thanks to the heavy traffic, frequent police sirens and seemingly impenetrable stream of tourists. But persevere and you'll be rewarded with a glimpse of some of Paris's key sights.

A Celtic tribe called the Parisii settled here in around 250BC. The Romans arrived 200 years later, building the town of Lutetia, which expanded onto the Left Bank. They built a governor's palace and fortress on the western side of the Île de la Cité. In AD508 the king of the Franks made the island his capital, and in the Middle Ages it again became a seat of political power, gaining a royal palace (now the Palais de Justice and Conciergerie). Much of the island was cleared in the 19th century during Baron Haussmann's re-drawing of Paris. Today, it is no longer a political power base, but it retains the Palais de Justice (the Law Courts) and the Préfecture de Police. The island is also the official heart of the city—distances from Paris to the rest of France are measured from the bronze star in the square in front of Notre-Dame.

WHAT TO SEE

KEY MONUMENTS
The Île de la Cité shelters three of Paris's most historic buildings—Notre-Dame (▷ 124–127), the Conciergerie (▷ 112–113) and Sainte-Chapelle (▷ 132–133). The most famous is the Cathedral of Notre-Dame, but it is worth fitting all three into your visit. The eerie Gothic halls of the Conciergerie contrast wonderfully with the brightness of nearby Sainte-Chapelle, which in turn seems less intimate than Notre-Dame, despite its smaller size.

THE QUIETER SIDE
When you have ticked off the key sights, there are quieter squares where you can relax and enjoy the views. The grassy square Jean XXIII is a good spot to sit and admire Notre-Dame, while square de l'Île de France, at the island's eastern tip, gives lovely views of the Seine and the Île St-Louis (▷ 116). It is also home to the Mémorial des Martyrs de la Déportation (▷ 117). The wonderful flower market in place Louis Lépine (▷ 140) sells anything from delicate blooms to trees.

Below *The Île de la Cité is the origin and heart of Paris*

ÎLE ST-LOUIS

This leafy island sits discreetly behind the more conspicuous Île de la Cité. Visitors pack its main road, the narrow rue St-Louis-en-l'Île, to browse in the shops and sample the famous ice cream at Maison Berthillon (www.berthillon.fr; closed Mon–Tue and Aug).

Architect Louis Le Vau designed many of the elegant town houses on the tiny island in the 17th century. He was so pleased with the result he decided to live there himself. You'll get wonderful views of Notre-Dame from the western tip of the island.

✚ 109 P8 ✉ Île St-Louis, 75004 🚇 Pont Marie, Sully Morland 🚌 67, 86, 87 🍴 Several cafés

INSTITUT DE FRANCE

www.institut-de-france.fr

The Institut de France, with its striking cupola, has a prime position on the Left Bank. The building was designed in 1663 by Louis Le Vau and financed by Cardinal Mazarin, as a college for provincial students. The college closed in 1790 and in 1805 Napoléon transferred the Institut de France to the building. The Institut, founded in 1795,

aims to protect the arts, literature and the sciences and is made up of five *académies:* Inscriptions et Belles-Lettres, Sciences, Beaux-Arts, Sciences Morales et Politiques and the prestigious Française. The Académie Française, founded in 1635, is limited to 40 members. Its rule over the standards of the French language is still very real and is embodied in the *Dictionnaire de la Langue Française.*

✚ 108 L7 ✉ 23 quai Conti, 75006 ☎ 01 44 41 44 41 🕐 Entry by guided tour only: Sat–Sun 10.30 and 3; advance booking obligatory (tel 01 44 41 45 32) 🖐 Adult €3.10 🚇 Pont Neuf, Odéon, Louvre-Rivoli 🚌 24, 27, 58, 70

INSTITUT DU MONDE ARABE

www.imarabe.org

In 1974, France and 19 Arab countries decided to create the Institut du Monde Arabe (the Arab World Institute). The foundation document was signed in 1980 and the institute opened on the Left Bank in 1987.

The stunning aluminium-and-glass building was dreamed up by a group of architects—Jean Nouvel, Pierre Soria, Gilbert Lezenes and Architecture Studio. Its design

combines modern materials with the spirit of traditional Arab architecture. The southern facade consists of 240 identical metal light-sensitive screens, adjusted every hour, which electronically filter the sunlight as it enters the building. Their design is taken from carved wooden screens called *moucharabiehs*, used in buildings from Morocco to southeast Asia. The high-speed transparent elevators alone make a visit worthwhile, so let them take you to the ninth floor, where you can admire the panoramic views of the river from the terrace or eat in the elegant restaurant.

The entrance to the museum is on the seventh floor and the displays move chronologically to the sixth and fourth floors, with more than 600 items on view. From Spain to India and from prehistoric times to the 19th century, the ceramics, bronzes, ivories, calligraphy, tapestries, textiles and carpets of this collection reflect the brilliance of the Arabic-Islamic civilization. There are also a variety of temporary exhibitions, including displays of photography and contemporary art.

The institute houses a facility for Arab language and civilization, a cinema, an auditorium, a library of more than 50,000 books, research facilities and an audiovisual venue, and it publishes two magazines. Events include lectures, music, dance and drama performances, creative workshops and other educational activities.

✚ 109 N8 ✉ 1 rue des Fossés–St-Bernard, 75005 ☎ 01 40 51 38 38 🕐 Tue–Sun 10–6. Library: Tue–Sat 1–8 🖐 Adult €6, child (13–17) €4 🚇 Jussieu, Cardinal Lemoine, Sully Morland 🚌 24, 63, 67, 86, 87, 89 📕 Guided tours (in French): Tue–Fri 3pm, Sat–Sun 3, 4.30. €5 🍴 Le Ziryab panoramic restaurant (ninth floor) ☕ Café Littéraire (ground floor) and Le Moucharabieh cafeteria (ninth floor) 🎁 Shop (ground floor) selling books, CDs, ceramics and gifts

Below *Aluminium and glass are used in an Arabic design in the Institut du Monde Arabe*

JARDIN DU LUXEMBOURG

▷ 118–119.

MANUFACTURE DES GOBELINS

Originally a dyeworks set up by the Gobelin brothers in the 15th century, the Manufacture des Gobelins attracted the attention of Colbert, Louis XIV's astute minister, and by 1662 it had become the royal tapestry factory. It rapidly expanded to include furniture and carpet workshops. Much of the interior decoration of Versailles was woven, carved or inlaid here.

Today you see the centuries-old looms clicking away, worked by expert weavers. The 90-minute guided tour also takes in some of the workshops of the famous Beauvais tapestry and Savonnerie carpet factories.

➕ 108 N11 ✉ 42 avenue des Gobelins, 75013 ☎ 01 44 08 53 49 or 0892 68 46 94 to book tickets 🕐 Tue–Sun 12.30–6.30 ✋ Adult €10, child (7–17) €7, under 7 free 🎫 Guided tour (in French): Tue–Thu at 1pm. Adult €9, child (12–17) €7. Arrive 10 min before the start of the tour 🚇 Les Gobelins 🚌 27, 47, 83, 91

MÉMORIAL DES MARTYRS DE LA DÉPORTATION

This monument commemorates the 200,000 French people who died in concentration camps during the Holocaust. The roof of the memorial sits in a peaceful grassy square on the eastern tip of the Île de la Cité, from where you can enjoy views of the river and the Île St-Louis. By contrast, walk down the narrow staircase into the shadowy crypt and you are limited to mere glimpses of the Seine through iron bars, a reminder of the incarceration experienced by the prisoners. A long, dark tunnel leading from the crypt is studded with 200,000 fragments of shining glass, one for each person who died. A light at the end symbolizes hope. This is no ordinary, lifeless monument—it gives an unsettling reminder of the horrors of World War II.

➕ 108 N8 ✉ square de l'Île de France, Île de la Cité, 75004 ☎ 01 46 33 87 56 🕐 Apr–Sep daily 10–12, 2–7; Oct–Mar 2–5 ✋ Free 🚇 Cité 🚌 24, 47 🚊 St-Michel Notre-Dame 🍴 Plenty on Île de la Cité

Above *A Moorish pink marble fountain and pool in the tranquil courtyard garden of La Mosquée, across the road from Jardin des Plantes*

LA MOSQUÉE

www.la-mosquee.com

A gem of 20th-century European Islamic architecture, with exquisitely carved arcades and a magnificent minaret, 33m (108ft) high. The splendid Paris Mosque is one of the Left Bank's most pleasant surprises, with its impressive square minaret and ornate decoration. It was built between 1922 and 1926, with French funds, to commemorate North African military support during World War I.

Faithful to ornate Hispano-Moorish architecture, its roofs are green tiled, its fountains are pink marbled and its doors are exquisitely carved. The grand patio was inspired by the Alhambra in Granada, Spain, and features decorative mosaics and fine woodwork. The finely carved arcades are also decorated with intricate mosaics. A spiritual base for Paris's Muslim community, the prayer room is exceptional for its ornamentation and fine carpets. The courtyard garden is a symbol of Muslim paradise. The Mosque is also home to a library and an Islamic teaching facility.

The rest of the Mosque complex is accessible from rue Geoffroy St-Hilaire and includes a restaurant, a salon de thé and the Hammam (Turkish baths). The Hammam is the perfect escape from the bustle of city life. Seated around a marble fountain, let your mind drift to exotic shores. Later, you can sit at an outdoor table in the pretty courtyard of the *salon de thé*, sipping mint tea and eating couscous. There is also a shop, reminiscent of a small souk, which is crammed with an array of distinctive items.

➕ 108 N9 ✉ La Mosquée: place du Puits-de-l'Ermite, 75005; Hammam: 39 rue Geoffroy St-Hilaire ☎ La Mosquée: 01 45 35 97 33; Hammam: 01 43 31 38 20 🕐 La Mosquée: guided tours in French: Sat–Thu 9–12, 2–6. Hammam: Men: Tue 2–9, Sun 10–9. Women: Mon, Wed–Thu, Sat 10–9, Fri 2–9 ✋ La Mosquée: adult €3, child (7–17) €2, under 7 free. Hammam: Entry only €15; prices vary for different treatments 🚇 Jussieu, Place Monge, Censier-Daubenton 🚌 47, 67, 89 🍴 Restaurant: 39 rue Geoffroy St-Hilaire 🍵 Salon de thé: 39 rue Geoffroy St-Hilaire 📖 Small bookshop at La Mosquée; a souk at 39 rue Geoffroy St-Hilaire sells ceramics, jewellery, bags, postcards, lampshades and other items

JARDIN DU LUXEMBOURG

INFORMATION

www.senat.fr

www.museeduluxembourg.fr

✚ 108 L9 ✉ rue de Vaugirard/rue de Médicis/boulevard St-Michel, 75006 ☎ Park: 01 42 34 23 89. Senate: 01 42 34 20 00. Musée du Luxembourg 01 40 13 62 00 🕐 Park: Times vary depending on season; generally dawn–dusk. Museum: Sun–Thu 10–8, Fri, Sat 10–10 💰 Park: free. Museum: Adult €13.50, child (13–18) €9 🚇 Odéon 🚌 21, 27, 38, 58, 63, 70, 82, 83, 84, 85, 87, 89 🚃 RER line B, Luxembourg 🔎 Guided tours of the Palais du Luxembourg on the 1st Sat of each month. To book a place call 01 44 54 19 49. To sit in on a Senate debate call 01 42 34 20 00 ☕ Open-air cafés, kiosk restaurant 🛒 Kiosk ❓ An oak tree dedicated to the victims of 9/11 has been planted near the Statue of Liberty

Above *Children enjoy donkey and pony rides in the Jardin du Luxembourg*

INTRODUCTION

The Jardin du Luxembourg, 24ha (60 acres), forms an attractive southern boundary to St-Germain-des-Prés and the Latin Quarter. Here, students come to relax after lectures and visitors find some breathing space between sightseeing. There are entrances all around the park and wide paths lead to the main attractions, including the octagonal pond and the Théâtre du Luxembourg. Plenty of seats and refreshments are available. The Palais du Luxembourg, home of the French Senate, is on the northern edge. You will need to make a reservation in advance for guided tours.

Bored with the Louvre, Marie de Médicis commissioned the gardens and palace in 1615, hoping for a reminder of her native Florence. She bought the land from Duke François of Luxembourg (hence the park's name) and asked architect Salomon de Brosse to use the Pitti Palace as inspiration. Work finished in the mid-1620s but Marie, widow of Henri IV, did not have long to enjoy her creation. She was exiled from France by the powerful Cardinal Richelieu and died penniless in Cologne.

A petition of 12,000 signatures failed to save certain parts of the gardens from Baron Haussmann's extensive development plans during the mid-19th century, but the remaining greenery continued to be a refuge for artists, writers and philosophers, including Ernest Hemingway, Victor Hugo and Jean-Paul Sartre.

WHAT TO SEE

RELAXING IN SCENIC SURROUNDINGS

The park contains some of the most beautiful public flower displays in Paris and is landscaped in an appealing mixture of French, English and Italian styles. The focal point is a large octagonal pond, elegantly encircled by stone urns and statues of French queens and other notable women. In good weather the park is full of Parisians sunbathing, playing either boules or chess, or jogging along the shady paths. Other attractions include tennis courts, a bandstand and, unusually, a bee-keeping school.

The Musée du Luxembourg occupies the former orangery. As well as showcasing works on the Renaissance and in memory of the Florentine queen Marie de Médicis, the museum stages excellent temporary art exhibitions.

Despite the crowds, the park is a welcome respite from the hectic Paris streets. But there is no forgetting you are in the heart of the city—the Eiffel Tower and Tour Montparnasse loom on the horizon.

PALAIS DU LUXEMBOURG
The Italianate Palais du Luxembourg is a reminder of the park's Florentine origins and is now home to the French Senate. It was commissioned by Marie de Médicis in the 17th century and during the Revolution was commandeered as a prison.

ACTIVITIES FOR CHILDREN
Children are well catered to, with pony rides (during French school holidays only), puppet shows in the Théâtre du Luxembourg (Wednesday, Saturday and Sunday from 2pm) and the usual swings and slides. They can also try their hand at being the skipper of a boat by renting remote-control model yachts to sail on the pond.

STATUES
The park contains more than a hundred statues, fountains and monuments. The Fontaine Médicis is a popular romantic spot to the east of the Palais du Luxembourg. The grotto was commissioned by Marie de Médicis in the 17th century and sculptures include allegorical characters representing the rivers Seine and Rhône, as well as the queen's coats of arms. Later, a sculpture showing the angry Polyphemus preparing to throw a rock at the innocent lovers Acis and Galatea was added. At the western end of the park you can see a miniature Statue of Liberty. This is the first model of New York's statue, created by Frédéric Bartholdi in 1870.

TIPS
» A programme of concerts and current exhibitions is posted at the *kiosque à musique* (music kiosk).
» The railings around the garden are often used as exhibition space.

Below left *Ball games are one of the many ways for children to let off steam in the park*
Below *Red, white and blue fowers thrive in an ornamental bed*

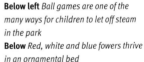

MUSÉE DU CINÉMA

www.cinematheque.fr

This new cinema museum is in the former American Cultural Center, a striking building created by architect Frank Gehry. The site includes the Henri Langlois Cinema Museum, four cinemas, the Cinémathèque Française, a film library, an exhibition room, a bookshop and a restaurant.

✚ 109 R10 ✉ 51 rue de Bercy, 75012 ☎ 01 71 19 33 33 🕐 La Cinémathèque Française–Musée du Cinéma: Mon, Wed–Sat 12–7 (also Thu 7–10), Sun 10–8 ✋ Adult €5, child (10–18) €4 🚇 Bercy 🚌 24, 64, 87

MUSÉE DE LA MONNAIE

www.monnaiedeparis.fr

Elegant Hôtel de la Monnaie, on the Left Bank alongside the Seine, housed the workshops of the Paris Mint from the 18th century until 1973. Today the workshops produce commemorative coins and medals. The *hôtel* is also home to a coin and medal museum, dating back to the 19th century, where you can learn about minting techniques.

✚ 108 M7 ✉ Hôtel de la Monnaie, 11 quai de Conti, 75006 ☎ 01 40 46 55 35 🕐 Tue–Fri 11–5.30, Sat–Sun 12–5.30 ✋ Adult €5, child (under 16) free, free to all on 1st Sun of month 🚇 Pont Neuf,

Odéon 🚌 27, 58, 70 🎧 Audioguide €3. Guided tour of the workshops (advance booking): Wed and Fri 2.15pm, €3 (free for under 16) 📖 ❓ The museum is closed for refurbishment until summer 2013

MUSÉE NATIONAL EUGÈNE DELACROIX

www.musee-delacroix.fr

Romantic painter Eugène Delacroix (1798–1863) spent the last six years of his life in this apartment. His living quarters and studio are now a small museum. On display are some of his paintings, drawings, pastels, sketches, furniture and personal documents.

✚ 108 L7 ✉ 6 rue de Furstemberg, 75006 ☎ 01 44 41 86 50 🕐 Wed–Mon 9.30–5 (last entry 4.30) ✋ Adult €5, child (under 26) free, free to all 1st Sun of month 🚇 St-Germain-des-Prés, Mabillon 🚌 39, 63, 70, 86, 95, 96

MUSÉE NATIONAL DU MOYEN ÂGE–THERMES DE CLUNY
▷ 122–123.

MUSÉUM NATIONAL D'HISTOIRE NATURELLE AND JARDIN DES PLANTES
▷ 121.

NOTRE-DAME
▷ 124–127.

PANTHÉON
▷ 128.

PONT DES ARTS

This is one of Paris's most romantic bridges, a popular place for street performances and impromptu parties. Also known as Passerelle (footbridge) des Arts, it links the Louvre with the Institut de France, and was rebuilt in 1984 with seven steel arches. Napoléon commissioned the original bridge.

✚ 108 L7 ✉ quai du Louvre/quai de Conti 🚇 Louvre-Rivoli 🚌 24, 27, 39, 69, 72, 75

PONT NEUF

Ironically, the New Bridge is actually Paris's oldest surviving bridge, dating from 1604. It was Henri II's idea, in 1556, to ease his journey between the Louvre palace and the abbey of St-Germain-des-Prés. The bridge opened almost half a century later, when Henri IV inaugurated it by galloping across on his charger. His equestrian statue stands there, although the original was melted down during the Revolution. In 1985, the land-artist Christo wrapped the entire bridge.

✚ 108 M7 ✉ Île de la Cité 🚇 Pont Neuf 🚌 24, 27, 58, 70, 75

Left *Pont Neuf is the oldest of Paris's bridges*
Above *The steel arches of Pont des Arts*

MUSÉUM NATIONAL D'HISTOIRE NATURELLE AND JARDIN DES PLANTES

The Jardin des Plantes is one of the city's prettiest parks and an ideal place for a stroll. Its wide tree-lined avenue, flanked by museums on one side and gardens on the other, is especially picturesque in autumn (fall) when the leaves are changing hue. Paths lead off to the gardens with flowers, statues and a great view of the striking Grande Galerie de l'Évolution (see below).

The Jardin des Plantes was founded in 1626 by two of Louis XIII's physicians as the royal garden of medicinal plants. It opened to the public in 1640 and was extended by the naturalist Buffon in the 18th century. At the heart of the garden, a new exhibition 'Le Cabinet d'historie' is dedicated to its topographical and architectural history—from its birth as the royal garden of medicinal plants in 1626 up to the present (open Wed–Mon 10–5; €3).

MUSÉUM NATIONAL D'HISTOIRE NATURELLE

The Natural History Museum is made up of several separate galleries within the Jardin des Plantes. The highlight is the Grande Galerie de l'Évolution, in a mammoth glass-roofed structure built in 1889 and renovated in the early 1990s. Contemporary displays cover themes ranging from evolution and the diversity of the living world to endangered and extinct species. The Galerie de Paléontologie, which opened in 1898, has fossils dating back millions of years. The Galerie d'Anatomie Comparée focuses on the classification of more than 1,000 vertebrates, while the Galerie de Minéralogie and Géologie displays gems, precious minerals and giant crystals.

PLANTS AND ANIMALS

Tropical greenhouses, including a winter garden and a Mexican greenhouse, shelter thousands of plant species. The Alpine garden is home to more than 2,000 species from mountainous regions including the Alps, Corsica and the Himalayas. The Ménagerie, which houses around 1,000 mammals, birds and reptiles, opened in 1794 and is currently closed while it undergoes a thorough redevelopment to bring it up to 21st-century standards.

INFORMATION

www.mnhn.fr (mainly in French)

✚ 109 P9 ☎ 01 40 79 56 01 🚇 Gare d'Austerlitz, Jussieu, Place Monge 🚌 24, 57, 61, 63, 67, 89, 91 🚃 🏧

Jardin des Plantes
www.jardindesplantes.net
✉ 57 rue Cuvier, 75005 ☎ 01 40 79 56 01 🕐 May–Oct daily 7.30–7.45; Nov–Apr 8–5.30 🖐 Free

Grande Galerie de l'Évolution
✉ 36 rue Geoffroy St-Hilaire, 75005
🕐 Wed–Mon 10–6 🖐 Adult €7, under 18 free 🚇 Censier-Daubenton

Galeries de Paléontologie et d'Anatomie Comparée
✉ 57 rue Cuvier, 75005 🕐 Wed–Mon 10–5 🖐 Adult €7, under 18 free

Galerie de Minéralogie & Géologie
✉ 36 rue Geoffroy St-Hilaire, 75005
🕐 Wed–Mon 10–6 🖐 Adult €8, child (4–13) €6

Les Serres (tropicales)
✉ 57 rue Cuvier, 75005 🕐 May–Oct daily 10–6; Nov–Apr 10–5 🖐 Adult €6, child (4–16) €4

Ménagerie (Zoo)
✉ 57 rue Cuvier, 75005 🕐 Closed for refurbishment until 2014

Above *The avenue in Jardin des Plantes*

INFORMATION

www.musee-moyenage.fr

108 M8 ✉ 6 place Paul-Painlevé, rue
du Sommerard, 75005 ☎ 01 53 73 78 16;
01 53 73 78 00 🕐 Wed–Mon 9.15–5.45
💶 Adult €8.50, under 18 free for
permanent exhibitions, free to all on 1st
Sun of month 🚇 Cluny-La Sorbonne, St-
Michel 🚌 21, 27, 38, 63, 85, 86, 87, 96
🚊 RER line B, C, St-Michel 🎧 Guided
tours available in English. Audioguide €1
📖 €22.80 🏪 Bookshop/gift shop

Above *A magnificent Gothic mansion
houses the Cluny Museum of the Middle
Ages on the site of Gallo-Roman baths*

INTRODUCTION

The Cluny Museum offers an intriguing glimpse into medieval life. Animated
tapestries, dazzling necklaces, headless statues and religious paraphernalia
are among the 23,000 exhibits, displayed in an intimate Gothic mansion in
the Latin Quarter. What makes the collection so compelling is that you get
a close-up view of objects that you usually admire only from a distance.
Vivid stained-glass windows you would normally crane your neck to see are
suddenly down at eye level, while altarpieces created to sit imposingly at
the far end of a church are right in front of you. The detail is exceptional. The
stained-glass exhibits are not only beautiful but enlightening, revealing the art
form through its three techniques: painting, fire and metal.

Entrance to the museum is through a splendid Gothic courtyard, whose
gargoyles and turrets put you in the mood for the exhibits inside. Pick up
a free plan at the ticket desk, then start your tour by walking through the
bookshop to room 2. From here it is easy to find your way around as you
simply follow the numerical order of the rooms, 2 to 12 on the lower floor
and 13 to 23 on the upper floor. After your visit, you can take a break in the
medieval gardens, whose entrance is on the corner of boulevards St-Michel
and St-Germain where, in the inner courtyard, you will find the 'Heavenly
Garden' and the 'Garden of Love'.

When the government, under the 'citizen king' Louis-Philippe of Orléans, decided to inaugurate a museum of the Middle Ages in Paris, the late-Gothic Hôtel de Cluny was the perfect location as it combined the great house with the Gallo-Roman baths. The museum was eventually opened in 1843. The turreted Hôtel de Cluny, one of Paris's oldest mansions, was built at the end of the 15th century as a pied-à-terre for a wealthy order of Benedictine monks from Cluny, in Burgundy. Illustrious residents included Mary Tudor, sister of Henry VIII, who was widowed at the age of 16 after a three-month marriage to Louis XII, and James V of Scotland. In the early 19th century the art collector Alexandre du Sommerard bought the property—and it is his rich finds that form the basis of the museum today.

WHAT TO SEE

TAPESTRIES

Vivid tapestries paint an enchanting, if idealized, picture of medieval life. Walking, bathing and reading are among the everyday activities portrayed in the 16th-century series *La Vie Seigneuriale* (Manorial Life; room 4). These activities include grooming, hunting, reading poetry, chivalrous conversations and courtly love. Artefacts such as combs, shoes and coins are also included. The floral background, known as *mille-fleurs*, was a popular artistic device at the time. Don't miss the 16th-century Les Vendanges (room 12), created in the southern Netherlands and portraying a busy grape harvest. The six allegorical tapestries of *La Dame à la Licorne* (The Lady and the Unicorn; room 13) were woven in silk and wool in the 15th century in the Netherlands. Each of the first five tapestries shows a lady acting out one of the five senses. In the enigmatic sixth piece, *À mon seul désir (To my only desire)*, she returns the necklace she has been wearing to its box, symbolizing, it is thought, a refusal to give in to worldly passions. Another tapestry to note is that depicting the life of St. Stephen, the first Christian martyr.

THE HEADS OF NOTRE-DAME

The concert hall (room 8) displays a surreal collection of heads that were knocked off statues on the west front of Notre-Dame by zealous Revolutionaries who thought they represented French kings. In fact, the statues, dating from the 13th century, were of biblical characters. Various other mutilated sculpture decorations originally came from the churches of St-Germain des Prés, Sainte-Geneviève, St-Denis and the Sainte-Chapelle. Historians assumed that many had been destroyed. In fact, they were brought together by a series of lucky coincidences, not least of which was the discovery in 1977 of dozens of them and other fragments in the vaults of a bank. As a consequence, it has been possible for scholars to trace the entire evolution of 12th- and 13th-century statuary in Paris.

GALLO-ROMAN BATHS

The museum is on the site of Paris's most ancient Gallo-Roman baths, the ruins of which can still be seen. In the second century AD, bathers would progress through three stone chambers offering different water temperatures—warm in the *tepidarium*, hot in the *caldarium* and cold in the *frigidarium*. Much of the vast *frigidarium* still remains and has been incorporated into the lower floor of the museum (room 9). It is an imposing chamber, with walls 2m (6ft) thick, rising 15m (49ft) high. In one corner stands Paris's oldest sculpture, the recently renovated *Pilier des Nautes* (AD30). A network of Roman vaults leads off from the *frigidarium*. Outside, you can see the ruins of the Roman gymnasium from the boulevard St-Germain. Along with the baths, which date back to the first and second centuries, the gymnasium represents the very few surviving remains of the Gallo-Roman civilization in Paris.

TIPS

» You don't have to pay to enter the Gothic courtyard off place Paul-Painlevé. It's a pleasant spot to sit for a few minutes and the turrets and gargoyles are worth a look.

» This is a good museum for English speakers, as the explanatory placards are written in English as well as French.

» Look for the figurine of the Madonna and Child carved out of ivory. It is one of the largest of its kind in the world.

» Take a look at the outside of the Hôtel de Cluny at night. Lighting engineers have illuminated the facade so that it appears to change in colour density the closer you come to it or the farther away you walk.

» A good example of the museum's medieval goldsmithing and enamelling exhibits is the Guarrazar Crowns from Toledo in Spain.

Below *Three carved stone spiral staircases connect the different levels of the Hôtel de Cluny*

INFORMATION

www.notredamedeparis.fr

Cathedral

✚ 108 N8 ✉ place du Parvis Notre-Dame, 75004 ☎ 01 42 34 56 10
🕐 Mon–Fri 8–6.45, Sat–Sun 8–7.15. Limited access on Sun ✋ Free 🚇 Cité, St-Michel, Châtelet 🚌 21, 24, 38, 47, 58, 70, 72, 74, 81, 82, 85, 96 🚉 RER lines B, C, St-Michel 📖 A wide choice 🚌 Guided tours: in French, Mon–Fri 2 and 3, Sat 2.30; in English, Wed–Thu at 2, Sat at 2.30. Extra tours in English in Aug 🍴 On Île de la Cité and in Latin Quarter 🎁 Bookshop and gift shop ❓ Organ recitals at 4.30 on Sun

Towers

www.monuments-nationaux.fr

✉ Rue du Cloître Notre-Dame (entrance is on the northwestern corner of the cathedral) ☎ 01 53 10 07 00
🕐 Jul–Aug Mon–Fri 10–6.30, Sat–Sun 10am–11pm; Apr–Jun, Sep daily 10–6.30; Oct–Mar daily 10–5.30; last entry 45 min before closing ✋ Adult €8, under 18 free 🚌 Guided tours by reservation (tel 01 44 54 19 30)

Treasury

✉ Entrance in cathedral, near the choir 🕐 Mon–Fri 9.30–6, Sat 9.30–6.30, Sun 1.30–6.30 ✋ Adult €3, child (6–12) €1

Crypt

www.paris.fr

✉ 1 place du Parvis Notre-Dame ☎ 01 55 42 50 10 🕐 Tue–Sun 10–6 ✋ Adult €4, child (14–26) €2, under 14 free

INTRODUCTION

Notre-Dame anchors the Île de la Cité with its powerful presence and more than 850 years of history. The cathedral is as famous a symbol of Paris as the Eiffel Tower and around 13 million people enter its doors each year. Despite this, it retains an inspiring sense of calm.

Entry is through the huge doorways of the west facade, in the touristy place du Parvis Notre-Dame. You can buy a guidebook at the bookstand just inside the cathedral, before wandering around the dimly lit interior. There are fewer crowds in the early morning, when the cathedral is also at its brightest. If you're not in a hurry, you may like to visit the Treasury, reached from the south side of the choir. The entrance to the crypt is outside, on place du Parvis Notre-Dame.

Keep some time for strolling around the outside of Notre-Dame to admire the architecture, including the buttresses. One of the best views of the exterior is from the Seine, on a boat trip that circles the Île de la Cité. Finally, if your legs will agree to it, there are wonderful views from the top of the towers. Queues are shortest in the morning, Tuesday to Friday.

In the 12th century, Bishop Maurice de Sully decided that Paris needed its own cathedral. Pope Alexander III laid the foundation stone in 1163 and the choir was constructed in just under 20 years. Guilds of carpenters, stone-carvers, iron forgers and glass craftsmen worked on the grand project but it took almost 200 years to complete, finishing in 1345. For years Notre-Dame doubled as a meeting place for trade unions and a dormitory for the homeless. Its cathedral school was renowned throughout Europe.

By the time Napoléon was crowned in the cathedral in 1804 Notre-Dame was in a state of disrepair. Victor Hugo, author of *The Hunchback of Notre-Dame*, campaigned for its restoration, concerned at the absence of countless statues (toppled during the Revolution), the lack of stained glass and the amputation of the spire in 1787. His ranting met with some success. The statues in the Gallery of Kings were eventually reproduced and a 90m (295ft) spire was erected. Viollet-le-Duc oversaw the restoration in the mid-19th century. His work included replacing some of the clear-glass windows with stained glass and modestly adding a statue of himself among the Apostles. It wasn't until after World War II that the rest of the windows were replaced. Today, Notre-Dame remains an important place of worship, as well as one of Paris's top visitor attractions.

WHAT TO SEE

WEST FACADE

The symmetrical west facade, dominated by Notre-Dame's towers, appears rather heavy and angular compared with the elegant curves and spires you see from the eastern side. But it is packed with sculptures, originally painted and intended as a Bible for the illiterate. The 28 large statues lined up between the doors and the windows form the Gallery of the Kings. Although the figures represent biblical characters, revolutionary zealots mistook them for French kings and beheaded them. The statues you see today are 19th-century replicas, but you can see some of the original heads at the Musée National du Moyen Âge (▷ 122–123). Below the Gallery of the Kings, the left portal is dedicated to the Virgin Mary, the central portal shows the Last Judgement and the right portal, dedicated to St. Anne, shows Mary holding the infant Jesus, while Louis VII and Bishop Sully kneel in worship.

TOWERS

It's a tough climb (387 steps and no elevator), but it is worth tackling the towers, 69m (226ft) high, for the views over Paris and a closer look at the gargoyles. You'll be following the fictional footsteps of Notre-Dame's bell ringer, Quasimodo. Two-thirds of the way up (and a mere 285 steps) is the gargoyle parapet known as the Galerie des Chimères, where you can enjoy views across the Latin Quarter to the Tour Montparnasse, as well as along the Seine and across the Île de la Cité to Sainte-Chapelle. This is a great place to photograph the quirky gargoyles, added in the 19th century by Viollet-le-Duc. A wooden staircase in the South Tower leads to the 13-tonne Emmanuel bell, recast in 1686 and evoking memories of a tormented Quasimodo.

A separate spiral staircase leads up to the top of the South Tower (another 115 steps), where the superb panoramic views take in Sacré-Cœur to the

TIPS

» Try to visit just before a service to experience the palpable sense of anticipation as lights are gradually turned on and people gather to worship.

» Instead of paying tourist prices in the nearby cafés and restaurants, enjoy a picnic in the grassy square Jean XXIII, on the southern side of the cathedral.

» There are classical and choral concerts held in the cathedral throughout the summer, usually on Tuesday evenings. For more details see www.musique-sacree-notredamedeparis.fr.

Opposite *At sunset Notre-Dame is silhouetted against the fiery sky*
Below *Climb the towers of the cathedral's west front for a close-up view of gargoyles*

FACTS AND FIGURES

» The cathedral is 128m (420ft) long and its transept is 48m (157ft) wide.

» The spire is 96m (315ft) high. The towers are 69m (226ft) high.

» More than 1,300 oak trees were felled to make the cathedral's wooden frame.

» The organ dates from the early 18th century and has 7,374 pipes.

» It is the most visited monument in France.

» It is a UNESCO World Heritage Site and attracts 13 million visitors a year.

north, the Arc de Triomphe to the west, the modern Bibliothèque Nationale to the east and the Panthéon to the south. At the top, take a moment to consider how the view spread out before you must have changed since the towers were completed in 1250.

THE WINDOWS

Notre-Dame has stunning stained glass and it is hard to imagine how the cathedral must have looked in the 18th century, when officials replaced many of the medieval windows with clear glass to let in more light. Much of the current stained glass dates from the 19th and 20th centuries. The south rose window, 13m (42ft) in diameter, is especially glorious when the sun shines through, adding extra vibrancy to the purple hues. Christ stands in the heart of the window, encircled by angels, Apostles, martyrs and scenes from the New Testament. Opposite, the middle of the north rose window shows Mary holding a young Jesus. Old Testament prophets, priests and kings fill the rest of the window, one of the cathedral's few originals.

CHOIR SCREEN, ALTAR AND NOTRE-DAME DE PARIS

Don't miss the cathedral's intricately carved and painted 14th-century choir screen, restored in the 1960s. Its enchanting depictions of gospel scenes include the Wise Men bringing their gifts to baby Jesus, Jesus riding into Jerusalem on a donkey, and the Last Supper.

The modern bronze high altar in the middle of the cathedral was consecrated in 1989. It depicts gospel writers Matthew, Mark, Luke and John and Old Testament prophets Isaiah, Ezekiel, Daniel and Jeremiah.

Nearby you can see the most famous of Notre-Dame's 37 statues of the Virgin Mary. Known as Notre-Dame de Paris, it dates from the 14th century and was installed in the cathedral in the 19th century.

Above *Intricate carvings decorate the arches of the west front*

CHAPELS

The cathedral is lined with small chapels, added during the 13th and 14th centuries and dedicated to saints. Guilds used to meet in these chapels and each May Day they would donate a painting to the cathedral. Some of these works of art remain on display today, including pieces by 17th-century artists Charles Le Brun and Eustache Le Sueur.

TREASURY AND CRYPT

Notre-Dame's Trésor holds medieval manuscripts, religious paraphernalia and relics, including the Crown of Thorns, bought for an exorbitant amount by Louis IX (▷ 132). It's not a vital part of the Notre-Dame experience, but the gold and jewel-encrusted items give an insight into the wealth and power wielded by the Church over the years. The cathedral's crypt is often overlooked by visitors, perhaps because the entrance is outside, on the opposite side of the place du Parvis Notre-Dame. Down here you'll see Roman foundations and archaeological finds.

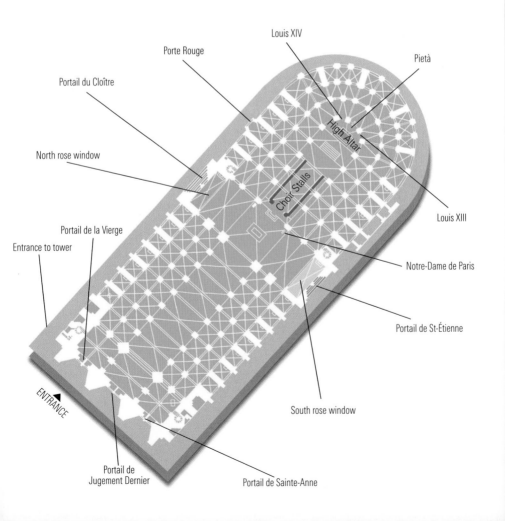

- Louis XIV
- Porte Rouge
- Pietà
- Portail du Cloître
- High Altar
- North rose window
- Choir Stalls
- Louis XIII
- Portail de la Vierge
- Entrance to tower
- Notre-Dame de Paris
- Portail de St-Étienne
- ENTRANCE
- South rose window
- Portail de Jugement Dernier
- Portail de Sainte-Anne

INFORMATION

www.monuments-nationaux.fr

✚ 108 M9 ✉ place du Panthéon, 75005 ☎ 01 44 32 18 00 🕐 Apr–Sep daily 10–6.30; Oct–Mar 10–6; last entrance 45 min before closing ✋ Adult €8 under 18 free 🚇 Cardinal Lemoine 🚌 21, 27, 38, 82, 84, 85, 89 🚆 RER B, Luxembourg 🎫 Guided tours in French. Ring ahead (tel 01 44 54 10 30) for other languages 📖 €7 🏛 Small bookshop/gift shop

TIPS

» See the noticeboard outside the Panthéon for times for the guided tours up to the dome's circular colonnade.

» If you don't feel like climbing to the colonnade, you can still enjoy views of the Eiffel Tower from the top of the Panthéon's steps.

Below A neoclassical peristyle makes an impressive entrance to the Panthéon

PANTHÉON

The neoclassical grandeur of the Panthéon is an arresting sight after you have wandered through the warren-like streets of the Latin Quarter to reach it. This colossal mausoleum contains the tombs of many illustrious citizens, including writers Victor Hugo, Émile Zola and Voltaire, scientists Marie and Pierre Curie, Braille inventor Louis Braille, and World War II Resistance martyr Jean Moulin. To be 'pantheonized' is one of the greatest accolades in France and arguments still ignite periodically about who merits a re-burial here.

GIVING THANKS

The monument was commissioned by Louis XV as a basilica dedicated to St. Geneviève, patron saint of Paris, in thanks for his recovery from gout. The king laid the foundation stone in 1764 and work finished in 1790, by which time the original architect, Jacques Germain Soufflot, had died. Only a year later, in 1791, the Revolutionaries seized the building, bricking up the windows and changing its function to a secular Temple of Fame.

VISITING THE PANTHÉON

You enter the building through an imposing peristyle, based on the grandiose frontage of Rome's Pantheon. The sculpted pediment portrays France's heroes receiving their rewards. Inside the vast, cross-shaped chamber the atmosphere feels austere. Religious heroes are prominent in many of the paintings in the naves, including St. Geneviève (western nave and choir), the beheaded St. Denis (western nave), Joan of Arc (northern nave) and St. Louis (northern nave). The Revolution also features in paintings and sculptures.

Look up into the dome—the scientist Foucault hung a pendulum here in 1851 to prove the earth rotates. To climb to the colonnade beneath the dome, 35m (115ft) high, you must take a guided tour—and tackle 206 steps. Downstairs in the huge, shadowy crypt you can see the tombs of author and playwright Alexandre Dumas, author and statesman André Malraux, philosopher Jean-Jacques Rousseau and many others.

QUARTIER LATIN
▷ 130–131.

RIVE GAUCHE
The Seine curves round the south of the city, known as the Left Bank, which is significantly smaller than the Right Bank. Despite this, many Left Bank residents claim they hardly ever cross the Seine; they have their Roman ruins, galleries, literary cafés and colleges. France's rulers sit in the Palais Bourbon and Palais du Luxembourg, and the 7th *arrondissement* is packed with stately residential avenues. Many of the landmarks that make up Paris's skyline are here: the Eiffel Tower, Les Invalides and the tall shadow of Tour Montparnasse. The four glass towers of the new national library, the Bibliothèque François Mitterrand, crown a huge redevelopment project in the 13th *arrondissement*.
✉ South of the Seine

SAINTE-CHAPELLE
▷ 132–133.

ST-ÉTIENNE-DU-MONT
www.saintetiennedumont.com
As you approach from place du Panthéon the church seems dwarfed by its mighty companion. But the closer you get, the more it steals your attention with its intricately carved facade and bell tower. Work started in 1492, replacing a smaller chapel of the abbey of Ste-Geneviève. It continued until 1626, which explains the architectural mix of Gothic, Renaissance and Classical. Paris's archbishop was assassinated in the church in 1857. The rood screen is a highlight.
✚ 108 N9 ✉ 1 place Ste-Geneviève, 75005 ☎ 01 43 54 11 79 ◷ Jul–Aug Tue–Sun 10–12, 2.30–7.45; Sep–Jun Tue–Fri 8.45–12, 2.30–7.30, Sat 8.45–12, 2–7.45, Sun 8.45–12, 2–7.45 ✋ Free ◻ Cardinal Lemoine ▣ 84, 89

ST-GERMAIN-DES-PRÉS
A charming district with narrow lanes, chic boutiques, the oldest

church in Paris and an abundance of cafés, restaurants, antiques shops and art galleries.

St-Germain-des-Prés, in the heart of the Left Bank, is a magnet to visitors and residents alike, with a more leisurely pace than on the other side of the river. At its core is the Église St-Germain-des-Prés (▷ 134), the oldest church in Paris, dating from the 11th century. Its picturesque bell tower is symbolic of the area. Nearby, in the tranquil rue de Furstemberg, is the Musée National Eugène Delacroix (▷ 120).

The pulse of the district is along the boulevard St-Germain, running west from the Latin Quarter to join the government buildings and bourgeois mansions of the 7th *arrondissement*. Lively cafés on this boulevard—the rendezvous of the literary elite—include the illustrious Café de Flore—once frequented by Jean-Paul Sartre—and Brasserie Lipp and Café Les Deux Magots, a former haunt of Ernest Hemingway.

South of the boulevard, the streets widen and the atmosphere changes. From the church of St-Sulpice (▷ 135) to the pretty Jardin du Luxembourg (▷ 118–119), through the shopping streets of rue Bonaparte, rue de Sèvres and rue de Grenelle, this is the St-Germain of fashion boutiques, publishing houses and trendy bars. Furniture shops line the boulevard Raspail leading to the crossroads of Sèvres-Babylone, home of Paris's first department store, Le Bon Marché.

North of the boulevard, towards the Seine, is an arty area, packed with small cinemas, art galleries, the École Nationale Supérieure des Beaux-Arts and the Hôtel de la Monnaie (▷ 120).
✚ 108 L7 ✉ 75006 ◻ St-Germain-des-Prés, Odéon, St-Sulpice, Mabillon ▣ 21, 38, 39, 63, 70, 85, 86, 87, 95, 96

Above *In the heart of St-Germain-des-Prés is its 11th-century church*

INFORMATION

INTRODUCTION

The Latin Quarter is an essential part of the Paris experience. Its picturesque
narrow side streets take you back to the Middle Ages, while the presence of
many students gives the area a refreshing vibrancy. No other district of Paris
claims so many bookshops or colleges, and there is also a host of historic
churches, cinemas, jazz clubs and restaurants. You'll find a relaxed and
youthful atmosphere compared with the frenetic, business-focused Right
Bank. Here, the cliché of students, artists and bohemians lingering for hours
in cafés is actually true.

Your first taste of the Latin Quarter is likely to be the busy place St-Michel,
with its imposing fountain symbolizing the archangel St. Michael slaying the
dragon. Two dragons flank the central statue spouting water into the fountain.
From here there are good views of Notre-Dame (▷ 124–127) on the nearby Île
de la Cité. The busy boulevard St-Michel (or *Boul Mich* to students), lined with
magazine kiosks, runs from place St-Michel along the length of the district
and teems with students and visitors. Unless you want to browse in its clothes
stores and bookshops, it is best to venture onto the picturesque side streets to
soak up more of the true Latin Quarter atmosphere.

The Latin Quarter owes its scholarly, literary and artistic reputation to the
founding of the Sorbonne university in the 13th century (▷ 135) in an area

Above *The Latin Quarter grew up around
the Sorbonne university*

known as the Montagne Ste-Geneviève. An animated crowd of European students soon flocked here, turning the university into a Catholic city-within-a-city. Other colleges grew up around the Sorbonne and the area gained the name Latin Quarter, after the language commonly used by the students for everyday conversation.

In the 15th century the introduction of printing presses made the rue St-Jacques France's publishing headquarters. Later, the district acquired a reputation for undisciplined and bohemian inhabitants, making it fertile soil for the Revolution. In May 1968, its rebellious streak re-emerged when students took to the streets (▷ 43).

WHAT TO SEE

WANDERING IN MEDIEVAL STREETS
The area to the east of place St-Michel is a warren of winding, historic alleyways, redolent of the Middle Ages. You'll find a variety small specialist shops in the streets off the *quais* and Greek restaurants in rue de la Huchette and rue de la Harpe.

It is worth seeking out the small 12th-century church of St-Julien-le-Pauvre (▷ 134) and the beautiful stained-glass windows of St-Séverin (▷ 134). The tranquil square René Viviani, off the quai de Montebello, is home to what is said to be Paris's oldest tree, planted in the early 17th century.

LITERARY LIFE
Farther south, in the area around the Sorbonne, you can plunge into the heart of academia and probably find a café once frequented by Latin Quarter intelligentsia such as Paul Verlaine or Jean-Paul Sartre. This is also where you'll find the Panthéon (▷ 128), final resting place of France's scientific, literary and political heroes.

GALLO-ROMAN BATHS
On the corner of boulevards St-Michel and St-Germain are the remains of the Gallo-Roman baths, the Thermes de Cluny. The vast stone chamber that housed the Frigidarium (cold bath) is now part of the Musée National du Moyen Âge (▷ 122–123).

GREEN LUNG
On the Latin Quarter's southern boundary, the flower-filled Jardin du Luxembourg (▷ 118–119) is the perfect place to rest your aching feet after a day exploring the streets.

TIPS
» For a stroll through the Latin Quarter ▷ 136–137.
» You could while away an hour or so browsing in the English-language bookshop Shakespeare and Company (▷ 140). Or head for the Gothic courtyard of the Musée National du Moyen Âge (▷ 122–123) to admire the turrets and gargoyles.

Below left *Book stalls and magazine kiosks line bustling boulevard St-Michel*
Below *Detail of the splendid fountain depicting St. Michael slaying the dragon in place St-Michel*

INFORMATION

www.monuments-nationaux.fr

✚ 108 M7 ✉ 4 boulevard du Palais, Île de la Cité, 75001 ☎ 01 53 40 60 80 ◷ Mar–Oct daily 9.30–6 (last entry 5.30); Nov–Feb 9–5 ✋ Adult €8, under 18 free. Joint ticket with Conciergerie €11 Ⓜ Cité, Châtelet 🚌 21, 24, 27, 38, 85, 96 Ⓡ RER line B, C, St-Michel-Notre-Dame ⬚ Guided tours by appointment only ☎ 01 44 54 19 33 📖 €7 🏠 Small gift shop in lower chapel

INTRODUCTION

It's not quite heaven, but the celestial rays of blue, red and golden light streaming through the windows of Sainte-Chapelle certainly seem out of this world. The only downside is the crowds, which, as with Rome's Sistine Chapel, can detract from what should be an awe-inspiring experience.

You reach the chapel through a shared entrance with the Palais de Justice, on the boulevard du Palais, where your bags will be screened. From here, walk round to the main entrance of the chapel. The wait for tickets can be long, but you can avoid this if you have a *Paris Museum Pass* (▷ 279) or a joint ticket with the Conciergerie (▷ 112–113). The entrance leads you first into the lower chapel, where there is a small gift shop. A steep spiral staircase takes you to the upper chapel.

Sainte-Chapelle was commissioned by the devout Louis IX (St. Louis) in the 13th century as a royal chapel, with direct access to the palace, principally to house holy relics and to promote the king's authority as a divinely appointed leader. It was constructed in the royal palace complex (now the Palais de Justice) in less than six years. The architect is not known for certain, although it was possibly Pierre de Montreuil, who rebuilt the apse of the Royal Abbey of Saint-Denis and also did the finishing work on the facade of Notre-Dame. He made clever use of discreet pillars to support the 670sq m (7,211sq ft) of stained glass without the need for walls.

The relics were displayed on a wooden-canopied platform that you can still see today in front of the altar. They included what was reputed to be the Crown of Thorns, pieces of the Holy Cross and drops of Christ's blood. King Louis IX was so eager to take possession of these objects that he paid the Emperor of Constantinople 135,000 livres for the Crown of Thorns alone— more than three times the building costs of the chapel. The Crown of Thorns is now kept in Notre-Dame's Treasury. The other relics, along with the silver- and copper-plated reliquary in which they were housed, were melted down during the course of the Revolution.

After the Revolution, the chapel was requisitioned for use as an archive for court documents. It was restored in the mid-19th century, under the direction of Eugène Viollet-le-Duc, when its fifth (and current) spire was constructed, rising 75m (245ft) above the ground. During the restoration some of the glass was destroyed or sold but, otherwise, the rest of the chapel is widely regarded as being true to the original drawings and descriptions of the building which survived. It was declared a national historic monument in 1862.

Above *Sainte-Chapelle is famed for its beautiful stained-glass windows*

WHAT TO SEE

THE WINDOWS

Sainte-Chapelle contains the largest expanse of 13th-century stained glass in the world. When you step into the upper chapel you are immediately hit by colour coming at you from all directions, not only from the glorious windows but also from the patterned floor, the golden columns and the painted lower walls. Fifteen windows, up to 15m (49ft) tall, and a glorious rose window depict more than 1,100 biblical scenes, from the Creation to the Apocalypse. Two-thirds of the windows are 13th-century originals, the oldest stained glass in Paris. The panels tell key biblical stories, starting with Genesis in the window on the left as you enter and working clockwise round the chapel to the Apocalypse in the rose window. The only non-biblical theme is in the final window, which tells how the holy relics came to Paris.

CARVINGS

Although the windows are undoubtedly the highlight of the upper chapel, take time to notice other features, such as the incredible detail of the sculpted golden foliage on the column capitals (including oak leaves, holly, thistle and hops) and the statues of the Apostles, which appear to be supporting the pillars (an allusion to their role as pillars of the Christian faith). Some are 19th-century copies—the originals are in the Musée National du Moyen Âge (▷ 122–123).

THE LOWER CHAPEL

Before reaching the brilliance of the upper chapel, you walk through the dark lower chapel, originally used by palace staff and dedicated to the Virgin Mary. Its blue, red and gold ceiling is decorated with fleurs-de-lys, symbol of the French monarchy, while some of the pillars bear Castilian towers, from the coat of arms of Louis IX's mother. The paintwork dates from the mid-19th century, when attempts were made to reproduce the medieval style. This followed damage caused during the Revolution, when the chapel was used as a warehouse to store flour.

TIPS

» The upper chapel can become extremely crowded. The quietest times to visit are Tuesday to Friday mornings.
» You can buy a joint ticket for the Conciergerie (▷ 112–113) and Sainte-Chapelle. Buy this at the Conciergerie, where the queues are often shorter.
» To help decipher the windows in the upper chapel, pick up an information card from the stand by the exit.
» A spiral staircase leads to the Upper Chapel—the view is well worth the climb.
» Try to visit when the sun is shining, to experience the windows at their iridescent best. Sunset is the best time to see the rose window, although the chapel is likely to be crowded then.
» If you have binoculars, bring them with you to help you see the higher windows.
» For details of the candlelit concerts held in the chapel, ask the ticket office or tourist information office.
» Strict security measures are in place here, so make sure bags are free of sharp objects as these may be confiscated.

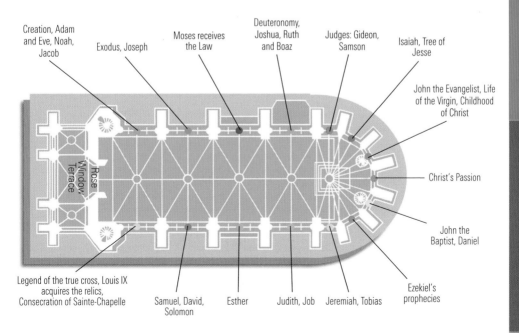

Creation, Adam and Eve, Noah, Jacob

Exodus, Joseph

Moses receives the Law

Deuteronomy, Joshua, Ruth and Boaz

Judges: Gideon, Samson

Isaiah, Tree of Jesse

John the Evangelist, Life of the Virgin, Childhood of Christ

Christ's Passion

John the Baptist, Daniel

Rose Window Terrace

Legend of the true cross, Louis IX acquires the relics, Consecration of Sainte-Chapelle

Samuel, David, Solomon

Esther

Judith, Job

Jeremiah, Tobias

Ezekiel's prophecies

ST-GERMAIN-DES-PRÉS (ÉGLISE)

www.eglise-sgp.org

The Église St-Germain-des-Prés is the oldest church in Paris and lies at the heart of the district that bears its name (▷ 129). The Merovingian king Childebert I founded an abbey on the site in the sixth century. The current church was consecrated by Pope Alexander III in 1163, although its bell tower dates from the previous century. The mix of Romanesque and Gothic styles is the result of many additions over the years. The structure was badly damaged during the Revolution and only one of the three original towers remains. The massive 12th-century flying buttresses are still intact. During the 19th century, the church underwent various restorations, and the murals in the nave and choir, by Flandrin, date from this period. The tomb of the philosopher René Descartes (1596–1650) lies in the St-Benoît side chapel.

✚ 108 L8 ✉ 3 place St-Germain-des-Prés, 75006 ☎ 01 55 42 81 33 ⓘ Mon–Sat 8–7.45, Sun 9–8 ✋ Free ⓜ St-Germain-des-Prés 🚌 39, 63, 86, 95

ST-JULIEN-LE-PAUVRE

www.sjlpmelkites.org

This small church, one of the oldest in Paris, is tucked away in a quiet corner of the Latin Quarter, near the tranquil square René Viviani (▷ 131). It dates from the 12th century and is said to stand on the site of a Merovingian burial ground. In the late Middle Ages the church had ties with the nearby university and elections for the rectors took place within its walls. During the Revolution it became a salt store, then in 1889 it was donated to the Melkite Church (Greek-Catholic). Inside the low-ceilinged building are various religious paintings and sculptures, although subdued lighting makes it hard to appreciate them fully. There is also an iconostasis (an Orthodox rood screen where icons hang) dating from around 1900. The church hosts classical music concerts.

✚ 108 M8 ✉ 1 rue Saint-Julien le Pauvre/23 quai de Montebello, 75005 ☎ 01 43 54 52 16 (for concert information call 01 42 28 43 85) ⓘ Daily 9.30–1, 3–6.30 ✋ Free ⓜ St-Michel 🚌 24, 47 🚇 RER lines B, C, St-Michel-Notre-Dame

ST-SÉVERIN

www.saint-severin.com

This beautiful church, in the Latin Quarter, would probably attract more visitors were it not for the grander Notre-Dame a few minutes' walk across the river (▷ 124–127). As it is, the Gothic St-Séverin remains a well-kept secret, but its beautiful stained glass makes it worth seeking out. Among the historic panes are some contemporary designs, installed in 1970, at the top end of the church. The vibrant windows, designed by Jean Bazaine, represent the Seven Sacraments. The church dates from the 13th century, although a fire led to much of it being rebuilt in the 15th century. Highlights include the Chapelle du St-Esprit, the double ambulatory and the palm-tree vaulting. The church originally took its name from a sixth-century hermit called Séverin the Solitary, although its allegiance later changed to a fifth-century Swiss abbot of the same name, whose statue now stands outside. Ask at the church office for the information leaflet (in English), which gives a plan of the building and details about its key features.

✚ 108 M8 ✉ 1 rue des Prêtres St-Séverin, 75005 ☎ 01 42 34 93 50 ⓘ Mon–Sat 11–7.30, Sun 9–8.30 ✋ Free ⓜ St-Michel 🚌 21, 24, 27, 38, 47, 85 🚇 RER lines B, C, St-Michel-Notre-Dame ❓ There is a ramp for wheelchair users at the back of the church, off rue St-Jacques

Above *The church of St-Germain-des-Prés seen from Les Deux Magots café*

ST-SULPICE

www.paroisse-saint-sulpice-paris.org

St-Sulpice is a masterpiece of classical architecture. It took six architects and 134 years to build the enormous church, 119m (390ft) long and 57m (187ft) wide. Work finished in 1780. The imposing facade is flanked by two asymmetrical towers; the south tower, still unfinished, is 5m (16ft) shorter than the north.

St-Sulpice is home to one of the world's largest church organs, but has many other treasures, including 17th-century stained-glass windows, paintings by Carle van Loo and carvings and statues by sculptors Edme Bouchardon, Jean-Baptiste Pigalle, the Slodtz brothers and Louis-Simon Boizot. The opulently carved and gilded pulpit was designed in 1788 by Charles de Wailly. Paintings by 17 renowned artists were commissioned to hang in the transept and the chapels in the 19th century. Murals by Eugène Delacroix are in the Chapelle des Anges, the first chapel on the right.

Look for the astronomical gnomon (sundial) in the form of a bronze meridian line stretching from the south to the north transept.

At noon on the winter solstice the image of the sun is reflected onto a white marble obelisk while at noon on the summer solstice the light falls onto a marble plaque in the south transept. In the past Charles Baudelaire and the Marquis de Sade were baptized here, Victor Hugo was married here and it still is favoured for society weddings, christenings and confirmations. Dan Brown's best-selling novel *The Da Vinci Code* has also brought St-Sulpice notoriety as the fictional setting for the keystone.

✚ 108 L8 ✉ place St-Sulpice, 75006 ☎ 01 46 33 21 78 or 01 46 33 21 78 🕐 Daily 7.30–7.30 ✋ Free 🚇 St-Sulpice 🚌 58, 63, 70, 86, 87, 95, 96

LA SORBONNE

www.sorbonne.fr

La Sorbonne university dates from the 13th century, when Robert de Sorbon, chaplain to St. Louis, set up a college to house the poorer theology students. For centuries the university maintained an independent attitude to the state, recognizing the English Henry V as King of France, condemning Joan of Arc and fiercely opposing the 18th-century philosophers. This continued into the 20th century, with the student revolt of 1968 (▷ 43). Cardinal Richelieu was responsible for rebuilding the college in the 17th century, although Jacques Lemercier's domed chapel, where the Cardinal now lies, is all that remains. Today's amphitheatres and corridors date from the 19th century. The premises are used by four universities—Paris Sorbonne, Sorbonne Nouvelle, Panthéon-Sorbonne and René Descartes.

Occasional exhibitions are held in the Chapelle de la Sorbonne and you can experience the college atmosphere in the student-filled place de la Sorbonne. Although the university is closed to the public, you can glimpse the courtyard off the rue de la Sorbonne. Parts are under renovation, due for completion in 2015.

✚ 108 M8 ✉ 47 rue des Écoles, 75005 ☎ 01 40 46 22 11 🕐 Closed to the public (guided tours are available for groups but you must telephone in advance for a reservation: 01 40 46 23 49; adult €9, child (4–18) €4) 🚇 Cluny-La Sorbonne 🚌 21, 27, 38, 63, 85, 86, 87 🚆 RER B, C, Cluny-La Sorbonne

Above *Place St-Sulpice has the fine Fountain of the Four Bishops at its heart*

QUARTIER LATIN

This walk takes you beyond the swarming boulevard St-Michel to the quiet cobbled alleyways, peaceful gardens, historic churches and laid-back cafés of the Latin Quarter.

THE WALK

Distance: 2.5km (1.5 miles)
Time: 1 hour 30 minutes
Start/end at: place St-Michel

HOW TO GET THERE

Take the Métro to St-Michel, buses 21, 24, 27, 38, 85, 96, RER line C to St-Michel-Notre-Dame.

★ Start at place St-Michel and walk across to the Fontaine St-Michel.

❶ The sculpture symbolizes St. Michael slaying a dragon. Place St-Michel is the main gateway to the Latin Quarter from the Île de la Cité. Numerous visitors, students and Parisians pass through.

Cross boulevard St-Michel and walk down the medieval rue de la Huchette. Cross over rue de Petit Pont. Turn left, then immediately right into rue de la Bûcherie, with its views of Notre-Dame. Continue to square René Viviani.

❷ This is a pleasant place to sit for a few moments, admiring the flowers and enjoying the gurgle of running water from the fountain. The acacia here is said to be one of the oldest trees in Paris, dating from the early 17th century.

Leave the square near the partly Gothic, partly Romanesque church of St-Julien-le-Pauvre (▷ 134).

❸ This small, low-ceilinged church is one of the oldest in Paris, having its origins in the 12th century. The church was remodelled in the 17th century; the present facade dates from that time.

From the church, follow the road round to rue St-Jacques. Cross rue St-Jacques and walk down rue St-Séverin, alongside the church of St-Séverin (▷ 134).

❹ To visit the Flamboyant Gothic church, turn left into rue des Prêtres St-Séverin. As well as gargoyles and beautiful stained glass, the church contains the oldest bell in Paris, cast in 1412.

Continue along rue St-Séverin to medieval rue de la Harpe, which, to the left, leads to boulevard St-Germain. Cross the boulevard to the medieval garden of the Musée National du Moyen Âge–

Opposite *Modern stained-glass windows in the church of St-Séverin*

Thermes de Cluny. Turn right up the boulevard, then left onto boulevard St-Michel.

❺ This traffic-thundering road, with its clothes stores, bookshops and news-stands, is the Latin Quarter's main artery.

Walk up boulevard St-Michel, then turn right onto rue de l'École de Médecine. Turn left onto rue André Dubois, then up the steps to reach rue Monsieur le Prince. Turn left onto this road.

❻ Rue Monsieur le Prince closely follows the line of Paris's old city wall, built by King Philippe-Auguste, who reigned in the late 12th and early 13th centuries. Today it has shops and restaurants, including the bistro Polidor at number 41, which was launched in 1845.

Just before Polidor, turn right into rue Racine, then walk along to place de l'Odéon, dominated by the 18th-century Odéon Théâtre de l'Europe. Wander down the rue de l'Odéon,

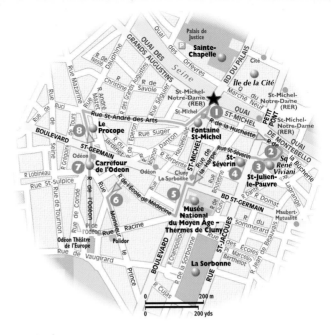

with its unusual shops, to reach Carrefour de l'Odéon.

❼ If you feel like a rest, you can stop for a coffee in one of the cafés.

Continue to boulevard St-Germain. Cross the boulevard and walk down rue de l'Ancienne Comédie.

❽ On your right you'll pass Paris's oldest café, Le Procope, founded in 1686 and now a restaurant (▷ 143).

At the Buci crossroads turn sharp right onto rue St-André des Arts. This leads back to place St-Michel. You could have a drink in one of the nearby cafés or cross the Pont St-Michel to explore the Île de la Cité.

WHEN TO GO
Daytime is best for this walk, when the shops and churches are open.

WHERE TO EAT
There is a choice of cafés on Carrefour de l'Odéon, or Pizza Milano at place St-Michel.

PLACES TO VISIT
The Latin Quarter has plenty to occupy you, including the Musée National du Moyen Âge–Thermes de Cluny (▷ 122–123), the stately Panthéon (▷ 128) and the refreshing Jardin du Luxembourg (▷ 118–119). You can while away a few hours in some of the many cafés or shop for clothes along boulevard St-Michel.

Left *Le Procope is the oldest café in Paris, now an excellent restaurant*

ST-GERMAIN-DES-PRÉS

This walk takes you through the picturesque lanes of St-Germain-des-Prés, along the Left Bank of the Seine and around the beautiful Jardin du Luxembourg.

THE WALK

Distance: 3km (2 miles)
Time: 2 hours 30 minutes
Start at: St-Sulpice Métro station
End at: St-Germain-des-Prés Métro station

HOW TO GET THERE

Take the Métro to St-Sulpice or buses 63, 70, 84, 86, 87 or 96.

★Leave St-Sulpice Métro station and walk east along rue du Vieux Colombier to place St-Sulpice. Straight ahead of you, across the square, you will see the Église St-Sulpice (▷ 135).

❶ St-Sulpice displays a mixture of architectural styles and dominates the square and its elaborate fountain. It took 134 years and six architects to build the church and even now the south tower remains unfinished. Treasures inside include murals by Eugène Delacroix, an extravagant pulpit and one of the world's largest organs.

From the main entrance of the church, head south down rue Férou. At the end, cross over rue de Vaugirard and turn right. Almost immediately on your left is an entrance to the Jardin du Luxembourg (▷ 118–119).

❷ The landscaped Jardin du Luxembourg, commissioned by Marie de Médicis in the early 17th century, is one of the most popular parks in Paris. The Palais du Luxembourg, within its grounds, is now home to the French Senate.

Leave the gardens by the northern exit, to the right of the Palais du Luxembourg. Cross the road and head north along rue Rotrou. Pass the neoclassical Odéon Théâtre de l'Europe on the right. When you reach place de l'Odéon turn around to admire the theatre's colonnaded facade. Walk across the square and carry on up rue de l'Odéon to the crossroads, carrefour de l'Odéon.

Continue north a short distance until you reach boulevard St-Germain. Cross over, turn right and then almost immediately left into the cour du Commerce St-André.

❸ This cobblestone passage was built in 1776 on the site of a tennis court. It became a hive of revolutionary activity, with Jean-Paul Marat printing his pamphlet at number eight, the anatomy professor Dr. Guillotin perfecting his 'philanthropic beheading machine' at number nine and revolutionary leader Georges Danton living at number twenty.

Turn left into rue St-André des Arts and almost immediately right at the carrefour de Buci into rue Dauphine. Walk to the end of this bustling street and you arrive at the Pont Neuf, the oldest bridge in Paris. Turn left, before the bridge, onto quai de Conti. On your left is the neoclassical Hôtel de la Monnaie.

4 The workshops of the Paris Mint were here from the 18th century. The *hôtel* now houses the Musée de la Monnaie (▷ 120), a coin and medal museum. Around 2,000 coins and hundreds of medals and tokens are on display, as well as prints, documents and engravings. The museum also explains minting techniques through the ages.

Cross over the road to walk along the edge of the Seine. Next to the Hôtel de la Monnaie, on the left, you'll see the splendid dome of the Institut de France (▷ 116), home of the Académie Française. Notice the beautiful Pont des Arts footbridge, composed of seven steel arches, spanning the river to the Louvre. As you walk along you'll see the *bouquinistes* (booksellers) lining the banks of the Seine.

5 Their green bookstalls, selling second-hand books, postcards and prints, have a history dating back 300 years. In the early days, the booksellers used to transport their goods in wheelbarrows across the river to sell them on the banks of the Seine.

Head south down rue Bonaparte. On your right you'll pass the most celebrated fine art school in Paris, the École Nationale Supérieure des Beaux-Arts. Turn left into rue Jacob and then right into rue de Furstemberg. At number 6, in the corner of a charming little square, you'll find the Musée National Eugène Delacroix (▷ 120).

6 The artist Eugène Delacroix lived in St-Germain-des-Prés for the last six years of his life, from 1857 to 1863. His apartment has been converted into a museum, where you can see some of his paintings and sketches, in addition to his personal possessions.

Head left down rue de l'Abbaye. Continue to head east on rue de Bourbon le Chateau. When you reach rue de Buci, home to one of Paris's most popular markets (closed Mondays), turn right. Turn right again and walk along boulevard St-Germain, passing the southern side of the Église St-Germain-des-Prés (▷ 134) on your right. Continue until you come to place St-Germain-des-Prés; turn

Opposite Café de Flore is a good place for refreshments at the end of the walk
Above *Street-side tables outside Les Deux Magots café on boulevard St-Germain*

right into the square, where you'll find the entrance to the church.

7 The Église St-Germain-des-Prés dates from the 11th century and is the oldest church in Paris. It is named after Germain, bishop of Paris in the sixth century, who was one of the administrators of the abbey originally on the site.

The walk ends at St-Germain-des-Prés Métro station, on boulevard St-Germain, on the southern side of the church.

WHEN TO GO

It is best to do this walk during the day, when the museums, gardens and churches are open. The market in the rue de Buci is closed on Mondays.

WHERE TO EAT

Two of the city's most famous and historic cafés can be found at the end of the walk (▷ 141). Les Deux Magots is on place St-Germain-des-Prés and Café de Flore is on boulevard St-Germain. There are also plenty of other cafés and restaurants along the route.

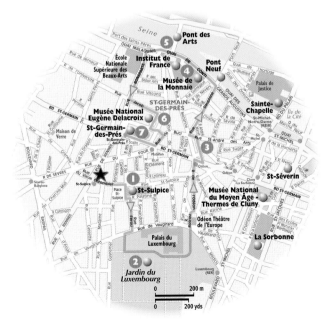

SHOPPING

ANDROUËT
www.androuet.com

Androuët stocks more than 200 types of cheese, serving discerning Parisian clients since 1909. All cheeses are made with unpasteurized milk and the staff offer advice on storing and serving.
✚ 146 N10 ✉ 134 rue Mouffetard, 75005 ☎ 01 45 87 85 05 🕓 Tue–Fri 9.30–1, 4–7.30, Sat 9.30–7.30, Sun 9.30–1.30 🚇 Censier-Daubenton

DE VINIS ILLUSTRIBUS
www.devinis.fr

This exceptional wine store sells rare vintages from 1811 to the present day, along with everyday wines and all the oenophile paraphernalia. A well-worn staircase leads down to the cavernous stone cellars dating from 1636, where the oldest vintages are stored.
✚ 146 N9 ✉ 48 rue de la Montagne Ste-Geneviève, 75005 ☎ 01 43 36 12 12 🕓 Tue–Sat 2–7 🚇 Maubert-Mutualité

DIPTIQUE
www.diptyqueparis.com

These are the ultimate in beautifully crafted candles and come in 48 different perfumes. They also have a divine range of eaux de cologne.
✚ 146 N8 ✉ 34 boulevard St-Germain, 75005 ☎ 01 43 26 77 44 🕓 Mon–Sat 10–7 🚇 Maubert-Mutualité

MARCHÉ DU BOULEVARD RASPAIL
There's a general market with fruit, vegetables and general produce, plus a Sunday organics market.
✚ 146 K8 ✉ boulevard Raspail, 75006 🕓 General market: Tue–Fri 7–2.20, organic market: Sun 9–1.30 🚇 Rennes

MARCHÉ AUX FLEURS
You'll find plants and flowers displayed near the banks of the river or in greenhouses, with specialist stands (such as orchids or herb gardens). On Sunday it becomes the Marché aux Oiseaux (Bird Market).
✚ 146 M7 ✉ place Louis Lépine, Île de la Cité, 75004 🕓 Mon–Sat 8–7.30; bird market, Sun 8–7 🚇 Cité

OLIVIERS & CO
www.oliviers-co.com

Dedicated to olive oil, Oliviers & Co stocks vintages from all over the Mediterranean, plus many products in which it is a core ingredient (tapenade, olive-oil biscuits). The company produces a range of organic cosmetics said to be high in antioxidants.
✚ 146 N8 ✉ 81 rue St-Louis en l'Île, 75004 ☎ 01 40 46 89 37 🕓 Daily 11–1.30, 2.30–7.30 🚇 Sully Morland, Pont Marie

POILÂNE
www.poilane.fr

Some of the best French bread is still baked here from secret family recipes, guarded by the Poilânes since the 1930s. The country nut-and-raisin bread is a must.
✚ 146 L8 ✉ 8 rue du Cherche-Midi, 75006 ☎ 01 45 48 42 59 🕓 Mon–Sat 7.15am–8.15pm 🚇 Sèvres-Babylone, St-Sulpice

SHAKESPEARE AND COMPANY
www.shakespeareandcompany.com

Shakespeare and Company (▷ 22) is named after the famous bookshop started by Sylvia Beach in the 1920s. This place is special, with its old floor tiles, little well full of coins and floor-to-ceiling shelves. The stock includes new and used books. There is a small library upstairs.
✚ 146 M8 ✉ 37 rue de la Bûcherie, 75005 ☎ 01 43 25 40 93 🕓 Mon–Sat 10am–11pm, Sun 11–11 🚇 St-Michel

Above *The flower market on Île de la Cité*

SONIA RYKIEL

www.soniarykiel.com

This is the designer's main ready-to-wear boutique: sexy, fluid clothes and lingerie, and accessories. The menswear shop is across the street.

🚇 146 L8 ✉ 175 boulevard St-Germain, 75006 ☎ 01 49 54 60 60 🕐 Mon–Sat 10.30–7 🚇 St-Germain-des-Prés, Sèvres Babylone

TASCHEN

www.taschen.com

This art bookshop is itself a work of art: Its interior was designed by Philippe Starck. Publications by this German publishing house include books on photography, design, painting and eroticism.

🚇 146 M8 ✉ 2 rue de Buci, 75006 ☎ 01 40 51 79 22 🕐 Mon–Thu 11–8, Fri–Sat 11am–midnight 🚇 Odéon

ENTERTAINMENT AND NIGHTLIFE

CAFÉ DE FLORE

www.cafedeflore.fr

Once the haunt of celebrated writers and philosophers (Jean-Paul Sartre, Simone de Beauvoir, Albert Camus and Samuel Beckett used to be regulars), this café welcomes customers for a snack or a drink in elegant surroundings.

🚇 146 L8 ✉ 172 boulevard St-Germain, 75006 ☎ 01 45 48 55 26 🕐 Daily 7am–2am 🚇 St-Germain-des-Prés

LE CHAMPO

www.lechampo.com

Numerous retrospectives of cult classics explore the work of directors such as the Marx Brothers, Claude Chabrol and Jacques Tati. Films are shown in their original language on two screens.

🚇 146 M8 ✉ 51 rue des Écoles, 75005 ☎ 01 43 54 51 60 🕐 Daily 1.50–10 ✋ Adult €8, under 20 €6 🚇 St-Michel, Odéon, Cluny-La Sorbonne

CURIO PARLOR

www.curioparlor.com

This stylized 'speakeasy' is one of the cool places of the *arrondissement* with an interior like a Victorian gentlemen's study. It also

houses the only Nikka (Japanese whisky) Bar outside Japan.

🚇 146 N8 ✉ 16 rue Bernardins, 75005 ☎ 01 44 07 12 47 🕐 Tue–Wed 8pm–2am, Thu–Sat 8pm–4am 🚇 Maubert-Mutualité

LES DEUX MAGOTS

www.lesdeuxmagots.fr

A hub for philosophers and artists in the 1950s, famously of Jean-Paul Sartre and Simone de Beauvoir and popular with Hemingway, this establishment has kept some of its literary feel thanks to the proximity of La Hune bookshop.

🚇 146 L7 ✉ 6 place St-Germain-des-Prés, 75006 ☎ 01 45 48 55 25 🕐 Daily 7.30am–1am 🚇 St-Germain des-Prés

LES ÉDITEURS

www.lesediteurs.fr

Les Éditeurs is frequented by the literary crowd. The warm, wooden interior, comfortable red velvet banquettes and subdued lighting make the perfect setting for reading—you're invited to pick up a book from the in-house library. The café is the venue of famous literary awards, including the Prix des Éditeurs.

🚇 146 M8 ✉ 4 carrefour de l'Odéon, 75006 ☎ 01 43 26 67 76 🕐 Daily 8am–2am 🚇 Odéon

MUSÉE NATIONAL DU MOYEN ÂGE–THERMES DE CLUNY

www.musee-moyenage.fr

This medieval mansion is home to a museum (▷ 122–123), and it also hosts classical and chamber music concerts. It's a unique setting.

🚇 146 M8 ✉ 6 place Paul-Painlevé, 75005 ☎ 01 53 73 78 16 🕐 Performances: Fri 12.30pm, Sat 4pm and occasional evenings at 7pm ✋ Free with admission to museum (€7.50). Evening performances €16 🚇 Cluny-La Sorbonne

PARADIS LATIN

www.paradislatin.com

Built by Gustave Eiffel at the same time as his tower, this cabaret found a new lease of life in the late 1970s. Its show Paradis d'Amour is dedicated to love in the true French cabaret tradition.

🚇 146 N8 ✉ 28 rue Cardinal Lemoine, 75005 ☎ 01 43 25 28 28 🕐 Wed–Mon 1.30pm, 8pm; show at 9.30pm ✋ Show: €55. Lunch and show: €65. Dinner and show: €149 🚇 Cardinal-Lemoine

THÉÂTRE MOUFFETARD

www.theatremouffetard.com

This theatre aims to appeal to all tastes and all ages with plays by classic and contemporary writers, shows sparkling with music and humour, and lively puppet shows.

🚇 146 N9 ✉ 73 rue Mouffetard, 75005 ☎ 01 43 31 11 99 🕐 Tue–Sat 7 or 9pm; children's show Wed 2.15pm, Sat 3pm and school holidays ✋ Evening: €14–€24; children's performances: €10 🚇 Place Monge

SPORTS AND ACTIVITIES

PISCINE JEAN TARIS

This pool's main attractions are its location and the view onto a leafy garden. There is one big pool and a smaller one for children. Credit cards are not accepted.

🚇 146 N9 ✉ 16 rue Thouin, 75005 ☎ 01 55 42 81 90 🕐 Tue, Thu 7–8.30, 11.30–1.30; Wed 7–8.30, 11.30–6; Fri 7–8.30, 11.30–1.30, 5–8; Sat 7–6; Sun 8–6 ✋ €3 🚇 Cardinal Lemoine

HEALTH AND BEAUTY

HAMMAM DE LA MOSQUÉE DE PARIS

▷ 117.

RASA YOGA RIVE GAUCHE

www.rasa-yogarivegauche.com

The well-established spa concentrates on yoga (including sessions for children), plus massage.

🚇 146 M8 ✉ 21 rue St-Jacques, 75005 ☎ 01 43 54 14 59 🕐 Mon, Wed, Fri 7am–9.30pm, Tue, Thu 10–9.30, Sat 10–4.30, Sun 11–6.30 ✋ Yoga class €20, 1-hour massage €70–€95 🚇 Cluny-La Sorbonne

FOR CHILDREN

MUSÉUM NATIONAL D'HISTOIRE NATURELLE

▷ 121.

THÉÂTRE MOUFFETARD

▷ above.

EATING

PRICES AND SYMBOLS
The prices given are the average for a two-course lunch (L) and a three-course dinner (D) for one person, without drinks. The wine price is for the least expensive bottle.

For a key to the symbols, ▷ 2.

ALCAZAR
www.alcazar.fr
English designer Terence Conran's bar-restaurant is popular with a fashionable Parisian crowd for some of the best fish in the capital. The menu also includes non-fish dishes such as grilled lamb. Upstairs there's a lounge-bar where international DJs take to the decks. Alcazar is also worth a visit for its Sunday brunch, which comes with the option of a head massage.

➕ 146 L8 ✉ 62 rue Mazarine, 75006, St-Germain-des-Prés ☎ 01 53 10 19 99 🕙 Sun–Thu 12–2.30, 7–1; Fri–Sat 12–2.30, 7–2 🖐 L €40, D €55, Wine €23 🚇 Odéon, St-Michel

AU RELAIS LOUIS XIII
www.relaislouis13.com
Manuel Martinez—previously chef at La Tour d'Argent (▷ 143)—set up his own restaurant in this 16th-century town house in 1996. You

can dine in the vaulted cellar, the oak-beamed main dining room or in the upstairs salon. The rich menu includes lobster, foie gras, cep ravioli, and vanilla and whisky *millefeuilles*.

➕ 146 M7 ✉ 8 rue des Grands-Augustins, 75006, St-Germain-des-Prés ☎ 01 43 26 75 96 🕙 Tue–Sat 12.15–2.30, 7.30–10.30 🖐 L €70, D €130, Wine €45 🚇 Odéon

BOUILLON RACINE
www.bouillon-racine.com
The bright and airy dining room is in a listed historic building, with a dazzling art nouveau interior. The excellent Belgian food includes *waterzooi* (a rich traditional Belgian soup made with herbs, vegetables and chicken, thickened with cream and egg yolk) and shrimp croquettes. As you would expect in a Belgian restaurant, there is a comprehensive range of beers.

➕ 146 M8 ✉ 3 rue Racine, 75006, Latin Quarter ☎ 01 44 32 15 60 🕙 Daily 12–12 (last orders 11) 🖐 L €25, D €35, Wine €25 🚇 Cluny-La Sorbonne, Odéon

COFFEE PARISIEN
As the name suggests, this is a hybrid of a place—a Parisian bistro serving American diner-style food,

in a picturesque pedestrian-only street. It's an excellent place for a lazy Sunday brunch, with American classics such as eggs Benedict, chicken wings, pastrami sandwiches and one of the best cheeseburgers in Paris.

➕ 146 L8 ✉ 4 rue Princesse, 75006, St-Germain-des-Prés ☎ 01 43 54 18 18 🕙 Daily 12–12 🖐 L €18, D €22, Coffee €3 🚇 Mabillon, St-Germain-des-Prés

LE COMPTOIR
www.hotel-paris-relais-saint-germain.com
Yves Cameborde is one of the city's most celebrated restaurateurs, and Le Comptoir, in the heart of the Left Bank, is one of a growing trend of gastro-bistros, championing simple food cooked well. There are no reservations for lunch (but try arriving after Parisians have finished eating, at around 2.30–3pm). You'll need to book well ahead to get a table for the gastronomic dinner.

➕ 146 M8 ✉ Hôtel Relais St-Germain, 9 carrefour de l'Odéon, 75006, St-Germain-des-Prés ☎ 01 44 27 07 97 🕙 Daily 12–12; bistro service 12–3 🖐 L €15, D €35, Wine €20 🚇 Odéon

Above *The rustic-style interior of Nos Ancêtres les Gaulois*

LA COUPOLE

www.flobrasseries.com

Dine in this Parisian institution and you'll be following in the footsteps of Pablo Picasso, Ernest Hemingway and Man Ray. The elegant art deco brasserie is a symbol of Montparnasse's artistic heyday. The bright and airy dining room has 33 fresco-adorned pillars, an imposing sculpture and Cubist floor tiles. You'll find all the brasserie classics on the menu, including seafood platters, sauerkraut and steak tartare, not forgetting the famous curried lamb.

✚ 146 L9 ✉ 102 boulevard du Montparnasse, 75014, Montparnasse ☎ 01 43 20 14 20 🕐 Sun–Thu 8.30am–10.30am, noon–1am, Fri–Sat 8.30am–10.30am, noon–1.30am 🖐 L €25, D €40, Wine €20 🚇 Vavin

JACQUES CAGNA

www.jacques-cagna.com

For more than 30 years, Jacques Cagna has been reinventing gourmet cuisine. Here you can expect delicacies such as veal rib in a ginger and lime sauce, and grilled langoustines. The restaurant, in a 17th-century town house, has Flemish paintings.

✚ 146 M7 ✉ 14 rue des Grands-Augustins, 75006, St-Germain-des-Prés ☎ 01 43 26 49 39 🕐 Tue–Fri 12–2, 7.30–10.15, Mon, Sat–Sun 7.30–10.15 🖐 L €60, D €110, Wine €30 🚇 St-Michel, Odéon

NOS ANCÊTRES LES GAULOIS

www.nosancetreslesgaulois.com

This fun Gallic-themed restaurant has been going since 1969. There's a rustic feel to the place, with stone walls, beamed ceilings and decorative agricultural tools. The idea is simple—one fixed-price menu, including unlimited wine from the barrel, an all-you-can-eat buffet of starters (cold meats and salads) and a choice of grilled kebabs, lamb chops, steaks and other meats from the open fireplace.

✚ 146 N8 ✉ 39 rue St-Louis en l'Île, 75004, Île St-Louis ☎ 01 46 33 66 07 🕐 Daily 7pm–2am 🖐 D €40 (including wine) 🚇 Pont-Marie

LE PETIT ST-BENOÎT

www.petit-st-benoit.com

This popular bistro is a St-Germain classic founded in 1901, and the look has barely changed since the 1930s when it was the haunt of writers and intellectuals whose pictures still hang on the wall. The menu includes soups, terrines and dishes such as rabbit with mustard. You can sit outside in summer. Credit cards are not accepted.

✚ 146 L7 ✉ 4 rue St-Benoît, 75006, St-Germain-des-Prés ☎ 01 42 60 27 92 🕐 Sep–Jul Mon–Sat 12–2.30, 7–10.30. Closed Aug 🖐 L €25, D €35, Wine €18 🚇 St-Germain-des-Prés

LE PROCOPE

www.procope.com

This former café, founded in 1686, now an elegant dining room, was frequented by the philosophers Voltaire and Rousseau. Benjamin Franklin is said to have drafted part of the American constitution here. The menu includes grilled beef fillet, coq au vin and basil sorbet. Fish fans can choose from mackerel terrine with potatoes, fish soup or a rich seafood platter.

✚ 146 M8 ✉ 13 rue de l'Ancienne-Comédie, 75006, St-Germain-des-Prés ☎ 01 40 46 79 00 🕐 Sun–Thu 11.30am–midnight, Fri–Sat 11.30am–1am 🖐 L €35, D €50, Wine €20 🚇 Odéon

LE REMINET

www.lereminet.com

This tiny restaurant is situated on the Left Bank in the picturesque old part of the Latin Quarter, a stone's throw from Notre-Dame. The inventive cuisine includes tasty modern-style dishes and traditional offerings such as snails. Note that Le Reminet is one of the rare bistros in Paris to be open on Sunday.

✚ 146 N8 ✉ 3 rue des Grands-Degrés, 75005, Latin Quarter ☎ 01 44 07 04 24 🕐 Daily 12–3, 7.30–11 🖐 L €25, D €35, Wine €18 🚇 Maubert-Mutualité

LA TOUR D'ARGENT

www.latourdargent.com

A Parisian institution since 1582, this is one of the best restaurants in France, if not the world. La Tour d'Argent sits on the sixth floor of a beautiful building overlooking the Seine, offering panoramic views. This is exquisite French cuisine at its finest, with lobster quenelles and duck being a couple of the well-known dishes. The wine cellar is exceptional.

✚ 146 N8 ✉ 15–17 quai de la Tournelle, 75005, Latin Quarter ☎ 01 43 54 23 31 🕐 Tue–Sun 12–1.30, 8–9.30 🖐 L €120, D €150, Wine €59 🚇 Pont Marie, Maubert-Mutualité

LA TRUFFIÈRE

www.la-truffiere.fr

Here you can dine by candlelight in the picturesque 17th-century vaulted cellar or in the attractive dining room with exposed beams. The gourmet French cuisine includes ingredients from southwest France, such as foie gras, duck and, above all, truffles. Start with duck foie gras with nuts, red wine and ginger jelly and baked apple, followed by *confit* of duck with mashed potato cake and black truffles; and for dessert, you could try a hot black truffle soufflé or caramelized custard cream with truffle. There is a good selection of wines and brandies.

✚ 146 N9 ✉ 4 rue Blainville, 75005, Latin Quarter ☎ 01 46 33 29 82 🕐 Tue–Sat 12–2, 7–10.30 🖐 L €60, D €80 (à la carte), Wine €17 🚇 Place Monge

ZE KITCHEN GALERIE

www.zekitchengalerie.fr

The deep-chestnut wooden floor adds warmth to the contemporary, functional setting of this trendy restaurant located close to the river. Chef William Ledeuil, who trained with Guy Savoy, can be seen at work in his kitchen: His innovative fusion cuisine combines Mediterranean flavours with an Asian touch and his menu changes every month.

✚ 146 M7 ✉ 4 rue des Grands-Augustins, 75006, St-Germain-des-Prés ☎ 01 44 32 00 32 🕐 Mon–Fri 12–2.30, 7–11, Sat 7–11 🖐 L €27, D €80, Wine €21 🚇 St-Michel

PRICES AND SYMBOLS

Prices are the lowest and highest for a double room for one night. Breakfast is included unless noted otherwise. All the hotels listed accept credit cards unless otherwise stated. Note that rates vary widely throughout the year.

For a key to the symbols, ▷ 2.

L'ATELIER SAINT GERMAIN

www.ateliersaintgermain.com
This 3-star hotel pays tribute to 1930s Montparnasse, with period furniture and mosaic reproductions of 1930s paintings in the bathrooms. Artists' haunts such as La Coupole (▷ 143) and Le Dôme brasseries are nearby. Facilities include a laundry service, room service, cable TV, WiFi, hairdryer and minibar.

➕ 146 L9 ✉ 49 rue Vavin, 75006, St-Germain-des-Prés ☎ 01 46 33 60 00 ✋ €100–€170, excluding breakfast ① 17 ⑤ ⬢ Vavin, Montparnasse

FAMILIA HÔTEL

www.hotel-paris-familia.com
This mid-19th-century mansion makes a comfortable 2-star base. There's period-style furniture in the public areas, plus wall frescoes.

A Continental breakfast is served downstairs. Rooms, some with balconies, are decorated in French style and come with WiFi facilities, satellite TV, fridge and hairdryer. There is guarded parking close by at an extra cost (€20 per day).

➕ 146 N9 ✉ 11 rue des Écoles, 75005, Latin Quarter ☎ 01 43 54 55 27 ✋ €99–€120, excluding breakfast ① 30 ⑤ ⬢ Jussieu, Cardinal Lemoine

GRAND HÔTEL DES BALCONS

www.balcons.com
This 2-star hotel is close to the Jardin du Luxembourg. Outside, there are flower-filled balconies; inside, the lobby and communal areas have an early 1900s feel, with period furniture and stained-glass windows. The bright and airy bedrooms have WiFi connection, cable and satellite TV and hairdryer.

➕ 146 M8 ✉ 3 rue Casimir-Delavigne, 75006, St-Germain-des-Prés ☎ 01 46 34 78 50 ✋ €112–€127, excluding breakfast ① 50 ⬢ Odéon

L'HÔTEL

www.l-hotel.com
This deluxe 4-star hotel, in a 19th-century pavilion, was fully renovated at the turn of the millennium. The

Above Historic hotels with period French detail abound in this region of the city

exuberantly elegant interior is by Jacques Garcia and the well-equipped rooms are named after famous people, such as Marco Polo, Mistinguett and Oscar Wilde (who breathed his last at this hotel in 1900). The restaurant (closed Sun, Mon and during Aug) has an impressive dome.

➕ 146 L7 ✉ 13 rue des Beaux-Arts, 75006, St-Germain-des-Prés ☎ 01 44 41 99 00 ✋ €245–€370, excluding breakfast ① 16 rooms, 4 suites ⑤ ⬢ Indoor ⬢ St-Germain-des-Prés

HÔTEL DE L'ABBAYE ST-GERMAIN

www.hotel-abbaye.com
Calm prevails at this 4-star hotel, on the site of a former abbey. The salon and most of the rooms look out onto a terrace; four suites have private terraces. The elegant interior has fine furniture and there is an antique fireplace in the salon. The hotel is close to the Jardin du Luxembourg. Facilities include a bar, a courtyard garden, room service, car rental and a laundry service. Bedrooms have

hairdryers, WiFi connections, safes and satellite TV.

🕂 146 L8 ✉ 10 rue Cassette, 75006 St-Germain-des-Prés ☎ 01 45 44 38 11 ✋ €246–€266 ⓘ 42 rooms, 4 suites 🅢 Ⓜ St-Sulpice, Sèvres-Babylone

HÔTEL ATLANTIS ST-GERMAIN-DES-PRÉS

www.atlantis-hotel.com

Most of the bright and airy rooms in this 2-star hotel face onto pretty place St-Sulpice. All have been beautifully decorated with soft tones, fine furniture and quilted bedspreads, and have telephone, cable and satellite TV, internet connection and a hairdryer. The communal areas are elegant and there is a grandfather clock in the breakfast room.

🕂 146 L8 ✉ 4 rue du Vieux-Colombier, 75006, St-Germain-des-Prés ☎ 01 45 48 31 81 ✋ €140–€210, excluding breakfast ⓘ 27 🅢 St-Sulpice

HÔTEL CLAUDE BERNARD

www.hotelclaudebernardparis.com

This 3-star hotel has a flamboyant, red lacquered facade and an elegant interior. Bright tones and flowers create a warm, welcoming atmosphere throughout, and there are fine fabrics and furniture in the bedrooms, which have balconies, WiFi and satellite TV. There is a bar, restaurant and internet booth.

🕂 146 M8 ✉ 43 rue des Écoles, 75005, Latin Quarter ☎ 01 43 26 32 52 ✋ €218–€228, excluding breakfast ⓘ 34 🅢 Ⓜ Maubert-Mutualité

HÔTEL DES DEUX ÎLES

www.deuxiles-paris-hotel.com

A 17th-century mansion on the picturesque Île St-Louis is home to this 3-star hotel. Provençal fabrics and painted rattan furniture enliven the comfortable bedrooms, which have cable TV and a hairdryer. WiFi connection is available. Paris's most famous ice-cream store, Berthillon, is nearby.

🕂 146 N8 ✉ 59 rue St-Louis en l'Île, 75004, Île St-Louis ☎ 01 43 26 13 35 ✋ €205, excluding breakfast ⓘ 17 🅢 Ⓜ Pont-Marie, St-Michel

HÔTEL DU GLOBE

www.hotelduglobeparis.com

A 2-star hotel with this much character is hard to find in Paris. There are beamed ceilings and antique furniture in the bedrooms and 18th-century bergère armchairs, and an 18th-century mirror in the salon. Facilities for the 21st century include TV, WiFi connection and phone. The hotel has the added bonus of being convenient for the Jardin du Luxembourg.

🕂 146 M8 ✉ 15 rue des Quatre-Vents, 75006, St-Germain-des-Prés ☎ 01 43 26 35 50 ✋ €99–€170, excluding breakfast ⓘ 14 Ⓜ Odéon

HÔTEL DES GRANDES ÉCOLES

www.hotel-grandes-ecoles.com

An oasis of peace in the lively Latin Quarter, this gem of a 3-star hotel is at the end of a cul-de-sac, with its own garden. It is decorated in elegant country-house style with wicker chairs and lace tablecloths in the breakfast room and floral wallpaper and quilted bedspreads in the bedrooms. Some rooms sleep up to four people. Hotel facilities include a babysitting service, a safe, WiFi and 15 covered parking spaces (extra fee). You can take your breakfast in the garden.

🕂 146 N9 ✉ 75 rue du Cardinal Lemoine, 75005, Latin Quarter ☎ 01 43 26 79 23 ✋ €118–€145, excluding breakfast ⓘ 51 Ⓜ Cardinal-Lemoine, Place Monge

HÔTEL MADISON

www.hotel-madison.com

Albert Camus finished writing his famous novel *L'Étranger (The Outsider*; 1942) at this elegant 3-star hotel. The celebrated café, Les Deux-Magots is opposite. The hotel has a beautiful 18th-century style salon with bergère armchairs, tapestries and wood panels, while the bedrooms have antique furniture, satellite TV, free internet access, minibar, safe and hairdryer.

🕂 146 L8 ✉ 143 boulevard St-Germain, 75006, St-Germain-des-Prés ☎ 01 40 51 60 00 ✋ €190–€310, excluding breakfast ⓘ 53 rooms and suites 🅢 Ⓜ St-Germain-des-Prés

HÔTEL LA PERLE

www.hotel-paris-laperle.com

This smart 3-star hotel, in a picturesque street near place St-Sulpice, is in a 17th-century mansion with its own courtyard. Bright tones add a contemporary note to the otherwise classic interior, which has fleur-de-lys carpets and beamed ceilings. Facilities include WiFi connection, cable and satellite TV, private safe and a laundry service.

🕂 146 L8 ✉ 14 rue des Canettes, 75006, St-Germain-des-Prés ☎ 01 43 29 10 10 ✋ €199–€250, excluding breakfast ⓘ 38 🅢 Ⓜ St-Germain-des-Prés, St-Sulpice, Mabillon

RELAIS ST-JACQUES

www.relais-saint-jacques.com

This building was a stopover for pilgrims on the route to Santiago de Compostela, in northwest Spain. It's now a stylish 4-star hotel with a 1920s-style bar and a Louis XV-style salon. The bedrooms are bright, airy and comfortable with 18th-century furniture. Some have views of the nearby Panthéon, while others have a jacuzzi in the bathroom. WiFi connection is available in the bedrooms and the lounge. Courtesy transport to the airport is provided.

🕂 146 M9 ✉ 3 rue de l'Abbé-de-l'Epée, 75005, Latin Quarter ☎ 01 53 73 26 00 ✋ €159–€279, excluding breakfast ⓘ 21 rooms, 1 suite 🅢 Ⓡ RER Luxembourg

LES RIVES DE NOTRE-DAME

www.rivesdenotredame.com

This 4-star hotel, housed in a small 16th-century building, overlooks the Seine and has wonderful views of the Île de la Cité. Beamed ceilings, marble tiling, tapestries and fine wrought-iron furniture are reminiscent of a Provençal or Tuscan villa. The bedrooms are large and two of them have sofas which can be converted into extra beds for children under 12 at no extra cost.

🕂 146 M8 ✉ 15 quai St-Michel, 75005, Latin Quarter ☎ 01 43 54 81 16 ✋ €175–€320, excluding breakfast ⓘ 9 rooms, 1 suite 🅢 Ⓜ St-Michel

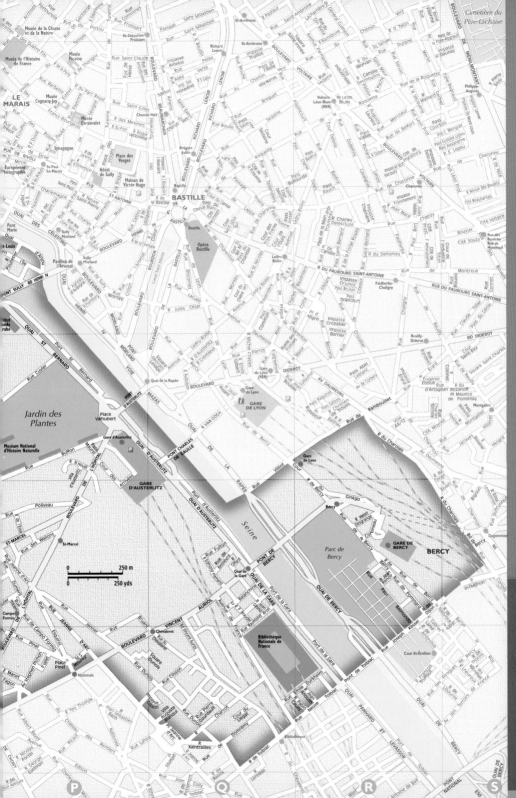

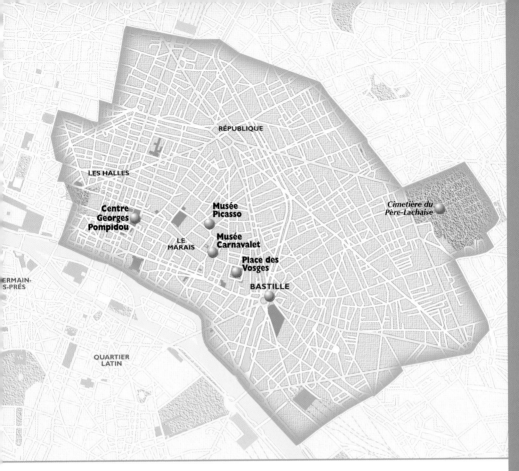

MARAIS AND BASTILLE

The Marais was once a marshland which became a fashionable residential district before its decline after World War II and, thanks to late-20th-century restoration, its sparkle has returned. At its heart is the early 17th-century place des Vosges, perhaps the most beautiful square in the world—certainly the oldest in Paris—and a perfect example of early town planning, creating tranquillity amid the city noise. Among the houses forming the square is Maison Victor Hugo, where visitors can explore the 19th-century literary world at the home of the great writer.

Like most of this area, the Bastille is now a bright, bustling district and home to the strikingly modern Opéra Bastille on the place de la Bastille, whose centrepiece is the Colonne de Juillet, topped by a winged *Spirit of Liberty*. The only reminder of the bloody events of 14 July 1789, when the Bastille prison was stormed, are paving stones marking its outline.

To the west is Les Halles, once known as the 'belly of Paris' for its food markets, but now a modern garden-cum-shopping-centre, close to the superb Renaissance Fontaine des Innocents. Marais, Bastille and Les Halles have a great many landmarks, galleries galore and tempting boutiques. Nearby the bizarre monument to modern art and Modernism, Centre Georges Pompidou is a treat for everyone, even the mildly curious; and the Musée Picasso features a huge number of the artist's works. Elsewhere, the Musée Carnivalet, set in two glorious mansions, affords visitors a first-hand experience of life in various exciting periods of Parisian history.

Over on the eastern edge of the region, the Cimetière Père-Lachaise is the world-famous burial ground, and the resting place of a veritable Who's Who of famous names from Molière to Edith Piaf. Close by is the Musée Edith Piaf where visitors can immerse themselves in her life and music.

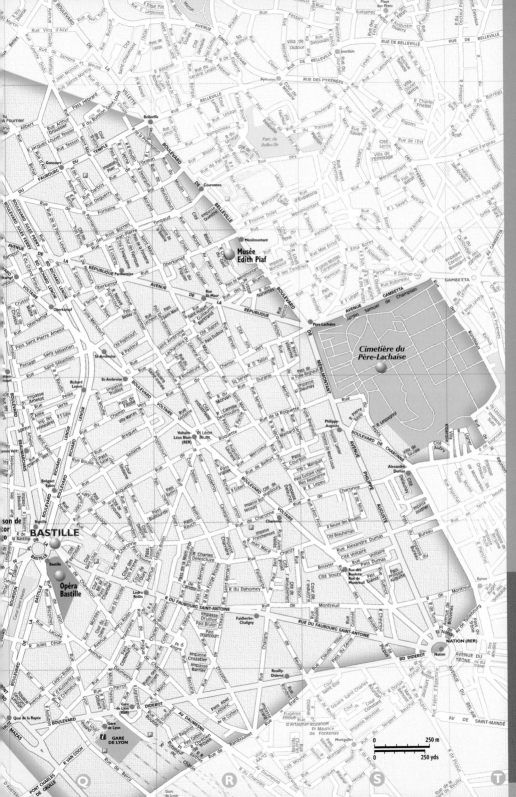

Musée
Edith Piaf

Cimetière du
Père-Lachaise

BASTILLE

Opéra
Bastille

GARE
DE LYON

250 m

250 yds

BASTILLE

Frenetic place de la Bastille, now bustling with street cafés and traffic, witnessed one of the pivotal events in France's history. Where in-line skaters and pedestrians now jostle for space, an angry Revolutionary mob stormed the Bastille prison in 1789 in a violent riot that signalled the bloody start of the French Revolution.

The Bastille was built in 1380 as a fortress guarding the eastern entrance to Paris. It later became a jail for political prisoners, including the Marquis de Sade and Voltaire. Nothing remains of the building, although paving stones mark its outline. A visual reminder of Paris's turbulent past is the Colonne de Juillet (July Column), which stands 50m (164ft) tall on place de la Bastille's busy roundabout. It was constructed in 1840 to commemorate the victims of another revolt, the 1830 Uprising which brought the 'citizen king' Louis-Philippe of Orléans to power, and is topped by the winged *Spirit of Liberty*.

The area, Bastille, has been considerably spruced up over recent years and is now a lively nightspot, with a wide choice of restaurants and bars. During the day you can shop in the hectic streets that radiate from the Colonne de Juillet. There is also a marina, art galleries and the ultra-modern Opéra Bastille (▷ 168).

Walk along the rue de Lyon and you'll come to the Viaduc des Arts, an old railway viaduct converted into craft workshops and artists' showrooms (9–129 avenue Daumesnil).

To escape the noise and traffic of the Bastille, head down rue St-Antoine, then turn right into the peaceful rue de Birague. Here, browse in shops selling paintings, rugs and ceramics, then walk back in time through an archway to the tranquil place des Vosges (▷ 169).

INFORMATION

✚ 151 Q8 ✉ place de la Bastille and surrounding area, 75004/75011/75012
🚇 Bastille 🚌 20, 29, 65, 69, 76, 86, 87, 91 🍴 A good selection of cafés and restaurants (▷ 176–177)

Opposite *The* Spirit of Liberty *crowns the July Column at the centre of busy place de la Bastille*
Above *Exterior detail of the Opéra Bastille*

CANAL ST-MARTIN

The Canal St-Martin, in the eastern part of the city, makes a peaceful alternative to a boat trip along the Seine. You can also stroll along the tree-lined canal paths. The canal, which opened in 1825, is around 5km (3 miles) long and passes through nine locks and two swing bridges. It is spanned by many picturesque curved metal footbridges. The canal featured in the 2001 film *Le Fabuleux Destin d'Amélie Poulain* and in Marcel Carné's 1938 film *Hôtel du Nord*.

 150 P4 ✉ Canal St-Martin Ⓜ République, Jaurès, Jacques Bonsergent, Goncourt 🚌 26, 46, 75 🚢 Several companies offer boat trips including Canauxrama

CENTRE GEORGES POMPIDOU
▷ 156–161.

CIMETIÈRE DU PÈRE-LACHAISE
▷ 155.

FONTAINE DES INNOCENTS

Water has gushed from this superb Renaissance fountain since the mid-16th century, although the fountain has not always stood on this spot. It was originally on the corner of the rue St-Denis but was moved to its current position in the late 18th century to replace a cemetery that had run out of soil. The cemetery's 2 million skeletons were transferred to the Catacombes (▷ 73). After the move, the fountain gained a fourth side, carved by Augustin Pajou. The original cascade was designed by Pierre Lescot and sculpted by Jean Goujon.

➕ 150 N7 ✉ square des Innocents, near Forum des Halles, 75001 Ⓜ Châtelet, Les Halles 🚌 38, 47 (and all buses going along rue de Rivoli) 🚇 Châtelet-Les-Halles 🍴 Plenty in Les Halles ❓ Don't visit the fountain alone at night

LES HALLES

www.forum-des-halles.com

'The belly of Paris' (so said writer Émile Zola) is a curious mixture of old and new, picturesque and seedy. It started life as a food market in the 12th century and continued this role until 1969, when the superb 1860s pavilions were demolished. A decade later they were replaced by the garish Forum des Halles, a vast underground shopping mall.

You can also visit the church of St-Eustache (▷ 168) and the Fontaine des Innocents (▷ left).

The early atmosphere of Les Halles remains in the surrounding streets, especially cobbled rue Montorgueil.

➕ 150 N6 ✉ 75001 (the area bordered by rue Beaubourg, rue du Louvre, rue Réaumur and rue de Rivoli) Ⓜ Les Halles 🚌 29, 38, 47, 67, 74, 85 and all routes up rue de Rivoli 🚇 Châtelet-Les-Halles 🍴 Au Pied de Cochon, 6 rue Coquillère ❓ Les Halles can be seedy at night, especially rue St-Denis

HÔTEL DE VILLE

www.paris.fr

The imposing town hall, built in neo-Renaissance style in the late 19th century, is home to the city council. Its predecessor was destroyed in the 1871 uprising. Place de l'Hôtel de Ville is a pedestrian-only haven in the middle of a mammoth traffic jam. Fountains at either end drown out some of the noise and it's a pleasant spot to admire the 136 statues of historical characters that decorate the town hall's facades.

➕ 150 N7 ✉ place de l'Hôtel de Ville, 75004 ☎ 01 42 76 40 40 🕐 Weekly guided tours in French, by appointment only; call 01 42 76 54 04 at least 7 days in advance ✋ Free guided tours Ⓜ Hôtel de Ville 🚌 38, 47, 58, 67, 70, 72, 74, 75, 96

***Below** A bridge over Canal St-Martin*

MARAIS AND BASTILLE • SIGHTS

REGIONS

CIMETIÈRE DU PÈRE-LACHAISE

You can visit the graves of luminaries such as Frédéric Chopin, Marcel Proust and Oscar Wilde at this vast cemetery, on the eastern edge of the city. Père-Lachaise covers 44ha (108 acres) on the slopes of Ménilmontant and contains around 70,000 tombs. Tree-lined, cobbled paths are bordered by ornate tombstones and mausoleums. Far from gloomy, it is a great place for a peaceful walk on a sunny day.

ENGLISH ORIGINS

The cemetery is named after Louis XIV's confessor, Père La Chaise, who once owned the land here. It was designed by Brongniart in 1803 to echo an English-style garden. At first, the cemetery was not popular with the people of Paris, but once the graves of writers Molière and Jean de La Fontaine and the tragic lovers Abélard and Héloïse had been transferred here—precisely to encourage other Parisians to follow suit—it soon became the most fashionable place to be buried in the city.

RESTING PLACE OF THE FAMOUS

Père-Lachaise has become a place of pilgrimage—among the famous people buried here are composers Frédéric Chopin and Georges Bizet, Paris town planner Baron Haussmann, artists Amedeo Modigliani and Eugène Delacroix, singers Edith Piaf and Maria Callas, writers Marcel Proust, Honoré de Balzac and Oscar Wilde, actresses Simone Signoret and Sarah Bernhardt, actor Yves Montand and dancer Isadora Duncan.

Of the more recent graves, one of the most visited is that of Jim Morrison, lead singer of The Doors, who died in Paris in 1971 at the age of 27, probably from a drugs overdose. Fans still leave cigarette stubs, flowers and beads as a mark of respect. In August 2003, French actress Marie Trintignant was buried in the cemetery.

MEMORIALS

The Mur des Fédérés, in the eastern corner of the cemetery, marks the site of the Communards' tragic last stand in 1871, when the 147 survivors of the Commune were lined up against the wall and executed by a government firing squad. They were buried where they fell, in a communal grave. There are also poignant memorials to the victims of Nazi concentration camps and to the Resistance fighters killed in World War II.

INFORMATION

www.pere-lachaise.com

✚ 151 S6 ✉ boulevard de Ménilmontant, 75020 ☎ 01 55 25 82 10
🕐 Mid-Mar to early Nov Mon–Fri 8–6, Sat 8.30–6, Sun 9–6; early Nov to mid-Mar Mon–Fri 8–5.30, Sat 8.30–5.30, Sun 9–5.30; last entry 15 min before closing
✋ Free
🚇 Père Lachaise, Gambetta 🚌 61, 69
🎫 Guided tours in English Jul–Aug Sat 3pm (€6) ❓ You can buy a map from the news vendors or florists near the main entrances (avenue Père Lachaise and boulevard de Ménilmontant). You can also obtain a map from the cemetery office by the Père Lachaise entrance at 16 rue du Repos

TIPS

» Try to avoid visiting on very windy days as there is a danger of falling branches.
» The cemetery is huge and maps are dotted about, but if you are keen to visit particular graves obtain your own map beforehand (see above) to help you find your way.

Above *Finding tranquil solitude in Père-Lachaise cemetery*

CENTRE GEORGES POMPIDOU

INTRODUCTION

Paris's wackiest building houses one of the largest collections of modern art in the world. Around six million visitors each year come to see works by Pablo Picasso, Andy Warhol, Jackson Pollock and many others. You'll either love or hate the brazen design of the Centre Georges Pompidou and you may well feel the same about the contemporary art it displays. The venue has sparked controversy since it opened in 1977, gracing the historic heart of Paris with a modern building that resembles a giant air-conditioning system.

The main entrance, off the lively place Georges-Pompidou, takes you to level zero, where you can pick up a plan of the building and buy museum and exhibition tickets. If you want to visit both the Musée National d'Art Moderne and the temporary exhibitions, an all-gallery pass may be your best ticket option. To reach the museum, take the escalator to the entrance on level four, where you can rent an audioguide. Once inside the museum you may prefer to head straight to level five, which covers the first half of the 20th century, before returning to level four to tackle works from the 1960s to the present day. Temporary exhibitions are on levels one and six. If you need a break from the galleries, you can get a bite to eat in the café on level one or browse in the bookshop on level zero or the boutique on level one.

The Centre Georges Pompidou was the inspiration of Georges Pompidou, president of France from 1969 until his death in 1974. His vision was a venue where people could enjoy contemporary film, drama, dance, music and visual art. The outlandish complex took five years to build and was a controversial addition to Beaubourg, a run-down district of 18th- and 19th-century town houses. The French press variously called the new centre an 'artistic cathedral', a 'cultural supermarket', a 'factory', 'refinery' and, more endearingly the 'Pompidoulium'. Designers Renzo Piano and Richard Rogers turned the building inside out by placing its 'guts' (all the piping) on the outside. This piping was coded using different shades of paint, with yellow for

INFORMATION

www.centrepompidou.fr

Centre Georges Pompidou

✚ 150 N7 ✉ place Georges-Pompidou, 75004 ☎ 01 44 78 12 33 ◉ Centre Georges Pompidou: Wed–Mon 11–10. Musée National d'Art Moderne and exhibitions: Wed–Mon 11–9 (last ticket 8), Thu until 11 for some exhibitions (last ticket 10). Closed 1 May. Library: Mon–Fri 12–10, Sat–Sun 11–10 💷 Adult all-gallery pass €10–€12 (depending on period), under 18 (museum and exhibition) free. Musée National d'Art Moderne: free 1st Sun of month. Exhibitions: prices vary ⓜ Rambuteau, Hôtel de Ville 🚌 29, 38, 47, 75 🚆 Châtelet-Les-Halles 🎧 Audioguide €5 📖 €12 (French, English, German, Italian, Spanish, Japanese) 🍽 Georges restaurant on 6th floor, with good views; tel 01 44 78 47 99 ☕ On 1st floor 📚 Bookshops on levels 0, 4, 6; boutique on 1; post office on 0

Opposite *The colourful centrepiece of the Stravinsky Fountain*
Above *This futuristic building is the inspired home of modern art*

LEVEL -1
Live events, Cinema 2

LEVEL 0
Lobby, including information, ticket office, post office, bookshop, Children's Gallery

LEVEL 1
Library, Cinema 1, exhibitions, café, design boutique

LEVELS 2 AND 3
Library

LEVELS 4 AND 5
Musée National d'Art Moderne

LEVEL 6
Exhibitions, restaurant, bookshop

electrics, blue for air-conditioning, green for water and red for the elevators. Pompidou did not live to see the opening in 1977, but his vision for the arts venue proved sagacious—it was soon attracting 22,000 visitors a day, rivalling the Louvre in popularity. It closed for two years for renovation work in the autumn of 1997, reopening just in time for the new millennium.

This inside-out gallery and performance centre, while named after Georges Pompidou, was greatly influenced by his wife, Claude. There is a widely held belief that Pompidou would have preferred a more classical approach and did not approve of the jury's choice of architects. It was said to be Claude's passion for modern art, particularly the work of the artist Yves Klein, that was the inspiration for her husband's crowning, posthumous achievement, the Pompidou Centre. It was Claude who instigated the redecoration of the Elysée Palace with cutting-edge contemporary design of the times, including painted aluminium walls and furniture by designer Pierre Paulin. Claude Pompidou remained committed to her various causes after her husband's death in 1974 and was a frequent visitor to the Pompidou Centre until her death in 2007. 'You feel better when you emerge,' she said. 'It is the salvation side of art.' And, with some 6 million people passing through its doors every year, its popularity shows no sign of dwindling.

WHAT TO SEE

MUSÉE NATIONAL D'ART MODERNE

Where the Musée d'Orsay (▷ 80–83) leaves off, the Museum of Modern Art takes over, featuring works from 1905 to the present day. Up to 2,000 pieces from the 60,000-strong collection are on display at any one time and range from Cubism by Georges Braque and Picasso to works by Surrealist Man Ray and video art by Korean artist Nam June Paik. The approach to the museum is almost as unusual as the art it contains. You step onto an escalator inside a giant transparent tube that runs up the outside of the building. This takes you to the fourth floor, which covers 1960 to the present day, including works by the French New Realists, photographers, architects and video artists. There

Below *The external escalator gives a close-up view of the building's facade*

are also rooms dedicated to graphic art and new media. Pieces on display change each autumn (fall). For a chronological overview, start on the fifth floor, tame in comparison, which takes you back to the first half of the 20th century. The displays here change each spring and include works by Henri Matisse, Picasso, Braque, Juan Gris and Pollock. On both floors, glass walls flood the interior with natural light and give wonderful views.

Despite the vast area of the exhibition halls, only a selection of works is shown at any given time. The works on view are alternated according to a display renewal policy and new acquisitions can be seen from time to time. Regular rehangings allow visitors to see as much of the huge collection of 60,000 works as possible. Room 14, for example, showcases the birth of Surrealism in the 1920s, following Apollinaire's coining of the phrase and featuring works by Dalí, Giacometti, Miró and Picasso; room 34 hosts a range of works by American neo-Dadaists that formed the link between Abstract Expressionism and Pop Art, including artists Jasper Johns and Robert Rauschenberg; while room 40 has the collected works of photographer Lucien Hervé, who concentrated on architecture, including a close collaboration with Le Corbusier. Featured artists include Francis Alÿs (b.1959), a Belgian visual artist currently based in Mexico City.

PANORAMA

Don't miss the view over Paris from the top floor. Landmarks you can spot include Sacré-Cœur, the Eiffel Tower, Notre-Dame and the Panthéon.

Left *Browsing in the level zero bookshop*
Below *An image of Georges Pompidou whose vision for a centre for the arts inspired the building*

IRCAM
www.ircam.fr
✉ 1 place Igor Stravinsky ☎ 01 44 78
48 43 or 01 44 78 15 45 ⓒ Pick up a
brochure or check the website for concert
details

Atelier Brancusi
✉ 55 rue Rambuteau ☎ 01 44 78 12 33
ⓒ Wed–Mon 2–6 ✋ Free

TEMPORARY EXHIBITIONS AND OTHER ATTRACTIONS

Temporary exhibitions, on the first and sixth floors, are as much a draw as the Musée National d'Art Moderne. Recent themes have ranged from 'Hitchcock and Art' to the designer Philippe Starck.

After the extensive renovation for the new millennium, the Bibliothèque Publique d'Information (public library) opened and is the largest library in France. It occupies the third and the second floors of the centre, with two million books, language laboratories, audio-visual equipment, newspapers and magazines from different countries. The Media Collection includes 1,200 video tapes, sound documents, CD-ROMs and websites of artists spanning more than 40 years of the history of image and sound in the main movements of contemporary art, covering performance and body art, minimal art, conceptual and post-conceptual art. There is also a performance stage, cinema and auditorium and a Galerie des Enfants which has workshops for children (entry is free to under-18s).

Nearby, at 1 place Igor Stravinsky, the experimental music venue IRCAM (Institut de Recherche et Coordination Acoustique Musique) stages concerts, workshops and lectures. On the other side of the Pompidou, on rue Rambuteau, the Atelier Brancusi is a reconstruction of Romanian sculptor Constantin Brancusi's workshop. Brancusi moved to Paris in 1904 and his studio has been re-created as he left it when he died in 1957.

OUTDOORS

On a sunny day, the square outside comes alive with jugglers, mime artists, fire-eaters and musicians. The Stravinsky Fountain, set in place Igor Stravinsky, was designed by Jean Tinguely and Niki de Saint-Phalle as part of the Pompidou Centre development. The inspiration for it was Stravinsky's ballet *The Firebird* and the zany bird centrepiece spins and sprays water at anyone who dares walk past. Finally, look out for Paris's newest public clock in rue Brantôme, the vicious-looking brass-and-steel *Le Défenseur du Temps* (The Defender of Time). The defender fights beasts, representing earth, water and air, on the hour but is seen at his most ferocious at noon, 6pm and 10pm.

Above *Air-conditioning pipework is painted blue*

MODERN ART FOR THE UNINITIATED—AN EXPLANATION OF SOME OF THE MOVEMENTS OF MODERN ART

Abstract Expressionism: This movement stemmed from the US and had two main subdivisions—Action Painting and Colour Field Painting. Action Painting focused on the act of painting, rather than the finished piece of art. The most famous artist of this genre was Jackson Pollock, who used sticks and syringes to drip paint onto the canvas, forming abstract shapes.

Arte Povera: Literally 'poor art', Arte Povera is an Italian-based genre that involves the use of cheap, everyday materials to create sculptures or art installations. Artists include Mario Merz and Giuseppe Penone.

Cubism: Created by Picasso, Braque, Fernand Léger and Gris in the early 20th century, Cubism was, in part, a backlash against Impressionism. People and objects are fragmented and portrayed using geometric shapes.

Fauvism: Uses bold blocks of pure colour, seen in the works of Matisse.

Fluxus: A movement launched in the 1960s. Rejected classic ideas of what a work of art is and focused on fluidity, chance, and everyday objects and events. Artists include Ben Vautier and Joseph Beuys.

Minimalism: The emphasis is on simplicity and repetition, such as the works of Donald Judd and Brice Marden.

New Realism: New Realists used everyday objects in their works, which would sometimes be smashed or burned as a statement against society or fine art. Arman's collection of gas masks, entitled *Home, Sweet Home,* is an example of the genre.

Pop Art: An artistic take on popular culture and advertising. One of the most famous Pop Art pieces is Andy Warhol's *Marilyn Monroe* silkscreen. Other artists include Claes Oldenburg, Roy Lichtenstein and David Hockney.

Surrealism: A rejection of logic and realism for a surreal dream world. This movement was popular in the 1920s and 1930s, with artists such as René Magritte and Salvador Dalí.

Video Art: Experimenting with video footage as art, for example in the work of Nam June Paik.

TIPS

» If you're a traditionalist when it comes to art, let yourself in (relatively) gently to the Museum of Modern Art by starting with the fifth floor (1905–1960) before tackling the more bemusing fourth floor (1960 to today).

» The museum's late opening hours allow you to enjoy a visit after an early evening meal (last ticket sold at 8pm; museum closes at 9pm).

» You may hear local people referring to the Centre Georges Pompidou as Beaubourg.

» The official guidebook has photos and information about 150 of the most important exhibits and is worth buying before you visit the Museum of Modern Art.

» If your mind is spinning from a day of modern art, you may enjoy a calming concert at the nearby church of St-Merri (▷ 168), on Saturdays at 9pm and Sundays at 4pm.

Below *Temporary exhibitions are as popular as the permanent collection*

MAISON EUROPÉENNE DE LA PHOTOGRAPHIE

www.mep-fr.org

The Maison Européenne de la Photographie is a stylish venue for dynamic exhibitions of contemporary photography. The galleries spread over five floors of the 18th-century Hôtel Hénault de Cantobre, as well as in a new wing, which opened in 1996. A 100-seat auditorium screens films related to the exhibitions, and there is also a library and video-viewing facilities.
✚ 150 P7 ✉ 5–7 rue de Fourcy, 75004 ☎ 01 44 78 75 00 🕐 Wed–Sun 11–8; closed during changeover of exhibitions 💷 Adult €7, child (8–16) €4, under 8 free 🚇 St-Paul 🚌 67, 69, 76, 96 🛗 In basement

MAISON DE VICTOR HUGO

www.musee-hugo.paris.fr

The quirky Maison de Victor Hugo conjures up a vivid impression of literary life in 19th-century Paris. It is in the Hôtel de Rohan-Guéménée, where Victor Hugo lived from 1832 to 1848 with his wife and four children. He wrote part of his world-famous novel *Les Misérables* here, and met with fellow writers such as Alexandre Dumas and Alphonse de Lamartine. As you climb the stone steps to the upper floors you'll see a series of old posters advertising various theatrical productions of *Les Misérables*. The luxurious wallpaper alone makes a visit to the permanent exhibitions on the second floor worthwhile. The *salon chinois* (Chinese room) is also striking. In the permanent exhibition on the second floor, the rooms are laid out to echo the interiors of Hugo's various homes, including one on the Channel Island of Guernsey, where he spent time in self-imposed political exile. Memorabilia include a bust of Hugo by Auguste Rodin and furniture from actress Juliette Drouet's room in Guernsey, some of it carved and decorated by Hugo. There is also a reconstruction of the room where Hugo died in 1885. Temporary exhibitions are staged on the first floor and there is a library on the third floor, although access to this is by appointment only.
✚ 151 P7 ✉ 6 place des Vosges, 75004 ☎ 01 42 72 10 16 🕐 Tue–Sun 10–6 💷 Permanent collections free. Temporary exhibitions vary 🚇 Bastille, St-Paul 🚌 20, 29, 65, 69, 96

LE MARAIS

Stretching west to east between Les Halles and the Bastille and north to south from the place de la République to the Seine, the Marais district has a beguiling combination of history, ornate architecture and trendy chic boutiques, bars, restaurants and galleries. The area was once an expanse of low-lying marshland, hence its name *marais* (marsh). Now it is home to cobblestone courtyards, medieval streets, beautiful mansions, a bustling Jewish quarter, and the oldest square in Paris—place des Vosges (▷ 169), where you can enjoy a leisurely drink.

During the 17th century, aristocrats competed here to build the most elegant mansion. The area subsequently fell into neglect until, in 1962, Culture Minister-cum-writer André Malraux pointed out the historic value of numerous crumbling monuments, and a restoration scheme began.

Today it is impossible to wander through the Marais without stumbling across architectural masterpieces, even if you can only admire them from their courtyards. Many of these mansions (called *hôtels*) now house museums, including the Musée Picasso (▷ 167), the Musée Carnavalet (▷ 164–165) and the Musée d'Art et d'Histoire du Judaïsme (▷ 163).
✚ 150 P7 ✉ Le Marais 🚇 St-Paul, Rambuteau, Hôtel de Ville, Bastille 🚌 29, 67, 69, 75, 76, 96

Above *The historic Marais district has been regenerated and restored, attracting a variety of small shops and boutiques*

MÉMORIAL DE LA SHOAH

www.memorialdelashoah.org

Inaugurated in January 2005 for the 60th anniversary of the liberation of Auschwitz, the Mémorial houses the tomb of the unknown Jewish martyr (in the crypt), the Mur des Noms bearing the names of the 76,000 Jews deported from France, and a museum relating the fate of the Jewish people during World War II. This comprehensive information and research centre is the largest of its kind in Europe.

✚ 150 N7 ✉ 17 rue Geoffroy-l'Asnier, 75004 ☎ 01 42 77 44 72 🕐 Sun–Fri 10–6 (also Museum Thu 6–10; Salle des Noms Thu 6–7.30) 🖐 Museum, crypt, multimedia centre and reading room: free; exhibition: adult €5, child (8–12) €3 🚇 St-Paul, Pont Marie 🚌 67, 69, 76, 96

MUSÉE D'ART ET D'HISTOIRE DU JUDAÏSME

www.mahj.org

Discover the rich cultural heritage of the Jewish community in France and beyond. This museum vividly illustrates the development of Jewish culture from the Middle Ages to the present day, in France and farther afield. It also highlights the contribution members of the Jewish community have made to European life and art. The main focus is on French Jews, although you can also see items from the rest of Europe, as well as North Africa.

An audioguide, included in the entry price, directs you chronologically through the museum. Themes include the Middle Ages, the Emancipation of the Jews after the French Revolution, intellectual and artistic achievements in the 19th century, and the tragedies and triumphs of the modern era. Medieval exhibits include a rare Hanukkah lamp, dating from before the expulsion of the Jews in the 14th century. Later items include a vivid Jewish marriage contract from 1752 and a 19th-century Algerian wedding outfit. Artists represented include Marc Chagall and Amedeo Modigliani. The

archives of the Dreyfus Affair contain around three thousand letters, photographs, books and official documents relating to the case of French Jewish army captain, Alfred Dreyfus, who was falsely convicted of passing secrets to the Germans in 1894. The museum opened in 1998 in the Hôtel de St-Aignan, a restored 17th-century mansion named after an early owner, the Duc de St-Aignan. The mansion became home to Jewish immigrants from Eastern Europe in the 19th century, and during World War II its residents were arrested by the German occupying forces and sent to concentration camps. Their memory is kept alive by an art installation by Christian Boltanski, called *Les habitants de l'Hôtel de Saint-Aignan en 1939* (1998).

✚ 150 N6 ✉ Hôtel de St-Aignan, 71 rue du Temple, 75003 ☎ 01 53 01 86 53

🕐 Mon–Fri 11–6, Sun 10–6. Closed Sat 🖐 Adult €6.80, under 18 free 🚇 Rambuteau, Hôtel de Ville 🚌 29, 38, 47, 75 🎧 Audioguide included in the entry price 🍴 Café 📖 Substantial bookshop

MUSÉE DES ARTS ET MÉTIERS

www.arts-et-metiers.net/

Art meets science at this quirky museum, with a collection of early scientific machinery, vintage cars and mechanical toys. You can see a primitive calculating machine invented by Blaise Pascal, one of Thomas Edison's phonographs and a mechanical toy created for Marie-Antoinette. A Formula 1 racing car sits incongruously in the former chapel.

✚ 150 N6 ✉ 60 rue Réaumur, 75003 ☎ 01 53 01 82 00 🕐 Tue–Sun 10–6 (also Thu 6pm–9.30pm) 🖐 Adult €6.50, under 18 free 🚇 Arts et Métiers, Réaumur-Sébastopol 🚌 20, 38, 39, 47 💻

Below *Christian Boltanski's* Les habitants de l'Hôtel de Saint-Aignan en 1939 *(1998)*

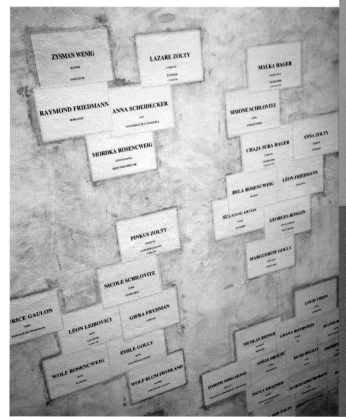

MUSÉE CARNAVALET

INFORMATION

www.carnavalet.paris.fr
✚ 150 P7 ✉ 23 rue de Sévigné,
75003 (also an entrance on rue des
Francs-Bourgeois) ☎ 01 44 59 58 58
🕙 Tue–Sun 10–6 🖐 Free (except
temporary exhibitions) 🚇 St-Paul 🚌 29,
69, 76, 96 🎧 Guided tours in French
and occasionally in English at various
times; information: 01 44 59 58 31 📖 €5
📖 Bookshop with a comprehensive
selection of history-related titles

INTRODUCTION

Step into these adjoining mansions and you'll be setting off on an intriguing journey through Paris-past. Paintings, memorabilia and sumptuous recreations of period rooms evoke the spirit of the city in previous eras, including the French Revolution and the reign of Napoléon I. The emphasis is on conveying an atmosphere rather than listing historical facts, so if you're expecting a detailed account of each era you may be disappointed. But if you want a taste of the high life during Louis XV's rule or a glimpse of the terrors of the Revolution, this is the place to come.

The museum is housed in two grand mansions—the Hôtel Carnavalet and the adjoining Hôtel Le Peletier de St-Fargeau. Use the main entrance on rue de Sévigné, rather than the entrance on rue des Francs-Bourgeois. This takes you straight into the Hôtel Carnavalet. There is an information desk here where you can ask for a plan of the museum (in English). Be sure to do this—you'll have little hope of making sense of the complex layout of the site without it. To reach the Hôtel Le Peletier de St-Fargeau, walk across the *galerie* on the first floor.

The building is a piece of history in itself—an ornate mansion built in the 1540s for the president of the Paris *parlement*, Jacques des Ligneris. Architect François Mansart put his stamp on the site in 1660, when he added a new wing. Shortly after, the celebrated lady of letters, Madame de Sévigné, moved in. The idea for a museum of Parisian history originally came from Baron Haussmann, the man responsible for reshaping the city in the 19th century (▷ 40). The Hôtel Carnavalet was chosen and the museum opened in 1880. More than a century later, in 1989, the collections were able to expand into the adjoining Hôtel Le Peletier de St-Fargeau.

WHAT TO SEE

THE REVOLUTION

The museum has a poignant collection of memorabilia from the French Revolution on the second floor of the Hôtel Le Peletier de St-Fargeau. You

Above *The pretty, formal garden of the Musée Carnavalet*

can see a set of keys from the Bastille prison, comic strips by Le Sueur and furniture used by the royal family while they were in prison. Paintings include works by Hubert Robert, who was imprisoned during the Revolution, and a portrait of the Revolutionary leader Robespierre, who later fell victim to the guillotine himself. A collection of fans, plates, clocks and furniture show that Revolutionary slogans infiltrated even household goods.

HOW THE OTHER HALF LIVED

A world away from the horrors of the Revolution, the lavish tastes of Paris's richer residents through the years are brought to life by vivid re-creations of their rooms.

On the ground floor of the Hôtel Carnavalet, the Grand Salon de l'Hôtel d'Uzès evokes the opulence of pre-Revolution days, with a profusion of gold, mirrors and chandeliers. Architect Claude-Nicolas Ledoux designed the original room in 1767.

On the first floor, rooms 21 to 23 are dedicated to the mansion's most famous resident, Madame de Sévigné, and include two portraits of her. Rooms 27 to 48 depict Paris during the reign of Louis XV (1715–1774). Literary and theatrical life is illustrated in room 47, with brightly painted wooden statuettes from the Théâtre Séraphin. The reign of Louis XVI (1774–1793) is covered in rooms 49 to 64. Don't miss the charming Boudoir Circulaire in room 51 and the stunning wallpaper throughout the first floor, made at the Gobelins workshops (▷ 117) and based on 18th-century designs.

19TH- AND 20TH-CENTURY DISPLAYS

Highlights from the Napoleonic era include the Emperor's 110-piece picnic case and his death mask (on the ground floor of the Hôtel Le Peletier de St-Fargeau). Reconstructions on the first floor of the Hôtel Le Peletier de St-Fargeau include the elegant art nouveau interior of the famous jewellers, Fouquet (1900), and Madame Wendel's 1920s Queen-of-Sheba ballroom. Also worth seeing is the re-creation of Marcel Proust's room, soundproofed with cork to protect the reclusive writer from unwanted noise.

TIPS

» Staff shortages mean some rooms are closed at times.

» Explanation panels are in French only, so you may like to buy the guidebook or borrow an audioguide before you begin your tour.

GALLERY GUIDE
HÔTEL CARNAVALET

Ground floor: Middle Ages to 16th century. Also Grand Salon de l'Hôtel d'Uzès.

1st floor: 17th and 18th centuries (to end of Louis XVI's reign).

HÔTEL LE PELETIER DE ST-FARGEAU

Ground floor: 19th century, from Napoléon I to 1848.

1st floor: 19th and 20th centuries (from Napoléon III).

2nd floor: the Revolution.

ORANGERIE

Paris's beginnings, from prehistory to Roman times.

Left and below *Exhibits on display in the Musée Carnavalet*

MUSÉE DE LA CHASSE ET DE LA NATURE

www.chassenature.org

Housed in two beautifully restored mansions—the Hôtel de Guénégard and the Hôtel de Mongelas—in the heart of the Marais district, the recently renovated Museum of Hunting and Nature is packed with stuffed animals, hunting weapons, paintings and decorative arts. It may not be to everyone's taste, but it gives an insight into an activity pursued since time immemorial. The collection of hunting weapons spans prehistory to the 19th century. Some displays are dedicated to big-game hunting, with souvenirs of the museum's founder, François Sommer. There are also hunting-related paintings, including works by François Desportes (court artist at Versailles), Jean-Baptiste-Siméon Chardin, Carle Vernet and a joint canvas created by Rubens and Jan Brueghel (the Elder).

✚ 150 P6 ✉ Hôtel Guénégaud, 60 rue des Archives, 75003 ☎ 01 53 01 92 40 ✪ Tue–Sun 11–6 💰 Adult €6, under 18 free 🚇 Rambuteau, Hôtel de Ville 🚌 29, 75

MUSÉE COGNACQ-JAY

www.paris.fr

The Musée Cognacq-Jay is a discreet, unassuming museum whose charm far exceeds its small size. Part of its appeal is the setting, in an elegant mansion furnished in 18th-century style. Narrow corridors and stairways lead to intimate chandeliered rooms, packed with paintings, porcelain, sculpture and objets d'art. The collection was put together in the early 20th century by Ernest Cognacq and his wife Louise Jay, founders of La Samaritaine department store. Their busts are displayed near the reception. In 1990 the collection was transferred to the 16th-century Hôtel Donon, in the Marais district. Works by Rembrandt, Jean Honoré Fragonard and Giovanni Battista Tiepolo are among the pieces on display. The Venetian scenes by Canaletto are impressive. There is also a garden (open summer only) and a bookshop. If you can read French, information cards placed at key points around the museum will fill you in on the collection. If not, just enjoy the refined atmosphere—a taste of the life led by wealthy Parisians in the 18th century.

✚ 150 P7 ✉ Hôtel Donon, 8 rue Elzévir, 75003 ☎ 01 40 27 07 21 ✪ Tue–Sun 10–6. Garden: open mid-May to mid-Sep (in good weather) 10–12.15, 4–5.35 💰 Free 🚇 St-Paul 🚌 29, 69, 76, 96

MUSÉE EDITH PIAF

Edith Piaf, the Little Sparrow, was born Edith Giovanna Gassion in 1915. Brought up in the working-class east end of Paris, she began her career as a singer in local bars and cafés. Although she achieved international acclaim in the 1930s, appearing in many plays and films, she is best remembered for songs such as *La vie en rose* and *Non, je ne regrette rien*. This small museum is crammed with Piaf memorabilia, including posters, letters, photographs, dresses and shoes. A visit is worthwhile if only to hear her original records playing in the background as you look around. Nearby is the Cimetière du Père-Lachaise (▷ 155) where you can visit her grave—thousands of people attended her funeral here in 1963.

✚ 151 R6 ✉ 5 rue Crespin du Gast, 75011 ☎ 01 43 55 52 72 ✪ Visit by appointment only so call in advance. Usually open Mon–Wed 1–6 💰 Free (donations appreciated) 🚇 Ménilmontant 🚌 96

MUSÉE DE L'HISTOIRE DE FRANCE (HÔTEL DE SOUBISE)

The star attraction of the Museum of French History is its sumptuous setting. The Hôtel de Soubise, in the Marais district, was built by Delamair in the early 18th century for the Princesse de Soubise at the same time as the Hôtel de Rohan on rue Vieille du Temple, intended for her son, the future Cardinal de Rohan. Delamair incorporated into his design the 14th-century double-towered entrance on the rue des Archives, a remnant of a medieval manor originally on the site. The Prince's Apartment *(Appartement du Prince)*, on the ground floor, is lavishly decorated by painters including Carle Van Loo and François Boucher. The artistry continues upstairs in the Princess's Apartment *(Appartement de la Princesse)*.

The history museum, housed in both mansions, is document-based and so probably not of great interest to non-French speakers. It draws on the National Archives for its exhibitions, a rich store that includes letters written by Charlemagne and Joan of Arc, the wills of Louis XIV and Napoléon I, and the last correspondence of Marie-Antoinette before her execution.

✚ 150 P7 ✉ Hôtel de Soubise, 60 rue des Francs-Bourgeois, Hôtel de Rohan, 87 rue Vieille du Temple, 75003 ☎ 01 40 27 60 96 ✪ Mon, Wed–Fri 10–12.30, 2–5.45, Sat–Sun 2–5.30 💰 Adult €3, under 18 free 🚇 Rambuteau, Hôtel de Ville 🚌 29, 75, 96 🏛 Gift shop/bookshop

Left *Detail of the ceiling of the Salon Ovale in Hôtel de Soubise, home of the Musée de l'Histoire de France*

MUSÉE PICASSO

The grand opening of this museum in 1985 put an end to 11 years of wrangling over the death duties of Pablo Picasso (1881–1973). Thanks to a law allowing payment of these duties in the form of works of art, the French State received one quarter of Picasso's collection from his heirs. The collection, including 203 paintings, 158 sculptures, 16 collages and more than 1,500 drawings and prints, was extended further after the death of Picasso's wife in 1990. Also on display is Picasso's personal collection of works by his mentors and contemporaries, including Paul Cézanne, Pierre-Auguste Renoir, Joan Miró, Georges Braque and Henri Matisse.

THE WORKS

The art is arranged chronologically, from Picasso's early 1900s Blue and Pink periods, through his years of Cubist experimentation with Georges Braque, to the 1930s and beyond. Look out for the *Trois Femmes à la Fontaine* (1921) at the top of the staircase to the left, and the sculpture of *La Guenon et Son Petit (the Baboon with Young;* 1951) in room 18, whose head is made from two toy cars.

Other highlights are his *Self-Portrait* (1901) in room 1, *The Goat* (1950) in room 16, *The Bathers* (1918) and *Two Women Running on the Beach* (1922) in room 6, and the tragic yet moving *Seated Old Man* (1970–71) in room 20. The collection captures the freshness and inventiveness that ran through the core of Picasso's long and creative life.

MANSION SETTING

Even for those who are not ardent Picasso fans, the museum is worth a visit to admire the interior of the magnificent Hôtel Salé, a beautiful 17th-century mansion in the Marais district. After changing hands several times, the mansion was acquired by the Ville de Paris in 1962, and in 1976 architect Roland Simounet began work to convert the interior to the Musée Picasso. The chandeliers and furniture were designed by Diego Giacometti and extensive, and expensive, renovation work was needed before the museum opened to the public. A small room dedicated to the history of the Hôtel Salé displays black-and-white photographs and information on the building and its occupants over the years. The nickname 'Salé' (salty) is in memory of the ostentatious tastes of the first owner, who made a fortune out of taxing salt.

INFORMATION

www.musee-picasso.fr (in French)
✚ 150 P7 ✉ Hôtel Salé, 5 rue de Thorigny, 75003 ☎ 01 42 71 25 21 ⏰ Wed–Mon 9.30–5.30; last entry 45 min before closing 👋 Adult €8.50, 18–25 €6.50, under 18 free for permanent collection; free to all on 1st Sun of month 🚇 St-Paul, Filles du Calvaire 🚌 29, 69, 75, 96 🎫 Guided tours Sep–Jun Mon, Fri 2.30 (€6.30) 📙 €3 ☕ Garden café, mid-Apr to mid-Oct 🛍 Bookshop and gift shop ❓ At the time of writing the museum is closed for extension and renovation and is due to reopen in early 2013.

TIP

» Wall plaques in each of the rooms give detailed information (in English) about the works on display.

Above *The Musée Picasso holds much of the artist's personal collection and a large proportion of all his works*

OPÉRA BASTILLE
www.opera-de-paris.fr

The geometric marble facade of this modern opera house dominates place de la Bastille (▷ 153), and the 2,700-seat auditorium hosts prestigious productions (▷ 175). The imposing building made its presence felt even before it was constructed. The project, championed by President Mitterrand in the early 1980s, ran into controversy when a design by a relatively unknown architect, Carlos Ott, was selected from more than 700 entries. The opera house attracted further criticism for its ungainly volume and its cost, but it was ready to open for the bicentenary of the French Revolution in 1989.

✚ 151 Q8 ✉ place de la Bastille (box office: 120 rue de Lyon), 75012 ☎ 01 40 01 19 70 (information); 0892 89 90 90 (reservations) 🕐 Box office: Mon–Sat 10–6.30 👋 Guided tours: adult €11, child (under 19) €6. Tickets only available at the box office 10 min before start of tour 🚇 Bastille 🚌 20, 29, 69, 76

PLACE DES VOSGES
▷ 169.

PONT MARIE
This stone bridge, linking the Île St-Louis with the Right Bank, had a controversial beginning. Île St-Louis property developer Christophe Marie first suggested the bridge in 1605, but completion was delayed until 1635. Disaster struck in the spring thaw of 1658. The bridge was top-heavy with tall houses (all the more profit for the developer) and a powerful flood caused two arches, along with the homes, shops and

occupants they supported, to topple into the Seine. The bridge was rebuilt—without any new houses.

✚ 150 P8 ✉ quai des Célestins/ Île St-Louis 🚇 Pont Marie 🚌 67

RIVE DROITE
The Right Bank (Rive Droite) is by far the larger of Paris's two parts and so is harder to define than the southern Left Bank (Rive Gauche). Kings built their palaces here, Baron Haussmann created his wide arteries and every ruler left at least one monument. The area boasts the Musée du Louvre, the outlandish Centre Georges Pompidou and two prestigious opera houses. Cushioning the grandeur are newer, burgeoning districts, including Bercy and La Villette, and spruced up older ones, such as the Marais. The Right Bank also contains the city's banking and business heart. In the far north is the former hilltop village of Montmartre.

✉ North of the Seine

ST-EUSTACHE
www.saint-eustache.org

Paris's second-largest church stands in the busy Les Halles district (▷ 154), next to the incongruously modern Forum des Halles. The Gothic structure is second in size only to Notre-Dame, on which it is based. Building work started in 1532 and continued for more than 100 years. Since then, the church has played a prominent role, hosting Louis XIV's first communion, Cardinal Richelieu's baptism and the premieres of Liszt's Grand Mass and Berlioz's Te Deum. The church's musical reputation continues today as a venue for regular concerts,

including organ recitals that take place on Sunday evenings.

✚ 150 M6 ✉ 2 rue du Jour, place du Jour, 75001 ☎ 01 42 36 31 05 🕐 Mon–Fri 9.30–7, Sat 10–7, Sun 9–7 👋 Free 🚇 Les Halles 🚌 29, 67, 74, 85 🚊 RER lines A, B, D, Châtelet-Les-Halles

ST-MERRI
St-Merri, a short walk from the Centre Georges Pompidou, is named after the Right Bank's patron saint. The 16th-century church is a superb example of Flamboyant Gothic. It contains Paris's oldest bell, made in 1331 and a remnant from the medieval chapel that once stood on the site. Inside, the stained-glass windows show Joseph in Egypt, St. Nicholas of Myre, St. Agnès and the Paris merchant Étienne Marcel. The ornate pulpit was carved in 1753 by the sculptor P.A. Slodtz, one of two brothers who worked on the church in the 18th century. The Carnaval des Animaux composer Camille Saint-Saëns was organist here in the 1850s. Today, you can enjoy free concerts usually on Saturdays and Sundays.

✚ 150 N7 ✉ 78 rue St-Martin, 75004 ☎ For concert information: 01 42 71 40 75 🕐 Daily 3–7 👋 Free 🚇 Hôtel de Ville 🚌 38, 47 🚊 RER lines A, B, D, Châtelet-Les-Halles

SYNAGOGUE
The synagogue lies in the heart of the Marais district's Jewish quarter (▷ 162). It was built in 1913 to designs by architect Hector Guimard, best remembered for his fanlighted Métro entrances. Guimard was one of the leading lights in the French art nouveau movement and was prolific between 1895 and 1910. He continued to work until 1930 but, distressed by the rise of Fascism, he emigrated to the United States, where he died in 1942.

✚ 150 P7 ✉ 10 rue Pavée, 75004 ☎ 01 48 87 21 54 🕐 Visits by request only. Telephone Sun–Thu between 10 and 4 👋 Free 🚇 St-Paul 🚌 69, 76, 96

Above The vast St-Eustache church

PLACE DES VOSGES

Paris's oldest square is the perfect place to while away a few hours, relaxing in an outdoor café or enjoying the fountains. Picturesque place des Vosges is steeped in history and only minutes away from the busy, modern Bastille district. It is a great example of the Paris phenomenon where you can be on a traffic-filled road teeming with people one minute, and in a quiet grassy square the next, seemingly miles from 21st-century bustle. Here you can browse in the boutiques, antiques shops and art galleries in the arcades surrounding the square or sip hot chocolate in one of the cafés.

PLACE ROYALE

A royal palace originally stood on this site but was demolished in the 16th century by Catherine de Médicis when her husband, Henri II, was killed in a tournament here. Later, Henri IV commissioned the elegant and symmetrical place Royale, one of the first examples of town planning in Paris. The square was inaugurated in 1612, amid spectacular celebrations. In 1800, it was renamed place des Vosges in tribute to the first French *département* to pay its new taxes.

SYMMETRY

The square's harmonious form is created by 36 red brick- and stone-faced houses, 9 on each side, with arcaded ground floors and steep pitched roofs. These striking buildings surround a formal garden containing fountains, trees, gravel paths, a children's play area, ornate lamp-posts and a statue of Louis XIII. The north and south facades of the square retain a royal touch, as each has a larger, central house, respectively the Pavillon de la Reine (Queen's pavilion) and the Pavillon du Roi (King's pavilion). The Pavillon de la Reine is now a 4-star hotel (▷ 179).

FAMOUS RESIDENTS

Many famous characters have inhabited the square's mansions and apartments across the centuries of its history. Princesses, duchesses, official mistresses, Cardinal Richelieu, the Duc de Sully, writer Alphonse Daudet and, more recently, the painter Francis Bacon and the architect Richard Rogers have all gazed out at its perfect symmetry. Another French author, Victor Hugo, penned many a manuscript at number six, his home from 1832 to 1848, and now a museum (▷ 162).

INFORMATION

✚ 150 P7 ✉ place des Vosges, 75004
🚇 Bastille, St-Paul, Chemin Vert 🚌 20, 29, 65, 96

TIPS

» Sunday afternoon is a good time to see the square, as this is when Parisians come for a stroll, to the accompaniment of outdoor musicians.
» To find out more about Paris life during the place des Vosges's heyday, visit the nearby Musée Carnavalet (▷ 164–165).

Below *Elegant and stately, historic place des Vosges is Paris's oldest square*

REGIONS   MARAIS AND BASTILLE • SIGHTS

THE EASTERN MARAIS

The Marais is one of the prettiest districts in central Paris, home to elaborate mansions (known as *hôtels*), medieval streets, huge doorways with ornate handles, charming gardens and squares, a bustling Jewish quarter and the oldest square in Paris, the place des Vosges.

THE WALK

Distance: 3km (2 miles)
Time: 2 hours
Start/end at St-Paul-Le Merais Métro station

HOW TO GET THERE

Take the Métro to St-Paul-Le Marais, or buses 69, 76 or 96.

★Leave St-Paul Métro station and head east along rue St-Antoine, passing the impressive facade of the church of St-Paul-St-Louis (1627–1641) on the right. At No. 62, on your left, is the Hôtel de Sully.

❶ This magnificent 17th-century mansion was once home to Henri IV's chief minister, the Duc de Sully. Today it houses the headquarters of the Centre des Monuments Nationaux.

Turn left into the peaceful rue de Birague which leads to the place des Vosges (▷ 169).

❷ This picturesque square was commissioned by Henri IV and completed in 1612. During the 17th century it was home to significant figures such as Cardinal Richelieu, Louis XIII's hypochondriac minister, and the playwright Molière. In the 19th century, writer Victor Hugo moved in. His house, number six, is now a museum (▷ 162).

Continue around the square, walking under the arcades, past restaurants and shops. Look into the garden entrance of number 28, the Pavillon de la Reine, now a hotel (▷ 179). If you feel like a drink, stop at a café under the arcades.

Leave the square by rue des Francs-Bourgeois. On your right is the Musée Carnavalet (▷ 164–165), built in 1548 and later home to the writer Madame de Sévigné. As you walk past you can see the beautiful courtyard and gardens.

❸ The Musée Carnavalet focuses on the story of Paris, from prehistory to the 20th century. The Revolution, Napoléon Bonaparte and art nouveau interiors are among its themes.

Turn right into rue Payenne. The gardens on the right and courtyards on the left are in typical 17th-century Marais style. Notice the elaborate wooden gates of the Hôtel de Chatillon, on your left, at number 13. Follow rue du Parc Royal to the

Left *The cloisters of one of the fine mansions which populate the Marais, a pretty medieval district*

left, walk around place de Thorigny and then turn right into rue de Thorigny, to reach the Hôtel Salé, built in 1656, and now home to the Musée Picasso (▷ 167; currently closed for expansion).

❹ Due to reopen in early 2013, this vast collection of Picasso's works contains more than 250 paintings, 160 sculptures and 1,500 drawings. There are also pieces by his contemporaries, notably Paul Cézanne, Joan Miró, Georges Braque and Henri Matisse.

Turn left along rue Debelleyme, past contemporary art galleries, and then left again down rue Vieille du Temple. On the left you will see the gardens of the Musée Picasso. Halfway down on your right at number 87, you pass the carved gates of the Hôtel de Rohan and, on the corner of rue des Francs-Bourgeois, the picturesque turret (1510) of the Maison de Jean Hérouët. Turn right here, past more

elegant mansions and the Crédit Municipal (municipal pawnshop) at number 55 on your left. On the right is the courtyard of the Hôtel de Soubise.

❺ This mansion was constructed between 1705 and 1708 and is now home to the National Archives and the Musée de l'Histoire de France (▷ 166).

Above Le Petit Fer à Cheval, *one of the traditional cafés in the Marais on rue Vieille du Temple*

Turn left into rue des Archives and take the next left into rue des Blancs Manteaux. This brings you back to rue Vieille du Temple. Turn right and after a short walk turn left to follow rue des Rosiers.

❻ This bustling street is the hub of the Jewish district, full of specialist shops as far as rue Pavée. Chic boutiques and trendy furniture stores trade alongside traditional Jewish fast-food stalls, cafés and bookshops.

Turn right into rue Pavée. On the left you'll pass the synagogue, designed by Hector Guimard (▷ 168).

Continue south to return to St-Paul-Le Marais Métro station.

WHEN TO GO
During the day, when the shops and museums are open.

WHERE TO EAT
The place des Vosges has plenty of cafés. Ma Bourgogne, at number 19, and L'Ambrosie, at number 9, both have outdoor tables set out under the arcades.

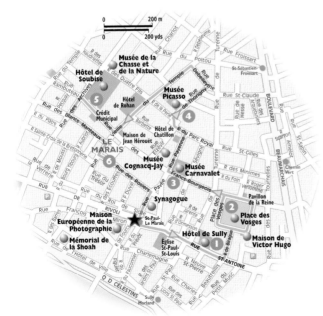

WALK

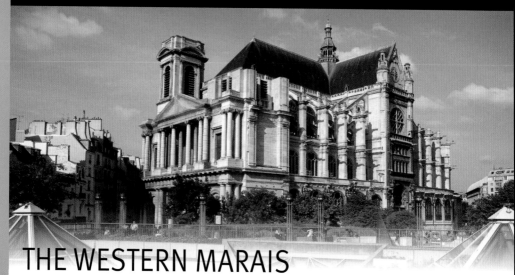

THE WESTERN MARAIS

This is a leisurely walk in the western Marais area, taking in Les Halles, with its warren of shops, and visiting the landmarks and some of Paris's great institutions.

THE WALK

Distance: 2.2km (1.4 miles)
Time: 1hr 40min
Start/end at: Hôtel de Ville

HOW TO GET THERE

Take the Métro to Hôtel de Ville, or buses 38, 47, 58, 62, 67, 70, 74, 75 or 96.

★ Start the walk at the exit from Hôtel de Ville Métro which faces the busy place de l'Hôtel de Ville in front of the Hôtel de Ville (▷ 154).

❶ What first comes into view in the square outside the Hôtel de Ville depends on the time of year—but it's bound to be crowded with tourists and Parisians at their leisure. In summer there is a tennis court and a children's games area, or there may be a giant TV screen relaying the French Open tennis or some other major sporting event. In high summer the riverfront at the far end becomes part of Paris Plage (▷ 44), a bespoke beach resort complete with sand, deck chairs, hammocks, palm trees and cocktail

kiosks. In the winter the square is a skating rink. The Hôtel de Ville (City Hall) building is in neo-Renaissance style dating from 1871, but there has been an administrative building on this spot since the 14th century.

From the Hôtel de Ville, head westward along rue de Rivoli—itself a chic shopping area—and on the left, just before the intersection with boulevard de Sébastopol, is the Tour Saint-Jacques.

❷ Built between 1508 and 1522, the 52m (170ft) Tour Saint-Jacques is the last remnant of a 16th-century church. Destroyed after the Revolution, the church had been a wayfaring stop for pilgrims on the way to Santiago de Compostela, in northern Spain. The interior commemorates the work of scientist Blaise Pascal (▷ 163), who conducted meteorological experiments here to refine his design of barometers.

Crossing rue de Rivoli from the tower and then crossing boulevard

de Sébastopol is a diagonal northwestward route from rue St-Denis, rue des Halles. Follow this in the direction of the Forum des Halles (▷ 154).

❸ From medieval times until the start of the 16th century this area was a marketplace which accommodated businesses and then specialized in food. In the mid-20th century the traditional meat, fruit and vegetable market was unceremoniously evicted to the suburbs at Rungis to make the modern city more navigable. What was left was a veritable hell-hole, literally *le trou des* (the hole of) Halles. The remedy to this unsightly cityscape was what we see today—a neat garden at ground level with a large underground shopping mall which is also home to museums, restaurants, discos and cinemas.

Walk across the garden to its northwestern edge where you will find the church of St-Eustache (▷ 168).

REGIONS MARAIS AND BASTILLE • WALK

❹ The Église de St-Eustache
began life in the 13th century as a
chapel dedicated to Ste. Agnès,
a Roman martyr, but it was another
martyr, St. Eustache, who gave the
church its name when it was rebuilt
in 1532. As the second-largest
church in Paris it is noted for the
baptisms of many royal, political
and musical figures, and itself has
a great musical reputation as the
setting for performances of works
by Liszt and Berlioz. Although
desecrated during the Revolution,
it still has a number of impressive
Rubens paintings.

With the church on your left and
Les Halles on your right, walk along
rue Rambuteau.

❺ Rue Rambuteau is lined with
shops and extends from the Église
St-Eustache and Les Halles to the
Centre Georges Pompidou and
the Marais. This road, built during
the post-revolutionary reign of
Louis-Philippe (▷ 40) in the 18th
century, was the first to penetrate
the medieval centre.

About two-thirds of the way along
the full length of rue Rambuteau,
take a break from the shops and
turn right into rue de Renard, which
is home to the Centre Georges
Pompidou (▷ 156–161).

❻ Visitors either love Centre
Georges Pompidou or hate it: No
one is indifferent to this ultra-
modern, inside-out building. The
square fronting the centre is alive
with jugglers, musicians, mime
artists and fire-eaters. To see inside,
you need much more time than a
walking schedule allows, but, by all
means, take a peep. Undeniably, it
has the world's largest collection
of modern art and is an outrageous
but wonderful spectacle to behold.

Backtrack to rue Rambuteau
and continue to where the road

intersects with rue du Temple.
On the left is the Musée d'Art et
d'Histoire du Judaïsme (▷ 163).

❼ The museum is based in the
Hôtel de St-Aignan, an attractive
17th-century mansion which has
associations with the Paris Jewish
community dating from the 19th
century. Inside, the exhibition
relates the story of the Jews in
Paris, France and beyond, and their
contribution to western culture.
As well as historically fascinating
objects and documents—including
archives of the Dreyfus affair
(▷ 163)—the museum has objets
d'art, textiles, manuscripts, and an
82-seat auditorium.

Outside the museum, rue du Temple
is a direct route back to the Hôtel de
Ville, though you could be tempted
to explore the remaining few metres
of rue Rambuteau before heading
back to the Métro.

WHEN TO GO
This is a good mid-morning walk in
spring or summer, when you can be
sure the shops are open. If you end
the walk at lunchtime at the Hôtel

de Ville the square is bound to be
full of Parisians taking it easy, having
fun and being themselves.

WHERE TO EAT
For a special treat why not visit
Georges, the restaurant on the top
of the Centre Georges Pompidou
(▷ 156–161). It's not cheap,
but is elegant, arty and offers
incomparable views over the heart
of Paris.

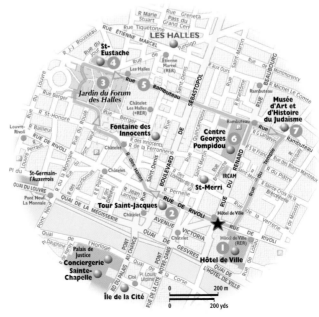

REGIONS   MARAIS AND BASTILLE • WALK

SHOPPING

ANTIK BATIK
www.antikbatik.fr
Come here for the finest of ethnic chic: embroidered blouses made of cotton or silk, long batik-printed stoles, bags and sexy lingerie.
✚ 180 P7 ✉ 18 rue de Turenne, 75004 ☎ 01 44 78 02 00 🕐 Tue–Sat 11–7, Sun–Mon 2–7 🚇 Hôtel de Ville

ANTOINE ET LILI
www.antoineetlili.com
Knick-knacks from all over the world, Asian beauty products and vivid outfits in luxurious fabrics. There are two shops—one for clothes, another for gifts—and also a small restaurant.
✚ 180 P4 ✉ 95 quai de Valmy, 75010 ☎ 01 40 37 41 55 🕐 Tue–Sat 10–7 🚇 Jacques Bonsergent, Gare de l'Est

BARBARA BUI
www.barbarabui.com
The lines are sleek, original and often have a sexy twist, but are never provocative. The collection is aimed at the urban woman and is classy, modern and feminine.
✚ 180 N6 ✉ 23 rue Étienne Marcel, 75001 ☎ 01 40 26 43 65 🕐 Daily 10.30–7.30 🚇 Étienne Marcel

BHV
www.bhv.fr
The City Hall Bazaar has been open since 1856. It sells just about everything you could possibly need.
✚ 180 N7 ✉ 42–55 rue de la Verrerie, 75004 ☎ 01 42 74 90 00 🕐 Mon–Tue, Thu–Fri 9.30–7.30, Wed 9.30–9, Sat 9.30–8 🚇 Hôtel de Ville

LA DROGUERIE
www.ladroguerie.com
This shop sells everything you'll need to make your own jewellery, to knit or to customize your home.
✚ 180 M6 ✉ 9 and 11 rue du Jour, 75001 ☎ 01 45 08 93 27 🕐 Tue–Sat 10.30–6.45, Mon 2–6.45 🚇 Les Halles

ISABEL MARANT
www.isabelmarant.fr
A regular on the catwalk, Isabel Marant has given Parisian elegance a bohemian bourgeois twist. Silk Paisley shirts, big woollen wrap-over tops: This is casual chic at its best.
✚ 181 Q8 ✉ 16 rue de Charonne, 75011 ☎ 01 49 29 71 55 🕐 Mon–Sat 10.30–7.30 🚇 Bastille

JEAN-CLAUDE MONDERER
On the picturesque rue des Francs-Bourgeois, this shop is for men and

Above *Mariage Frères tea house*

women who love elegant, original footwear. Fine materials, remarkable finishing and interesting designs.
✚ 180 P7 ✉ 22 rue des Francs-Bourgeois, 75004 ☎ 01 48 04 51 41 🕐 Tue–Sat 10.30–7.30, Sun 2–7, Mon 10.30–7 🚇 St-Paul

KILIWATCH
www.espacekiliwatch.fr
Kiliwatch offers the very best in retro gear that's carefully chosen for its classic styling, then cleaned and pressed before being put on sale. Every garment is very good quality, so often come at a price.
✚ 180 M6 ✉ 64 rue Tiquetone, 75002 ☎ 01 42 21 17 37 🕐 Tue–Fri 11–7, Sat 11–7.30, Mon 2–7 🚇 Étienne Marcel

MARIAGE FRÈRES
www.mariagefreres.com
Founded in 1854, this tea house is a Parisian institution. It stocks hundreds of teas from all over the world. The Tea Museum displays rare objects from the 17th century onwards; copies are on sale.
✚ 180 N7 ✉ 30 rue du Bourg-Tibourg, 75004 ☎ 01 42 72 28 11 🕐 Daily 10.30–7.30 🚇 Hôtel de Ville

ENTERTAINMENT AND NIGHTLIFE

CAFÉ BEAUBOURG
This modern, stylish café-restaurant has a terrace spilling out onto the piazza Beaubourg. It is one of the best spots for people-watching in Paris.
➕ 180 N6 ✉ 100 rue Saint-Martin, 75004 ☎ 01 48 87 63 96 🕐 Sun–Thu 8am–1am, Fri–Sat 8am–2am 🚇 Rambuteau

DUC DES LOMBARDS
www.ducdeslombards.com
A Parisian institution, the most prestigious jazz musicians regularly perform at this intimate club. Performances often culminate in memorable jam sessions.
➕ 180 N7 ✉ 42 rue des Lombards, 75001 ☎ 01 42 33 22 88 🕐 Performance: Mon–Sat 9pm 🖐 €30–€40 🚇 Châtelet

FORUM DES IMAGES
www.forumdesimages.net
This complex offers four different screenings daily of films illustrating themes and retrospectives of Paris. There are also children's afternoons, and films about the city which can be viewed on individual screens.
➕ 180 M6 ✉ 2 Grande Galerie, Porte St-Eustache, Forum des Halles, 75001 ☎ 01 44 76 63 00 🕐 Tue 1–10, Wed–Sun 1–9 🖐 Day pass: adult €9, child (under 12) €5 🚇 Les Halles, Châtelet

JAVA
www.la-java.fr
Latino bands often play at this concert hall and DJs mix salsa and latin strains to keep you dancing until the early hours. The venue saw Edith Piaf make her debut.
➕ 181 Q5 ✉ 105 rue du Faubourg du Temple, 75010 ☎ 01 42 02 20 52 🕐 Concerts: 8.30pm 🖐 €6–€8 🚇 Goncourt

LIZARD LOUNGE
www.cheapblonde.com
This lively pub has a wooden interior and beer on tap. Concerts take place in the basement.
➕ 181 N7 ✉ 18 rue du Bourg-Tibourg, 75004 ☎ 01 42 72 81 34 🕐 Daily noon–2am 🚇 Hôtel de Ville

OPÉRA BASTILLE
www.operadeparis.fr
This massive modern auditorium opened in 1989 (▷ 168). Operas and symphony orchestras benefit from its exceptional acoustics, and there is also some ballet.
➕ 181 Q8 ✉ 120 rue de Lyon, 75012 ☎ 0892 89 90 90 🖐 €5–€180 🚇 Bastille

THÉÂTRE DE LA BASTILLE
www.theatre-bastille.com
Formerly a cinema, this venue shows avant-garde plays and dance performances featuring new talent as well as big names.
➕ 181 Q7 ✉ 76 rue de la Roquette, 75011 ☎ 01 43 57 42 14 🕐 Performances: Tue–Sat 7.30pm, 9pm, Sun 5pm 🖐 €24 🚇 Bastille

THÉÂTRE MOLIÈRE—MAISON DE LA POÉSIE
www.maisondelapoesieparis.com
The Molière theatre, dating from 1791, is home to the 'House of Poetry'. Activities include readings, sometimes with music or dance.
➕ 180 N6 ✉ 157 rue St-Martin, 75003 ☎ 01 44 54 53 00 🖐 €11–€21 🚇 Rambuteau

THÉÂTRE MUSICAL PARIS CHÂTELET
www.chatelet-theatre.com
Built in 1862, this venue is famed for its grandeur, with candelabra and gilded mouldings. It attracts an audience of classical music lovers who like to dress up for orchestral concerts, ballet and opera.
➕ 180 M7 ✉ 1 place du Chatelet, 75001 ☎ 01 40 28 28 40 🕐 Performance: daily (concerts 8pm/opera 7.30pm) 🖐 €11–€101 🚇 Châtelet

THÉÂTRE DE LA VILLE
www.theatredelaville-paris.com
Forever associated with Sarah Bernhardt, who used to play here at the beginning of the 20th century, this grand theatre (1,000 seats) hosts plays and modern dance.
➕ 180 M7 ✉ 2 place du Châtelet, 75004 ☎ 01 42 74 22 77 🕐 Performances: Mon–Fri 8.30pm, Sat 5pm, 8.30pm 🖐 €16–€34 🚇 Châtelet

SPORTS AND ACTIVITIES

PARIS À VÉLO C'EST SYMPA
www.parisvelosympa.com
Guided bicycle tours are available in French and English. Unaccompanied bicycle and tandem rental is also available.
➕ 181 Q6 ✉ 22 rue Alphonse-Baudin, 75011 ☎ 01 48 87 60 01 🕐 Tours: Apr, Oct Wed, Sat–Sun 10am, Nov–Mar Sat–Sun 10am, May–Sep Sat 8.30pm 🖐 €34 for a 3-hour ride 🚇 Richard-Lenoir

RANDONNÉE EN ROLLERS
www.pari-rollers.com
The Rollers and Coquillages Society organizes mass in-line skating through Paris every Friday evening and Sunday afternoon. The three-hour routes changes regularly.
➕ 181 Q8 ✉ Office at Nomades, 37 boulevard Bourdon, 75004 ☎ 01 44 54 07 44 🕐 Fri 9pm, Sun 2pm 🖐 Free 🔹 Meet Fridays at base of Tour Montparnasse, Sundays at place de la Bastille 🚇 Bastille

HEALTH AND BEAUTY

LES BAINS DU MARAIS
www.lesbainsdumarais.com
In this hammam (Turkish bath) and spa you can sip mint tea after the hammam. Brisk massages as well as relaxing facials and other treatments are available.
➕ 180 N7 ✉ 31–33 rue des Blancs-Manteaux, 75014 ☎ 01 44 61 02 02 🕐 Women: Mon 10–8, Tue 10am–11pm, Wed 10–7. Men: Thu 10am–11pm, Fri 10–8. Mixed: Wed 7pm–11pm, Sat 10–8, Sun 10am–11pm 🖐 Hammam €35; oil massage €70 🚇 St-Paul

FOR CHILDREN

FORUM DES HALLES
▷ 154.

MUSEE DE LA POUPÉE
www.museedelapoupeeparis.com
This delightful collection of more than 500 French dolls from 1800 to 1919 is displayed in enchanting settings. There is a doll's hospital, and workshops and storytelling.
➕ 180 N6 ✉ Impasse Berthaud, 75003 ☎ 01 42 72 73 11 🕐 Tue–Sun 10–6 🖐 Adult €8, child (3–11) €4 🚇 Rambuteau

EATING

PRICES AND SYMBOLS

The prices given are the average for a two-course lunch (L) and a three-course dinner (D) for one person, without drinks. The wine price is for the least expensive bottle.

For a key to the symbols, ▷ 2.

AMBASSADE D'AUVERGNE

www.ambassade-auvergne.com
Ambassade d'Auvergne brings the finest regional cooking from the heart of the Auvergne, with ingredients such as foie gras, mushrooms and lentils complementing meats including duck, guinea fowl and veal. The interior combines formal table settings with a touch of mountain lodge on the walls. This is an excellent choice if you want to steer clear of modern bistro-style eateries and try hearty French dishes.
✚ 180 N6 ✉ 22 rue du Grenier St-Lazare, 75003, Les Halles ☎ 01 42 72 31 22 ◷ Daily 12–2, 7.30–last food orders at 10 ✋ L €30, D €45, Wine €19 Ⓜ Rambuteau

AU PIED DE COCHON

www.pieddecochon.com
This Parisian institution is a blessing for hungry night owls. It has been open around the clock, every day of the week, since 1946. Take your place in the elegant dining room, feast your eyes on the fresco-covered walls and the beautiful lighting, then your palate with one of France's regional special dishes. Vegetarians will want to avoid the pig's trotters, the house signature dish. Seafood is plentiful and the French onion soup a must.
✚ 180 M6 ✉ 6 rue Coquillère, 75001, Les Halles ☎ 01 40 13 77 00 ◷ Daily 24 hours ✋ L €30, D €45, Wine €19 Ⓜ Châtelet

LE BAR À SOUPES

www.lebarasoupes.com
At this brightly painted venue in the trendy Bastille district, you can choose from six varieties of fresh soup each day, with options including creamed tomato and red pepper, pumpkin and bacon, chick peas Eastern style, and coconut milk and carrot. Inside it's like a simple but charming cantina, with plain tables and chairs and large paintings of vegetables.
✚ 181 Q8 ✉ 33 rue de Charonne, 75011, Bastille ☎ 01 43 57 53 79 ◷ Mon–Sat 12–3, 6.30–11 ✋ Bowl of soup, bread and salad €10 Ⓜ Bastille, Ledru Rollin

Above *Turn back time at Brasserie Flo*

BISTROT L'OULETTE

www.l-oulette.com
A truly honest, no-frills but typically Parisian bistrot, serving good French dishes like Burgundian snails, confit and fresh apple tart, all made with the ingredients of southwest France. Owned by Marcel Baudis and his wife, Marie-Noëlle, who also run the upmarket l'Oulette in the 12th *arrondissement*, it's popular with locals looking for good value, and those on a more limited budget won't be disappointed.
✚ 181 Q7 ✉ 38 rue des Tournelles, 75011, Bastille ☎ 01 42 71 43 33 ◷ Mon–Fri 12–2.15, 7–12; Sat 7–12 ✋ L €30, D €44, Wine €15 Ⓜ Bastille

BISTROT DU PEINTRE

www.bistrotdupeintre.com
This beautiful art nouveau bistro, established in 1903, has wood panels, soft lighting and large mirrors. Not surprisingly, the 'painter's bistro' displays numerous paintings, including a beautiful oil of La Goulue, the celebrated cancan dancer. You can eat in the welcoming bar, in the other dining room upstairs or on the small

terrace in spring and summer. The high-quality traditional French cuisine includes chicory, diced bacon and poached egg salad, duck à l'orange and steak tartare.

⊞ 181 R8 ✉ 116 avenue Ledru-Rollin, 75011, Bastille ☎ 01 47 00 34 39 ◷ Daily 7am–midnight 🖐 L €25, D €40, Wine €11 Ⓜ Ledru Rollin

BOFINGER

www.bofingerparis.com

This elegant brasserie, dating from 1860, claims to be the oldest in Paris. It has a lavish art nouveau interior with an impressive stained-glass ceiling, mirrors, plenty of carved wood and lots of plants. The beautifully prepared French classic dishes include lobster, oysters, duck and steak tartare.

⊞ 181 Q8 ✉ 5–7 rue de la Bastille, 75004, Bastille ☎ 01 42 72 87 82 ◷ Mon–Fri 12–3, 6.30–1, Sat–Sun noon–1am 🖐 L €30, D €40, Wine €20 Ⓜ Bastille

BRASSERIE FLO

www.floparis.com

Brasserie Flo is a Parisian institution, established in 1886. It is housed in a listed building with a wonderful turn-of-the-20th-century interior, stained-glass panels, green leather booths and wooden panels on the ceiling. The menu includes steak, fresh seafood and Alsatian special dishes such as sauerkraut. For dessert, try the profiteroles or vacherin (ice cream and meringue).

⊞ 180 N5 ✉ 7 cour des Petites Écuries, 75010, Grands Boulevards ☎ 01 47 70 13 59 ◷ Daily 12–3, 7–1.30 🖐 L €28, D €42, Wine €25 Ⓜ Château-d'Eau

CHEZ JENNY

www.chez-jenny.com

Chez Jenny is named after the Alsatian Robert Jenny, who established the restaurant in 1930. Several types of sauerkraut are on offer—including one with champagne—and you can also choose seafood and special dishes such as saveloy sausage salad. Desserts include iced gugelhupf (cake) with egg custard. The decoration also pays tribute to the

northeastern region of France, with frescoes depicting its landscapes and marquetry by regional artist Charles Spindler.

⊞ 180 P6 ✉ 39 boulevard du Temple, 75003, République ☎ 01 44 54 39 00 ◷ Daily 12–12, Fri–Sat noon–1am 🖐 L €30, D €55, Wine €20 Ⓜ République

CHEZ PAUL

www.chezpaul.com

An old school bistro that hasn't changed much in the last 50 years (except to adhere to the smoking ban), the menu is simple but delicious and the decor is 100 per cent turn of the century—19th to 20th century that is. It's a no-frills place but exceptionally authentic.

⊞ 181 Q8 ✉ 13 rue de Charonne, 75011 ☎ 01 47 00 34 57 ◷ Mon–Fri 12–3, 7–12.30am, Sat–Sun noon–12.30am 🖐 L €30, D €40, Wine €17 Ⓜ Bastille, Ledru Rollin

CHEZ PRUNE

The terrace gives lovely views of the Canal St-Martin and the interior reflects the owner's enthusiasm for salvaging items. The bistro is perfect for a drink or light bite (try a cheese and cold meat platter) or for brunch, a feast of croissant, scrambled eggs, ham, salmon, orange juice and tea or coffee.

⊞ 180 P5 ✉ 36 rue Beaurepaire, 75010, République ☎ 01 42 41 30 47 ◷ Mon–Sat 8am–2am, Sun 10am–2am 🖐 Cold meat or cheese plate €10, brunch €18, beer €2.50 Ⓜ Jacques Bonsergent, République

LES GRANDES MARCHES

Les grandes marches (the big steps) refer to those of the Opéra Bastille, although this open two-floor house also has its own stylish staircase. Go to the upper floor for wonderful views of place de la Bastille. The modern decoration includes plenty of steel surfaces and subtle lighting. The menu includes innovative French dishes such as Loué chicken with pistachio and mustard juice, and caramel-coated monkfish with butter orange juice. The restaurant is also renowned for its seafood platters.

⊞ 181 Q8 ✉ 6 place de la Bastille, 75012, Bastille ☎ 01 43 42 90 32 ◷ Daily 9am–4am 🖐 L €25, D €45, Wine €19 Ⓜ Bastille

JOE ALLEN RESTAURANT

www.joeallenparis.com

In a small street in the bustling Les Halles district is one of four internationally famous American bar/restaurants under the Joe Allen banner. Its brick walls are covered with pictures and you dine by candlelight in the evenings. The venue has been a hit with the show-business crowd since it opened in 1972, partly due to the professional barmen, but also because of the high quality of the all-American food.

⊞ 180 N6 ✉ 30 rue Pierre Lescot, 75001, Les Halles ☎ 01 42 36 70 13 ◷ Sun–Wed 12–12, Thu–Sat noon–1am 🖐 L €25, D €35, Wine €17 Ⓜ Etienne-Marcel

LE PHARAMOND

www.pharamond.fr

This restaurant, established in 1832, is in a listed historic building. It has an extravagant art nouveau interior with ceramic murals, floor tiles, huge mirrors, mosaics and a dramatic spiral staircase. They serve traditional food from the Normandy region such as Caen-style tripe with cider, calvados (apple brandy) and potatoes, and melt-in-the-mouth chocolate cake. This is a Parisian institution, in keeping with the best tradition of Les Halles.

⊞ 180 N6 ✉ 24 rue de la Grande-Truanderie, 75001, Les Halles ☎ 01 40 28 45 18 ◷ Mon–Sat 12–2.30, 7.30–10.30 🖐 L €40, D €60, Wine €18 Ⓜ Les Halles

LE TRAIN BLEU

www.le-train-bleu.com

To step inside this historic restaurant is to take a journey back to 1900 when it was inaugurated as the new station buffet. The classic French cuisine includes sole meunière, roast lamb with gratinéed potatoes, and crème brûlée.

⊞ 181 Q9 ✉ Gare de Lyon, 75012, Bastille ☎ 01 43 43 09 06 ◷ Daily 11.30–3, 7–11 🖐 L €45, D €80, Wine €30 Ⓜ Gare de Lyon

Above *Reception at Hôtel St-Paul Le Marais*

PRICES AND SYMBOLS

Prices are the lowest and highest for a double room for one night. Breakfast is included unless noted otherwise. All the hotels listed accept credit cards unless otherwise stated. Note that rates vary widely throughout the year.

For a key to the symbols, ▷ 2.

AUBERGE INTERNATIONALE DES JEUNES

www.aijparis.com
These lodgings are at rock-bottom prices. The rooms are clean and the atmosphere friendly. Four-bed rooms have a separate bathroom and shower, while rooms for two or three people have a bathroom on each floor. There is internet access. Bed linen and blankets are provided.  181 R8 ✉ 10 rue Trousseau, 75011, Bastille ☎ 01 47 00 62 00 ✋ Jul–Aug €21 per person; Mar–Jun, Sep, Oct €20; Nov–Feb €17 ⓘ 100 rooms; 250 beds ⓜ Ledru Rollin, Bastille

AUBERGE DE JEUNESSE JULES FERRY

www.fuaj.org/Paris-Jules-Ferry
Ideally placed for strolls along the Canal St-Martin, this youth hostel has six-bed dormitories as well as

some rooms for couples. Facilities include a laundry, electronic lockers and internet terminals. Breakfast is available but no cooking facilities. ✚ 181 Q6 ✉ 8 boulevard Jules Ferry, 75011, Canal St-Martin ☎ 01 43 57 55 60 ✋ €25 per person ⓘ 99 beds ⓜ République

BOURG TIBOURG

www.hotelbourgtibourg.com
Superstar designer Jacques Garcia has created this charming boutique hotel in a fantasy of styles in the heart of the Marais. Choose from Venetian to Eastern and from Romantic to baroque—where the small rooms are all exquisitely furnished, exotic and intimate. ✚ 180 N7 ✉ 19 rue du Bourg-Tibourg, 75004, Le Marais ☎ 01 42 78 47 39 ✋ €250–€370, excluding breakfast ⓘ 30 ⓜ Hôtel de Ville

CASTEX HOTEL

www.castexhotelparis.com
Situated on the border of the historic Marais and Bastille districts, this 3-star hotel deliberately emphasizes its 17th-century features: period furniture in the reception areas and bedrooms, picturesque breakfast room with

stone walls and vaulted ceiling. The stylish bedrooms are equipped with telephone, satellite TV and safe. ✚ 180 P8 ✉ 5 rue Castex, 75004, Marais ☎ 01 42 72 31 52 ✋ €84–€150, excluding breakfast ⓘ 30 ⓢ ⓜ Bastille

CORAIL HÔTEL

www.corailparishotel.com
This 3-star hotel is popular with the business crowd, being close to the Gare de Lyon, with its Métro, RER and mainline train services. Rooms may be slightly lacking in character, but come equipped with a hairdryer, private safe, telephone, WiFi and satellite TV. ✚ 181 Q9 ✉ 23 rue de Lyon, 75012, Gare de Lyon ☎ 01 43 43 23 54 ✋ €69–€110, excluding breakfast ⓘ 50 ⓢ ⓜ Gare de Lyon

HOSTELLERIE DU MARAIS

www.hostelleriedumarais.com
A stone's throw from the place des Vosges, this small 3-star hotel was totally renovated in 2008. The vaulted cellar has remnants of the original 17th-century building, while the bedrooms are spacious with clean lines, designer touches

and WiFi. Warm hues and exposed stone and wood floors grace the reception, lounge and bar areas.

⊞ 180 P7 ✉ 30 rue de Turenne, 75003, Le Marais ☎ 01 42 72 73 47 ⚲ €132–€230, excluding breakfast ① 24 ⓜ St-Paul, Chemin Vert

HÔTEL BELLEVUE ET DU CHARIOT D'OR

www.hotelbellevue75.com

Dating from the mid 19th century, the hotel's grand Haussmann-style facade belies the simple bedrooms within, but this 2-star establishment is comfortable and good value. Located just north of the Pompidou Centre and close to the Forum des Halles, all rooms have private bathrooms and WiFi, and there is an elevator.

⊞ 180 N6 ✉ 39 rue de Turbigo, 75003, Le Marais ☎ 01 48 87 45 60 ⚲ €70–€72, excluding breakfast ① 59 ⓜ Châtelet-Les Halles, Réaumur-Sebastopol

HÔTEL LOUVRE RIVOLI

www.paris-hotel-rivoli.com

This 3-star hotel, within walking distance of the Louvre, Notre-Dame and Centre Georges Pompidou, has a welcoming salon, a water bar, and a 16th-century vaulted breakfast room. Rooms and public areas are cool and contemporary.

⊞ 180 M7 ✉ 7 rue Jean Lantier, 75001, Châtelet ☎ 01 42 33 45 38 ⚲ €90–€130, excluding breakfast ① 30 ⓜ Châtelet

HÔTEL MURANO

www.muranoresort.com

A pop-art bar, white marble, 21st-century-style frosted glass and steel fittings housed in a 19th-century classical building make this a hip designer establishment. It is like a playground for the young, cool and chic with a DJ bar, glittering red elevator and moody lighting. The spacious bedrooms are decorated in shades from sunshine yellow and lilac to sky blue and emerald green, while the suites have minipools or gas fireplaces—and entry to all is by fingerprint scanner. The Murano is under the same ownership as the Kube in Montmartre.

⊞ 180 P6 ✉ 13 boulevard du Temple, 75003, Le Marais ☎ 01 42 71 20 00 ⚲ €350–€2,500, excluding breakfast ① 49 rooms, 2 suites ⓢ ⓜ Filles du Calvaire

HÔTEL DU PETIT MOULIN

www.hoteldupetitmoulin.com

Once the oldest bakery in Paris where Victor Hugo bought his baguettes, this 1900s building is now a showcase for designer Christian Lacroix. Each of the 17 rooms bears his hallmark with designs ranging from rustic to zen, or from traditional to playful. Lawn-green corridors and black lacquered doors contrast with traditional and modern furnishings and splendid art by the couturier himself. This is high fashion in the Haut Marais.

⊞ 180 P6 ✉ 29 rue du Poitou, 75003, Le Marais ☎ 01 42 74 10 10 ⚲ €110–€230, excluding breakfast ① 17 ⓢ ⓜ St-Sébastien Froissart

HÔTEL ST-MERRY

www.hotelmarais.com

If you choose room nine of this 3-star hotel you'll be sleeping under a flying buttress! The hotel was built during the Renaissance as the presbytery of the church of St-Merri. Its highly original interior also has many late-Gothic features, including sculptures, carved woodwork and beamed ceilings.

⊞ 180 N7 ✉ 78 rue de la Verrerie, 75004, Le Marais ☎ 01 42 78 14 15 ⚲ €160–€230, excluding breakfast ① 11 rooms, 1 suite ⓜ Hôtel-de-Ville, Châtelet

HÔTEL ST-PAUL LE MARAIS

www.hotel-paris-marais.com

A former 17th-century convent houses this 3-star hotel, near the Musée Carnavalet. The bar and salon have burgundy carpets and plenty of mahogany, and there is an internet area. Bedrooms have cable TV, telephone, WiFi and tea- and coffee-making facilities, and breakfast is served in a fine stone-vaulted room.

⊞ 180 P7 ✉ 8 rue de Sévigné, 75004, Le Marais ☎ 01 48 04 97 27 ⚲ €135–€290, excluding breakfast ① 28 ⓢ ⓜ St-Paul

HÔTEL SAINTONGE

www.hotelsaintongeparis.com

This small, 3-star hotel is in a quiet street in the Marais in a tall 17th-century former private mansion. Exposed stonework, beams and vaulted ceilings all add to its traditional, rustic charm. Rooms tend to be on the small size but, to compensate, they are light and attractively decorated. Breakfast (not included) is served in the atmospheric former cellar.

⊞ 180 P6 ✉ 16 rue Saintonge, 75003, Le Marais ☎ 01 42 77 91 13 ⚲ €115; suites €170, excluding breakfast ① 23 ⓜ République, Filles du Calvaire

LES JARDINS DU MARAIS

www.lesjardinsdumarais.com

Providing that rare balance of peace and solitude in an area that is generally bustling with shoppers and tourists sightseeing, near the Picasso Museum, Les Jardins du Marais was completely refurbished in 2009 but has retained a brighter version of its original 1930s features. It has every modern amenity, including facilities for visitors with disabilities, and a fitness centre.

⊞ 181 Q7 ✉ 228 rue Amelot, 75011, Marais ☎ 01 40 21 20 00 ⚲ €135–€350, excluding breakfast ① 255 ⓢ ⓥ ⓜ St-Sébastien Froissart

PAVILLON DE LA REINE

www.pavillon-de-la-reine.com

It would be hard to find a more perfect setting for a 4-star hotel than this 17th-century building on the historic place des Vosges. This was the residence of Anne of Austria, Louis XIII's wife, and the exquisite interior retains much of its period furniture, with an imposing fireplace in the salon. The vaulted cellar is now a breakfast room, with tapestries adorning the walls. Bedrooms have satellite TV, WiFi, bathrobe and slippers, and some have delightful canopy beds.

⊞ 181 P7 ✉ 28 place des Vosges, 75003, Le Marais ☎ 01 40 29 19 19 ⚲ €360–€490, excluding breakfast ① 40 rooms, 14 suites ⓢ ⓜ Bastille, St-Paul

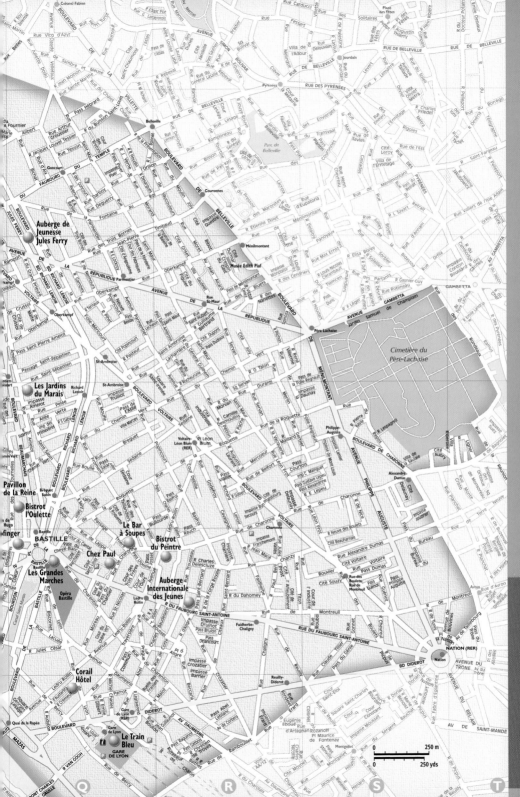

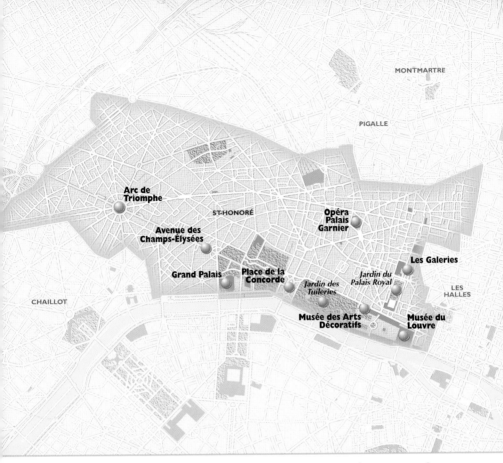

LOUVRE AND CHAMPS-ÉLYSÉES

This is arguably the most grandiosely attractive area of Paris, with many of its most important buildings and monuments, and the world's largest and most glamorous museum, the Louvre. The Arc de Triomphe and Champs-Élysées are, in combination, Paris's most famous street and its crowning glory. The Arc, erected as a symbol of French national might, is still the focus of major commemorations, and the 2km (1.2 miles) leafy Champs-Élysées, which started life as a driveway in 1616, is permanently bustling with tourists and Parisians engaged in some serious shopping.

The area's other major shopping centres are Les Galeries, a network of four 19th-century malls near the Jardin du Palais Royal. This is close to the Louvre and one of Paris's most famous gardens, the Tuileries. In the vicinity there's the Musée des Arts Décoratifs, whose collection of decorative arts includes some from the Middle Ages. Other distinguished museums include the Musée Cernuschi, which has ancient Oriental art exhibits, and the Musée Fragonard which tells the history of perfume.

Set in a lavish palace, the Bibliothèque National de France–Site Richelieu has been the country's official library since the early 18th century. A little north of here the French stock exchange, La Bourse, is to be found, and the Opéra Palais Garnier, the lavish theatre which was the largest in the world when it opened in 1875, is unmissable. Place de la Concorde, itself an imposing sight with an ancient obelisk at the centre of the city's largest square, is also a wonderful place from which to get an overall visual taste of Paris. From here in various directions you can see the Champs-Élysées, the Arc de Triomphe, the Tuileries, the Louvre, the church of La Madeleine, the Pont de la Concorde and the Palais Bourbon, home of the Assemblée Nationale.

INTRODUCTION

The wide, leafy Champs-Élysées is a focal point for the French nation, witness to momentous events such as de Gaulle's triumphal liberation march in 1944 and the soccer World Cup celebrations in 1998. Despite the avenue's glamorous reputation, be prepared also for streams of traffic, swarms of busy people and rather brash cinemas, car showrooms and chain stores.

If the Arc de Triomphe is your main goal, take the Métro to Charles-de-Gaulle–Étoile, which drops you just outside. However, if you don't mind a 20-minute stroll, a good place to begin is two-thirds of the way down, at Métro Champs-Élysées-Clemenceau. Leave the Métro station and take a look at the imposing Grand Palais on avenue Winston Churchill (▷ 192), then walk towards place Charles-de-Gaulle, with the Arc de Triomphe looming up majestically in front of you. You'll see greenery as far as the Rond-Point des Champs-Élysées, at which point the commercial side of the avenue takes over. At the top, use the underpass to cross to the Arc, where you can climb the 234 steps to the roof. The views are stunning. Once back down, you could get a bite to eat at one of the nearby cafés or hop on the Métro and travel the four stops to Concorde to see the start of the avenue. This is guarded by copies of the Marly Horses—the originals are in the Louvre.

The Champs-Élysées dates back to 1616, when Marie de Médicis turned the area into a fashionable driveway. Then, landscape designer André Le Nôtre

INFORMATION

www.monuments-nationaux.fr
Arc de Triomphe
✚ 184 G5 ✉ place Charles-de-Gaulle, 75008 ☎ 01 55 37 73 77
🕐 Apr–Sep daily 10am–11pm; Oct–Mar 10am–10.30pm. Closed 14 July pm, 11 Nov pm 🖐 Free to wander around the base. Rooftop: adult €9.50, under 18 free
🚇 Charles de Gaulle-Étoile 🚌 22, 30, 31, 52, 73, 92 🚈 RER line A, Charles de Gaulle-Étoile 🖐 For information on guided tours call Centre de Monuments Nationaux on 01 44 54 19 30 📖 €7
🎁 Gift shop ❓ There is a ceremony at the Tomb of the Unknown Soldier daily at 6.30pm

Opposite *Tomb of the Unknown Soldier*
Above *The Arc de Triomphe at night*

AVENUE DES CHAMPS-ÉLYSÉES

✚ 184 J5 ✉ 75008 🚇 Charles de Gaulle–Étoile, Georges V, Franklin D. Roosevelt, Champs-Élysées-Clemenceau 🚌 32, 42, 73 and others 🚃 Charles de Gaulle-Étoile 🍴 🖥 Wide selection 🏬 Plenty of shops

TIPS

» It takes at least 30 minutes to walk from one end of the Champs-Élysées to the other. You may prefer to take the Métro—Line 1 (yellow) runs the length of the avenue.

» Most cafés and restaurants are at the Arc de Triomphe end, although you may find better value in establishments in the side streets.

» The best time for photos from the top of the arch is just after it opens, when the light is clearer, or just before sunset.

Above left *Louis Vuitton is one of the many stores on the Champs-Élysées*
Above right La Marseillaise *sculpture by François Rude on the Arc de Triomphe*

(of Versailles fame) added alleys of trees and gardens, prompting its current name, Elysian Fields. Walkways and fountains were installed in 1824 and the avenue became crowded with cafés, restaurants and a stylish clientele.

Napoléon Bonaparte commissioned the Arc de Triomphe in 1806, demanding an awesome memorial to the French army. In 1810 a wooden, life-size model was installed to celebrate the Emperor's marriage to Marie-Louise, but the real thing was not ready until after his death. Various architects and sculptors worked on the monument, inspired by Rome's Arch of Titus and Arch of Septimius Severus. The arch's symbolic role was confirmed after World War I, when parades of victorious troops marched through.

WHAT TO SEE

ARC DE TRIOMPHE

Napoléon conceived the Arc de Triomphe as a symbol of his military might, modelled on the triumphal arches of ancient Rome—specifically the Arch of Titus but, at 50m (164ft) high, more than three times bigger. Two centuries on, the colossal monument is still an image of national pride. It plays a central role in many of France's key commemorations, including VE Day (8 May), Bastille Day (14 July) and Remembrance Day (11 November). Within its grounds are the Tomb of the Unknown Soldier, installed in 1920 after World War I, and a poignant Memorial Flame, added three years later.

Access to the Arc de Triomphe is gained via the stairs on the north corner of the Champs-Élysées. There are wonderful views from the rooftop, which is reached via 234 steps. In the museum hall of the Arc de Triomphe, greatly modernized and modified from its original pre-World War II fittings (see We Are Flying, ▷ panel, right), visitors are invited to view the 12 avenues, which radiate from Étoile. Most of these avenues bear the name of a famous battle fought (and won) by Napoléon, such as Friedland and Wagram. From the top you can admire Haussmann's web-like street design and look along the Grand Axis (▷ panel, right) towards place de la Concorde in one direction and the Grande Arche in the other. At night the city shimmers with lights. There is a small shop and museum on the way up.

Back at ground level, save some time to admire the magnificent sculpted facade, the work of three different artists. Don't miss the fearsome winged figure of Liberty on François Rude's sculpture, *La Marseillaise,* calling the French to defend their nation (northeastern pillar, facing the Champs-Élysées). On the southeast pillar Napoléon is depicted as a victorious Roman emperor. The 30 shields studding the crown of the arch each bear the name of a Revolutionary or Imperial victory.

AVENUE DES CHAMPS-ÉLYSÉES

This famous avenue is packed with cinemas, shops, cafés and car showrooms, and bustling with life. Although it is high on most visitors' itineraries, you are as likely to see Parisians going about their business as camera-snapping sightseers. The tree-lined avenue is more than 2km (1.2 miles) long and 71m (232ft) wide, stretching between two of the city's most illustrious monuments—the Arc de Triomphe and the Egyptian obelisk in place de la Concorde. A short detour will lead you to other key buildings, including the Grand Palais (▷ 192) and the Palais de l'Élysée, official residence of the French president.

The French come here to celebrate, whether it be winning the soccer World Cup or welcoming home participants in the Tour de France cycle race. The avenue has hosted some of France's most prestigious processions, including the funeral of writer Victor Hugo in 1885, General de Gaulle's liberation march in 1944 and the bicentenary celebrations of the French Revolution in 1989. Catch it on 14 July (Bastille Day) when most of the French army rolls past in the traditional parade. Another good time to visit is during the Christmas illuminations in November and December.

GRAND AXIS

The Arc de Triomphe is a key element of the Grand Axis that runs in an imaginary straight line across the city from the Louvre's Arc de Triomphe du Carrousel to the Grande Arche at La Défense (▷ 254). To emphasize the progression along this route, the Grande Arche is twice as tall as the Arc de Triomphe, which in turn is twice as tall as the Arc de Triomphe du Carrousel.

ÉTOILE

The Arc de Triomphe's traffic-ridden roundabout is still known as the Étoile (star), despite an official name-change to place Charles-de-Gaulle. The Étoile label comes from the 12 avenues that radiate from it like the tips of a star, a layout designed by Baron Haussmann in the 19th century. It may look impressive from the roof of the Arc de Triomphe but at ground level it seems to have resulted in all the cars in the capital converging on this one point!

WE ARE FLYING

Modernization work in 2008 replaced some of the outdated pre-World War II fittings inside the Arc, so that major historical events are shown on touch-sensitive screens. The display also retraces the construction of the monument, highlighting its architecture and decoration. Also a 'real time' film is projected on the floor, giving visitors the impression they are flying 31m (102ft) above the forecourt and the commemorative flame.

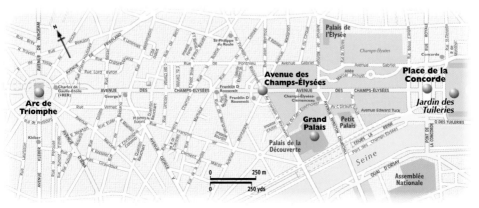

BIBLIOTHÈQUE NATIONALE DE FRANCE–SITE RICHELIEU

www.bnf.fr

This former palace has been the base for France's national library since the early 18th century. It is close to the Louvre and Palais Royal and was once home to Cardinal Mazarin, Louis XIII's First Minister. In 1996 part of its collection moved to the new François-Mitterrand site (▷ 111), creating space to focus on manuscripts, maps, music, prints, photos and coins. Reading room access is reserved for those who prove a genuine research need, but you can see temporary exhibitions in the Galerie Mansart (devoted to photography), Galerie Mazarine and the Crypte. The Galerie Mazarine has a wonderful painted ceiling.

✚ 185 M6 ✉ 58 rue de Richelieu, 75002 ☎ 01 53 79 59 59 ⓘ Library: Reading Room advisory service: Mon–Fri 10–5, Sat 10–12.30, 1.30–5; rooms vary; Galerie Mansart, Galerie Mazarine and Crypte: Tue–Sat 10–7, Sun 12–7 (during exhibitions only) ✋ Adult €7, under 18 free ⓜ Bourse ⓑ 20, 29, 39, 48, 67, 74 ⛴ Guided visits 1st Tue of month

LA BOURSE

Paris's money-spinning hub is in the Palais de la Bourse. Designed by architect Alexandre Brongniart, this neoclassical Napoleonic creation was built between 1808 and 1826. In 1902 and 1907 two wings were added, giving the building the shape of a cross. After more than 150 years of the clamour of stockbrokers, in 1987 silence finally reigned in the Palais Brongniart when the stock exchange was computerized. Glass cubicles and a blackboard displaying stocks and shares recreate the atmosphere of the trading floor.

✚ 185 M5 ✉ Palais Brongniart, rue Vivienne, 75002 ☎ 01 49 27 14 70 ⓘ Closed to the public for 2012 ⓜ Bourse ⓑ 20, 29, 39, 74, 85

Right *Statue of Jean-Paul Sartre outside the Bibliothèque Nationale de France*
Opposite *Galerie Vivienne*

DROUOT

www.drouot.fr

Paris's leading auction house was founded in the 19th century and takes its name from the Comte de Drouot, Napoléon's aide-de-camp. There are 16 auction rooms and the auctions, in French, usually begin at 2pm. Viewing is from 11 to 6 the day before the sale and 11 to noon on the day of the sale. You'll find details on the website and in *La Gazette de l'Hôtel Drouot*, published weekly.

✚ 185 M5 ✉ 9 rue Drouot, 75009 ☎ 01 48 00 20 20 ⓘ Sep–Jul Mon–Sat 11–6, Sun times vary ✋ Free ⓜ Richelieu-Drouot, Le Peletier ⓑ 20, 39, 48, 67, 74, 85

LES GALERIES

▷ 191.

GRAND PALAIS

▷ 192.

JARDIN DU PALAIS ROYALE

▷ 193.

JARDIN DES TUILERIES

▷ 194.

JEU DE PAUME

www.jeudepaume.org

The Jeu de Paume is part of the Centre National de la Photographie. It combines its efforts with the Site Sully, housed in the 17th-century Hôtel de Sully in Le Marais, to present the art of photography from the 19th to the 21st centuries through temporary exhibitions. The airy, neoclassical Jeu de Paume, idyllically located in the Jardin des Tuileries (▷ 194), was commissioned by Napoléon III as an indoor court for *réal* (royal) tennis, played with the *paume* (palm) of the hand. When lawn tennis took over in popularity, the court was used for art exhibitions and after World War II it became one of the world's finest Impressionist museums, until the exodus of its rich collection to the Musée d'Orsay in 1986.

✚ 185 K6 ✉ 1 place de la Concorde, 75008 ☎ 01 47 03 12 50 ⓘ Tue–Fri 12–7, Sat–Sun 10–7, also Tue 7–9 ✋ Adult €8.50, under 18 free ⓜ Concorde ⓑ 24, 42, 52, 72, 73, 84 🛈 ❓ Closed between temporary exhibitions; programme available on 01 47 03 12 52 (recorded information)

LES GALERIES

Between the late 18th and early 19th century a network of *galeries* was built on the Right Bank. Fewer than 30 of the original 140 passages survive. Many have been restored; others are dusty reminders of a bygone age.

Les Galeries, often referred to as 'the passages', were the forerunners of the modern shopping mall conceived and built in the early 19th century. The idea of locating shops and cafés under cover in linked passageways was partly inspired by the souks of the Arabian world, affording elegant Parisian shoppers the comfort of weather-proof alleys out of the way of mud-splattering carriages. When the department stores arrived, Les Galeries fell into decay, but some were restored to former glory in the late 20th century.

WHAT TO SEE IN THE GALERIES

Elegant Galerie Vivienne, built in 1823, is perhaps the most fashionable, with its ornate cast-iron gates, high glass roofs, chandeliers and mosaic floors. It is home to Legrand—one of Paris's best wine-merchants—a toy shop, a bookshop established in 1826, stylish boutiques and a chic *salon de thé* with tables spilling out under the lofty skylights.

Parallel to it is the much-restored Galerie Colbert, dating from 1826 and now an annexe of the Bibliothèque Nationale. It has interesting shops and a sophisticated brasserie, the Grand Colbert (▷ 214–215). Exhibitions are sometimes held in its galleries and auditorium. The Passage des Panoramas, built in 1800, is today a hive of specialist shops with eateries.

The picturesque 1826 Galerie Véro-Dodat is named after two butchers and was one of the first streets in Paris to be illuminated by gas. Today its black-and-white tiled floor, window boxes and carved wooden mouldings make a shadowy, harmonious setting for an old-world restaurant, antiques shops and galleries. Passages Jouffroy and Verdeau are also worth visiting. Both passages have a range of antiquarian bookshops and specialty stores and passage Jouffroy is home to the Musée Grévin waxwork museum (▷ 196).

INFORMATION

http://parisinconnu.com/passages

Galerie Vivienne ✚ 185 M6 ✉ 4 rue des Petits-Champs/6 rue Vivienne/5 rue de la Banque, 75002 🚇 Bourse

Galerie Colbert ✚ 185 M6 ✉ 6 rue des Petits-Champs, 75002 🚇 Bourse

Passage des Panoramas ✚ 185 M5 ✉ 11 boulevard Montmartre/10 rue St-Marc, 75002 🚇 Grands Boulevards

Galerie Véro-Dodat ✚ 185 M6 ✉ 19 rue Jean-Jacques Rousseau, 75001 🚇 Palais-Royal–Musée du Louvre

Passage Jouffroy ✚ 185 M5 ✉ 10 boulevard Montmartre, 75009 🚇 Grands Boulevards

Passage Verdeau ✚ 185 M5 ✉ 31 bis rue du Faubourg-Montmartre, 75009 🚇 Le Peletier

TIPS

» The *galeries* are an ideal place to visit on a rainy day. Browse in the boutiques, window shop or simply enjoy the ornate architecture, glass roofs and decorative tile floors.

» If your feet are aching, relax in a café under the skylights and let the surroundings waft you back to 19th-century Paris.

GRAND PALAIS

The Grand Palais, with its soaring glass and iron domes, occupies a commanding position between the Seine and the Champs-Élysées and faces the Petit Palais across avenue Winston Churchill. It was built for the 1900 Universal Exhibition, along with the nearby Pont Alexandre III and Petit Palais. The aim was to form a prestigious axis running from the golden-domed Les Invalides to the Champs-Élysées. The colossal building is a striking mix of art nouveau and neoclassical and it is well worth walking around the outside before venturing inside to see the high-profile exhibitions. There are wonderful friezes on the eastern and western facades of the Grand Palais.

INSIDE THE GRAND PALAIS

The Palais falls under the auspices of the Réunion des Musées Nationaux, which hosts a continuous series of temporary exhibitions at the venue. On the western side, the Palais de la Découverte is a hands-on science museum aimed primarily at children, with a Planetarium (the exhibits may be of limited interest to children who do not speak French). Topics range from climate change to the workings of the human heart. Even if you don't want to visit the science museum, take a peek at its foyer, with mosaic floor and glass-domed ceiling. As well as the science museum and the main exhibition hall, there is also an events hall which is variously the venue for car shows, fashion shows and other grand events.

RESTORATION

The Grand Palais is the world's largest structure of ironwork and glass. In 1993 one of the glass-panel ceilings of the palace fell in and it was closed for more than a dozen years, reopening fully only in 2007, after a major €100 million face-lift.

PETIT PALAIS

The Palais is home to the Musée des Beaux-Arts de la Ville de Paris, offering an eclectic and surprising collection of 17th- and 20th-century paintings, including works by Cézanne, Courbet, Delacroix, Gaugin, Renoir, and Rodin.

JARDIN DU PALAIS ROYAL

This tranquil garden is the perfect place to recharge your batteries after a visit to the Louvre. The flower-filled enclave is separated from the 21st century by a cordon of handsome 18th-century arcades. These shelter traditional *salons de thé* and quirky shops selling anything from art, jewellery and clothes to pipes, silverware and model soldiers.

In good weather the gardens are full of Parisians resting, reading and playing boules. The flower beds are vibrant, and a central statue and refreshing fountain add to the elegant calm. Children come to roller-skate around the rather incongruous grey-and-white striped mini-columns in the Cour d'Honneur, a controversial 1986 addition by artist Daniel Buren. The courtyard's sleek water features blend more easily with the rest of the garden.

THE PALACE

The Palais Royal was commissioned by Louis XIII's advisor, Cardinal Richelieu, in the 17th century and was originally called the Palais-Cardinal. Molière and his troupe of actors used to perform in the Théâtre du Petit Cardinal, which once stood at the southern corner of the palace. It was here in 1673 that the illustrious playwright fell ill, ironically during a production of *Le Malade Imaginaire* (The Hypochondriac). He died a few hours later. The nearby Comédie Française still stages his plays today.

Louis XIV spent part of his childhood in the Palais Royal and authors Colette and Jean Cocteau lived in residences within the grounds. Now the building houses the offices of the French Ministry of Culture and is not open to the general public.

UPRISING

The arcades and apartments surrounding the palace garden were constructed in the 18th century. Only a few years later, on 12 July 1789, Camille Desmoulins made a passionate speech in the garden that sparked the uprising and the storming of the Bastille two days later (▷ 37) signalling the start of the Revolution.

INFORMATION

www.monuments-nationaux.fr

✚ 185 M6 ✉ place du Palais-Royal, 75001 (entrance to the gardens is through an arch to the left of the Palais Royal) ◷ Jun–Aug daily 7am–11pm; Apr–May 7am–10.15pm; Sep 7am–9.30pm; Oct–Mar 7.30am–8.30pm ✋ Free ⓜ Palais Royal/Musée du Louvre 🚌 21, 48, 67, 69, 72, 81 🍴 Restaurants and tea rooms around the outside, including Muscade tea room (▷ 215) 🛍 Plenty of small shops in the arcades

Opposite *The glass-domed Grand Palais*
Above *An intriguing fountain of giant boules in the Cour d'Honneur*

INFORMATION

⊕ 185 K6 ✉ place de la Concorde, 75001 ☎ 01 40 20 90 43 🕐 Jun–Aug daily 7am–11pm; Apr–May 7am–9pm; Sep–Mar 9.30–7.30 ✋ Free 🚇 Tuileries, Concorde 🚌 24, 68, 72, 73, 84, 94 🅿 €7 ☕ Open-air cafés 📖 Bookshop at Concorde end ❓ No dogs allowed

TIPS

» Children can rent model yachts to sail on the pond at the Louvre end of the park.
» Free guided tours take place during the summer months. For more information see the noticeboards or call 01 49 96 19 33.

JARDIN DES TUILERIES

Dominated at one end by the hectic place de la Concorde and at the other by the mighty Louvre, this is not one of those parks that lets you forget you're in the heart of the city. But what the elegant, French-style grounds lack in seclusion they make up for in photo opportunities, offering marvellous views of the Louvre, Eiffel Tower, Arc de Triomphe, Musée d'Orsay and the Egyptian obelisk in place de la Concorde. The park, once considered the best-kept in Europe, runs alongside the Seine.

ART AND NATURE

The grandest way to enter is through the gilded gates at the Concorde end. This brings you to the first of two large ponds, balanced at either end of the park—ideal for relaxing with a book. Two art galleries stand on terraces either side of this first pond, the Jeu de Paume (▷ 190) and the Musée de l'Orangerie (▷ 197). Look out for Henry Moore's *Reclining Figure* (1951), which sits on the steps leading up to the Musée de l'Orangerie.

Follow the wide central avenue towards the Louvre and the gravel of the western half of the park gradually gives way to grass and well-tended flower beds. You'll pass allegorical statues, open-air cafés and children's playgrounds. All around people are relaxing. At the other end of the park, the neoclassical Arc du Carrousel acts as a symbolic gateway to the Louvre and is also the first arch in Paris's *Grand Axis*, the imaginary straight line linking the Louvre, the Arc de Triomphe and the Grande Arche.

ITALIAN ORIGINS

The park was the inspiration of Catherine de Médicis, who wanted an Italian-style garden to complement the Tuileries Palace, built in 1564. Lavish balls, concerts and fireworks ensured her garden became a key social venue. The park as we know it today dates from 1649, when Louis XIV asked landscape gardener, André Le Nôtre, to redesign it in the formal French style. He added the central avenue, as well as two raised walkways running along either side, and the garden soon became a fashionable promenading area. The palace went up in smoke at the hands of the Communards in 1871 but the garden survived. After years of neglect and pollution in the 20th century, it received a make-over in time for the start of the 21st century.

Above *A formal French garden between the Louvre and place de la Concorde, Jardin des Tuileries affords fine views*

MUSÉE DES ARTS DÉCORATIFS

The Union Centrale des Arts Décoratifs (UCAD) was founded in the late 19th century by a group of industrialists whose aim was to display beauty in function. Today UCAD comprises a decorative arts library, three schools and four museums. Three of the museums, including the Musée des Arts Décoratifs, are in the Pavillon de Marsan and the Louvre's Rohan wing.

THE COLLECTION

The Musée des Arts Décoratifs has more than 150,000 items covering almost every aspect of the decorative arts, from ceramics, glass and embroidery to wood and metalwork. Collections include the Middle Ages and Renaissance, art nouveau, art deco, modern and contemporary, and a further five specialist departments: glass, toys, drawings, wallpaper and a dazzling display of 1,200 items of jewellery from the Middle Ages to today.

The art nouveau collection includes several pieces of furniture by Emile Gallé, one of the masters of the genre. The Middle Ages and Renaissance galleries contain a rich collection reflecting religious art and domestic life from the 13th to 16th centuries. The Galerie des Retables contains a fine collection of European altarpieces carved in wood and stone. Tapestries are on display in the Salle de la Vie Rurale dans la Tapisserie. The Salle du Maître de la Madeleine contains medieval sculptures and paintings, and the Cabinet de Travail, a delightful period room, is decorated with refined marquetry panelling. The Salle des Vitraux contains French and Italian furniture, Flemish tapestries, 16th-century stained glass and objets d'art.

OTHER COLLECTIONS

The Musée Nissim de Camondo, the grand collection of objets d'art amassed by the Comte de Camondo during the late 18th century, is housed in an early 19th-century family home (▷ 197).

INFORMATION

www.lesartsdecoratifs.fr

✚ 185 L6 ✉ 107 rue de Rivoli, 75001
☎ 01 44 55 57 50 🕐 Tue–Wed, Fri–Sun 11–6, Thu 6–9 🎟 Adult €9, under 18 free; €17.50 for all four museums
🚇 Palais-Royal/Musée du Louvre, Tuileries 🚌 21, 27, 39, 48, 69, 72, 81, 95 ☛ Phone in advance for details of guided tours: tel 01 44 55 59 26
🏛 Bookshop and gift shop

Below *Iconic chair designs on display in the Musée des Arts Décoratifs*

REGIONS LOUVRE AND CHAMPS-ÉLYSÉES • SIGHTS

195

MUSÉE CERNUSCHI

www.paris.fr

Banker Henri Cernuschi went on an 18-month world tour in the 1870s and came back with an enchanting assortment of ancient art from China and Japan. On his death in 1896 he left the collection to the city, along with his neoclassical mansion next to Parc Monceau (▷ 205). Since then, further items have been added, including the prized eighth-century painting *Chevaux et Palefrenier (Horses and Groom)*. Ancient statuettes, jade objects and pottery are all on display, as well as contemporary Chinese paintings. The approach to the museum is attractive, whether through the picturesque Parc de Monceau or the beautiful gilded gates that lead into avenue Vélasquez from the boulevard Malesherbes.

✚ 185 J4 ✉ 7 avenue Vélasquez, 75008 ☎ 01 53 96 21 50 ⏰ Tue–Sun 10–6 🖐 Free (except temporary exhibitions: adult €7.50, under 14 free) Ⓜ Monceau, Villiers 🚌 30, 94

MUSÉE FRAGONARD

www.fragonard.com

This museum tells the story of perfume-making over 3,000 years, from Ancient Egyptian times to the present day. It is split into two parts, in two buildings near the Opéra Palais Garnier. The Musée du Parfum is in a 19th-century town house in rue Scribe, and the Théâtre-Musée des Capucines is in an attractive theatre dating from 1895. Both are home to fascinating collections of perfumery paraphernalia, from bottles and burners to paintings and photographs. There are displays explaining how perfume is made, including an overview of the raw materials. At the Musée des Capucines a miniature factory with 19th-century copper-distilling equipment demonstrates various extraction methods.

Fragonard has been creating perfumes since 1926 and uses a mixture of traditional and modern techniques. Products are on sale at

Above *The shop at Musée Fragonard sells the famous perfumier's fragrant products at reduced factory prices*

factory prices in the gift shops.

✚ 185 L5 ✉ Musée du Parfum: 9 rue Scribe, 75009. Théâtre-Musée des Capucines: 39 boulevard des Capucines, 75002 ☎ Musée du Parfum: 01 47 42 04 56. Théâtre-Musée des Capucines: 01 42 60 37 14 ⏰ Mon–Sat 9–6 🖐 Free Ⓜ Opéra 🚌 21, 27, 42, 68

MUSÉE GRÉVIN

www.grevin.com

If you are hoping to spot a celebrity or two while in Paris, why not cheat a little and visit this waxwork museum? Here you can mingle with Sean Connery, Julia Roberts and Bruce Willis at a cocktail party, join Barack Obama, Queen Elizabeth II and Vladimir Putin in the Élysée Palace and watch Auguste Rodin and Salvador Dalí at work in their studios. You'll find the ubiquitous Elvis Presley and Marilyn Monroe among the 300 waxwork models, and even Lara Croft. When you've had enough of 21st-century glitz, step back in time to Paris's turbulent past. The French Revolution is re-created with plenty of blood and gore, and you can also witness the assassination of Henri IV and meet Napoléon and Louis XIV.

The Musée Grévin (also known simply as Grévin) is the Parisian answer to Madame Tussaud's and was launched in 1882 by cartoonist and sculptor Alfred Grévin and

journalist Arthur Meyer. Since 2001, a group of journalists known as the Académie Grévin has met twice a year to decide which famous faces should be immortalized in wax. Recent additions include philosopher Bernard-Henri Lévy, US senator Hillary Clinton, singer Céline Dion, chef Alain Ducasse and France's glamorous 'first lady' Carla Bruni-Sarkozy.

✚ 185 M5 ✉ 10 boulevard Montmartre, 75009 ☎ 01 47 70 85 05 ⏰ Mon–Fri 10–6.30, Sat–Sun 10–7 (last entry 1 hour before closing) 🖐 Adult €21, child (6–14) €13, under 6 free Ⓜ Grands Boulevards 🚌 20, 39, 48, 74, 85 ❓ You can buy tickets in advance at FNAC, Carrefour, Auchan, Virgin Megastore and the tourist office

MUSÉE JACQUEMART ANDRÉ

www.musee-jacquemart-andre.com

Banker Edouard André and his painter wife Nélie Jacquemart were keen collectors of European art and amassed an impressive private collection of European masterpieces. In 1875 they built a stately mansion to display their acquisitions, complete with a ballroom, picture gallery and ornate swirling staircase. Nélie outlived her husband, but when she died she respected his wish to donate the mansion and its contents to the Institut de France. It opened as a museum in 1913. More than 90 years on you can wander through the elegant picture gallery, music room, grand salon and other parts of the mansion where paintings, sculptures and tapestries are displayed. The former dining room (now the café) has a ceiling painted by Giovanni Battista Tiepolo. The walls are decorated with 17th-century tapestries from Brussels. The collection includes paintings and sculptures by Italian artists (including Canaletto, Botticelli and Della Robbia), Flemish and Dutch masters (Van Dyck, Rembrandt and Hals) and French artists (Boucher, David and Fragonard). As well as the permanent collection, the museum hosts popular temporary exhibitions. An audioguide is included in the entry price.

✚ 184 J4 ✉ 158 boulevard Haussmann, 75008 ☎ 01 45 62 11 59 🕓 Daily 10–6 ✋ Adult €10, child €8.50, under 7 free 🍽 Daily 10–6 Ⓜ St-Philippe-du-Roule, Miromesnil 🚌 22, 28, 43, 52, 80, 83, 84, 93 🚆 RER line A, Charles-de-Gaulle-Étoile

MUSÉE DU LOUVRE
▷ 198–203.

MUSÉE NISSIM DE CAMONDO
www.lesartsdecoratifs.fr

The elegance of the furniture and ornaments on display in this stylish town house hides a tragic family story. Moïse de Camondo left his house and collection to the State on his death in 1935, stipulating that it should be named in memory of his son, Nissim, who was killed in action during World War I. Within 10 years of Moïse's death, his daughter and her family were killed at Auschwitz. The mansion is laid out as an 18th-century home and contains Moïse's tasteful collection of decorative arts, mainly from the second half of the 18th century. Vases once owned by Marie-Antoinette are among the items on display. You can also see a silver dinner service made for Empress Catherine II of Russia. Despite its 18th-century furnishings, the mansion was built in the early 20th century to designs inspired by Versailles's Petit Trianon.

✚ 185 J4 ✉ 63 rue de Monceau, 75008 ☎ 01 53 89 06 50 🕓 Wed–Sun 10–5.30 ✋ Adult €7, under 18 free. Cumulative tickets for the Rivoli museums and Musée Nissim de Camondo €17.50 Ⓜ Villiers, Monceau 🚌 30, 84, 94

OPÉRA PALAIS GARNIER
▷ 204.

MUSÉE DE L'ORANGERIE
www.musee-orangerie.fr

The Orangerie started life as a greenhouse but is now an art gallery displaying eight of Monet's world-famous *Water Lily* paintings. It was constructed in 1852, in Second Empire style, to overwinter orange trees from the Jardin des Tuileries (▷ 194). It became an art gallery in the early 20th century, and houses 144 Impressionist and 20th-century paintings. Artists represented include Pierre-Auguste Renoir, Paul Cézanne and Pablo Picasso.

✚ 185 K6 ✉ Jardin des Tuileries, 75001 ☎ 01 44 77 80 07 🕓 Wed–Mon 9–6 ✋ Adult €7.50, under 18 free (temporary exhibitions €2 extra) Ⓜ Concorde 🚌 24, 42, 52, 72, 73, 84, 94

Below *Monet's* Water Lily *paintings are displayed in the Musée de l'Orangerie*

INTRODUCTION

The Louvre is one of the most famous art galleries in the world and it covers a vast period, from around 7,000BC to 1848. There is no way you'll be able to see all 35,000 works on display in one visit, so you need to be selective. If you don't know where to begin, consider taking one of the *Visite-Découverte* guided tours. The free museum plan, available from the information desk, also highlights the key works.

The main entrance is through I.M. Pei's striking glass pyramid in the middle of the large Napoléon Courtyard. From here escalators take you down to the gleaming marble underground foyer, with its cloakroom, information desk and entrances to the museum's three wings: Richelieu, Sully and Denon. If you already have a ticket or a museum pass, you can enter through the passage Richelieu, off the rue de Rivoli, where the wait is usually shorter. Other access points are through the Carrousel du Louvre shopping area and the Porte des Lions (closed on Fridays). When it's time for a break, the museum has a choice of cafés and restaurants. Alternatively, you can leave the site and find a café nearby, as your ticket allows re-entry on the same day.

The building dates back to the 14th century, when Charles V transformed Philippe-Auguste's 12th-century fortress into a medieval castle. Nearly two centuries later, the wily Renaissance king François I instigated considerable rebuilding, and also launched the Louvre's art collection, bringing the *Mona Lisa* and its creator, Leonardo da Vinci, to France. Various kings carried out improvements to the building, until Louis XIV moved the court to Versailles in the 17th century. During the Revolution, an art museum opened to the public in the Grand Galerie.

Napoléon celebrated his marriage to Marie-Louise in the Louvre in 1810, and lived in the nearby Tuileries Palace, which has since burned down. He set about creating a central courtyard dominated by the Arc du Carrousel, building a new wing and adding floors. His numerous victories overseas, and the subsequent looting, added significantly to the Louvre's stock.

Improvements, in the 1980s and 1990s, saw the creation of I.M. Pei's stunning glass pyramid, as well as extensive renovations to the museum's galleries. The new Department of Islamic Art is scheduled to open in 2012 in a new gallery in the Cour Visconti, showcasing 2,000 objects spanning the creativity of the Islamic lands over 13 centuries and three continents.

The Louvre is already the largest museum in the world, but it has no intention of resting on its laurels. Farther afield it is spawning offshoots in the northern French city of Lens (due to open in 2012) and in Abu Dhabi in the United Arab Emirates—scheduled for completion in 2013. France's entry into the culture export business has not pleased many traditionalists who have accused the Louvre of cultural prostitution. The same purists were scornful of the blockbusting 'Picasso and the Masters' exhibition in 2008 held in the Louvre, Grand Palais and the Musée d'Orsay, which they claimed was aimed at mass culture. The debate continues between the modernizers and purists, but the present director's drive to renew the Louvre's historic vocation as a universal museum seems to be finding favour—with the public at least. The number of visitors today is annually more than eight million—60 per cent more than in 2001.

When I.M. Pei's glass pyramid was unveiled in 1989 it triggered a great deal of controversy. Twenty years on, this stunning piece of architecture has come to be loved by most, representing the successful fusion of the classical with the ultra modern. Under the pyramid, the Hall Napoléon is the starting point for *The Da Vinci Code* trail—an audio guide designed by the Louvre, in

INFORMATION

www.louvre.fr

✚ 185 M7 ✉ 99 rue de Rivoli, 75001 ☎ 01 40 20 50 50. Information in French and English: 01 40 20 53 17. Auditorium: 01 40 20 55 55 🕐 Thu, Sat–Mon 9–6, Wed, Fri 9am–9.45pm (last entry 45 min before closing). Some rooms closed in rotation 🖐 Adult €10, under 18 free. Temporary exhibitions in the Hall Napoléon €11; cumulative tickets for Hall Napoléon and permanent exhibitions €14. Tickets are valid all day, so re-entry is allowed. Tickets combining entrance and rail travel are available at railway stations. The museum is free on the 1st Sun of each month and 14 July (except for exhibitions in the Hall Napoléon) 🚇 Palais Royal/Musée du Louvre 🚌 21, 24, 27, 39, 48, 68, 69, 72, 76, 81, 95 🚊 Châtelet-Les-Halles 🔲 Various guided tours are available in English and French, including the *Visite-Découverte* (Discovery Visit, €9) in English at 11 and 2 (not 1st Sun of month) and in French Sat–Sun at 11.30. Audioguides are available in French, English, German, Spanish, Italian and Japanese. Pick them up from the entrances to the three wings of the museum (€6). Special tours are available for those with reduced mobility. There is also a sculpture gallery for those with visual impairments. Ask at the information desk for a leaflet about disability access 📖 Range of guidebooks. Free leaflet available at information desk 🍴 Cafés and restaurants 📗 Large bookshop

Opposite Beneath the glass pyramid in the Louvre

FACTS AND FIGURES

» The Louvre has 1,100 security guards clad in uniforms by Balenciaga and a 24-hour fire brigade of 46 *pompiers* (firefighters).

» The oldest work in the collection is a 9,000 year-old plaster statue of a human figure found in Jordan. The most recent is a painting of corpses from the riots of Paris in 1848.

» All the events relating to the Louvre in the book and subsequent film of *The Da Vinci Code* take place in the Denon wing (named after Dominique-Vivant Denon, the museum's first director between 1802 and 1815).

Above *Papyrus depicting a man being transported on a barque to the afterlife by gods Thoth and Khepri*

response to public demand. It is an amusing wander in the footsteps of the 'symbologist' Robert Langdon and the 'cryptologist' Sophie Neveu, the main characters in the book and film. While not taking sides for or against this work of fiction, it presents the Louvre in a new and light-hearted vein, and is full of factual information, laying some glaring inaccuracies to rest. There was a rumour, for example, spread in the mid 1980s by those against the pyramid's construction, that it was composed of 666 panes of glass—the same number as the Beast in the Book of Revelation (New Testament). This 'satanic' number is incorrect: in reality the pyramid comprises 673 diamond-shaped and triangular panes of glass, excluding the doors.

WHAT TO SEE

MONA LISA

When Leonardo da Vinci set up his easel in Florence in the early 16th century to paint the *Mona Lisa*, little did he know he was creating what was to become one of the world's most famous works of art. The diminutive painting, only 77cm (30in) tall and 53cm (20in) wide, is on the first floor of the Denon wing, surrounded by bullet-proof glass and a constant crowd. The identity of the woman is not known for certain, although she is believed to be the wife of Francesco del Giocondo, hence the portrait's other name, *La Gioconda*. Da Vinci painted the work between 1503 and 1506. François I obtained the painting soon after its completion. It has since spent time in Versailles and in the former Tuileries Palace and has even hung in Napoléon's bedroom.

In 1911 an Italian stole the portrait from the Louvre, wanting to return it to its native Florence. It was recovered two years later, after a police hunt that won it worldwide fame.

VENUS DE MILO AND THE WINGED VICTORY OF SAMOTHRACE

The eternally serene *Venus de Milo* (ground floor, Sully) is the most famous of the Louvre's Greek antiquities. She was discovered on the island of Melos in 1820. As Aphrodite, the goddess of love, she portrays the Greek image of perfect beauty. The marble statue was created around 100BC, during Greece's Hellenistic period, although its style harks back to Classical Greek sculpture.

Among the other Greek antiquities, don't miss the *Winged Victory of Samothrace* (first-floor landing, Denon), soaring 3m (9.8ft) high. The statue was sculpted in 190BC to celebrate a maritime victory and shows the goddess Victory. The fluid style of the carving gives the impression the sea wind is blowing through her dress and wings. The sculpture had to be painstakingly reassembled from 300 pieces found on the island of Samothrace in 1863.

ETRUSCAN AND ROMAN ART

While Ancient Greek civilization was thriving, the Etruscans were carving out their own civilization in northern Italy. Highlights of their art include a terracotta sarcophagus (c.530BC) showing a husband and wife reclining on wineskins (ground floor, Denon). Both wear the contented smiles that are a feature of Etruscan sculpture. The Louvre's collection of Roman art (ground floor, Denon) includes mosaics, sculpture, plates, vases and sarcophagi.

TIPS

» Don't miss the Galerie d'Apollon (Denon, 1st floor) reopened at the end of 2004. Commissioned by Louis XIV, it inspired the Hall of Mirrors at Versailles and was embellished for 200 years by artists from Le Brun to Delacroix. It now displays the Crown Jewels.

» The museum is usually less crowded on Wednesday and Friday evenings when it stays open until 9.45pm.

» To avoid long waits for tickets, use a Paris Museum Pass (▷ 279) or prebook your ticket by phone, internet, FNAC (tel 01 41 57 32 28; small commission charged) or at certain department stores (Auchan, Bon Marché, Galeries Lafayette, Virgin). This allows you to use the passage Richelieu entrance.

Below *The Louvre has a marvellous collection of sculpture*

TIPS

» You can view many of the Louvre's paintings and other exhibits on the website, allowing you to decide before your visit where to focus your attention.

» The information desk has free maps—useful for planning your visit and showing which rooms are closed.

» Staff shortages mean that not all the rooms are open every day. If there are particular things you want to see, check the website for the schedule of closures.

» Purchase your tickets in advance. When you come out of the Métro (Carrousel exit) there are ticket machines at the Carrousel du Louvre entrance (99 rue de Rivoli, 75001). Alternatively, turn right by the jewellery shop Cécile Jeanne—the Tabac also sells tickets.

» The entrance ticket is valid on the same day for the collections and temporary exhibitions of the Musée National Eugène Delacroix (▷ 120).

» Cameras are not allowed inside the Louvre.

» The best of the cafés and restaurants in the museum is the Café Richelieu (first floor of the Richelieu wing). Outside the museum, but only a short walk east is the untouristy Le Fumoir bar/restaurant (6 rue de l'Amiral Coligny; www.lefumoir.com).

Above left Leonardo da Vinci's Mona Lisa *is one of the most famous artworks*
Above right *One of the sculpture galleries*

THE EGYPTIAN COLLECTION

You are offered a captivating glimpse of life at the time of the pharaohs, as much as 5,000 years ago, in the Egyptian rooms. The collection is the largest of its kind outside Egypt, containing 55,000 items, around 5,000 of which are on show. There are commanding sphinxes and statues of the all-powerful pharaohs, but just as fascinating are the smaller, everyday items, including mirrors, combs, necklaces and intricately carved spoons used for applying cosmetics. Don't miss the pink granite Grand Sphinx, part pharaoh, part lion, that once protected the corridors of a holy shrine (ground floor, Sully). Its precise age is unknown, but stylistic details suggest it could be more than 4,600 years old.

The collections are presented thematically on the ground floor of the Sully wing, where topics include fishing, funerals and writing. On the first floor the displays are chronological, starting with prehistory, tracing the rule of the pharaohs and ending just before the arrival of the Romans in 333BC. To see how Egyptian culture developed under Roman rule and during the Coptic Christian era you can continue your tour in the lower floor of the Denon wing.

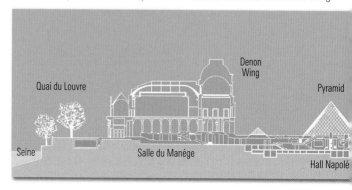

FRENCH HISTORICAL/ALLEGORICAL PAINTINGS

These vast paintings, on the first floor of the Denon wing, draw you into the action not simply through their immense size but also in the vivid detail. Some of the subjects would have seemed uncomfortably contemporary when the paintings were first unveiled. Théodore Géricault's *The Raft of the Medusa* (1819) portrays a controversial French shipwreck that took place near Senegal three years earlier. Only 15 of the 150-strong crew survived, clinging to a hastily constructed raft, and there were rumours of cannibalism and treachery. Early viewers of the paintings were shocked by the realism of the corpses.

Dead bodies also appear in Eugène Delacroix's *Liberty Leading the People* (1830), although the presence of the allegorical figure Liberty brings a sense of triumph to the destruction and chaos. The painting depicts the uprising of 1830. Jacques-Louis David's neoclassical painting *The Coronation of Napoléon I* seems rather cold when set against the passion of Delacroix and Géricault's works. Almost 10m (33ft) wide, it was commissioned by the Emperor himself, and completed in 1807.

OTHER HIGHLIGHTS

- *The Lacemaker* by Jan Vermeer (1669–1670; Richelieu, second floor)
- *Dying Slave* by Michelangelo (1513–1515; Denon, ground floor)
- *The Marly Horses* by Coustou (1743–1745; Richelieu, Cour Marly)
- Cour Khorsabad (Richelieu, ground floor)
- *The Wedding Feast at Cana* by Veronese (1562–1563; Denon, first floor)
- Medieval fortifications (lower ground floor)

The Louvre operates a useful system of colour-coding on its maps. The departments are:

Egyptian Antiquities (green): The main collection is on the ground and first floor of Sully. Roman and Coptic Egypt are on the lower floor of Denon.

Greek, Etruscan and Roman Antiquities (blue): First and ground floor of Sully, ground floor of Denon. Pre-Classical Greece is on Denon's lower floor.

Oriental Antiquities (yellow) and Arts of Islam (dark green): Arts of Islam are on the lower ground floor of Richelieu. The Cour Khorsabad is on the ground floor of Richelieu, and Antique Iran and Levant are on the ground floor of Sully.

Paintings (red): Paintings from France, Flanders, Holland and Germany are on the second floor of Richelieu and Sully; large French paintings are on the first floor of Denon. Italian and Spanish paintings are on the first floor of Denon; English on the first floor of Sully.

Drawings and Prints (pink): French drawings are on the second floor of Sully; German, Flemish and Dutch on the second floor of Richelieu; Italian on the first floor of Denon.

Objets d'Art (mauve): First floor of Richelieu, Denon and Sully.

Sculptures (beige): French sculptures are on the ground and lower ground floors of Richelieu. Italian sculptures are on the ground and lower ground floors of Denon.

History of the Louvre (brown): Remains of the medieval fortress are on Sully's lower ground floor.

Arts of Africa, Asia, Oceania and the Americas (white): Denon ground floor (on loan from the Musée du Quai Branly, ▷ 84).

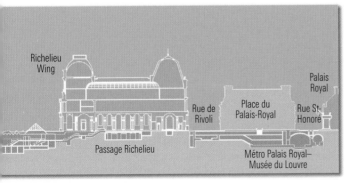

Above *The ceilings of the Louvre were installed when it was a royal palace, from the 15th to the 17th centuries*

INFORMATION

www.operadeparis.fr

✚ 185 L5 ✉ place de l'Opéra, 75009
☎ 01 40 04 24 93. Box office and
museum: 0892 89 90 90. 🕐 Daily
10–5, 10–1 during matinée performances.
Closed 1 Jan, 1 May and when there is a
matinée performance/special event. The
auditorium is closed during rehearsals
and shows ✋ Adult €9, child (10–19)
€6, under 10 free 🚇 Opéra 🚌 20,
21, 22, 27, 29, 42, 52, 53, 66, 68, 81, 95
🚶 Guided tours last
1 hr 30 min and cost €12.50 (child €9.50);
in French Wed, Sat– Sun at 11.30 and
3.30; in English Wed, Sat–Sun at 11.30
and 2.30. Telephone in advance. 📖 €7
🎁 Gift shop

Below *Likened to a wedding cake, the
baroque Opéra Palais Garnier opened
in 1875*

OPÉRA PALAIS GARNIER

The sumptuous Opéra Palais Garnier was commissioned by Napoléon III
and inaugurated in 1875. Charles Garnier beat more than 170 hopefuls in
a competition to design the prestigious building. Work finished 15 years
after the official acceptance of his riotous design and was hampered by the
nightmarish discovery by Charles Garnier of an underground expanse of water.
This deep lake was the inspiration for the writer Gaston Leroux's *Phantom
of the Opera*. The decorative facade has been likened to a huge ornamental
wedding cake. Look for Carrier-Belleuse's provocative lamp-bearing statues
and the copy of Jean-Baptiste Carpeaux's sculpted group *La Danse* to the
right of the front arcade (the 1869 original is now in the Musée d'Orsay).

INSIDE THE OPÉRA PALAIS GARNIER

When it opened, the opera house was the largest theatre in the world at
11,000sq m (118,404sq ft), a fittingly lavish epitaph to the architecture of
the Second Empire. The splendid marble and gilt Grand Staircase and the
baroque Grand Foyer are highlights inside. The stage can accommodate
up to 450 performers and the fabulous auditorium holds around 2,000
spectators under a domed ceiling painted by Marc Chagall in 1964. The
Italianate, horseshoe-shaped auditorium has opulent red and gold furnishings
and a huge crystal chandelier (weighing 8 tonnes). A small library-museum
presents the history of the Opéra and includes paintings, photographs and
memorabilia. Temporary exhibitions are held throughout the year. Many
operatic performances are staged at the Opéra Bastille (▷ 168). The Opéra
Palais Garnier is almost exclusively devoted to ballet (▷ 213).

PARC MONCEAU

www.paris.fr

It's worth taking a trip out to this timeless park, northeast of the Arc de Triomphe, with its fake ruins, tree-shaded pond and magnificent gates. The weekend is best, when the park buzzes with joggers, families and residents of the classy surrounding area. From the Métro station, with its art nouveau entrance, you enter the park through gilded wrought-iron gates. Inside, there's a pond bordered with fake Roman columns, a pyramid, a rotunda, various statues and plenty of trees and flowers. For children there are donkey rides, swings and a merry-go-round. The park was landscaped in the English style by Thomas Blaikie in 1783 and became a public park in 1861. Nearby attractions include the Musée Cernuschi (▷ 196) and the Musée Nissim de Camondo (▷ 197).

☩ 184 H4 ☒ boulevard de Courcelles, 75008 ☎ Mairie de Paris information 39 75 ⊕ Apr–Sep daily 7am–10pm; Oct–Mar 7am–8pm ⊌ Free ⊜ Monceau ⊟ 30, 84, 94 ▣

PLACE DE LA CONCORDE

▷ 206.

PLACE DE LA MADELEINE

The colossal church of La Madeleine (open daily 9–7) is supported by 52 enormous Corinthian pillars and resembles a Greek temple. The triangular pediment bears a sculpted frieze of the Last Judgement. Construction began in 1764, but did not finish until 1842. The church has had a varied career, narrowly avoiding becoming a railway station, stock exchange, bank and another temple to Napoléon. It is now a popular venue for society weddings and funerals and has seen the coffins of notables such as Frédéric Chopin and Marlene Dietrich.

After you have climbed the steps to the main entrance, turn around to admire the view down the rue Royale to the obelisk in the place de la Concorde (▷ 206), across the river to the Palais Bourbon (▷ 73) and beyond to the golden cupola of Les Invalides (▷ 74–75). Food connoisseurs should try to make time to visit Fauchon, the exclusive foodstore synonymous with the best of French food. There are plenty of other food shops and restaurants on the square, as well as a small flower market.

☩ 185 K5 ☒ place de la Madeleine, 75008 ⊜ Madeleine ⊟ 24, 42, 52, 84, 94

PLACE VENDÔME

www.paris.fr

Stately place Vendôme is the symbol of Parisian chic. You'll need a hefty bank balance to venture into its exclusive jewellery stores, and its hotel, the Ritz, is among the most prestigious in the world. Noted residents of the square have included Frédéric Chopin, who died at number 12, and Anton Mesmer, founder of the theory of mesmerism, who held experiments at number 16. Marcel Proust, Ernest Hemingway and Coco Chanel were guests at the Ritz, and Diana, Princess of Wales, dined there before her fateful car journey across Paris in August 1997.

Louis XIV commissioned the classical square in 1685, choosing Versailles architect Jules Hardouin-Mansart, who had impressed him with his design for place des Victoires (▷ 207). The focal point was an equestrian statue of the king, but this fell victim to the mob during the Revolution. In 1810 it was replaced by a 44m (144ft) bronze column, based on Trajan's column in Rome, but this was pulled to the ground during another revolution, the Paris Commune of 1871. It was rebuilt and now supports a Caesar-like statue of Napoléon. The square's turbulent past has caused its name to be changed frequently over the years, with titles including place des Conquêtes, place Louis le Grand, place des Piques and place Internationale. Keep an eye out for traffic while admiring the square—despite the cobbles, it is not pedestrian-only.

☩ 185 L5 ☒ place Vendôme, 75001 ⊜ Opéra, Tuileries ⊟ 21, 27, 29, 68, 72, 81, 95

Above *Napoléon presides over place Vendôme from his brass column*

INFORMATION

✚ 185 K6 ✉ place de la Concorde, 75008 ✋ Free 🚇 Concorde 🚌 24, 42, 72, 73, 84, 94

TIPS

» Use the pedestrian crossing when walking to the middle of the square — but be careful, as the traffic does not always stop when it should.

» Take time to appreciate the wonderful views from the heart of the square, especially up the Champs-Élysées.

PLACE DE LA CONCORDE

Hectic place de la Concorde was once an area of swampland but now buzzes with people and traffic. It sits on the intersection of two principal axes and, braving the traffic to stand in the middle of the square, you are rewarded with four dramatic views. To the west is the Champs-Élysées (▷ 189), leading to the Arc de Triomphe (▷ 188–189), and to the east you can look past the ornate gates of the Jardin des Tuileries (▷ 194) down towards the Louvre (▷ 198–203). North along the rue Royale is La Madeleine church (▷ 205) and to the south, across the Pont de la Concorde, is the colonnaded Palais Bourbon, home to the Assemblée Nationale (▷ 73).

ROYAL DESIGN

The square was designed by Jacques-Ange Gabriel and laid out between 1755 and 1775 to accommodate an equestrian statue of the reigning king, Louis XV. Gabriel designed the two properties flanking the rue Royale — the Hôtel Crillon and the Hôtel de la Marine — in addition to the stone pedestals in each corner of the octagonal square. These are topped with female statues each representing a major French city — Lille, Strasbourg, Lyon, Marseille, Bordeaux, Nantes, Brest and Rouen.

HORRORS OF THE REVOLUTION

The square was originally called place Louis XV but was renamed place de la Révolution during the Revolution. The statue of Louis XV was removed and the guillotine erected in its stead. Between 1793 and 1795 more than 1,300 people were beheaded here, including Louis XVI and his queen, Marie-Antoinette. With the cooling of revolutionary passions in 1795, the square was renamed the place de la Concorde, in the hope of a less troubled future. Soon after, Guillaume I Coustou's two magnificent *Chevaux de Marly* (1743–45), sculpted from Carrara marble, were installed at the entrance of the Champs-Élysées. The statues you see today are replicas, however — the originals are now on display in the Louvre.

EGYPTIAN OBELISK

In 1833 Mohammed Ali, Viceroy of Egypt, presented King Louis-Philippe with a 230-tonne, pink granite obelisk, 23m (75ft) high. It is around 3,300 years old, engraved with hieroglyphics, and was once used to measure the sun's shadow at the Temple of Thebes.

Above *One of two neoclassical maritime-themed fountains designed by Jacques-Ignace Hittorff*

PLACE DES VICTOIRES

www.paris.fr

Elegant, circular place des Victoires is tucked quietly at the end of the busy shopping street, rue Étienne Marcel. Its curved mansions house the chic boutiques of Kenzo, Cacharel and other leading fashion names. The square was laid out in 1685 by the architect Jules Hardouin-Mansart, who also worked on Versailles. It was commissioned by the Maréchal de la Feuillade to celebrate the victories of the Sun King, Louis XIV. A statue of the king was destroyed during the Revolution and later replaced by an equestrian sculpture by Bosio. Look down rue Catinat to see the imposing Banque de France.

✚ 185 M6 ✉ place des Victoires, 75002 Ⓜ Bourse, Sentier 🚌 29

ST-GERMAIN-L'AUXERROIS

Kings and royal families from the nearby Louvre palace used St-Germain-l'Auxerrois as their parish church until the Revolution and you can still see the royal pew, near the pulpit. Other highlights include the beautiful stained-glass windows, the carved choir screen and the 18th-century organ, moved from Sainte-Chapelle in 1791.

The site's religious connections date back to AD500, when an oratory was built here. In later years it was used to hastily baptize children whose lives were in danger from floods. The current church was constructed between the 13th and 16th centuries but lost its religious role during the Revolution and became, for a time, a police station, town hall, barn and printers' workshop. Architect and medieval specialist Viollet-le-Duc restored the building in the 19th century. The church's bell (1527) notoriously signalled the onset of the bloody St. Bartholomew's Day Massacre in 1572 (▷ 31). The church is a tranquil and pleasant place for a stop after a visit to the Louvre (▷ 198–203). You can sit on benches on the grassy area outside the church and admire the Louvre's facade.

✚ 185 M7 ✉ 2 place du Louvre, 75001 ☎ 01 42 60 13 96 🕓 Early Jul–early Sep Mon–Sat 9.30–7.30, Sun 9–8; early Sep–early Jul Mon–Fri 8–7, Sat–Sun 9–8 (except during mass services) 🎟 Free Ⓜ Louvre-Rivoli, Pont Neuf 🚌 21, 24, 27, 67, 69, 70, 74, 75, 76, 85

Below *A stained-glass window in the church of St-Germain-l'Auxerrois*

RIVE DROITE

A relaxing walk from place de la Concorde that combines restful gardens with chic Parisian shops.

THE WALK

Distance: 3.5km (2 miles)
Time: 2 hours
Start/end at: place de la Concorde

HOW TO GET THERE

Take the Métro to Concorde, or buses 24, 42, 72, 73, 84 or 94.

★Carefully cross the stream of traffic flowing through place de la Concorde to look at the obelisk in the heart of this historic square.

❶ Place de la Concorde (▷ 206), titled place de la Révolution for the two and a half years when the notorious guillotine was installed as its centrepiece, was designed as an open octagon. Only the northern side has buildings. The pink granite obelisk that now graces the square came to Paris from Luxor, Egypt, in the 1830s.

Cross to the ornate gates of the Jardin des Tuileries and stroll through this vibrant public garden.

❷ The Tuileries (▷ 194) is one of the oldest public gardens in Paris and offers fabulous views of the Louvre, the Eiffel Tower, place de la Concorde and the Arc de Triomphe. Parisians come here to relax by the two large ponds when the sun comes out, or to stroll along the terraces on either side of the park.

At the end of the park, turn left to rue de Rivoli. Turn right onto rue de Rivoli and walk beside the Louvre.

❸ Many of France's rulers have left their mark on the Louvre (▷ 198–203), including Charles V, François I and Napoléon. The original medieval fortress was transformed into a castle in the 14th century, then a royal palace, before assuming its present role as one of the world's most prestigious museums.

Cross rue de Rivoli into place du Palais Royal. From here, cross rue St-Honoré and bear left, towards the Comédie Française. Enter the Jardin du Palais Royal through a discrete arch on the left of the palace.

❹ This garden (▷ 193) is only moments from the traffic and crowds of rue de Rivoli but a million miles away in atmosphere. You enter through a courtyard decorated with curious grey-and-white striped mini-columns, designed by the artist Daniel Buren in 1986. The garden, with its vivid flowerbeds, is surrounded by elegant 18th-century arcades with individual shops.

Walk to the end of the garden and leave on the left side, past the historic restaurant Le Grand Véfour—look through the window at the lovely painted ceiling. This brings you to rue de Beaujolais. Turn right here, left up rue Vivienne, followed by a left turn onto rue des Petits Champs. You'll pass the Bibliothèque Nationale de France.

❺ This building (▷ 190) was once the palace of 17th-century prime

Opposite *Detail of one of the fountains in place de la Concorde*

minister Cardinal Mazarin, but has housed France's national library since the 18th century. By the 1990s the mammoth collection had outgrown the site and in 1996 an additional library (▷ 111) opened in the 13th *arrondissement*, named after former president Mitterrand.

Continue until you reach avenue de l'Opéra. Cross the avenue and walk up towards the opera house.

❻ The sumptuous Opéra Palais Garnier (▷ 204) was designed by Charles Garnier and opened in 1875. It is an extravagance of marble, gold and sculpture and was once the largest opera house in the world.

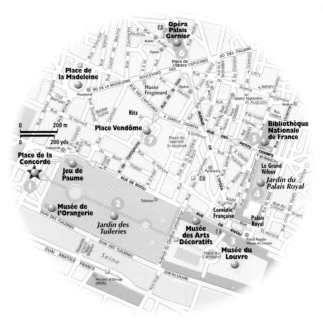

Just before place de l'Opéra, turn left down rue de la Paix, brimming with elegant jewellery shops. This leads to the even more exclusive place Vendôme (▷ 205).

❼ More chic jewellery shops and the world-famous Paris Ritz Hotel are among the occupants of place Vendôme. Be careful of the traffic while you admire the wares and the architecture—the cobbles give the false impression that the square is pedestrian-only.

Cross the square and walk down rue de Castiglione, with its elegant shopping arcades. Turn right onto rue de Rivoli, which returns you to place de la Concorde. Back in the square, don't miss the view down the Champs-Élysées to the Arc de Triomphe.

WHEN TO GO
The best time to do this walk is during the day, when the shops are open and the Jardin des Tuileries is at its best. If you decide to take an evening stroll, avoid the Jardin des Tuileries and walk up rue de Rivoli instead.

WHERE TO EAT
For a meal try the chic but traditional brasserie Le Grand Colbert, at 4 rue Vivienne, near the Jardin du Palais Royal (▷ 214–215). For tea and cake visit the chic Muscade tea room, within the *jardin* grounds, at 36 rue Montpensier (▷ 215).

Left *Flowers in the lovely Jardin du Palais Royal*

REGIONS LOUVRE AND CHAMPS-ÉLYSÉES • WALK

209

ALONG THE SEINE

A river cruise along the Seine is a great way to view some of the key sights from a different perspective. It is also ideal if you are short on time—in just over an hour you can see many of the famous landmarks.

THE RIVER TRIP

Distance: 11km (7 miles)
Time: Just over 1 hour
Start/end at: square du Vert-Galant, Pont Neuf

HOW TO GET THERE

Take the Métro to Pont Neuf, or buses 24, 27, 58, 67, 70, 72, 74 or 75. From the Métro station walk over Pont Neuf. Just over halfway across, on the right, is a sign for the Vedettes du Pont Neuf. Go down the steps to the square du Vert-Galant, on the Île de la Cité, and turn right. The boarding platform is ahead.

★ The boat leaves from the pretty square du Vert-Galant and heads west. The first bridge you pass under is the pedestrian-only Pont des Arts. This was originally built in 1804 but replaced in 1984. It is one of the most romantic bridges in Paris and is also a popular meeting place for artists. On the Right Bank you can see the Museé du Louvre.

❶ The Louvre (▷ 198–203), one of the largest museums in the world, was once the residence of the kings and queens of France. It now houses an outstanding collection of art, from ancient times to the 19th century.

After passing under the Pont du Carrousel and the Pont Royal you'll see the facade of the Musée d'Orsay on the Left Bank.

❷ This excellent museum (▷ 80–83) in the former Orsay railway station has displays of fine and applied arts from 1848 to 1914. It has one of the world's best Impressionist collections.

The next two bridges are the Passerelle de Solférino, spanning the river between the Jardin des Tuileries and the Musée d'Orsay, and the Pont de la Concorde, built with stones from the Bastille prison, which was destroyed during the

French Revolution. On the Left Bank stands the home of France's Assemblée Nationale, the 18th-century Palais Bourbon (▷ 73), and on the Right Bank is place de la Concorde.

❸ Place de la Concorde (▷ 206), laid out between 1755 and 1775, is the largest square in Paris at more than 8ha (20 acres). At its heart stands the city's oldest monument, an ancient Egyptian obelisk 23m (75ft) high.

The boat passes under the ornate Pont Alexandre III, built for the 1900 Exposition Universelle and dedicated to the Franco-Russian alliance. On the Right Bank you can see the Grand Palais and Petit Palais (▷ 192) and on the Left Bank, in the distance, is Les Invalides.

❹ Within Les Invalides (▷ 74–75) you'll find the Musée de l'Armée, with fascinating displays of military

Opposite *A bateau mouche passes under the Pont des Arts*

art and equipment. Napoléon's tomb is in the Église du Dôme.

After passing under the Pont des Invalides, the Pont de l'Alma and the Passerelle Debilly, the boat rounds a bend and you are greeted by a spectacular view of the Eiffel Tower on the Left Bank.

⑤ The Eiffel Tower (▷ 90–95), symbol of Paris, was constructed between 1887 and 1889, is 324m (1,063ft) high and has around seven million visitors each year. The views from the top are breathtaking.

The Pont d'Iéna spans the river between the Eiffel Tower on the Left Bank and the Jardins du Trocadéro on the Right Bank. The boat passes under this bridge before turning and heading back in the opposite direction to the Île de la Cité. As you sail along look out for the houseboats and brightly painted restaurant-barges moored along the banks of the Seine. You'll see the grand cupola of the Institut de France on the right before you pass under the southern side of the Pont Neuf.

⑥ The 'new bridge' is actually the oldest in Paris, dating from the 17th century. It was the first bridge across the Seine to be built without houses on it.

The next two bridges are the Pont St-Michel, leading to the Latin Quarter and the Sorbonne university (▷ 135), and the Petit Pont, the smallest bridge in Paris. On the Île de la Cité you can see the beautiful Cathedral of Notre-Dame.

⑦ Notre-Dame (▷ 124–127) was constructed between the 12th and 14th centuries and is a masterpiece of Gothic architecture. Notice its impressive flying buttresses and its spire, 96m (315ft) high.

Several bridges farther along the river, to your right, lies the Institut du Monde Arabe (▷ 116) and the outdoor sculptures of the Musée de la Sculpture en Plein Air. The boat now turns to circle around the picturesque Île St-Louis (▷ 116). After three more bridges, including the romantic Pont Marie, you can see Paris's town hall, the Hôtel de Ville (▷ 154), on the Right Bank.

As the boat sails back along the other side of the Île de la Cité (and under another three bridges), you'll pass the city's oldest hospital, the Hôtel-Dieu, and the Conciergerie.

⑧ Originally part of a royal palace, the Conciergerie (▷ 112–113)

later became a prison. More than 2,600 people held here during the Revolution were sent to the guillotine, including Queen Marie-Antoinette. Look for the 16th-century clock, the Tour de l'Horloge, on the facade of the Conciergerie.

The boat passes back under the Pont Neuf and the cruise ends where it began.

INFORMATION
www.vedettesdupontneuf.com
☎ 01 46 33 98 38 ⏰ Mid-Mar to end Oct daily 10.30, 11.15, 12 and every half-hour from 1.30 to 7, then 8, 9, 9.30, 10 and 10.30; end Oct to mid-Mar Mon–Thu 10.30, 11.15, 12, 2, 2.45, 3.30, 4.15, 5, 5.45, 6.30, 8 and 10, Fri–Sun 10.30, 11.15, 12 and every 45 minutes from 2 to 6.30, then 8, 9, 9.30, 10 and 10.30. Times may vary 🖐 Adult €13, child (4–12) €6.50, under 4 free 📖 Pick up a free route map from the boarding platform

WHEN TO GO
Evening is a great time to go on this trip, when the monuments are lit up. Day or night, try to go when the weather is good so you can sit on deck and get the best views.

WHERE TO EAT
There is a small bar on the boarding platform and vending machines on the boat. There is also the Captain's Bar on the Bateaux les Vedettes.

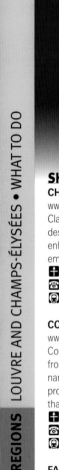

SHOPPING

CHANEL
www.chanel.com
Classy, sexy and feminine, the designs of this fashion house, enhanced by exclusive perfumes, embody Parisian elegance.
✚ 219 K5 ✉ 31 rue Cambon, 75001 ☎ 01 42 86 28 00 🕐 Mon–Sat 10–7 🚇 Madeleine, Concorde

COLETTE
www.colette.fr
Come here for cutting-edge design from one of the industry's rising names, or for imported beauty products. The water bar offers more than 100 brands of water.
✚ 219 L6 ✉ 213 rue St-Honoré, 75001 ☎ 01 55 35 33 90 🕐 Mon–Sat 11–7 🚇 Tuileries, Pyramides

FAUCHON
www.fauchon.fr
The very best of French cuisine has been available here since 1886. Beluga caviar, the best vintages of the finest spirits, and many more exotic delicacies can also be found.
✚ 219 K5 ✉ 26 and 30 place de la Madeleine, 75008 ☎ 01 70 39 38 00 🕐 No. 26: Mon–Sat 8am–9pm. No. 30: Mon–Sat 9–8:30 🚇 Madeleine

GALERIES LAFAYETTE
www.galerieslafayette.com
The main building of this grand 1912 department store has a stained-glass dome, balconies and gilded balustrades. It is a luxurious setting for hundreds of brands.
✚ 219 L5 ✉ 40 boulevard Haussmann, 75009 ☎ 01 42 82 34 56 🕐 Mon–Wed, Fri–Sat 9.30–8, Thu 9.30–9 🚇 Chaussée d'Antin

JAMIN PUECH
www.jamin-puech.com
Each bag is a work of art. Jamin Puech has brought jewellery to leather craft and is now one of Paris's fashion-scene darlings.
✚ 219 off M4 ✉ 61 rue d'Hauteville, 75010 ☎ 01 40 22 08 32 🕐 Tue–Fri 10–7, Mon, Sat 11–7 🚇 Poissonnière, Bonne Nouvelle

LAVINIA
www.lavinia.fr
You'll find more than 5,000 wines and 1,000 spirits spread over three floors here. There is also a bar and a restaurant where you can buy the finest French wines by the glass.
✚ 219 K5 ✉ 3–5 boulevard de la Madeleine, 75001 ☎ 01 42 97 20 20 🕐 Mon–Sat 10–8 🚇 Madeleine

Above *Fauchon sells the best of French food*

LENÔTRE
www.lenotre.fr
Lenôtre has long been famous for its fine foods and pastries, but the launch of the *macarré*, a square-shaped macaroon, has made it even more fashionable. Unusual varieties include chocolate-cherry and aniseed-blackcurrant.
✚ 219 J3 ✉ 15 boulevard de Coucelles, 75008 ☎ 01 45 63 87 63 🕐 Daily 9–9 🚇 Villiers

LOUIS VUITTON
www.louisvuitton.com
The beige and brown chequered pattern and the interlaced LV initials are the house's signature and a symbol of chic par excellence.
✚ 218 H5 ✉ 101 avenue des Champs-Élysées, 75008 ☎ 01 53 57 20 00 🕐 Mon–Sat 10–8, Sun 11–7 🚇 George V

MARCHÉ AUX TIMBRES
Stamp lovers, professionals and amateurs alike, meet every week in this fashionable area.
✚ 219 J5 ✉ On the corner of avenue de Marigny and avenue Gabriel, 75008 🕐 Thu, Sat–Sun 9–6 🚇 Champs-Élysées-Clemenceau

PRINTEMPS

www.printemps.com

Under the store's stained-glass cupola, there are six floors of women's fashion and Europe's largest perfume department. There is also a men's store, and a home decoration department.

✚ 219 L5 ✉ 64 boulevard Haussmann, 75009 ☎ 01 42 82 50 00 🕐 Mon–Wed, Fri–Sat 9.35–8, Thu 9.35am–10pm 🚇 Havre-Caumartin

ENTERTAINMENT AND NIGHTLIFE

L'ARC

www.larc-paris.com

Dressing smartly should grant you the right to enter this temple of chic and trendy Parisian nightlife. Disco, dance and techno are played, and the terrace has a superb view of the Arc de Triomphe.

✚ 218 G5 ✉ 12 rue de Presbourg, 75016 ☎ 01 45 00 78 70 🕐 Restaurant: Mon–Fri 12–3, 7.30–11, Sat 7.30–11; club: Thu–Sat 11.30–4 ✋ Free 🚇 Charles de Gaulle-Étoile

BAR HEMINGWAY

www.ritzparis.com

Within the Ritz hotel, this bar pays tribute to the celebrated writer. Papa himself used to enjoy the elegant atmosphere, malts and champagne.

✚ 219 L6 ✉ Hôtel Ritz, 15 place Vendôme, 75001 ☎ 01 43 16 33 65 🕐 Daily 10.30am–2am 🚇 Opéra, Madeleine

BARRAMUNDI

www.barramundi.fr

India meets Africa for the style, and chill-out world music spices up the atmosphere. Popular with the fashion crowd.

✚ 219 L5 ✉ 3 rue Taitbout, 75009 ☎ 01 47 70 21 21 🕐 Mon–Fri 12–3.30, 6.30–2, Sat 7pm–5am 🚇 Richelieu-Drouot

BUDDHA BAR

www.buddha-bar.com

Trendy bar and restaurant where you go to spot celebrities as much as to listen to the music and admire the decor. As a result the place is crowded and the service can be indifferent, unless you are famous.

✚ 219 K5 ✉ 8 rue Boissy d'Anglas, 75008 ☎ 01 53 05 90 00 🕐 Bar and restaurant: Mon–Fri from noon, Sat–Sun from 4pm 🚇 Concorde

CRAZY HORSE

www.lecrazyhorseparis.com

This Parisian institution was established in 1951. Its *Taboo* show presents dancers who appear to be almost nude. Dinner is served.

✚ 218 H6 ✉ 12 avenue George V, 75008 ☎ 01 47 23 32 32 🕐 Show: Sun–Fri 8.15pm, 10.45pm, Sat 7pm, 9.30pm, 11.45pm ✋ Show and dinner: €155; champagne and show: €70 🚇 Alma-Marceau, George V

HARRY'S NEW YORK BAR

www.harrys-bar.fr

Hundreds of cocktails are on offer here, perfectly mastered by highly professional barmen.

✚ 219 L5 ✉ 5 rue Daunou, 75002 ☎ 01 42 61 71 14 🕐 Daily 10am–4am 🚇 Opéra

LIDO DE PARIS

www.lido.fr

This cabaret offers a titillating show, with the legendary topless Bluebell Girls and magic tricks, and some fine French cuisine, under the direction of chef Philippe Lacroix.

✚ 218 H5 ✉ 116 bis avenue des Champs-Élysées, 75008 ☎ 01 40 76 56 10 🕐 Show: daily 7.30pm ✋ Dinner and show: €150–€280; champagne and show: €100 🚇 George V

OPÉRA PALAIS GARNIER

www.opera-de-paris.fr

This architectural masterpiece (▷ 204) provides a lavish, prestigious setting for visiting ballet and opera companies, and orchestras.

✚ 219 L5 ✉ place de l'Opéra, 75009 ☎ 0892 89 90 90 ✋ €5–€180 🚇 Opéra

PARIS STORY

www.paris-story.com

This thrilling 45-minute multimedia show illustrates Paris's history over the past 2,000 years to music by Berlioz, Gounod and Saint-Saëns.

✚ 219 L5 ✉ 11 bis rue Scribe, 75009 ☎ 01 42 66 62 06 🕐 Daily 10–6 on the hour; available in 12 languages through headsets ✋ Adult €10, child (6–17) €6, family €26 🚇 Opéra

QUEEN

www.queen.fr

This trendy club attracts a straight and a gay crowd. House and garage music is mixed by international DJs.

✚ 218 H5 ✉ 102 avenue des Champs-Élysées, 75008 ☎ 01 53 89 08 90 🕐 Daily 11.30pm–6am ✋ €15 Mon–Thu and Sun, €20 Fri–Sat 🚇 George V

SPORTS AND ACTIVITIES

RITZ ESCOFFIER SCHOOL

The height of culinary practice, the Escoffier School offers two-and-a-half-hour cookery lessons.

✚ 219 L5 ✉ Hôtel Ritz, 15 place Vendôme, 75001 ☎ 01 43 16 30 30 🕐 Wed 2.30–5 ✋ €100 🚇 Opéra, Madeleine

HEALTH AND BEAUTY

BASTIEN GONZALEZ HOTEL LE BRISTOL DAY SPA

www.bastiengonzalez.com

Pedicurist to the stars, Bastien Gonzalez has a unique approach to feet and can make toenails shine for up to three months without varnish.

✚ 218 J5 ✉ 108 rue de Faubourg St-Honoré, 75008 ☎ 01 42 66 24 22 🕐 By appointment ✋ €130 🚇 St-Philippe du Roule

VILLA THALGO

www.thalgo.fr

A seven-hour thalassotherapy session includes bodyscrub, seaweed wrap, balneotherapy, jet shower, aquagym and massages.

✚ 219 L5 ✉ 11 rue du 4 Septembre, 75002 ☎ 01 42 96 42 76 🕐 Mon–Wed 8.30–7, Thu–Fri 8.30–7.30 ✋ 60-min treatment around €75, 40-min around €50 🚇 Quatre Septembre

FOR CHILDREN

MUSÉE GRÉVIN

▷ 196.

PALAIS DE LA DÉCOUVERTE

▷ 192.

PARC MONCEAU

▷ 205.

PRICES AND SYMBOLS

The prices given are the average for a two-course lunch (L) and a three-course dinner (D) for one person, without drinks. The wine price is for the least expensive bottle.

For a key to the symbols, ▷ 2.

6 NEW YORK

www.paris-restaurant-6newyork.com

This restaurant, named after its address, is reminiscent of an elegant Manhattan dining room. The interior is strikingly contemporary, with a great view of the Eiffel Tower. On the menu you'll find fusion dishes such as lobster and sun-dried tomato risotto, black and white chocolate *millefeuille*, and traditional dishes.

✚ 218 H6 ✉ 6 avenue de New York, 75016, Champs-Élysées ☎ 01 40 70 03 30 🕐 Mon–Fri 12.30–2, 6–11, Sat 6–11 ✋ L €35, D €60, Wine €23 🚇 Alma Marceau

L'ALSACE

www.restaurantalsace.com

This little piece of eastern France is an integral part of the Parisian landscape. Brasserie-style cuisine forms the menu, with a choice of seafood platters, sauerkraut, apple

strudel and iced *gugelhupf* (cake). The interior is equally regional, and there is a pleasant terrace for spring and summer days.

✚ 218 H5 ✉ 39 avenue des Champs-Élysées, 75008, Champs-Élysées ☎ 01 53 93 97 00 🕐 Daily 24 hours ✋ L €30, D €50, Wine €19 🚇 Franklin D. Roosevelt

L'APPART

The dining room in this house is meant to look like an apartment, but looks more like a comfortable library, lined with bookshelves. Expect inventive cuisine with a Mediterranean accent, such as pan-roasted veal in a creamy mustard and mushroom sauce. Before Sunday brunch, there's a children's brunch with a pastry workshop.

✚ 218 H5 ✉ 9–11 rue du Colisée, 75008, Champs-Élysées ☎ 01 53 75 42 00 🕐 Daily 12–2.30, 7–11.30, Sun brunch 12–3 ✋ L €35, D €50, Wine €20 🚇 Franklin D. Roosevelt

CAFÉ MARLY

There are wonderful views of the Louvre pyramid from this elegant brasserie. There are sleek armchairs and gilt-edged black wood panels. The menu has typical brasserie food such as rare tuna in a sesame crust.

Above *This region has varied dining choices*

✚ 219 L6 ✉ 93 rue de Rivoli, 75001, Louvre/Palais Royal ☎ 01 49 26 06 60 🕐 Daily 8am–2am ✋ L €40, D €55, Wine €22 🚇 Palais-Royal/Musée du Louvre, Tuileries

LE GRAND CAFÉ

www.legrandcafe.com

Inaugurated in 1875 this restaurant is open day and night. The interior is beautiful, art nouveau, with an impressive stained-glass ceiling and fanciful furniture. Fish is king here and is served grilled, poached or meunière (in lemon and butter). The menu also includes some French meat dishes, such as fillet of Charolais beef with peppercorns or grilled with a Béarnaise sauce.

✚ 219 L5 ✉ 4 boulevard des Capucines, 75009, Grands Boulevards ☎ 01 43 12 19 00 🕐 Daily 24 hours ✋ L €35, D €55, Wine €20 🚇 Opéra

LE GRAND COLBERT

www.legrandcolbert.fr

This chic brasserie, which dates from 1830 has high ceilings, black-and-white floor tiles, Café-de-Paris-style lamps and an army of highly professional waiters wearing the traditional black-and-white *garçon* uniform. The menu includes seafood platters, sauerkraut and steaks.

➕ 219 M6 ✉ 2 rue Vivienne, 75002, Louvre/Palais Royal ☎ 01 42 86 87 88 ⏰ Daily noon–1am (last orders midnight) 🖐 L €28, D €45, Wine €22 🚇 Bourse, Palais-Royal/Musée du Louvre

GUY SAVOY

ww.guysavoy.com

Guy Savoy's menu features delicacies such as poached-grilled pigeon and giblets in a beetroot and mushroom *millefeuille*, or langoustines with citrus and peas. This is a true culinary experience.

➕ 218 G4 ✉ 18 rue Troyon, 75017, Champs-Élysées ☎ 01 43 80 40 61 ⏰ Mon–Fri 12–2, 7–10.30, Sat 7–10.30 🖐 L €200, D €300, Wine €90 🚇 Charles de Gaulle-Étoile

MARKET

www.jean-georges.com

There is a pared-down approach to the menu here, which offers the produce of a raw bar, notably a choice of oysters, and fusion food by chef Jean-Georges Vongerichten. Try the black truffle pizza or the hors d'œuvre selection that includes shrimps on a skewer, ginger lobster roll, raw tuna and spiced quail.

➕ 219 J5 ✉ 15 avenue Matignon, 75008, Champs-Élysées ☎ 01 56 43 40 90 ⏰ Mon–Fri 8am–11am, 12–3, 7–11, Sat, Sun 12–4.30, 7–11.30 🖐 L €40, D €60, Wine €30 🚇 Franklin D. Roosevelt, Champs-Élysées-Clemenceau

MAXIM'S

www.maxims-de-paris.com

This belle-époque restaurant was established in 1893 by café waiter Maxime Gaillard and acquired in 1981 by designer Pierre Cardin. It is now a hub of Parisian social life and has proved so successful that other Maxims have opened across the world. Attentive service, refined French cuisine and a prestigious location all give a touch of class.

➕ 219 K6 ✉ 3 rue Royale, 75008, Concorde ☎ 01 42 65 27 94 ⏰ Tue–Fri 12.30–2, 7.30–10, Sat 7.30–10 🖐 L €130, D €175, Wine €40 🚇 Concorde

MUSCADE

www.muscade-palais-royal.com

This high-class venue has an exceptional setting in the Palais Royal gardens. It has a particularly elegant interior, with black-and-white floor tiles and Regency chairs. At Muscade they are passionate about cakes and gateaux, which you can enjoy as a dessert or as part of a traditional afternoon tea. This includes chocolate macaroons, fig and saffron caramel *pastilla* (a Middle Eastern filo-pastry dish) and ginger and lemon cake. Other delicacies include muffins and chocolate gateaux.

➕ 219 L6 ✉ 36 rue Montpensier, 75001, Louvre/Palais Royal ☎ 01 42 97 51 36 ⏰ Tea room: Tue–Sun 10–7; restaurant: Tue–Sat 10am–10.30pm, Sun 10–3 🖐 Tea €4, slice of cake €6 🚇 Pyramides, Palais-Royal/Louvre

PIERRE GAGNAIRE

www.pierre-gagnaire.fr

Gagnaire is a 3-star chef from the Lyon region, who delights gourmets with his boundless creativity using the simplest ingredients. Dishes include mild-onion marmalade, veal and foie gras with figs and salted raw ham, bitter orange and carrot paste and creamed parsnip and chocolate. A real treat for special occasions.

➕ 218 H5 ✉ 6 rue Balzac, 75008, Champs-Élysées ☎ 01 58 36 12 50 ⏰ Mon–Fri 12–1.30, 7.30–9.30, Sun 7.30–9.30 🖐 L €130, D €250, Wine €60 🚇 George V

POMZE

www.pomze.com

A boutique, a restaurant and a bar all dedicated to…apples! Stéphane Oliver's inventive cooking is based on this universal ingredient and the shop offers a wide choice of ciders, jams, chutneys as well as six pure juices, each made from a single variety of fruit.

➕ 219 J4 ✉ 109 boulevard Haussmann, 75008, Grands Boulevards ☎ 01 42 65 65 83 ⏰ Mon–Fri 8.30am–10.30pm, Sat 3pm–10.30pm 🖐 L €35, D €50, Wine €21 🚇 St-Augustin

SPOON

www.spoon.tm.fr

Sleek lines and deep purple walls are enhanced by the pastels of the chair cushions. There's just as much creativity in the kitchen, where celebrated chef Alain Ducasse dreams up highly personalized menus—you choose the sauce and accompaniment to your meal. The menu combines French, American and Asian influences with plenty for vegetarians. Unusually, the wine list has mostly American and New World wines (California is particularly well represented), and some wines are available by the glass each day.

➕ 218 H5 ✉ 14 rue de Marignan, 75008, Champs-Élysées ☎ 01 40 76 34 44 ⏰ Mon–Fri 12–2, 7–11 🖐 L €44, D €55, Wine €24 🚇 Franklin D. Roosevelt

SPRING

www.springparis.fr

When American Daniel Rose came to Paris to study he had a yen to open a restaurant in the gourmet city—and what a madcap place it is. It's truly unmissable. There is no menu, just a set four-course dinner made from the day's freshest ingredients, and it's served on the dot at 8.30pm. In all other respects this is an easy-going establishment.

➕ 219 M6 ✉ 6 rue Bailleul, 75001 ☎ 01 45 96 05 72 ⏰ Fri 12–2.30, Tue–Sat 8.30pm–10.30pm (one sitting—don't be late) 🖐 L €64, D €64, Wine €32 🚇 Louvre Rivoli

VILLA SPICY

www.spicyrestaurant.com

Be prepared for inventive cuisine that explodes with taste. The menu changes with the seasons but includes surprising examples such as tartare of salmon or stir-fried vegetables with pistou. There's also an organic detox menu (€36) which is delicious but light on delicate digestive systems. The interior is in the style of a classical Mediterranean villa.

➕ 218 J5 ✉ 8 avenue Franklin D. Roosevelt, 75008, Champs-Élysées ☎ 01 56 59 62 59 ⏰ Daily 12–3, 7–12 🖐 L €30, D €40, Wine €20 🚇 Franklin D. Roosevelt

PRICES AND SYMBOLS

Prices are the lowest and highest for a double room for one night. Breakfast is included unless noted otherwise. All the hotels listed accept credit cards unless otherwise stated. Note that rates vary widely throughout the year.

For a key to the symbols, ▷ 2.

HÔTEL ASTRID

www.hotel-astrid.com
This 3-star hotel is in a peaceful side street close to the Champs-Élysées. No two bedrooms are the same—styles include romantic (think brass bedframe, chandelier and pink curtains) and country (pine furniture and blue wallpaper). Facilities include a safe, hairdryer, WiFi internet access and satellite TV. There are parking spaces nearby.
✚ 218 G4 ✉ 27 avenue Carnot, 75017, Champs-Élysées ☎ 01 44 09 26 00 ✋ €159–€169, excluding breakfast 🛏 40 🔁 🚇 Charles de Gaulle-Étoile

HÔTEL DU BOIS

www.hoteldubois.com
Designer Michel Jouannet has transformed this 3-star hotel from a palace of chintz to a chic, bright place to stay. Rooms are calm with earthy colours and artist Gotof has

supplied the paintings, which are available for purchase. Satellite TV with international channels and WiFi are provided.
✚ 218 G5 ✉ 11 rue du Dôme, 75016, Champs-Élysées ☎ 01 45 00 31 96 ✋ €126–€285, excluding breakfast 🛏 39 🚇 Kléber, Charles de Gaulle-Étoile

HÔTEL COSTES

www.hotelcostes.com
A very popular jet-set hang-out which is curiously cosy with lavish yet discreet furnishings, and nooks and crannies to allow guests to be private in public. This luxury 5-star hotel is the place to be seen in Paris—if only in its equally luxurious restaurant. Right in the heart of a fashionable district, originally a Napoléon III mansion, it opened as a hotel in 1991.
✚ 219 K6 ✉ 239 rue St-Honoré, 75001, Concorde ☎ 01 42 44 50 00 ✋ €385–€650, excluding breakfast 🛏 82 rooms, 3 suites 🔁 🏊 🍴 🚇 Concorde

HÔTEL ÉLYSÉES CERAMIC

www.elysees-ceramic.com
Behind its opulent, historic art nouveau facade, which features sculpted painted ceramics, lies a charming belle époque interior—all just a few minutes' stroll from the

Arc de Triomphe, the Champs-Élysées and the luxury shops of rue du Faubourg Saint-Honoré. The feeling of being in another age happily does not extend to the facilities which, like the bathrooms, are right up to date.
✚ 218 G4 ✉ 34 avenue de Wagram, 75008, Arc de Triomphe ☎ 01 42 27 29 30 ✋ €220–€230, breakfast not included 🛏 57 🔁 🚇 Ternes

HÔTEL FRANKLIN ROOSEVELT

www.hroosevelt.com
This hotel is in a great position, close to the Champs-Élysées and avenue Montaigne, with its world-famous couture shops. Inside, there is a fine blend of subtle lighting, thick fitted carpets, rich red fabrics and dark wood. If you're looking for a bit of luxury, the suite on the sixth floor has a king-size bed and a jacuzzi. Facilities include a bar, reading room and winter garden.
✚ 218 H5 ✉ 18 rue Clément Marot, 75008, Champs-Élysées ☎ 01 53 57 49 50 ✋ €220–€280, excluding breakfast 🛏 48 🔁 🚇 Franklin D. Roosevelt, Alma Marceau

Above *The elegant and lavish Salon Cambon at the Ritz*

INTERCONTINENTAL PARIS AVENUE MARCEAU

www.ic-marceau.com

Total refurbishment in 2010 has turned this old 4-star property into a sleek, contemporary 5-star boutique hotel close to all the major attractions. Communal areas have striking wall art while each room is individually furnished, some with antique pieces and ceiling frescoes. High levels of service and amenities including Wii console rental and Nespresso machines.

🚼 218 G5 ✉ 64 avenue Marceau, 75017, Champs-Élysées ☎ 01 44 43 36 36 ✋ €210–€950 🚹 56 🔂 🜢 🚇 Charles de Gaulle-Étoile

HÔTEL LAUTREC OPÉRA

www.paris-hotel-lautrec.com

This 3-star hotel is named after the celebrated artist Henri Toulouse-Lautrec, who once lived here. The building is classified as an historic monument and has a beautiful 18th-century facade. Inside, there's a more contemporary feel, with pale wood furniture and blue and yellow upholstery. Some of the guest bedrooms have walls of bare brickwork and there are exposed beams in the ceilings. All rooms have satellite TV.

🚼 219 M5 ✉ 8–10 rue d'Amboise, 75002, Opéra ☎ 01 42 96 67 90 ✋ €115–€165, excluding breakfast 🚹 59 🔂 🚇 Richelieu-Drouot

HÔTEL QUEEN MARY

www.hotelqueenmary.com

Elegance is the hallmark of this 3-star hotel, near the Opéra Palais Garnier. The salon has moulded ceilings and printed fitted carpets, while the large dining room has a tromp-l'œil painting. The spacious bedrooms are decorated with mahogany wood and burgundy fabrics. There's a small terrace and the usual facilities of cable TV, WiFi connection, safe, hairdryer and minibar in the bedrooms.

🚼 219 K5 ✉ 9 rue Greffulhe, 75008, Opéra ☎ 01 42 66 40 50 ✋ €130–€209, excluding breakfast 🚹 35 rooms, 1 suite 🔂 🚇 Madeleine, Havre-Caumartin

HÔTEL RESIDENCE FOCH

www.foch-paris-hotel.com

A charming 3-star residence with well-appointed rooms filled with quality furniture and traditional French touches but also modern necessities like WiFi. There's a bright bar on the ground floor and the hotel benefits from a private courtyard garden where you can relax over breakfast or a drink.

🚼 218 F4 ✉ 10 rue Marbeau, 75116, Champs-Élysées ☎ 01 45 00 46 50 ✋ €180–€200, excluding breakfast 🚹 25 🔂 🚇 Porte Dauphine

HÔTEL SPLENDID ÉTOILE

www.hsplendid.com

Remarkably well priced for a hotel in such a rich location, the building of the Splendid Étoile is a fine example of Haussmann construction, dating back to 1880. The hotel lacks nothing in facilities.

🚼 218 G4 ✉ 1 bis avenue-Carnot, 75017, Arc de Triomphe ☎ 01 45 72 72 00 ✋ €250–€380 for room with Arc de Triomphe view 🚹 54 rooms, 3 suites 🔂 🚇 Charles de Gaulle-Étoile

HÔTEL TILSITT

www.tilsitt.com

This 3-star hotel is a great find. Set close to the Arc de Triomphe, the location is good and the furnishings are a melange of sleek Scandinavian style combined with a touch of classical Greek, set inside the typically Gallic structure. The furnishings have a luxurious feel, though the rooms can be compact. Each bedroom has a wide-screen TV and WiFi internet. The lounge bar opens 24 hours.

🚼 218 G4 ✉ 23 rue Brey, 75017, Champs-Élysées ☎ 01 43 80 39 71 ✋ €90–€165, excluding breakfast 🚹 38 🔂 🚇 Charles de Gaulle-Étoile 🇷 RER: Charles de Gaulle-Étoile

HÔTEL DE VENDÔME

www.hoteldevendome.com

Handy for all the main sights of the central Right Bank, and close to the Ritz (see below), Hôtel de Vendôme is a small gem furnished in the best of French decorative arts

style, yet with an international air. Built in 1832, it was restored in the 1990s to its original grandeur and today the hotel has an inviting piano bar, a traditional restaurant and a penthouse meeting room.

🚼 219 L6 ✉ 1 place Vendôme, 75001, Opéra ☎ 01 55 04 55 00 ✋ €450–€865, excluding breakfast 🚹 19 rooms, 10 suites 🔂 🚇 Opéra

HÔTEL WASHINGTON OPÉRA

www.hotelwashingtonopera.com

Madame de Pompadour, mistress of Louis XV, once lived here. Her home is now a lavish 4-star hotel. The bedrooms have Directoire-style furniture and marble bathrooms; some have canopy beds.

🚼 219 L6 ✉ 50 rue de Richelieu, 75001, Palais Royal ☎ 01 42 96 68 06 ✋ €215–€275, excluding breakfast 🚹 36 🔂 🚇 Palais-Royal/Musée-du-Louvre

LE MEURICE

www.lemeurice.com

A historic landmark established specifically to attract 19th-century English visitors, Le Meurice is the ultimate in luxury, with its own restaurant and every amenity from WiFi internet to an iPod radio alarm. Possibly too expensive for most, but certainly worth a visit.

🚼 219 L6 ✉ 228 rue de Rivoli, 75001, Tuileries ☎ 01 44 58 10 10 ✋ €720–€1,020, excluding breakfast 🚹 115 rooms, 23 suites 🔂 🜢 Spa 🚇 Tuileries

RITZ

www.ritzparis.com

This world-famous hotel has been the epitome of elegance and luxury since it opened in 1898. Coco Chanel, Ernest Hemingway and Marcel Proust were regular guests here. The lavish interior is decorated with antiques and chandeliers. The hotel has a club, several restaurants, bars and private salons, conference rooms and the gourmet cookery school, Ritz-Escoffier.

🚼 219 L5 ✉ 15 place Vendôme, 75001, Opéra ☎ 01 43 16 30 30 ✋ €850–€970, excluding breakfast 🚹 103 rooms, 56 suites 🔂 🏊 🜢 🚇 Tuileries, Pyramides, Madeleine, Concorde

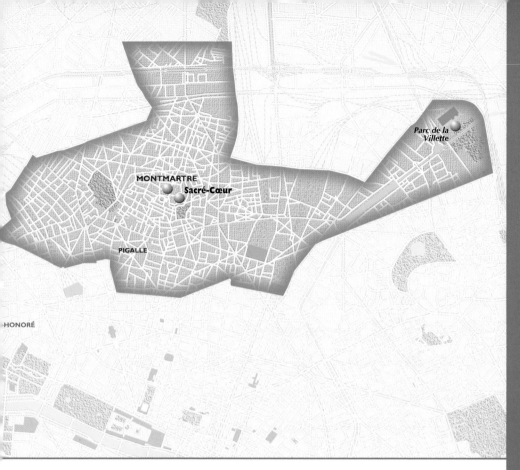

Parc de la
Villette

MONTMARTRE
Sacré-Cœur

PIGALLE

HONORÉ

MONTMARTRE

Montmartre is the icing on the rich confection of culture, romance and imagination that constitutes Paris. It is a village within a city, with cobbled streets and an innate cosiness.

After the Eiffel Tower, the second-highest point in Paris is the great dome of the gleaming white Sacré-Cœur basilica at the very top of Montmartre hill which offers stunning views of up to 50km (30 miles). As well as being one of the most visible landmarks in the city, and a beautiful one at that, the basilica also has the most exquisite interior featuring a breathtaking golden mosaic.

The Moulin Rouge, Paris's top cabaret spot and one-time stomping ground for artist Toulouse-Lautrec, is, like the Sacré-Cœur, virtually the 'badge' of Montmartre—and a 'must see' for every visitor. So, too, are the Cimetière de Montmartre, resting place of many famous Parisians, and the Marché aux Puces de St-Ouen antiques market. Also on Montmartre hill, the place du Tertre is a huge outdoor artists' colony. Indeed, there are plenty of reminders of artists who originally flourished here. Espace Montmartre–Salvador Dalí has France's largest collection of work by the zany Catalan painter, and Musée Gustave Moreau is a studio-museum which shows how the 19th-century painter lived, on the edge of Pigalle, the area famous for the sex trade that once flourished there.

Visitors can learn the history of the area from its actual and fabled beginnings at the Musée de Montmartre. But for a taste of the 21st century, the ultra-modern 55ha (135-acre) Parc de la Villette is a futuristic world in an innovatively landscaped park on either side of the Canal de l'Ourcq. Its range of cultural and leisure activities include a science museum, music complex, hemispheric cinema, exhibition centre and concert hall.

objects, ranging from Louis XV mirrors and luxurious 19th-century chandeliers to weird and wacky 1970s furniture. Don't be put off by the cluster of tacky stands along the approach to the market. Walk past them, under the flyover, then decide which of the 13 official markets you'll tackle first. There are around 2,000 shops and stalls to choose from. Watch out for pickpockets and remember that prices fluctuate with the weather, so be prepared to haggle. Sunday afternoons are busy.

➕ Off map 223 M1 ✉ Porte de Clignancourt, 75018 (from the Métro station turn right onto avenue de la Porte de Clignancourt, past the tacky unofficial stands. Walk under the flyover and the market is on your left) ☎ 01 40 12 32 58 🕐 Sat 9–6, Sun 10–6, Mon 11–5. Many stalls close 1–15 Aug ✋ Free 🚇 Porte de Clignancourt 🚌 56, 85 🍴 Cafés and restaurants on rue des Rosiers ❓ Beware of pickpockets

CIMETIÈRE DE MONTMARTRE

Montmartre's cemetery is packed with graves of the famous, including composers Hector Berlioz and Jacques Offenbach, writers Henri Stendhal and Alexandre Dumas, and artists Edgar Degas and Jean-Baptiste Greuze. The imposing tomb of Émile Zola is close to the flower-filled roundabout near the main entrance, although the writer's remains were moved to the Panthéon (▷ 128) in 1906. The cemetery, opened in 1825, also holds the grave of Louise Weber, the Moulin Rouge dancer known as La Goulue, who appeared in paintings by Toulouse-Lautrec. Jazz fans may be interested in finding the tomb of the saxophone inventor, Adolphe Sax.

A noticeboard at the main entrance gives times and dates of guided visits.

➕ 222 L2 ✉ 20 avenue Rachel, 75018 ☎ 01 53 42 36 30 🕐 Mid-Mar to early Nov Mon–Fri 8–6, Sat 8.30–6, Sun 9–8.30; early Nov to mid-Mar Mon–Fri 8–5.30, Sat 8.30–5.30, Sun 9–5.30 ✋ Free 🚇 Place de Clichy/Blanche 🚌 30, 54, 74, 80, 95

ESPACE MONTMARTRE—SALVADOR DALÍ

www.daliparis.com

This surreal museum displays more than 300 weird and wonderful works by the Catalan artist Salvador Dalí (1904–1989), who came to live in Paris in the late 1920s. The disconcerting black-walled interior is a fitting backdrop for the sculptures and illustrations, which form the biggest Dalí collection in France.

➕ 223 M3 ✉ 11 rue Poulbot (off place du Tertre), 75018 ☎ 01 42 64 10 10 🕐 Jul–Aug daily 10–8, Sep–Jun 10–6 ✋ Adult €10, child €6, under 8 free. Audioguide €2 🚇 Abbesses, Anvers 🚌 50, 80, Montmartrobus

MARCHÉ AUX PUCES DE ST-OUEN

www.parispuces.com

Pick up a piece of bygone Paris—or a cheap imitation—at what claims to be the world's largest antiques market, spread over 7ha (17 acres) north of Montmartre, just beyond the *périphérique*. Even if you have no intention of buying, you'll find an Aladdin's Cave of fascinating

MONTMARTRE

▷ 226–227.

MOULIN ROUGE

www.moulinrouge.fr

The Moulin Rouge is the famous symbol of Montmartre. Its decadent reputation was initially fuelled by Toulouse-Lautrec's posters and more recently by the 2001 film *Moulin Rouge*. The 'Red Windmill' was never actually a windmill but was launched as a cabaret venue in 1889. It soon became known for its saucy shows, featuring scantily clad cancan girls. Over the years stars have made guest appearances, including Edith Piaf, Frank Sinatra, Liza Minnelli and Elton John. You can still see lively shows here (at a price), complete with the famous *cancaneuses* dancers.

➕ 222 L3 ✉ 82 boulevard de Clichy, 75018 ☎ 01 53 09 82 82 🕐 Shows nightly at 9pm and 11pm; dinner at 7pm ✋ Show and dinner: €150–€180; show and champagne: €102, show: €90 🚇 Blanche 🚌 30, 54, 68, 74

Opposite *The legendary Moulin Rouge*
Above *Stall at Marché aux Puces de St-Ouen*

MONTMARTRE

INFORMATION

www.montmartrenet.com

✚ 223 M2 ✉ 75018 Ⓜ Anvers, Abbesses, Blanche, Lamarck

Ⓜ Montmartrobus; 30, 31, 54, 60, 67, 68, 74, 80, 81, 85, 95 have stops around the edge of Montmartre 🍴 La Maison Rose, rue de l'Abreuvoir (tel 01 42 57 66 75; open 12–3, 7–11; closed Wed lunch and Tue and Thu dinner). There are plenty of restaurants and cafés in the area, many of them very touristy 🎫 A selection

INTRODUCTION

The hilltop village of Montmartre, to the north of the city core, has a split personality. There are teeming tourist traps, including place du Tertre and the front steps of Sacré-Cœur, but venture a few minutes off the beaten track and you'll find quiet cobbled streets, whitewashed cottages and all the atmosphere of a small village. The Métro will take you to the outskirts of the district, but to reach the key sights you'll have to either walk or take the Montmartrobus, which runs a circular route from place Pigalle, past Sacré-Cœur, and north to the Métro station Jules Joffrin. You can avoid the daunting walk up the steps to Sacré-Cœur by taking the funicular from square Willette (costing one Métro ticket each way).

Montmartre started life as a place of worship, a far cry from its later hedonistic reputation. The Romans built a temple to Mercury here, naming the hill Mons Mercurii. It was later called Mont des Martyrs, following the murder of Paris's first bishop, St. Denis, in the third century AD. He was said to have picked up his head and taken it to a nearby fountain to wash away the blood, before collapsing (see his statue in square Suzanne-Buisson). Montmartre's religious connection was renewed in the 12th century, when Louis VI founded a Benedictine Abbey there. With monks around, the area was soon filled with vineyards. By the end of the 17th century around 30 windmills stood on the hill and Montmartre prospered with the production of wine, flour and gypsum (plaster of Paris) for the city below. Gypsum quarrying stopped in the early 19th century because the hill was in danger of collapsing. Montmartre became known for its decadent cabarets at the end of the 19th century. Nowadays the district is no longer the hub of Paris's nightlife, but visitors still come to La Butte (the mound) for a taste of its Bohemian past.

WHAT TO SEE

TOURIST MONTMARTRE

Montmartre is crowned by the Basilique du Sacré-Cœur (▷ 232–235), a dazzling white neo-Byzantine creation whose domes and turrets look stunning against a blue sky. There are sweeping views over Paris from its front steps. The nearby place du Tertre (literally 'Hillock Square') is Paris's highest point

Above *Postcards celebrate Montmartre's former famous residents*

and swarms with visitors and street artists. The restaurant La Mère Catherine, at number 6, was founded in 1793 and was said to have given rise to the name *bistro*. Legend has it that in 1814, Russian troops, who had become regulars at the restaurant, would shout *bystro* (quickly) to hurry along their food (▷ 39). You can sometimes try Montmartre's own wine here, made from grapes grown in the area's only remaining vineyard, on rue des Saules.

VILLAGE MONTMARTRE

Place du Tertre is tourist Montmartre at its peak, but only a few minutes' walk away are quieter streets, including rue de l'Abreuvoir, rue des Saules and rue Girardon. Make sure you save some time to wander through this less showy side of Montmartre (see walk, ▷ 236–237), where you'll find cobblestones, tree-lined steps and even two windmills. It's hard to remember you're still in France's capital. At 22 rue des Saules is the tiny but legendary cabaret venue Au Lapin Agile (▷ 238), once frequented by Picasso and still providing entertainment. Nearby, at 12 rue Cortot, is the Musée de Montmartre (▷ 228), where you can learn more about the history of the area. A short walk away, off rue Lepic, is one of Montmartre's two remaining windmills, the Moulin de la Galette, built in 1622 and formerly known as Le Moulin du Blute-fin. Legend claims that one of its millers, Pierre-Charles Debray, was strung up on its sails in 1814 for trying to stop the invading Cossacks, although it is more likely he was killed by a stray bullet. Later in the 19th century the Debray family converted the mill into a popular open-air dance hall, providing inspiration for many artists, including Renoir and Vincent Van Gogh. Nearby is the Moulin Radet, now part of a restaurant called Le Moulin de la Galette (▷ 241).

ARTISTS' MONTMARTRE

Montmartre earned an almost mythical status at the end of the 19th century, thanks to its community of artists and its raunchy nightlife. Toulouse-Lautrec immortalized scenes at the world-famous cabaret Moulin Rouge (▷ 225), while Renoir captured the exuberance of a ball at the Moulin de la Galette. Twentieth-century artists who converged on Montmartre included Picasso and Georges Braque, who gave birth to Cubism in the Bateau-Lavoir studios, on place Emile-Goudeau. The original timber building burned down in 1970 and was replaced by a concrete studio, now closed to the public. For 20th-century art head for the surreal Espace Montmartre–Salvador Dalí (▷ 225).

TIPS

» Le Petit Train de Montmartre (Promotrain; www.promotrain.fr) offers a 40-minute tour of Montmartre's main sights, starting from place Blanche (10–6; until midnight at weekends and during July and August; adult €6, child (under 12) €3.50). The Montmartrain runs a similar circuit.
» Montmartre's cemetery (▷ 225) is well worth a visit to search out the graves of Hector Berlioz, Jacques Offenbach, Émile Zola and other composers and writers.

Below left *A baker's art nouveau shopfront in Montmartre*
Below *The tomb of Alexandre Dumas in Montmartre's cemetery*

MUSÉE GUSTAVE MOREAU

www.musee-moreau.fr

This studio-museum, on the edge of Pigalle, offers an intriguing view of how a late-19th-century artist lived. On the lower floors you'll find the studios of the Symbolist painter Gustave Moreau (1826–1898), teacher to Henri Matisse. Upstairs is a reconstruction of his private apartment, where you can see the kind of paintings, objects and furniture he chose to surround himself with. Paintings gracing his walls included works by Edgar Degas and Théodore Chassériau. Moreau wanted his house to be preserved as a museum. His wish has been granted and the museum displays around 1,300 of his works.
✚ 222 L4 ✉ 14 rue de la Rochefoucauld, 75009 ☎ 01 48 74 38 50 🕐 Mon, Wed–Thu 10–12.45, 2–5.45, Fri–Sun 10–5.15 🖐 Adult €5, under 18 free, free to all on 1st Sun of month 🚇 Trinité, St-Georges

MUSÉE DE MONTMARTRE

www.museedemontmartre.fr

Montmartre's history is arguably the most enchanting of all Paris's districts, with its walking beheaded saint, prosperous windmills and infamous nightlife. You can find out more at the Musée de Montmartre, in a 17th-century mansion that once belonged to Rose de Rosimond, a member of Molière's stage troupe. The house, behind Montmartre's remaining vineyard, later was home to painter Pierre-Auguste Renoir.
✚ 223 M2 ✉ 12 rue Cortot, 75018 ☎ 01 49 25 89 37 🕐 Daily 10–6 🖐 Adult €8, child €6, under 10 free 🚇 Lamarck-Caulaincourt 🚌 80, Montmartrobus

PARC DE LA VILLETTE

▷ 230–231.

PIGALLE

The name Pigalle is synonymous with the blatant sex trade that has flourished there for decades. There are sleazy bars, sex shops and peep shows in the boulevard Rochechouart and surrounding streets. In the 19th century, the painters Pierre-Auguste Renoir and Henri de Toulouse-Lautrec were frequent visitors, scouting around place Pigalle looking for models.
✚ 223 L3 ✉ South of Montmartre, from place d'Anvers to place de Clichy, 75009/75018 🚇 Pigalle 🚌 30, 54, 67; Montmartrobus

PLACE DES ABBESSES

Place des Abbesses is less touristy than place du Tertre, farther up the Montmartre hill, so makes a quieter coffee stop.

The square has a magnificent art nouveau Métro entrance, that leads into Paris's deepest station, 40m (131ft) below ground. The church of St-Jean-de-Montmartre (1904) picks up on the art nouveau theme, with decorative windows that enliven the rather ugly red-brick cladding. This conspicuous brickwork earned it the nickname St-Jean-des-Briques. The square takes its name from the abbey that once stood on the site. A mischievous legend claims that Henri de Navarre, who later became King Henri IV, had a fling with the abbess in 1590.

Seek out the Mur des Je t'Aime (▷ 24) where 'I love you' is declared in 311 languages.
✚ 223 M3 ✉ place des Abbesses, Montmartre, 75018 🚇 Abbesses 🚌 Montmartrobus 🚋 A selection

Below *Hector Guimard's art nouveau entrance to Abbesses Métro station*
Opposite *Stone carving detail on the Musée Gustave Moreau*

PARC DE LA VILLETTE

INFORMATION

www.villette.com

✚ Off map 223 P3 ✉ 211 avenue Jean-Jaurès, 75019 ☎ 01 40 03 75 75 🚇 Porte de la Villette 🚌 75, PC2, PC3

Cité des Sciences et de l'Industrie

www.cite-sciences.fr
www.lageode.fr

✚ Off map 223 P3 ✉ 30 avenue Corentin-Cariou, 75019 ☎ 01 40 05 80 00 (recorded information) 🌐 Explora exhibitions: Tue–Sat 10–6, Sun 10–7. Planetarium: Tue–Sun, shows every hour from 11–5 (except 1pm). La Géode: Tue–Sun 10.30–8.30 (times vary Mon and public hols). *L'Argonaute*: Tue–Sat 10.30–5, Sun 10–6.30. Cinaxe: Tue–Sun, shows every 15 min from 11–1 and 2–5 (times vary on public hols) ✋ Explora exhibitions: adult €8, child €6, under 6 free. Planetarium: adult €3 (plus admission to Explora), under 6 free. Cité des Enfants: €8 per person for a 90-min session. La Géode: €10.50, child €9 (mid-week only). *L'Argonaute*: €3. Cinaxe: €5.40, child €4.80 🚇 Porte de la Villette 🚌 75, PC2, PC3 🚤 Canauxrama canal trips to Parc de la Villette, ▷ 264 📷 La Géode: Headsets free from the information point 🍴 Le Hublot, level 2 🛍 📚 Gifts and books ⓘ Children under 3 not admitted to La Géode, *L'Argonaute*, Cinaxe, Planetarium and Cité des Enfants

INTRODUCTION

The ultra-modern Parc de la Villette catapults you into a futuristic world. Its innovatively landscaped 55ha (135 acres) is the largest green area in Paris. There is a range of cultural and leisure activities, including a science museum, music complex, hemispheric cinema, exhibition venue and concert hall.

The park is northeast of the city's heart and is easily reached by Métro. For the Cité des Sciences et de l'Industrie take Line 7 to Porte de la Villette. For the Cité de la Musique take Line 5 to Porte de Pantin. A covered walkway runs the length of the park, linking the two attractions. The walk takes around 15 minutes. The reception desks in the Cité des Sciences et de l'Industrie have information in several languages. You can also pick up a schedule *(Le Programme)* of the shows, films and presentations here. Reserve shows, films and activities as soon as you arrive at the Cité des Sciences et de l'Industrie because they are very popular.

Parc de la Villette was created in the 1980s, designed by architect Bernard Tschumi. He transformed the former abattoir into landscaped grounds containing water features, themed gardens, children's playgrounds, cultural sites, cafés and events venues. The site straddles the Canal de l'Ourcq and is decorated with red metal follies. The city abattoirs stood here from 1867 until 1974 and their cattle hall was transformed into La Grande Halle, now used for trade fairs and concerts. The Cité des Sciences et de l'Industrie opened in 1986, on the same day that Halley's Comet passed near the earth. Its concrete, steel and glass building, surrounded by a moat, was designed by Adrien Fainsilber. The Cité de la Musique, designed by Christian de Portzamparc, opened in 1995.

WHAT TO SEE

CITÉ DES SCIENCES ET DE L'INDUSTRIE

This giant, futuristic science and technology venue is packed with high-tech, hands-on displays, in addition to shows, audiovisual presentations, optical illusions and interactive experiments. The Explora exhibitions, on levels 1 and 2, cover five main themes: The Universe; Water and the Earth; Challenges of the Living World; Industry; and Communication. There is a planetarium on level 2 and the excellent Cité des Enfants on level 0. The 'Nouvelle Cité des Enfants' caters for two to seven year olds. Here games and fun experiments encourage children to learn. The Louis-Lumière cinema, on level 0, shows 3D films and the exhibition 'Ocean, Climate and Us' on level 2 explores the effect of climate change on the world's oceans and seas. The Cité des

Sciences et de l'Industrie also has a Médiathèque (a multimedia library), a health village (offering information), a cyber-base and the Cité des Métiers (providing careers guidance).

LA GÉODE, *L'ARGONAUTE* AND LE CINAXE

Just south of the Cité des Sciences, across the moat, stands the space-age Géode cinema. This gigantic sphere measures 36m (118ft) in diameter. The exterior is covered with curved triangles of polished steel, creating a spectacular distorted mirrored effect. Inside, you can see films on a 1,000sq-m (10,764sq-ft) hemispheric screen—the images are 10 times larger than in a normal cinema. Next to the Géode you can explore *L'Argonaute*, a military submarine that was launched in 1957 and served in the Toulon submarine squadron for 24 years. On the western side of the Cité des Sciences stands the 56-seater Cinaxe—one of the biggest simulator cinemas in the world. The high-tech simulator moves in synchronization with the film.

CITÉ DE LA MUSIQUE

The highlight here is the Musée de la Musique, a fascinating music museum displaying around 900 musical instruments, dating from the Renaissance to the present day. As you walk around, an infrared audioguide plays the music of the instruments in front of you. Paintings, sculptures and beautiful models of concert halls are also displayed. Concerts are staged in the amphitheatre, with its baroque organ. The Cité also contains research facilities, a media library, music and dance information rooms and the Conservatoire National Supérieur de Musique de Paris.

On the eastern edge of the park, a 6,000-seat venue called Zénith stages pop and rock concerts. Other music events are also held in the 15,000-seat Grande Halle.

Cité de la Musique
www.citedelamusique.fr
➕ Off map 223 P3 ✉ 221 avenue Jean-Jaurès, 75019 ☎ 01 44 84 44 84 (information and reservations) ◷ Tue–Sat 12–6, Sun 10–6 (concert times vary). Ticket office closes 45 min before closing
👋 Museum: adult €8, under 6 free
🚇 Porte de Pantin 🚌 75, PC2, PC3
☕ Café de la Musique 📖 Bookshop and gift shop

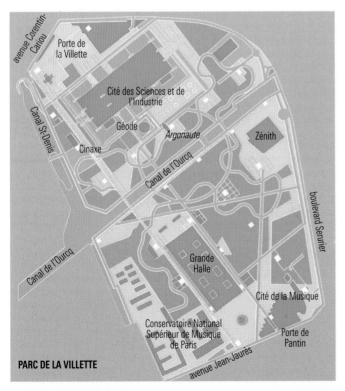

avenue Corentin-Cariou
Porte de la Villette
Cité des Sciences et de l'Industrie
Géode
Argonaute
Zénith
Cinaxe
Canal St-Denis
Canal de l'Ourcq
Canal de l'Ourcq
boulevard Serurier
Grande Halle
Cité de la Musique
Conservatoire National Supérieur de Musique de Paris
Porte de Pantin
PARC DE LA VILLETTE
avenue Jean-Jaurès

Opposite *Cité de la Musique is one of the array of cultural and leisure activities at Parc de la Villette*

INTRODUCTION

The mighty Sacré-Cœur basilica is one of Paris's most prominent landmarks, shimmering at the top of Montmartre's hill. Its eastern-inspired dome is the second-highest point in Paris and the views from the top stretch up to 50km (31 miles). This sweeping panorama is the main attraction for its many visitors, who gather in hordes on the front steps. But walk inside the hushed interior, especially during Mass, and it is an altogether more spiritual experience. The basilica is not the most accessible place, sitting north of central Paris, without a Métro station. Take the Métro to Anvers or Abbesses, then walk to square Willette, where a funicular (or a flight of steep steps for the energetic) takes you the final way up the hill. Enter the basilica from the front doors on place du Parvis du Sacré-Cœur. If Mass is in progress, you may find your movements restricted, but otherwise you are free to roam. To climb to the dome or to visit the crypt, leave the basilica and turn right, to a side door on the west of the building. Tickets for the dome are issued from a machine here.

Sacré-Cœur was commissioned as atonement for the deaths of 58,000 people during the Franco-Prussian war of 1870–1871 and the bloody events of the Commune (▷ 41). Money was donated from across France and the first stone was laid in 1875.

INFORMATION

www.sacre-coeur-montmartre.com

✚ 223 M2 ✉ place du Parvis du Sacré-Cœur ☎ 01 53 41 89 00 ◉ Basilica: daily 6am–10.30pm. Dome and crypt: daily 9–5.45 (also 5.30–7 in summer) ✋ Basilica: free. Dome: adult/child €5 ⊚ Anvers/Abbesses, then walk to funicular 🚌 Montmartrobus 📖 €5 (in French, English, German, Spanish and Italian) 🍴 Cafés and restaurants in Montmartre (▷ 240–241) 📖 Small bookshop/gift shop ❓ There is an elevator at 35 rue du Chevalier de la Barre to help people with disabilities gain access to the basilica

Opposite and above *Sacré-Cœur basilica sits at the top of the hill of Montmartre*

TIPS

» Sacré-Cœur is a 10-minute walk from Abbesses or Anvers Métro stations. Or you could take the Montmartrobus to the base of the funicular.

» The funicular costs one Métro ticket each way—you'll probably consider it worthwhile when you see how many steps lead up to the basilica!

» Try to visit just before a service takes place (times are posted on the website). The basilica can seem rather sombre otherwise.

Above *A neo-Byzantine gem, Sacré-Cœur took 39 years to complete*

The basilica was originally designed by Paul Abadie, a pupil of Viollet-le-Duc, although six more architects were called in over the 39-year building project. Various problems hampered the building work, including unstable ground on a hill full of gypsum quarries, and the basilica was not ready until 1914. Then World War I intervened, and Parisians had to wait until 1919 for the consecration. The stained-glass windows were destroyed by bombs in 1944. Despite its setbacks—and the constant stream of visitors—the basilica has not lost its focus as a place of worship. More than 130 years after the vow to build Sacré-Cœur, priests still work in relays to maintain constant prayer for forgiveness for the horrors of war.

WHAT TO SEE

PANORAMA

The views from Sacré-Cœur make the trip out here worthwhile even if you don't want to visit the basilica itself. Try to choose a clear day, when you'll see farther across the city and when the contrast between the glistening white domes of the basilica and the blue sky behind is at its most dramatic. If you are short of time, the view from the front terrace should keep your camera satisfied. Among the landmarks you can see are Notre-Dame, the gold dome of Les Invalides, and Tour Montparnasse. For striking views of the Eiffel Tower, head round the corner into rue Azaïs. If you have the time (and energy), it is worth climbing the dome. The entrance, shared with the crypt, is on the western side of the basilica, in rue du Cardinal Guibert. A steep spiral staircase of 234 steps leads to the colonnade, where you'll have a vertigo-inducing view down into the basilica, as well as out across Paris. The bronze statue you see just in front of the colonnade shows St. Michael killing a demon. Behind the dome stands the main bell tower, which houses one of the world's largest bells, and the largest in France, the 19-tonne La Savoyarde.

The basilica itself is best viewed below, in place St-Pierre, from where the turrets and towers seem to bridge the metaphorical gap between earth and heaven. To find some more unusual views of the building, wander around the back of the basilica and into Parc de la Turlure (see walk, ▷ 237).

MOSAIC

Inside the basilica, the vast golden mosaic that hovers over the choir is a striking focal point. It is one of the largest of its kind, covering 475sq m (5,112sq ft), and was created by Luc-Olivier Merson between 1900 and 1922. Christ stands in the middle, with outstretched arms and a golden heart. Immediately surrounding him, the Virgin Mary, Joan of Arc, St. Michael, the Pope and a figure representing France look up in reverence.

Farther to the left, the characters in the lower row represent the earthly church, while above you can see members of the heavenly church, including St. Peter and St. Paul. To the right, the lower row portrays the builders of Sacré-Cœur, while above them are French saints, including St. Louis and St. Geneviève. God the Father and the Holy Spirit are represented on the ceiling, and the Latin inscription below the mosaic reads 'To the most holy Heart of Jesus, France, fervent, penitent and grateful'.

SCULPTURES

Joan of Arc and St. Louis guard the entrance to the basilica, on horseback in sculpted bronze. A stone statue of Christ stands high above them, in an arched recess. Gospel stories are portrayed on the bronze doors. Inside, look for the statue of *Our Lady of Peace*, in the Virgin Chapel, by Georges Serraz. Other sculptures include a silver statue of Christ, *Le Sacré-Cœur*, by Eugène Benet, and a silver *Virgin and Child* by Paul Brunet. Further statues can be seen in the crypt, including archbishop Cardinal Guibert, who approved the building of the basilica in 1872, and a *Pietà* by Jules Coutan.

Opposite *Shimmering gold, a beautiful mosaic of Christ hangs over the choir*
Below *A gargoyle on the south side of Sacré-Cœur*

MONTMARTRE

There is so much more to Montmartre than the towering Sacré-Cœur basilica, impressive though this is. This walk shows you the lesser-known side of Paris's hilltop village, with its picturesque cottages, cobbled streets and panoramic views.

THE WALK

Distance: 3km (2 miles)
Time: 2 hours
Start at: place Blanche
End at: place des Abbesses

HOW TO GET THERE

Take the Métro to Blanche, or buses 30, 54, 67, 68 or 74.

★ Starting from place Blanche, walk west along boulevard de Clichy, past the Moulin Rouge on your right.

❶ When the Moulin Rouge (▷ 225) first opened its doors in 1889, its vivacious cancan dancers were an immediate hit. The venue still stages shows, now aimed at visitors.

Turn right into avenue Rachel and carry on to the entrance of the Cimetière de Montmartre.

❷ In the Cimetière de Montmartre (▷ 225) you can seek out the tombs of the writer Stendhal, composer Hector Berlioz and saxophone inventor Adolphe Sax.

Leave the cemetery at avenue Rachel and walk up the steps on the right to rue Caulaincourt (a flyover). Turn right onto this road and walk to the junction with rue Joseph de Maistre. Turn right and after a few minutes, turn sharp left up rue Lepic. Van Gogh lived at number 54 of this winding road from 1886 to 1888. Follow the curve until you come to the junction with rue Tholozé. Look up to the left, past the green arch, to the Moulin de la Galette. Farther along the road, on the corner with rue Girardon, is the Moulin Radet.

❸ The Moulin de la Galette (literally the 'biscuit windmill') became a dance hall in the 19th century and was the inspiration behind Pierre-Auguste Renoir's painting *Le Bal du Moulin de la Galette* (1876). The Moulin Radet now forms part of a restaurant, confusingly called the Moulin de la Galette.

Turn left into rue Girardon, cross avenue Junot and enter the square Suzanne-Buisson, on the left.

❹ The square is named after a World War II resistance heroine. The statue is of the third-century bishop St. Denis, who was beheaded by the Romans. Legend has it that he picked up his head and washed off the blood in a fountain on this spot.

Facing the statue, turn right and leave the square into place Casadesus, in rue Simon Dereure. Turn right into the allée des Brouillards. Renoir lived in one of the houses on the left in the 1890s. The 18th-century mansion on the right was once a dance hall and a shelter for homeless artists.

Continue to place Dalida, named after the singer and actress who died in 1987, then walk up the cobbled rue de l'Abreuvoir. Formerly a country lane, the road takes its name from the watering trough *(l'abreuvoir)* that once stood at number 15. Number 14 attracted many of Montmartre's artists when it was the Café de l'Abreuvoir, while number 12 was home to Camille Pissarro from 1888 to 1892. If you're feeling hungry, stop for lunch at La Maison Rose.

Turn left after La Maison Rose and walk down the steep cobbled rue des Saules to the legendary cabaret spot, Au Lapin Agile (▷ 238). Turn right (east) along rue St-Vincent, past Montmartre's vineyard on your right. Cross rue du Mont Cenis, once home to Hector Berlioz (number 22), and walk uphill to rue de la Bonne. This leads into the hidden-away Parc de la Turlure.

❺ This tranquil park, well off the tourist trail, gives you magnificent views over Paris, as well as an unusual perspective on Sacré-Cœur.

Wander up through the park, then exit onto rue du Chevalier de la Barre. Continue along rue du Cardinal Guibert to the entrance to Sacré-Cœur, on place du Parvis du Sacré-Cœur.

❻ The neo-Byzantine basilica of Sacré-Cœur (▷ 232–235) was commissioned as atonement after the Franco-Prussian war (1870–1871). Building work took nearly 40 years.

Leave Sacré-Cœur and turn right along rue Azaïs, with its stunning views over the city. Turn right up rue St-Eleuthère to St-Pierre-de-Montmartre.

❼ Humbler than its grand companion, this peaceful church

was originally part of the 12th-century Benedictine abbey of Montmartre.

Enter the touristy place du Tertre (▷ 227) and leave by the gift-shop strewn rue Norvins. Turn second left, through place Jean-Baptiste Clément. Turn right into rue Ravignan, and continue round to the left into the tree-shaded place Émile-Goudeau.

❽ On the right of this square, look for the Bateau Lavoir, where Pablo Picasso, Juan Gris and Georges Braque had studios and where Cubism was born. The original ramshackle wooden building burned down in 1970, but has since been rebuilt.

To leave the square, walk down a small flight of steps and continue down rue Ravignan until you reach rue des Abbesses. Turn left here to place des Abbesses.

❾ Before stopping for a drink at place des Abbesses (▷ 228), take a look at the art nouveau Métro entrance and the unusual facade

of the church of St-Jean-l'Evangeliste-de-Montmartre (1904), nicknamed St-Jean-des-Briques for its profusion of red bricks.

WHEN TO GO
It is best to follow this walk during the day, as parts of Montmartre can be seedy at night.

WHERE TO EAT
Try La Maison Rose or one of the cafés around place des Abbesses.

TIP
» For another stunning view of Sacré-Cœur, head from place des Abbesses down rue Yvonne Le Tac to the base of the funicular.

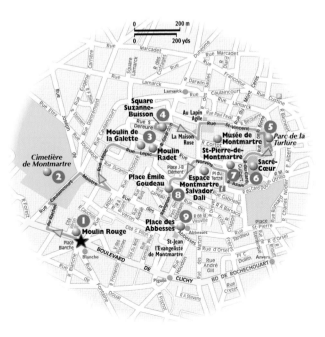

SHOPPING

LA BOUTIQUE DES ANGES
www.boutiquedesanges.fr
You'll find angels of all shapes and sizes, and made out of many materials at this specialist shop, buy one for the wall at home or one for your purse to carry with you.
✚ 245 M3 ✉ 2 rue Yvonne le Tac, 75018 ☎ 01 42 57 74 38 ◷ Mon–Sat 10.30–7.15, Sun 11–7 🚇 Abbesses, Anvers

GALERIE W
www.galeriew.com
For serious collectors of contemporary art make your way through the street artists and portrait sketchers to Galerie W. Eric Landau, which represents and displays work by more than 20 artists and also hosts temporary exhibitions throughout the year.
✚ 244 L2 ✉ 44 rue Lepic, 75018 ☎ 01 42 54 80 24 ◷ Daily 10.30–8 🚇 Abbesses, Pigalle

JUDITH LACROIX
www.judithlacroix.com
This young designer made her name with her successful children's range—using a fabric that resembled a page from a child's homework book. After her work was distributed at leading outlets such as Barneys in New York, she opened her own boutique in 2002 and extended her range to include womenswear.
✚ 244 L4 ✉ 3 rue Henri Monnier, 75009 ☎ 01 48 78 22 37 ◷ Mon–Sat 10–7 🚇 St-Georges

MARCHÉ BARBÈS
Especially colourful on Saturday, this market is where Africans in *boubous*, Arabs in burnouses and night-owls rub shoulders looking for ethnic wares, fruit and vegetables.
✚ 245 P3 ✉ boulevard de la Chapelle, 75018 ◷ Sat 7–3, Wed 7–2.30 🚇 Barbès-Rochechouart

ENTERTAINMENT AND NIGHTLIFE

AU LAPIN AGILE
www.au-lapin-agile.com
This Montmartre cabaret has been a meeting place for artists for nearly 150 years. On the walls, many souvenirs tell of its glorious past. French singers and poets perform here Tuesday to Sunday in a cordial but intimate atmosphere. Credit cards are not accepted.
✚ 245 M2 ✉ 22 rue des Saules, 75018 ☎ 01 46 06 85 87 ◷ Show:

Above *Moulin Rouge, a world-famous venue*

Tue–Sun 9pm–2am ✋ Show and drink: €24 🚇 Lamarck-Caulaincourt

LA BOULE NOIRE/LA CIGALE
www.laboule-noire.fr
www.lacigale.fr
Plenty of famous names have played at La Boule Noire, a diminutive venue in the heart of Pigalle, including Franz Ferdinand, Jamie Cullum, Metallica and The Dandy Warhols. It is linked to the grand former theatre La Cigale, which has now been modernized with a striking black and red theme, and hosts musicals, rock and pop, and music festivals.
✚ 245 M3 ✉ 120 boulevard Rochechouart, 75018 ☎ 01 49 25 81 75 🚇 Pigalle, Anvers

CARROUSEL DE PARIS
www.carrouseldeparis.fr
A show that combines cabaret, music hall and a little risqué cancan dancing, the Carrousel has been part of the Paris scene since 1926.
✚ 244 L3 ✉ 40 rue Pierre Fontaine, 75009 ☎ 01 40 16 49 51 ◷ Dinner daily 8.30 ✋ Show and dinner: €50–€75 🚇 Blanche

CINÉMA DES CINÉASTES

www.larp.fr

In a former cabaret venue designed by Gustave Eiffel, this three-screen complex shows avant-garde films, usually in their original language. Bar-restaurant on site.

➕ 244 K3 ✉ 7 avenue de Clichy, 75017 ☎ 01 53 42 40 00 🕐 Daily 1.30–10.30 🎟 Adult €9, child €7 🚇 Place de Clichy

LE DIVAN DU MONDE

www.divandumonde.com

This small concert hall runs theme nights, with an emphasis on world music. It welcomes new talent and lively Saturday evenings feature names like Groovy People Party.

➕ 245 M3 ✉ 75 rue des Martyrs, 75018 ☎ 01 40 05 06 99 🎟 €5–€15 🚇 Pigalle, Abbesses

ÉLYSÉE MONTMARTRE

www.elyseemontmartre.com

Over a century old, this establishment has retained its original interior and is now host to some of the best pop-rock concerts. It is also famous for its ball and techno nights.

➕ 245 M3 ✉ 72 boulevard Rochechouart, 75018 ☎ 01 44 92 45 47 🎟 €10–€20 🚇 Anvers

LE FOLIES PIGALLE

www.lefoliespigalle.com

A nightclub emblematic of Paris's red-light district, this is a favourite haunt of the gay community. A young crowd moves to the sound of house in a highly charged atmosphere. On Sundays the rhythms are more varied and there's a gay tea dance.

➕ 244 L3 ✉ 11 place Pigalle, 75009 ☎ 01 48 78 55 25 🕐 Mon–Thu midnight–6am, Fri–Sat noon–6am, Sun 6pm–6am 🎟 €20 (includes one drink), Sun €7 🚇 Pigalle

FOURMI

Named 'La Fourmi' (the Ant) in reference to La Fontaine's fable, this convivial venue—popular with the arty crowd—has a beautiful retro style with a large bar, small wooden tables and ochre walls.

The concert hall La Cigale (▷ 238) is nearby.

➕ 245 M3 ✉ 74 rue des Martyrs, 75018 ☎ 01 42 64 70 35 🕐 Mon–Thu 8am–2am, Fri–Sat 8am–4am, Sun 10am–2am 🚇 Pigalle

LE FREQUENCE CAFÉ

www.frequencecafe.com

An eclectic mix of bright pink walls, massive mirrors and red plastic chairs makes the interior unforgettable. Have a meal before joining the DJ.

➕ 244 L4 ✉ 56 rue Notre Dame de Lorette, 75009 ☎ 01 42 82 95 06 🕐 Tue–Sat 9pm–dawn 🎟 Menus from €26, entry to nightclub included 🚇 St-Georges

LA MACHINE

www.lamachinedumoulinrouge.com

Club and concert venue featuring a range of live acts. There's also a cocktail bar and an open-air terrace on site.

➕ 244 L3 ✉ 90 boulevard de Clichy, 75018 ☎ 01 53 41 88 89 🕐 Wed–Sat 9pm–4am 🎟 €15–€25 🚇 Blanche

MOULIN ROUGE

www.moulin-rouge.fr

The 'Red Windmill' opened in 1889 and is a Parisian institution (▷ 225). Fine food is served while you watch the titillating *Féerie* show.

➕ 244 L3 ✉ 82 boulevard de Clichy, 75018 ☎ 01 53 09 82 82 🕐 Shows: daily 9pm, 11pm 🎟 Show: €90; show and champagne €102, show and dinner: €150–€180 🚇 Blanche

NO STRESS CAFÉ

In the peaceful Nouvelle-Athènes district, south of Pigalle, this café extends a relaxed yet lively welcome; tables spill onto the tiny square when the sun comes out.

➕ 244 L4 ✉ 2 place Gustave-Toudouze, 75009 ☎ 01 48 78 00 27 🕐 Daily 11.30am–1.30am; Dec–Mar closed Mon 🚇 St-Georges

THÉÂTRE FONTAINE

www.theatrefontaine.com

This 650-seat former dance hall stages contemporary plays and enduring classics.

➕ 244 L3 ✉ 10 rue Fontaine, 75009 ☎ 01 48 74 74 40 🕐 Performances: Wed–Fri 8.30pm, Sat 6pm, 9pm 🎟 €12–€37 🚇 Blanche, St-Georges, Pigalle

THÉÂTRE DE LA VILLE–SALLE DES ABBESSES

www.theatredelaville-paris.com

This auditorium offers contemporary plays and dance performances.

➕ 244 L3 ✉ 31 rue des Abbesses, 75018 ☎ 01 42 74 22 77 🕐 Performances: daily 8.30pm 🎟 €28–€34 🚇 Abbesses

SPORTS AND ACTIVITIES

CERCLE CLICHY–MONTMARTRE

www.cerclecm.com

Occupying a former brasserie built in 1880, this billiard hall has a lot of character. Play American and French billiards, snooker and pool.

➕ 244 L3 ✉ 84 rue de Clichy, 75009 ☎ 01 48 78 32 85 🕐 Daily 1pm–6am 🎟 Around €10 per hour. Proof of identity is required 🚇 Place de Clichy

SQUASH MONTMARTRE

www.squashmontmartre.fr

Facilities at this friendly squash club include four courts, a gym, sauna, solarium, clubhouse and restaurant.

➕ 244 L2 ✉ 14 rue Achille Martinet, 75018 ☎ 01 42 55 38 30 🕐 Mon–Fri 10am–11pm, Sat–Sun 10–8 🎟 €16 per session 🚇 Lamarck-Caulaincourt

HEALTH AND BEAUTY

L'INSTITUT DES ABBESSES

www.linstitutdesabbesses.com

A well-established spa and beauty parlour offering a range of facials and body treatments, plus face and body epilation.

➕ 245 M3 ✉ 4 rue Houdon, 75018 ☎ 01 46 06 01 23 🕐 Mon–Fri 10–9, Sat 10–7 🎟 Facial 1 hour from €50 🚇 Abbesses, Pigalle

FOR CHILDREN

PROMOTRAIN

www.promotrain.fr

Give the steps a miss and, for the price of a Métro ticket, take the funicular from the bottom to the top of Sacré-Cœur.

➕ 245 N1 ✉ 131 rue de Clignancourt, 75018 ☎ 01 42 62 24 00 🚇 Simplon

EATING

PRICES AND SYMBOLS

The prices given are the average for a two-course lunch (L) and a three-course dinner (D) for one person, without drinks. The wine price is for the least expensive bottle.

For a key to the symbols, ▷ 2.

BISTRO POULBOT

www.bistropoulbot.com

A *fin de siècle* setting for this celebrated eatery that's been given a 21st-century lease of life by Veronique Melloul. Having travelled the world, she has returned to her homeland, traditional bistro cooking (lunchtime) but with touches of creativity (evening menu).

✚ 245 M2 ✉ 39 rue Lamarck, 75018, Montmartre ☎ 01 46 06 86 00 ⏱ Mon–Sat 12–3, 7–10.30 🖐 L €25, D €45, Wine €18 Ⓜ Lamarck-Caulaincourt

CHAMARRÉ MONTMARTRE

www.chamarre-montmartre.com

Previously well known as A. Beauvilliers, this long-standing restaurant has had a name change and facelift courtesy of chef Antoine Heerah. The decor is now smart and contemporary and Antoine combines elements of his native Mauritian dishes with classic

French cuisine, to great aplomb.

✚ 245 M2 ✉ 52 rue Lamarck, 75018, Montmartre ☎ 01 42 55 05 42 ⏱ Tue–Fri 12–2.30, 7–10 🖐 L €45, D €60, Wine €21 Ⓜ Lamarck-Caulaincourt

AU PIED DU SACRÉ-CŒUR

www.aupieddusacrecoeur.com

As the name suggests, this restaurant is at the foot of Sacré-Cœur. Warm tones and wooden furniture define the stylish, inviting interior. In fair weather you can eat out on the terrace. The cuisine ranges from traditional dishes such as pan-fried foie gras or grilled steak in pepper sauce to more exotic creations such as tagine of lamb with spices. The finest French ingredients are always used.

✚ 244 L2 ✉ 85 rue Lamarck, 75018, Montmartre ☎ 01 46 06 15 26 ⏱ Daily 12–2.30, 6–10.30 🖐 L €25, D €40, Wine €18 Ⓜ Lamarck-Caulaincourt

AU VIRAGE LEPIC

Book ahead for this welcoming bistro, in Montmartre's windmill-crowned rue Lepic. You'll find meat-based main courses, tasty puddings and a good wine list. In summer you can sit outside.

✚ 244 L2 ✉ 61 rue Lepic, 75018,

Above *Enjoy fine wines in Montmartre*

Montmartre ☎ 01 42 52 46 79 ⏱ Wed–Mon 7–11.30 🖐 D €30, Wine €19 Ⓜ Blanche, Abbesses

AUX CADET DE GASCOGNE

www.cadet-de-gascogne.com

This is a traditional but somewhat touristy restaurant in the artistic heart of Montmartre where artists congregate. It's a pleasant refuge for lunch when the throng of the square gets too much to bear. Try their avocado with shrimps or their Auvergnate salad (walnuts, ham and blue cheese).

✚ 245 M3 ✉ 4 place du Tertre, 75018, Montmartre ☎ 01 46 06 71 73 ⏱ Daily 12–2.30, 7.30–10.30 🖐 L €26, D €35, Wine €20 Ⓜ Abbesses

LA BONNE FRANQUETTE

www.labonnefranquette.com

Over 400 years old (originally named after a billiard-style game Aux Billards en Bois), this eaterie specializes in traditional French fare. You feel almost compelled to start with French onion soup or Burgundy snails and then to have the beef stew à la Bourguignonne. The interior harks back to the 19th century when it was a meeting place for the artists of Montmartre. ✠ 245 M2 ✉ 18 rue Saint-Rustique, 75018, Montmartre ☎ 01 42 52 02 42 ◷ Daily 12–2.30, 7.30–10.30 🍴 L €30, D €43, Wine €19 🚇 Abbesses

LA CRÉMAILLÈRE 1900
www.cremaillere1900.com
At the top of the steep steps on place du Tertre, this restaurant doubles as a cabaret and serves a good selection of traditional and international dishes. The interior is in the style of La Belle Époque and, although it's popular with tourists, it also attracts locals. Its garden is a pleasure in summer, but it can also be covered and heated during inclement weather.
✠ 245 M3 ✉ 15 place du Tertre, 75018, Montmartre ☎ 01 46 06 58 59 ◷ Daily 9–12.30 🍴 L €23, D €33, Wine €19 🚇 Abbesses

GEORGETTE
Easy on the eye, easy on the pocket, this little bistro to the far south of Montmartre has the feel of the Sixties with formica tabletops. It has a menu to satisfy most palates, from the simple (Auvergne ham with poached egg) to the classic *croustillant de veau pommes sautées,* finishing off with rice pudding for the sweet-toothed.
✠ 244 L4 ✉ 29 rue St-Georges, 75009, Montmartre ☎ 01 42 80 39 13 ◷ Tue–Fri 11.30–10.30 🍴 L €28, D €40, Wine €20 🚇 Notre-Dame-de-Lorette

LE MOULIN DE LA GALETTE
www.lemoulindelagalette.fr
Incorporating one of the surviving windmills on the hill of Montmartre, Le Moulin de la Galette was the subject of many paintings by great artists including Van Gogh and Toulouse-Lautrec. These days, at the restaurant that has taken its name, they still take an artistic pride in its heritage and, equally, a pride in their cuisine. It's worth being prepared to pay a little more than the fixed-price menus to experiment with some of their more exotic dishes.
✠ 244 L2 ✉ 83 rue Lepic, 75018,

Montmartre ☎ 01 46 06 84 77 ◷ Daily 12–11 🍴 L €35, D €50, Wine €21 🚇 Notre-Dame-de-Lorette

L'ORIENTAL
www.loriental-restaurant.com
Although this restaurant is close to touristy Montmartre, you could be in another world. Lanterns, mosaics, curtains, mirrors and a fountain imported from Marrakesh create a Moroccan palace feel. The cuisine is North African, with *pastillas* (dishes based on filo pastry), *tagines* such as king's lamb with figs, almonds and dates, the essential couscous and a mint tea to conclude.
✠ 245 M3 ✉ 47 avenue Trudaine, 75009, Montmartre ☎ 01 42 64 39 80 ◷ Daily 12–2.30, 7.30–10 🍴 L €30, D €40, Wine €26 🚇 Pigalle

PÉTRELLE
www.petrelle.fr
Slightly off the beaten track, but Madonna managed to find her way here when she was in Paris some years ago. Indeed, this is a haunt of the film and fashion celebrities who feel at home in its designer clutter. Tournados Rossini is the speciality. Perhaps too showy for some, but the handwritten menus are a nice touch.
✠ 245 M3 ✉ 34 rue Pétrelle, 75009, Montmartre ☎ 01 42 82 11 02 ◷ Tue–Sat 8–10 🍴 D €80, Wine €30 🚇 Anvers

LA POUTRE
www.restaurantlapoutre.fr
Visitors to this charming restaurant are invited to sample a fondue served in the traditional way. It's delicious and the surroundings are charming. Diners who have been horrified by high prices in tourist areas will find respite here.
✠ 245 M3 ✉ 10 rue des Trois Feres, 75009, Montmartre ☎ 01 42 57 45 04 ◷ Mon–Fri 12–2.30, 7.30–10.30, Sat 7.30–10.30, Sun 12–2.30 🍴 L €23, D €33, Wine €19 🚇 Anvers

LE RESTAURANT
www.lerestaurant.fr
Le Restaurant has been serving clients since 1989 and today its

success is down to a combination of old-style French bistro attitude (good food and good prices) with contemporary decor. There's a choice of seven or eight fixed-price starters and main courses that are typical of the bistro style.
✠ 244 L3 ✉ 32 rue Véron, 75018 ☎ 01 42 23 06 22 ◷ Daily 12–2.30, 7–11.30 🍴 L €27, D €35, Wine €18 🚇 Blanche, Abbesses

ROSE BAKERY
This English-style eatery has based its success on the quality of its organic products and on its healthy, delicious recipes. These include fresh soups, salads and pastries, to be eaten in the dining area or taken away. There is a weekend brunch menu and a grocery store (City Organic) in the nearby rue Milton.
✠ 245 M4 ✉ 46 rue des Martyrs, 75009, Montmartre ☎ 01 42 82 12 80 ◷ Tue–Fri 9–7, Sat–Sun 10–5. Lunch served from noon 🍴 L €12.50, Wine €3.50 per glass, Tea €4–€6 🚇 Notre-Dame-de-Lorette

LA TABLE D'EUGENE
Chef Geoffroy Maillard worked as part of the team at the Hotel Bristol before striking out on his own. The result is a splendid bistro contemporary in design and with dishes of finesse without a heavy price tag. Dorade tartare is a current signature dish.
✠ 245 M2 ✉ 18 rue Eugène Sue, 75018 ☎ 01 42 55 61 64 ◷ Tue–Sat 12–3, 7–10 🍴 L €25, D €35, Wine €22 🚇 Marcadet-Poissonniers

WEPLER
www.wepler.fr
Opened in 1892, this period eatery has seen a host of famous clients including Picasso and Henry Miller. It's renowned for its seafood, though it serves a full traditional brasserie menu. Come for the gargantuan seafood platter (€98) but note that the dining room gets crowded as the evening progresses.
✠ 244 K3 ✉ 14 place de Clichy, 75018 ☎ 01 45 22 53 24 ◷ Daily 8.30am–12.30pm 🍴 L €35, D €50, Wine €18 🚇 Place de Clichy

PRICES AND SYMBOLS

Prices are the lowest and highest for a double room for one night. Breakfast is included unless noted otherwise. All the hotels listed accept credit cards unless otherwise stated. Note that rates vary widely throughout the year.

For a key to the symbols, ▷ 2.

AUBERGE DE JEUNESSE CITÉ DES SCIENCES

www.hihostels.com

Dormitories at this youth hostel have four or six beds and there are electronic lockers, internet terminals, a terrace, TV room, laundry, bicycle rental and a kitchen.
 Off map 245 P3 ✉ 24 rue des Sept Arpents, 93310, Le Pré St-Gervais, La Villette ☎ 01 48 43 24 11 ✋ €25 per person ❶ 185 beds Ⓜ Hoche

AUBERGE DE JEUNESSE CLICHY

www.hihostels.com

On the northwestern outskirts, this youth hostel has rooms for two to six people, as well as a TV room, laundry, lockers, internet terminals and a restaurant (open in summer).
✚ Off map 244 J1 ✉ 107 rue Martre, 92110, Clichy ☎ 01 41 27 26 90 ✋ €24 per person ❶ 338 beds Ⓜ Mairie de Clichy

CHAT NOIR DESIGN HÔTEL

www.lesrelaisdeparis.fr

Housed in what used to be a Parisian cabaret club, this hotel is full of design touches based on the red and black design of the 'Chat Noir'—a stylized depiction of Theophile Steinlen's famed 1896 poster Le Chat Noir can be seen throughout the hotel. Rooms are bright and well equipped (WiFi, DVD, etc), featuring modern furnishings and good bathrooms.
✚ 244 L3 ✉ 68 boulevard de Clichy, 75018 ☎ 01 42 64 15 26 ✋ €139–€215, excluding breakfast ❶ 40 🅢 Ⓜ Blanche

HÔTEL AMOUR

www.hotelamourparis.fr

Cute and uncluttered by gadgetry, the Hotel Amour is located in the up-and-coming area known these days as SoPi (for South Pigalle). The hotel is owned by a group of local artists and some of its rooms have been decorated by their friends. The place has a decidedly 1970s, youthful feel about it. The furnishings are quaintly chaotic. It also has a great restaurant, popular with locals and tourists, which spills out into the leafy courtyard in nice weather.
✚ 245 M4 ✉ 8 rue Navarin, 75019, Pigalle ☎ 01 48 74 14 09 ✋ €140–€165, excluding breakfast ❶ 20 Ⓜ St-Georges

HÔTEL DAMRÉMONT

www.damremont-paris-hotel.com

On the northern outer edge of Montmartre, the 2-star Hotel Damrémont is still within walking distance of all the attractions of the area and just 15 minutes away by Métro from place Madeleine, Opéra, Galeries Lafayette, the Stade de France and the Champs-Élysées. The amenities are pretty standard, but it is a comfortable, quiet place.
✚ 244 L2 ✉ 100 rue Damrémont, 75018, Montmartre ☎ 01 42 64 25 75 ✋ €75–€140, excluding breakfast ❶ 35 Ⓜ Jules Joffrin

HÔTEL ELDORADO

www.eldoradohotel.fr

On the edge of Montmartre but still quite close to the big attractions, the Eldorado is rated among the best budget hotels in the city. Try to get a garden pavilion room. The Bistrot des Dames is the place to eat. The hotel is not great on amenities, though there is WiFi, but think of the money you're saving.

Above *Montmartre has a wide range of accommodation choices*

🚇 244 K3 ✉ 18 rue des Dames, 75017, Montmartre ☎ 01 45 22 35 21
✋ €58–€85, excluding breakfast 🛏 33
🚇 Place de Clichy

HÔTEL ERMITAGE

www.ermitagesacrecoeur.fr

The 2-star Ermitage has the atmosphere of a village inn. The out-of-the-way two-storey building dates back to 1870 when it was a mansion, in Napoléon III architectural style. There are exposed beams in some rooms, adding to the auberge effect. Others have chandeliers, and all have flowery decorations. Outside, there's a well-kept country-style garden. Free WiFi is available. Credit cards are not accepted.

🚇 245 M2 ✉ 24 rue Lamarck, 75018, Montmartre ☎ 01 42 64 79 22 ✋ €99–€105 🛏 12 🚇 Lamarck-Caulaincourt

HÔTEL KUBE

www.kubehotel.com

Just up the road from La Chapelle Métro, nestling in the backstreets and just five minutes from the Eurostar terminal at Gare du Nord, there's a hotel which can best be described as a technophobe's nightmare. For all that, the city's first ice-bar is a remarkable, private place. The reception is inside a great glass cube on the outside which means no one gets a peep inside unless they're guests. The rooms are ultra-chic and decked out with techno-gadgetry (it goes without saying that WiFi internet contact is on tap), and the hotel lacks nothing in facilities: there's even work-out equipment.

🚇 245 P2 ✉ 1 passage Ruelle, 75018, Gare du Nord ☎ 01 42 05 20 00 ✋ €318–€424, excluding breakfast 🛏 41
🚇 La Chapelle

HÔTEL PARTICULIER

www.hotel-particulier-montmartre.com

If you're looking for a luxury option in this part of the city, this sumptuous bijou suite hotel is a good option. The property is opulent with lavish treatments courtesy of designer Morgane Rousseau. Each suite is individually furnished and there's a salon to relax in and a verdant garden. The house is used for many artist soirées and is filled with objets d'art.

🚇 244 L2 ✉ 23 avenue Junot, 75018, Pavillon D, Montmartre ☎ 01 53 41 81 40 ✋ €290–€590, excluding breakfast 🛏 5
🚇 Blanche, Lamarck-Caulaincourt

IBIS HÔTEL SACRÉ-COEUR

www.ibishotel.com

Nestling in the busy Montmartre streets at the foot of the Butte de Montmartre, just a few hundred metres from Sacré-Cœur Basilica, this branch of the Ibis chain may be short on grandeur, but it's big on location and economy. The staff here take care of their guests tirelessly and enthusiastically. All the rooms, which do sacrifice style to functionality, are cosy and have WiFi internet access. Apart from breakfast which is available from 4am, the dining facilities are limited to the bar where snacks are available. But, being in Montmartre there are plenty of atmospheric restaurants nearby. Public undercover pay parking is available for guests.

🚇 245 M3 ✉ 100 boulevard Rochechouart, 75018, Montmartre ☎ 01 46 06 99 17 ✋ €69–€115, excluding breakfast 🛏 68 🚇 Anvers, Pigalle

MERCURE MONTMARTRE

www.accorhotels.com

This modern 3-star hotel is unable to provide the olde-worlde charm of many of the hotels around here, but makes up for the lack of atmosphere by its location and amenities. The hotel bar, L'Atelier, is open from 5pm to 1am. The rooms have a view of Sacré-Cœur Basilica to the north or of the Eiffel Tower to the south, and fittings and facilities include a minibar, safe, radio, satellite TV, telephone with voicemail, WiFi internet access and a security peephole.

🚇 244 L3 ✉ 3 rue Caulaincourt, 75018, Montmartre ☎ 0825 80 79 79 ✋ €129–€245, excluding breakfast 🛏 305
🚇 Place de Clichy

PREMIUM HOTEL MONTMARTRE

www.hotelpremiummontmartre.com

Originally a dormitory for Moulin Rouge dancers when Toulouse-Lautrec was painting them, this 3-star hotel lies between Sacré-Cœur and Moulin Rouge. Today it has WiFi access, telephone, safe, desk and television. The sixth floor rooms have the best views.

🚇 244 L2 ✉ 5 rue Tholozé, 75018, Montmartre ☎ 01 46 06 30 52 ✋ €90–€160, excluding breakfast 🛏 50
🚇 Blanche

ROMA SACRÉ-COEUR

www.hotelroma.fr

This is a 2-star gem with four rooms on the seventh (top) floor, themed on works by Georges Braque who lived in the Roma in 1913. Set in the heart of the Butte Montmartre, it is rated one of the best hotels in its class. It doesn't have a restaurant, but has an arrangement with nearby Chez Ginette. All the attractions of Montmartre are within walking distance and the nearest Métro is literally on its doorstep.

🚇 245 M2 ✉ 101 rue Caulaincourt, 75018, Montmartre ☎ 01 42 62 02 02 ✋ €90–€200, excluding breakfast 🛏 57
🚇 Lamarck-Caulaincourt

VILLA ROYALE

www.villa-royale.com

This is the place to call up the spirit of La Belle Époque. Even the plasma TV, the jacuzzis and the modern fireplaces are camouflaged by ingenious techniques to erase any sense of anachronism or intrusion on the illusion. The rooms each have a minibar and WiFi on demand, and are named after various figures from French history and they are decked out in rich crimsons of the neo-baroque, with velvet drapes and mirrors framed in a gold cornice. And the view outside is just as impressive, with all the main sightseeing attractions just a few steps away.

🚇 244 L3 ✉ 2 rue Deperré, 75009, Pigalle ☎ 01 55 31 78 78 ✋ €199–€309, excluding breakfast 🛏 34 🚇 Pigalle

Auberge de Jeunesse Clichy

Hôtel Damrémont

Au Pied du Sacré-Cœur

Hôtel Particulier

Au Virage Lepic

Le Moulin de la Galette

Premium Hôtel Montmartre

Mercure Montmartre

Le Restaurant

Hôtel Eldorado

Wepler

Chat Noir Design Hôtel

Villa Royale

No Stress Café

Musée Gustave Moreau

Georgette

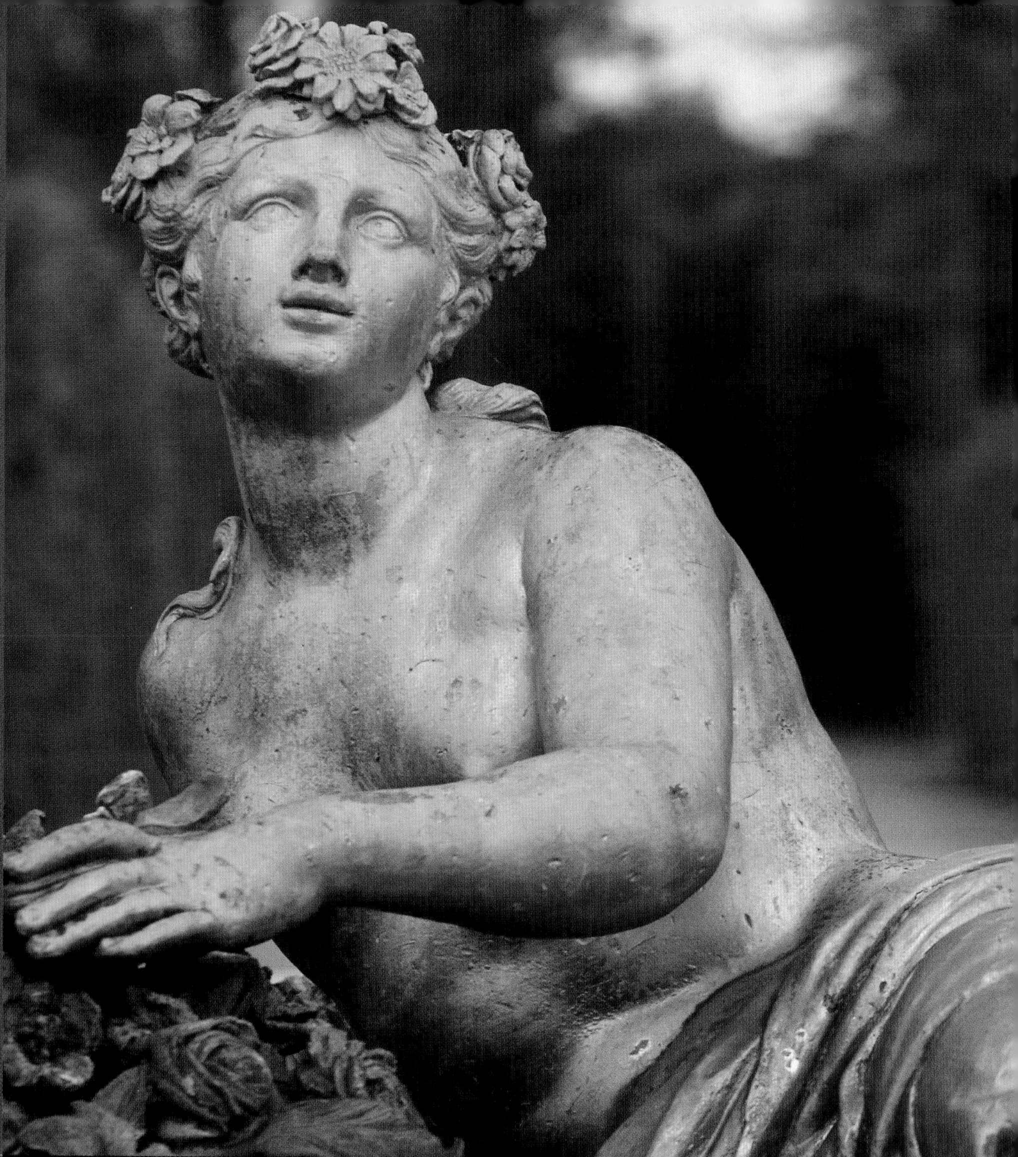

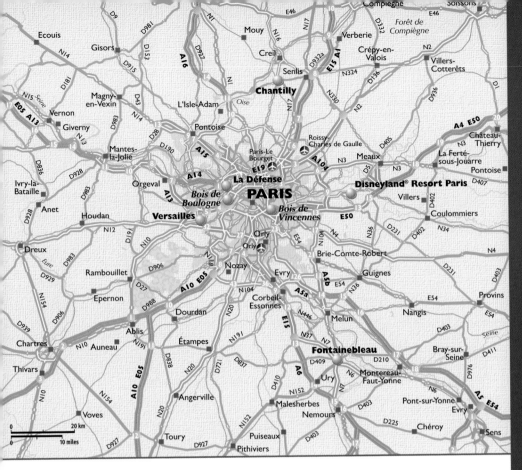

EXCURSIONS

Paris may be a glittering gem, but visitors shouldn't let its dazzle blind them to some of the treasures just beyond the city limits. Among many enriching outings around the city, the Bois de Boulogne just to the west forms part of the forest that surrounded ancient Paris. Once a hunting ground, it is now the Parisians' favourite green retreat—a haven of lakes, flower gardens and waterfalls spread over more than 800ha (2,000 acres). And for lovers of today's chase, the two horse-racing courses, Longchamp and Auteuil, attract millions of racegoers every year. Beyond the city boundary to the east, the Bois de Vincennes is Paris's largest park, with three lakes, a floral park and historic castle, and criss-crossed with car-free roads. Like the Bois de Boulogne, it was part of the royal hunting forest and is now the perfect recreation ground for a refreshing escape; it's easily accessible by a short Métro or bus ride. If it's charming fairytale castles that you seek, then take a 25-mile trip north to the Château de Chantilly, surrounded by gorgeous parkland and home to a superb art collection. At La Défense, Paris's out-of-town high-rise business park, the big attraction is the monumental 110m (360ft) high Grande Arche, large enough to contain Notre-Dame.

To escape a little farther afield, less than an hour's train ride from Paris puts you down at the Château de Fontainebleau, the opulent repository of French and Parisian history. The handsome building has 1,900 rooms and its vast grounds include more than 16,000ha (40,000 acres) of forest where royals strolled, hunted and learned the art of chivalry. In historical importance Fontainebleau rivals but cannot eclipse Versailles which is a mere 30-minute train ride from Paris. Versailles represents the ultimate in French royal palaces: It is a glistening wonderland of gardens, fountains, lavish state apartments and spectacular mirrors suffused in light.

Finally, if there are children in your party, there's one out-of-town excursion you can't escape—Disneyland® Resort Paris set in five different 'lands' with their themed rides, restaurants and shops. It's great fun.

EXCURSIONS PARIS

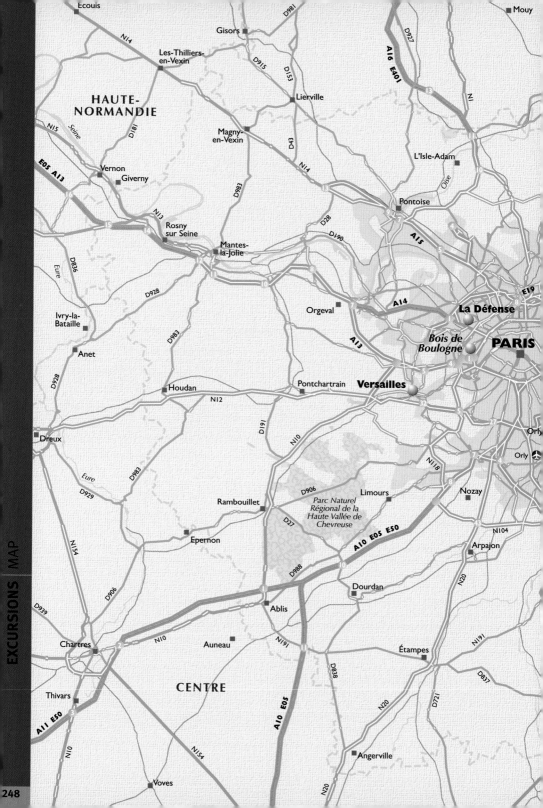

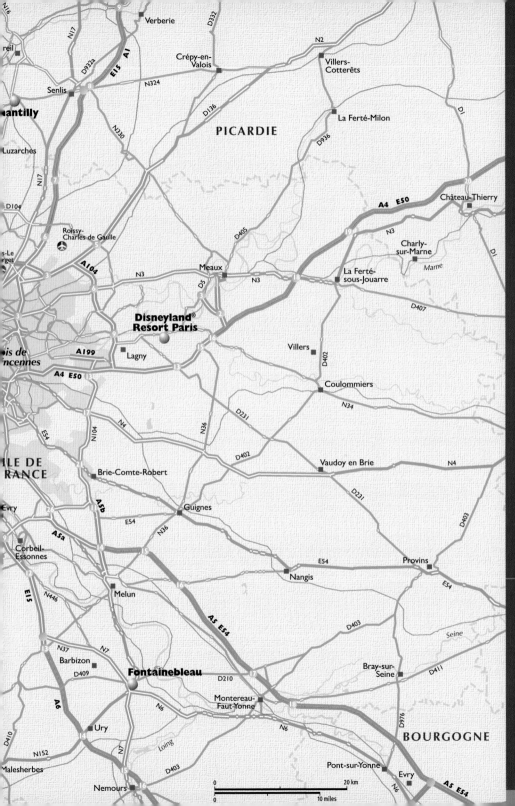

HOW TO GET THERE

The Bois de Boulogne is 4km (2.5 miles) west of central Paris 🚇 Porte Maillot, Porte Dauphine, Porte d'Auteuil

PLACES TO VISIT
PARC DE BAGATELLE

✉ route de Sèvres à Neuilly, 75016 ☎ 01 53 64 53 80 🕐 Daily, hours vary according to time of year. Jul–Aug 9.30–8 ✋ Free, except during temporary exhibitions: Adult €5, child (7–25) €2.50, under 7 free 🚇 Pont de Neuilly, then bus 43 or 93; Porte Maillot, then bus 244

JARDIN D'ACCLIMATATION

www.jardindacclimatation.fr
✉ boulevard des Sablons ☎ 01 40 67 90 85 🕐 Apr–Sep daily 10–7; Oct–Mar 10–6 ✋ Adult and child (3–18) €3, under 3 free 🚇 Les Sablons

JARDIN SHAKESPEARE

✉ Pré-Catelan ☎ 01 40 19 95 33 🕐 Daily, hours vary ✋ Free 🚇 Porte Maillot, then bus 244

JARDIN DES SERRES D'AUTEUIL

✉ 3 avenue de la Porte d'Auteuil ☎ 01 71 28 50 82 🕐 Daily 9–4.45 ✋ Free 🚇 Porte d'Auteuil

BOIS DE BOULOGNE

The Bois de Boulogne is Paris's western lung. Among its 845ha (2,090 acres) of green space you will find extensive landscaped parkland with lakes, flower gardens and waterfalls, as well as the Roland-Garros tennis stadium and the famous Longchamp racecourse.

Like the Bois de Vincennes on the eastern side of the city (▷ 251), the Bois de Boulogne was used for hunting in medieval times and for the construction of ships for the navy during the reign of Louis XIV, before becoming an aristocratic leisure ground in the 18th century. Napoléon III and his town planner Baron Haussmann were responsible for the park's current layout.

GREEN SPACE

The Bois de Boulogne lies just outside the *périphérique* and draws joggers, bicyclists and people who want to escape the city for an hour or two. There are cafés and restaurants, two lakes linked by waterfalls, follies, winding paths, an open-air theatre, two racecourses and more than 140,000 trees.

A highlight is the Parc de Bagatelle, on the northwestern edge. Its small chateau, built in 1775, looks out over a romantic park laid out by landscape gardener Thomas Blaike. There are more than 700 types of roses.

The Jardin d'Acclimatation, farther north, is good for children, with playgrounds, minigolf, puppet shows, toy train and Explor@dome.

Moving south, the Jardin Shakespeare has an open-air theatre staging productions in French and English, as well as a garden laid out with flowers, herbs and trees mentioned in Shakespeare's plays and sonnets. In the Jardin des Serres d'Auteuil, in the south, 19th-century greenhouses shelter tropical plants. A short walk away is Roland-Garros, home of the French Tennis Open.

There are 35km (22 miles) of bicycle routes in the Bois de Boulogne. Bicycles may be hired opposite the main entrance of the Jardin d'Acclimatation (mid-Oct to mid-Apr daily; mid-Apr to mid-Oct Wed, Sat–Sun and public hols).

After dusk the Bois de Boulogne becomes a very adult playground indeed and certainly justifies its notoriously risqué reputation.

BOIS DE VINCENNES

The Bois de Vincennes forms the perfect antidote to city life. Only a Métro ride from central Paris, it has three lakes, a historic castle, a beautiful floral park and one of France's largest zoos. There is a hippodrome staging trotting races and a velodrome for bicycling events, football and rugby matches.

The Bois de Vincennes was a rich royal hunting ground in the 12th century, sectioned off by one of Philippe-Auguste's walls. By Louis XV's reign it had become a popular promenading area and in the 19th century Baron Haussmann landscaped it for the working-class population of eastern Paris. The woods suffered serious damage in the storms of 1999. The *donjon* (dungeon) of the Château has just reopened after 12 years' restoration. Originally completed by Charles V in 1365, it held many famous prisoners, including the infamous Marquis de Sade.

CHÂTEAU DE VINCENNES

The Château de Vincennes has led a far from quiet life, despite its peaceful surroundings. Louis XIV spent his honeymoon within these walls, Winston Churchill attended a war conference in the underground chambers and the German forces executed their prisoners in the courtyards during the Occupation of Paris.

Today, you can wander around the grounds and try to piece together the range of architectural styles, from the 14th-century medieval keep to the 17th-century classical Pavillon du Roi and Pavillon de la Reine and the 19th-century Pavillon des Armes. The keep has been restored, and you can take a guided tour around Charles V's study and the chapel, based on Paris's Sainte-Chapelle. Inside you can see Paris's second-oldest bell, the 700kg (1,540lb) Vincennes bell, commissioned for the keep by Charles V in 1369. Whole sections of the chapel's windows were destroyed during the storms of 1999, although the stunning Rose Window survived.

PARC ZOOLOGIQUE DE PARIS

The city zoo began its life in 1793 from the remains of the royal estate. During the early 19th century it was the largest collection in Europe. Many of the animal enclosures date from the late 19th- to the mid 20th-century, which does not sit with the 21st-century remit of the organization, so the zoo has closed its doors and a major refurbishment is currently underway.

PARC FLORAL

The flower garden is a lovely place to wander after a visit to the nearby Château de Vincennes. The flower displays are exceptional and attractions for children include minigolf, quad-biking and the Théâtre pour Enfants (certain days only). The park has a striking dahlia garden, an iris garden, medicinal plants, a Valley of Flowers, and forests of rhododendrons and azaleas. It also houses France's national collection of camellias and geraniums. A jazz festival gets the park jiving from early June to the end of July and classical music concerts are held in August and September.

INFORMATION
www.boisdevincennes.com

HOW TO GET THERE
The Bois de Vincennes is 6km (4 miles) east of central Paris
🚇 Château de Vincennes for the chateau and the Parc Floral
🚌 46 and 56 to Chateau de Vincennes, routes 86 and PC2 to Porte de Vincennes, 46 for the Parc Floral

PLACES TO VISIT
CHÂTEAU DE VINCENNES
www.monuments-nationaux.fr
✉ Avenue de Paris, 94300 Vincennes
☎ 01 48 08 31 20 🕐 Apr–Sep daily 10–6.15; Oct–Mar Keep: 10–5.15 with access to chapel at 10.15, 11.15, 2.30, 3.30 and 4.30. Last ticket sold 45 min before closing ✋ Grounds: free. Château: €8 (under 18 free)

PARC ZOOLOGIQUE DE PARIS
www.mnhn.fr
✉ 53 avenue de St-Maurice, 75012
☎ 01 44 75 20 14 🕐 Closed for renovation until 2014

PARC FLORAL
www.parcfloraldeparis.com
✉ route du Champ de Manœuvre, 75012
☎ 01 49 57 24 84 🕐 Apr–Sep 9.30–8; Oct–Mar 9.30–5 ✋ Adult €5, child €2.50
🍴 Two cafés, open daily in summer, Wed, Sat–Sun in winter

TIP
» If your French is not very strong, think twice before embarking on the Château de Vincennes tour.

Opposite *Strolling in the Bois de Boulogne*
Above *Boating in the Bois de Vincennes*

INFORMATION

www.chantilly-tourisme.com

HOW TO GET THERE

Chantilly is 40km (25 miles) north of Paris
🚆 Gare du Nord to Chantilly-Gouvieux
(30 min). It takes around 30 min to walk
from the train station to the chateau.
RER: line D from Châtelet les Halles (takes
around 45 minutes from central Paris).
There are occasional buses or you can get
a taxi from outside the station (around €8)
🚗 Take the autoroute du Nord (A1)
and leave on the Survilliers-St-Witz exit.
Alternatively take the N16 or N17

INTRODUCTION

The town of Chantilly is one of the leading training venues in Europe for
racehorses and is home to a world-famous racecourse and the Musée Vivant
du Cheval horse museum. Chantilly has two culinary claims to fame—the
delicious whipped and sweetened cream known as *crème chantilly* and
the 17th-century master chef Vatel. He met a tragic end in 1671, when he
committed suicide because he didn't have enough fish to feed Louis XIV
and his courtiers.

The fairytale Renaissance Château de Chantilly, surrounded by a moat,
sits in beautiful parkland and is home to an outstanding art collection. The
chateau is one of the most picturesque castles in the region. It is surrounded
by attractive parkland, with the forest of Chantilly beyond, and contains a
magnificent art collection.

WHAT TO SEE

CHÂTEAU DE CHANTILLY

Chantilly was founded by a Roman named Cantilius but it was the famous
head of the French army, High Constable Anne de Montmorency, who played
a key role in developing the site in the 16th century. He decided to transform
the medieval castle into a Renaissance chateau, and added the Petit Château,
which still survives today. The chateau passed into the hands of the powerful
Condé family in the mid-17th century and the prince, known as the Grand

Above *Picturesque Château de Chantilly*

Condé, called in Versailles landscape architect André Le Nôtre to create the Grand Canal, lakes, waterfalls, ornamental ponds and a maze. The chateau became a popular venue for festivals and other gatherings, and literati included Jean de La Fontaine and Molière.

During the Revolution much of the Grand Château was pillaged and destroyed and the building was used as a prison. In around 1830 Henri d'Orléans, Duke of Aumale, inherited the property, then commissioned Honoré Daumet to carry out a major restoration in 1875. In 1886 the duke gave Chantilly to the Institut de France, stipulating that his art collections should be preserved and the chateau must open to the public. The Musée Condé opened in April 1898, less than a year after his death.

MUSÉE CONDÉ

The art and furnishings on display here date from the Renaissance to the 19th century. The picture galleries have works by French, Italian, Dutch, English, Flemish and Spanish painters, in addition to 18th-century Chantilly porcelain and 19th-century Chantilly lace. Look out for works by Raphael, Jean Fouquet, Fra Angelico, Eugène Delacroix and Camille Corot. In a skylit room called The Tribune there are masterpieces by Antoine Watteau, Eugène Delacroix and Jean-Auguste Dominique Ingres. The Psyche Gallery has 42 stunning 16th-century grisaille stained-glass windows and The Sanctuary exhibits Raphael's *Trois Grâces* (1500–1505) and 40 miniatures by Jean Fouquet (1445). The library has a vast collection of rare and important books—don't miss a reproduction of the illuminated medieval manuscript *Très Riches Heures du Duc de Berry* (15th century). The chapel has beautiful stained-glass windows, and the word *L'Espérance* (Hope) decorates the ceiling.

Tours of the Large Apartments take in the Prince's Bedchamber, the Music Room and the Great Condé Victory Gallery. The sumptuously furnished Small Apartments of the Duke and Duchess of Aumale (guided tours only) were decorated in the 19th century with wood panels, marquetry furniture, brocade drapes and portraits. The Small Monkey Gallery, painted in the 18th century, is covered in decorative panels with monkey motifs.

THE PARK

The grounds cover around 115ha (284 acres) and are ideal for strolling. Attractions include the Grand Canal, the waterfall, the 18th-century Anglo-Chinese garden, Le Nôtre's 17th-century French gardens, the Maison de Sylvie and the romantic English Garden with its Island of Love, Swan Lake, Temple of Venus and Beauvais waterfall. There is also the Enghien Castle, a children's play area, a kangaroo enclosure and Le Hameau (the Hamlet), all built in 1774 for the Prince of Condé.

In the spring and summer you can sail along the moats and canals in an electric boat, take a nostalgic trip in a horse-drawn carriage or go for a ride on a little train.

MUSÉE VIVANT DU CHEVAL

The stables (Grandes Écuries), with their striking facade, were built for Louis-Henri, Duke of Bourbon, in the 18th century. According to legend, he believed he would be reincarnated as a horse after his death. The stables, 186m (610ft) long, were intended to accommodate 240 horses and more than 400 hounds for stag and boar hunts.

Today the stables are devoted to the Living Horse Museum. Created in 1982 by Yves Bienaimé, this internationally renowned museum is considered the biggest and most beautiful of its kind. You can see horses of different breeds, equestrian exhibits, works of art and riding demonstrations. The rooms of this museum are closed for renovation until 2014, but the stable, dome and gallery are open (Wed–Mon 2–5).

TIPS

» There are information cards in several languages in each room of the Musée Condé.

» Holders of a Paris Museum Pass (▷ 279) receive free entry to the Musée Condé.

WHERE TO EAT

Château de Chantilly: The tea room and restaurant, La Capitainerie, is open throughout the year (closed Tue and evenings; tel 03 44 57 15 89).

Le Hameau: Les Goûters Champêtres restaurant serves regional dishes (mid-Mar to mid-Nov; tel 03 44 57 46 21).

Park: La Courtille, in the English Garden, offers snacks, drinks and ice creams (Mar to mid-Nov; tel 03 44 57 46 21).

PLACES TO VISIT
CHÂTEAU DE CHANTILLY—MUSÉE CONDÉ

www.chateaudechantilly.com

✉ BP 70243, 60631, Chantilly ☎ 03 44 27 31 80 🕐 Early Apr–early Nov Wed–Mon 10–6 (park 10–8); early Nov–early Apr Wed–Mon 10.30–5 (park 10.30–5) ✋ Museum and park: adult €11, under 18 free. Park: adult €5, under 18 free 🎧 Guided tours need to be booked in advance; audioguides €2 🗣 Several to choose from; prices vary 🎁 Gift shop ❓ The Small Apartments by guided tour only. Buy tickets from the gift shop

MUSÉE VIVANT DU CHEVAL

www.museevivantducheval.fr

✉ Grandes Écuries, BP 60242, 60631, Chantilly ☎ 03 44 57 40 40; tourist office 03 44 67 37 37 🕐 The new equestrian spectacle 'The Princes of Chantilly' is a 1-hour show of dressage and equine feats run during the afternoon. Tickets are available from 1pm at the ticket office or can be booked online 🖐 Adult €20, child (4–17) €15.50. Pass Domaine Chantilly (admission to both attractions, including spectacle and park) adult €28.50, child (4–17) €15.50

INFORMATION
www.ladefense.fr

HOW TO GET THERE
La Défense is 6km (4 miles) west of the centre of Paris

🚇 Grande Arche de La Défense
🚆 RER line A, La Défense
🚌 No. 73 from central Paris

TIPS
» The best view of the Arc de Triomphe is not from the roof of the Grande Arche but from the top of the 54 marble steps leading up to the elevators.
» To experience the bustle of business-focused La Défense, visit on a weekday.

PLACES TO VISIT
GRANDE ARCHE
www.grandearche.com
✉ 1 parvis de la Défense, 92044
☎ 01 49 07 27 27 ❓ The exterior is a must-see sight, but the interior of the building is not open to the public

Opposite and above The Grande Arche is the focal point of La Défense

LA DÉFENSE

You couldn't find a starker contrast with Paris's historic core than this high-rise business district on the city's western edge. In addition to office blocks, you'll find Les Quatre Temps shopping complex and the CNIT building (Centre of New Industries and Technologies), looking like an upturned shell, and Paris's most striking modern monument.

The main draw for visitors to La Défense is the imposing Grande Arche, which rises 110m (360ft) above the enormous pedestrian-only square called Le Parvis. Stand on the white marble steps of this giant and the people wandering across the vast square seem utterly dwarfed by skyscrapers.

Today, La Défense has a population of 20,000 and in addition to being an important business hub continues to push the boundaries of urban architecture. In 2013, L'eco-quartier Hoche, a new housing district of more than 600 homes will open, featuring the latest building materials and energy-saving technologies.

GRANDE ARCHE

The Grande Arche was the culmination of many unsuccessful attempts to find a nucleus for La Défense in the 1970s. The design, by Danish architect Johan Otto von Spreckelsen, was finally chosen in 1983 and the venture became one of President Mitterrand's *Grand Projets* (▷ 43).

The Grande Arche sits at the northwesternmost end of the Grand Axis—an *axe historique* or historical axis—a straight route that runs through Paris from the Louvre (▷ 198–203) and place de la Concorde (▷ 206), up the Champs-Élysées (▷ 187–189), under the Arc de Triomphe (▷ 187–189) and along the avenue de la Grande Armée, finding a suitably fitting end at the arch.

From architect Sully, minister to Henri IV in the 16th century, it was seen as desirable to construct urban landscapes according to strict principles. This route was founded in order for the Kings of France to leave their palace and depart the city quickly to reach their royal hunting grounds to the north. Today it allows modern visitors a chance to glimpse some of the city's finest monuments dating from the 14th century to the 20th century—a view that encapsulates what is so fascinating about this vibrant capital.

Standing below the Grande Arche is an unnerving experience, as you look up at 300,000 tonnes of concrete, marble-cladding and glass rising above the ground. The Grande Arche is best admired from below, looking up into the vast chasm that is greater than the height of Notre-Dame and the width of the Champs-Élysées. The futuristic monument-cum-office block was designed as a symbolic western gateway to Paris and focal point of the new business district. Work finished in 1989, in time for the bicentenary of the Revolution.

INFORMATION

www.disneylandparis.com

✉ BP 100, Marne-la-Vallée, 77777 CEDEX 4 ☎ 01 60 30 60 30 or local number (from France) 08 25 30 02 22

🕐 Disneyland® Park: Hours variable throughout the year, but generally Mon–Fri 10–7, Sat–Sun 10–10 Walt Disney Studios® Park: Hours variable throughout the year, but generally daily 10–7 💰 1-day/1-park ticket: adult €57, child (3–11) €41, under 3 free. 1-day/2-parks Hopper ticket: adult €69, child €51. 2-day/2-parks Hopper ticket: adult €122, child €109. Prices vary according to season. Parking: €15 per day; free if you are staying at a Disneyland Resort Paris hotel 🏬 Shops and boutiques sell a huge range of items 🔲 Height and age restrictions apply to some of the rides. Hours, prices and information on Disney products are subject to change or cancellation without prior notice.

Above *Sleeping Beauty Castle*
Opposite *Adventure Isle in Adventureland*

INTRODUCTION

Experience the magic of Disneyland—a must for kids of all ages. Disneyland Resort Paris is easily accessible from Paris and makes a terrific day trip.

Disneyland Resort Paris attracts millions of visitors to its two theme Parks—Disneyland® Park and Walt Disney Studios® Park. Other attractions include the Disney Village, Disney themed hotels and a 27-hole golf course.

The resort, in the Marne-la-Vallée countryside east of Paris, opened in 1992 to a blaze of publicity. It was Disney's fourth Park, following in the footsteps of California, Florida and Tokyo. The Walt Disney Studios Park opened in 2002.

WHAT TO SEE

DISNEYLAND® PARK

You can visit five different 'lands' at the 56ha (140-acre) Disneyland® Park, each with its own themed rides, restaurants and shops. Main Street, USA takes you back in time with its nostalgic scenes from an American town at the turn of the 19th century. Seasonal parades bring scenes from Disney's animated films to life, with dancers and, of course, the famous Disney characters (see the website for dates and times). Fantasyland, especially popular with younger children, includes Sleeping Beauty Castle and the 'It's a Small World' ride. Adventureland boasts the swashbuckling Pirates of the Caribbean, Adventure Isle and the high-speed Indiana Jones and the Temple of Peril ride. Frontierland, with its canyons, gold mines and rivers, offers two thrill-seeker attractions—the Big Thunder Mountain runaway train and the ghostly Phantom Manor. Discoveryland was inspired by Jules Verne's visions of the future, and the Mystery of the Nautilus ride is based on the film *20,000 Leagues Under the Sea*. Reaching top speeds of 68kph (43mph), the Space Mountain: Mission 2 roller coaster is not for the faint-hearted. The spectacular

Star Tours flight simulator whisks visitors onto an interplanetary journey.

Other attractions include the high-tech blockbuster Buzz Lightyear Laser Blast® inspired by Disney. Pixar's *Toy Story 2*—expect long queues—in Discoveryland.

WALT DISNEY STUDIOS® PARK

The Walt Disney Studios® Park is divided into four zones, each aiming to create the atmosphere of a real film studio. Studio 1 gives an insight into what goes on behind the scenes in the world of cinema. In Toon Studio you can watch the Animagique 3D animated show and let yourself be whirled away on the Flying Carpets over Agrabah ride. Production Courtyard offers the thrilling Twilight Zone Tower of Terror™, while in Backlot you can experience the excitement of the Rock 'n' Roller Coaster Starring Aerosmith and the fantastic Moteurs…Action Stunt Show Spectacular® featuring Lightening McQueen and try the amazing rollercoaster ride Crush's Coaster, inspired by Disney. Pixar's *Finding Nemo*.

DISNEY® VILLAGE

The entertainment complex Disney Village sits between both Disney® Parks and the Disney® hotels. The Village is bustling with bars, shops, street artists and multi-screen cinemas. You could end the day with the popular dinner-spectacular Buffalo Bill's Wild West Show, or stop for a meal at one of the dozens of restaurants to choose from, serving French, Italian, English, Bavarian, Mexican and American cuisine. There are waiter-service and self-service restaurants as well as an array of snack bars.

HOW TO GET THERE

Disneyland Resort Paris is 32km (20 miles) east of Paris

🚃 RER line A runs from Châtelet-les-Halles and Gare de Lyon to Marne-la-Vallée/Chessy (around 40 min). The station is 100m (320ft) from the entrances to both Disneyland Park and Walt Disney Studios Park

🚗 Take the A4 motorway (Autoroute de l'Est), in the direction of Metz/Nancy. Leave at exit 14, to Parcs Disneyland

TIPS

» Look for the information areas (City Hall in Disneyland Park and Studio Services in Walt Disney Studios Park), which provide entertainment schedules, maps and general information.

» The free FASTPASS system is available on some of the more popular rides in Disneyland Park, reducing waiting time.

» Booking in advance is recommended for the popular sit-down restaurants (tel 01 60 30 40 50).

INTRODUCTION

The Château de Fontainebleau rivals Versailles (▷ 260–263) in grandeur and historic interest but has the bonus of attracting fewer crowds. It is steeped in regal and imperial resplendence, with 1,900 opulent rooms and exquisite landscaped gardens.

Fontainebleau has witnessed some momentous events in French history, including the birth of Louis XIII in 1601 and Napoléon signing his deed of abdication in 1814. The site was popular with royalty as far back as the 12th century, when kings went hunting in the 17,000ha (42,000 acres) of forest. The keep in the Oval Courtyard is the only remnant of a medieval castle dating from these times.

The pivotal period for Fontainebleau was the 16th century, when François I commissioned a sumptuous royal residence, enticed by the hunting opportunities. He employed the cream of Italy's artists and craftsmen to decorate the palace's interior and laid out the garden with lakes and canals.

A century later, the gardens were re-landscaped by André Le Nôtre, the man responsible for Versailles's stately parterres. Subsequent rulers put their stamp on the palace with numerous modifications, including Napoléon, who chose it as a suitably majestic base and had it completely refurnished in 1804.

WHAT TO SEE

RENAISSANCE ROOMS

François I wanted Fontainebleau to be packed with prestigious art and this is reflected in the lavish decoration of Les Salles Renaissance.

The highlight is the Salle de Bal, the ceremonial ballroom, which hosted many a glittering occasion. The dazzling 30m (98ft) hall is decorated with wood panels and frescoes illustrating mythological and hunting themes. Vast windows bathe the room in light and give lovely views over the Oval Courtyard on one side and the Grand Parterre on the other. An imposing fireplace by Philibert Delorme stands at the far end. Pre-recorded Renaissance music helps you imagine the festivities once enjoyed here. In the Galerie François I you can see frescoes painted by the Florentine artist Rosso, a disciple of Michelangelo. For years they lay hidden behind other paintings and were rediscovered only in the 20th century.

Above Magnificent Fontainebleau rivals Versailles in all but the number of visitors

Opposite The fabulous Galerie François I is the most extraordinary example of Renaissance decorative arts in France

SOVEREIGN'S STATE APARTMENTS

Les Grands Appartements des Souverains are even more opulent than the Renaissance Rooms. Hardly an inch of space on the walls or ceilings has escaped intricate decoration. Don't miss the huge tapestries in the Salon François I and in the next-door Tapestry Room, created at the Gobelins factory. The ornate bed in the Empress's Bedchamber was made for Marie-Antoinette, although she never actually slept in it.

Napoléon Bonaparte converted the former king's bedchamber into a Salle du Trône (throne room) in 1808. The preposterously extravagant room is a decorative mixture of Louis XIII, XIV and XV styles.

NAPOLÉON I'S IMPERIAL APARTMENT

These rooms offer a fascinating insight into some of the more personal aspects of Napoléon's life, although they are not his private apartments (Small Apartments)—they can be seen by guided tour only. His ceremonial bedchamber is suitably lavish, while the Petite Chambre à Coucher de l'Empereur is more humble, with a camp bed. This room doubled as Napoléon's study, as you can see from the large desk. The Salon Particulier de l'Empereur witnessed a key moment in France's history on 6 April 1814, when Napoléon signed his abdication papers at its round table.

THE GROUNDS

Fontainebleau's grounds are stunning and in good weather you should allow at least an hour to wander through them. For a self-guided walk (8km/5 miles), pick up the *circuit découverte* leaflet at the information desk.

A good place to start is the stately Cour du Cheval Blanc (Courtyard of the White Horse), at the entrance to the chateau. Napoléon bid farewell to his Imperial Guard at the 17th-century horseshoe staircase here in April 1814, before his exile on the island of Elba. The courtyard is also known as the Cour des Adieux in his memory.

To the right of the courtyard (as you face the chateau) is the Jardin Anglais (English Garden), dating from the early 19th century. To the left is the Jardin de Diane. From here, a pleasant stroll around the chateau leads to the elegant Grand Parterre, with its square central pond. Beyond is the 1.2km (0.75-mile) canal, created in 1606 by Henri IV. Be sure to continue round to the vast Carp Pond, separating the Jardin Anglais from the Grand Parterre and formerly used for water tournaments.

HOW TO GET THERE

Fontainebleau is 55km (34 miles) south of the centre of Paris

🚆 Gare de Lyon to Fontainebleau-Avon, trains run roughly every hour, on the Transilien line (around 45 min). From Fontainebleau-Avon station the A/B bus takes you to the chateau in around 15 min

🚌 Take the A6 motorway from the Porte d'Orléans and leave at the Fontainebleau exit

TIPS

» Gare de Lyon is a large station and finding the correct platform for Fontainebleau can be confusing. It helps to know that the lettered platforms are in the main concourse area, while the numbered platforms are at the end of platform A. For a timetable of trains to Fontainebleau-Avon, ask at the ticket desk that deals with RER and Métro trains.

» Combined rail and entrance tickets are available.

» Holders of a *Paris Museum Pass* (▷ 279) receive free entry to the castle.

» The Jardin Anglais closes one hour before the other gardens.

WHERE TO EAT

There is no café. Picnics are allowed in the park, but not in the gardens. There are cafés and restaurants in the town.

INFORMATION

www.chateauversailles.fr

✉ Versailles, 78000 ☎ 01 30 83 78 00
🕐 State Apartments: Apr–Oct Tue–Sun
9–6.30; Nov–Mar 9–5.30 (last admission
30 min before closing). Grand and Petit
Trianon: Apr–Oct daily 12–6.30; Nov–Mar
12–5.30. Gardens: daily 8am–dusk
(6pm or 8.30pm depending on month).
Park: summer daily 7am–dusk; winter
8am–dusk. On public hols phone ahead
to check opening times 🚶 See Getting
Your Bearings, ▷ 263 🍴 La Flottille
(tel 01 39 51 41 58) and La Petite Venise
(tel 01 39 53 25 69) 🍵 Café in the Cour
de la Chapelle. Two snack bars in the
grounds 🎧 Guided tours are available.
Book at 9am. Audioguides for the State
Apartments free. You need to leave a
passport, credit card or driving licence as
a deposit ♿ Entrance H is for visitors
with disabilities. There is an elevator to
the State Apartments

INTRODUCTION

Versailles is France's ultimate royal palace, an opulent monument to the super
ego of the Sun King, Louis XIV. More like a town than a chateau, it was the
seat of French power for more than 100 years and kept members of the royal
family safely cushioned from their subjects in Paris—until the invasion of the
Revolutionary mob. Now the invaders are visitors, who come to see the lavish
State Apartments and fountain-filled gardens.

Versailles had relatively humble beginnings, as a hunting lodge for
Louis XIII. In 1661, Louis XIV decided to move his court to the deserted
swamp, 20km (12.5 miles) southwest of Paris, an astute way of isolating the
nobility and his ministers while keeping an eye on his not-too-distant capital.
He brought in the greatest architects of the day, Louis Le Vau and Jules
Hardouin-Mansart, and building work continued up to his death in 1715. A
town soon sprang up to accommodate the court, and the smaller palaces of
the Grand Trianon and the Petit Trianon were later created as royal love nests.
The building project put a severe strain on France's finances but the palace
remained the seat of power until 1789, when a revolutionary mob seized
Louis XVI and forced him back to Paris.

WHAT TO SEE

KING'S STATE APARTMENT

The Appartement du Roi, part of the Grands Appartements, is a shrine to the
power and grandeur of Louis XIV. The ceilings are painted with scenes of
thunderous gods and the walls are richly clad with marble and gilded bronze.
Each room is dedicated to an Olympian deity symbolizing a royal virtue or

duty. The sun god Apollo, closely linked to the cult of the Sun King (Louis XIV), gives his name to the throne room. The ceiling painting by François Le Moyne in the Hercules Drawing Room on the first floor depicts 142 characters.

HALL OF MIRRORS

The Galerie des Glaces, also part of the Grands Appartements, bathes you in a sea of chandeliers, natural light and opulence. More than 350 mirrors catch the light pouring in through the huge arched windows, which in turn give spectacular views of the gardens and canal. The hall, 73m (240ft) long, was designed by Jules Hardouin-Mansart and completed in 1686. Since then it has served as a venue for royal wedding celebrations, a place for greeting foreign dignitaries and even a corridor. The Treaty of Versailles was ratified here in 1919. The omnipresent Louis XIV is depicted in the ceiling paintings by Charles Le Brun, showing episodes from the king's reign.

QUEEN'S APARTMENT

The Appartement de la Reine runs parallel to the King's State Apartment, with the Hall of Mirrors forming a lavish corridor between the two. In the Queen's Bedchamber the Queen suffered the ordeal of giving birth in public, to prove royal heirs were genuine. Marie-Antoinette was the last queen to occupy the

HOW TO GET THERE

Versailles is 20km (12 miles) southwest of the centre of Paris

🚆 RER line C takes 30 min to Versailles Rive-Gauche, followed by a 10-min walk to the palace. A mainline train from Gare Montparnasse takes 15 min to Versailles Chantiers, followed by a 20-min walk. The mainline train from Gare St-Lazare takes 25 min to Versailles Rive-Droite, followed by a 15-min walk

🚌 Take autoroute A13 to the Versailles–Château exit, then follow signs to the chateau

Opposite *The manicured gardens and Latona Fountain*
Below *Dazzling in its opulence is the Hall of Mirrors, scene of many lavish events*

TIPS

» The busiest days are Tuesday and Sunday, as well as holiday weekends. The palace is closed on Mondays.

» Be prepared for lots of waiting in line—for a ticket, for an audioguide and for the toilets.

Above *One of the most beautiful examples of 18th-century French architecture*

room and portraits of her family decorate the walls. The exuberant feather-canopied bed is a copy. A poignant portrait of the queen with three of her children hangs in the Antechamber of the Grand Couvert. The empty crib is a moving reference to her youngest daughter, Sophie, who died before the portrait was painted.

FOUNTAINS

Versailles's fountains are famous and it is a pity that on most days they remain still. To catch them in full flow, visit during one of the *Grandes Eaux Musicales* (Apr–Oct Sat–Sun and public hols; mid-May to mid-Jun Tue; Jun to mid-Jul Thu; times vary. Grand Evening Fountain Displays mid-Jun to Aug. Booking advised; for dates and reservations tel 01 30 83 78 89 or visit www.chateauversailles-spectacles.fr). It comes as no surprise that Louis XIV's most-loved deity, the sun god Apollo, plays a prominent role. The Apollo Fountain, guarding the entrance to the Grand Canal, shows the sun god rising out of the water on a chariot, symbolizing the rise of the Sun King's reign. Closer to the chateau, the Latona Fountain depicts Apollo's mother asking Jupiter to turn the Lycian peasants into frogs. Don't miss the Neptune Fountain, past the North Parterre.

THE GROUNDS

Versailles has the largest palace grounds in Europe (100ha/247 acres), which were tamed by André Le Nôtre into a geometry so perfect that even nature seemed to obey the Sun King's commands. Work began in 1661 and took 40 years to complete. Though many areas have been reworked over time, the Grove of the Three Fountains is one part of the garden that was featured in the original plans and the King is said to have stamped his own ideas on Le Nôtre's 1677 design of the terraced fountains here. The grove was restored and renovated to this original plan in 2005. Louis XIV sailed a flotilla of ships on the 1.6km (1-mile) Grand Canal—today, you can rent rowing boats.

GETTING YOUR BEARINGS

Many people expect to be immediately overawed by the grandeur of Versailles, but instead, your first impression could well be confusion. The palace has a bewildering number of entrances and ticket options, and when you finally start the tour you'll find very few of the rooms have information boards. It's a good idea to rent an audioguide before you start.

Once at the chateau a *'passeport'* gives access to all the areas of the chateau, the park, Châteaux de Trianon, including the restored Petit Trianon and Marie-Antoinette's Estate as well as an audioguide in one of ten languages (adult €15, child (under 18) free).

For a less hectic day limit yourself to the Château (adult €15, child (under 18) free, audioguide included) and its immediate gardens. With this ticket you can enjoy all the public areas of the vast building, including the Grands Appartements, the Hall of Mirrors and the Queen's Apartments, along with the Chambre de Roi and the Petits Appartements.

If you still have the energy, you can then enjoy the Domaine de Marie-Antoinette (adult €10, child (under 18) free) the parts of the grounds loved by the doomed queen, including the Grand Trianon and Petit Trianon. These are a 25-minute stroll away, or take the mini train (adult €7, child (11–18) €5.50, under 11 free). You can buy a Paris Museum Pass (▷ 279), which gives free access to the Grands Appartements, the Grand Trianon and Petit Trianon, however, some restrictions apply so read the small print to make sure the ticket fits your needs. Entrance to Versailles is free for under-18s and for citizens under 26 of EU member countries, and for everyone on the first Sunday of the month (October to end March). You can buy *'passeport'* tickets and RER travel tickets to the chateau online from the Paris tourist office website www.parisinfo.com.

Above *Le Hameau watermill in the grounds*

WHERE TO EAT

There are two restaurants, a café and two snack bars. On a summer Sunday it is best to book ahead for the restaurants. Alternatively, you can bring a picnic to eat in the park.

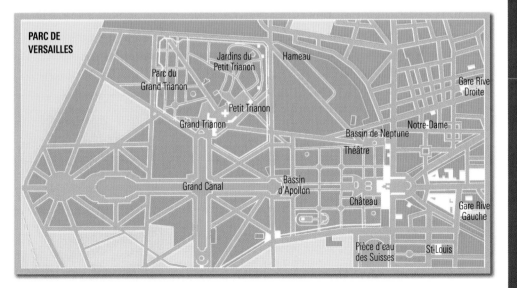

PARC DE
VERSAILLES

Parc du
Grand Trianon

Jardins du
Petit Trianon

Hameau

Gare Rive
Droite

Petit Trianon

Grand Trianon

Notre-Dame

Bassin de Neptune

Théâtre

Grand Canal

Bassin
d'Apollon

Château

Gare Rive
Gauche

Pièce d'eau
des Suisses

St-Louis

No visit to Paris is complete without a boat trip down the Seine (▷ 210–211). Bus tours can also be worthwhile if you want a quick and comfortable introduction to the city. Alternatively, to really get under the skin of a *quartier*, try a walking tour.

BICYCLE TOURS
▷ 61.

BOAT TRIPS
BATEAUX MOUCHES
www.bateaux-mouches.fr
Board at the Pont de l'Alma for a trip down the Seine in a glass-roofed boat. The tour lasts 70 minutes. Dinner cruises are available.
☎ 01 42 25 96 10 (reservations)
⏰ Sailings: Apr–Sep 10.15, 11, 11.30, 12.15, 1, 1.45. 2.30, 3, 3.30, 4, 4.30, 5, 5.30, 6, 6.30, 7, and every 20 min from 7–11; Oct–Mar 11, 12, 1, 1.45. 2.30, 3.15, 4, 5, 6, 7, 7.45, 8.30, 9 (50-person minimum in low season) ✋ Adult €11, child (4–11) €5.50

BATEAUX PARISIENS
www.bateauxparisiens.com
Take a one-hour cruise along the Seine in a glass-topped boat. Audioguides are available. Board near the Eiffel Tower.
☎ 0825 01 01 01 ⏰ Apr–Oct daily 10am–10.30pm every 30 min (except 1.30 and 7.30); Nov–Mar 10–10 every hour ✋ Adult €12, child (3–12) €5, under 3 free

BATOBUS
www.batobus.com
Hop on and off as you please between eight stops from the Champs-Élysées to the Tour Eiffel.
✉ Port de la Bourdonnais, 75007 ☎ 0825 05 01 01 ⏰ Jun–Aug daily 10–9.30, every 17 minutes; Apr–May, Sep–early Nov 10–7, every 25 minutes; early Nov–early Jan, early Feb–May 10–4.30, every 35 minutes. Closed early Jan–early Feb ✋ 1-day pass: adult €14, child (under 16) €9. 2-day pass: adult €18, child €12

CANAUXRAMA
www.canauxrama.com
Take a trip along the picturesque Canal St-Martin, the waterway that featured in the 2001 film *Le Fabuleux Destin d'Amélie Poulain*.

The trip, lasting two hours and thirty minutes, starts at Port de l'Arsenal, at Bastille, and takes you up to Parc de la Villette. Book ahead.
☎ 01 42 39 15 00 ⏰ Daily 9.45, 2.30 (in summer boats also leave from La Villette at 9.45, 2.45) ✋ Mon–Fri adult €16, child (4–12) €8.50, Sat–Sun €10 to all

VEDETTES DU PONT NEUF
www.vedettesdupontneuf.com
Cruises along the Seine, starting from Pont Neuf. The trip lasts one hour and takes you up to the Eiffel Tower, and round the Île de la Cité.
☎ 01 46 33 98 38 ⏰ ▷ 211 ✋ Adult €13, child (4–12) €6, under 4 free

BUS TOURS
LES CARS ROUGES
www.carsrouges.com
See the major sights from an open double-decker bus, hopping on and off when you like. Commentary is available in French and English. The circuit lasts 2 hours 15 minutes.
☎ 01 53 95 39 53 ⏰ Daily 9.30–8 every 10–20 min (last tour starts at 6) ✋ 2-day pass: adult €26, child (4–12) €13, under 4 free

CITYRAMA TOUR
www.pariscityrama.com
Cityrama offers a 90-minute city tour on a double-decker bus, with commentary in 13 languages. Other excursions include Paris by Night, Versailles and Giverny.
✉ 2 rue des Pyramides ☎ 01 44 55 61 00 ⏰ Tours: Apr–Sep daily 9, 10.30, 12 and 2.45; Oct–Mar 10, 11.45, 2.45 ✋ City tour: adult €18, child (4–11) €9

L'OPEN TOUR
www.pariscityrama.com
Hop-on, hop-off open-top double-decker buses run four circuits—the Paris Grand Tour, Montmartre Grands Boulevards, Montparnasse/

St-Germain and Bastille/Bercy. There is commentary in French and English.
☎ 01 42 66 56 56 ⏰ Apr–Oct daily every 10–15 min, first bus 9.20am, last round trip 6pm; Nov–Mar every 25–30 min, first bus 9.45, last round trip 4pm ✋ 1-day pass: adult €29, child (4–11) €15, under 4 free; 2-day pass: adult €32, child (4–11) €15, under 4 free

PARIS VISION
www.parisvision.com
Paris Vision offer tours by bus and minibus. These range from the two-hour Paris Express Tour around the city, with commentary, to trips to Versailles, Giverny and Chartres.
✉ 214 rue de Rivoli, 75001 ☎ 01 44 55 60 00 ⏰ Discovery Tour: daily 9, 12 and 3 ✋ Discovery tour: adult €18, child (4–11) €9

WALKING TOURS
PARIS WALKS
www.paris-walks.com
Take a two-hour walking tour, with English commentary. Themes range from Hemingway's Paris to the French Revolution.
☎ 01 48 09 21 40 ⏰ Call ahead for times and places, or visit the website ✋ Adult €12, child (under 15) €8

Below *Cruise on the Seine* by bateau mouche

PRACTICALITIES

Practicalities gives you all the important practical information you will need during your visit from money matters to emergency phone numbers.

PRACTICALITIES PARIS

PARIS

TEMPERATURE

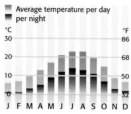

RAINFALL

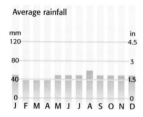

BEFORE YOU GO

CLIMATE

» Paris's climate is generally not subject to extremes. Winters are cool, but rarely bitterly cold, while summers are warm, but not rain-free. Although the city has a reasonably low rainfall overall, be prepared for showers.

» The cliché of 'Paris in the spring' does not usually apply until well into May, when the weather finally warms up.

» Summer (June to the end of August) can be glorious. The longest days are in June and July, when you're likely to enjoy the

most sunshine and comfortable temperatures. August can be hot, oppressive and stormy—Parisians who haven't fled the city tend to head down to the *quais* beside the Seine for a fresher breeze.

» If you are lucky, you'll have crisp, sunny days in autumn (September to November).

» Snow is rare in winter.

WHEN TO GO

» Spring is a pleasant time to visit Paris, when the chestnut trees are in blossom and the weather is warming up.

» If you choose hot and sunny July you'll be battling with many other visitors, but time it right and you'll experience the Bastille Day celebrations (14 July). August is quieter, as many Parisians flee to other parts of France to escape the oppressive heat or to 'Paris Plage' in July and August. Some restaurants close for the whole month and there are fewer cultural activities.

» The weather can be pleasant in autumn but hotel rooms are harder to find as the trade fair season is in full swing. If you don't mind the cooler winter weather, December can be a magical time, with the Christmas lights glowing.

» Most monuments and museums close on 1 January, 1 May, 1 November, 11 November and 25 December. There are fewer bus, train and Métro services on France's national holidays (▷ 279), so try to avoid arriving on those dates.

TIME ZONES

CITY	TIME DIFFERENCE	TIME AT 12 NOON IN FRANCE
Amsterdam	0	12 noon
Berlin	0	12 noon
Brussels	0	12 noon
Chicago	-7	5am
Dublin	-1	11am
Johannesburg	+1*	1pm
London	-1	11am
Madrid	0	12 noon
Montréal	-6	6am
New York	-6	6am
Perth, Australia	+7*	7pm
Rome	0	12 noon
San Francisco	-9	3am
Sydney	+9*	9pm
Tokyo	+8*	8pm

Clocks in France go forward one hour on the last Sunday in March, until the last Sunday in October.

* One hour less during French Summer Time.

WHAT TO TAKE

» The key things to remember are your passport, travel documents, money, credit cards and any medication you need. You'll also need your driving licence if you plan to rent a car while in France, and car registration and insurance documents if you are taking your own car (▷ 63).

» Take clothing for a range of weather, even in summer. Make sure you have walking shoes, an umbrella, a raincoat and sunglasses (in spring/summer). In summer you'll also need sunscreen.

WEATHER WEBSITES AND TELEPHONE NUMBERS

ORGANIZATION	TELEPHONE	NOTES	WEBSITE
Météo France	0892 68 02 75, €0.34 per minute (within France)	Forecasts for Paris and the rest of France	www.meteofrance.com
The Met Office (UK)	0870 900 0100, £0.60 per minute (within UK)	Five-day forecasts for Paris, as well as information about the UV index	www.metoffice.gov.uk
Paris Tourist Office		Provides a link to the Météo France website, as well as information on air quality in Paris	www.parisinfo.com
Weather Channel (US)		Links to Paris forecasts from the website of the US-based Weather Channel	www.weather.com

» A small backpack or shoulder bag is useful for sightseeing. But keep your money tucked away safely and keep an eye on your bag in crowded places (see Finding Help, ▷ 274).

» Take the addresses and phone numbers of emergency contacts, including the numbers to call if your credit cards are stolen.

» It is wise to take photocopies of tickets and insurance documents and keep them separately from the originals, in case of loss. Keep a note of your credit card numbers.

» There is a language guide in this book (▷ 294–299), but a separate phrase book might be helpful.

» A first-aid kit is a good precaution. Useful items include antiseptic cream, sticking plasters (Band-Aids), painkillers and diarrhoea medicine.

» If you wear glasses, take a spare pair, in case of any damage, or your prescription so you can buy a replacement pair.

PASSPORTS AND VISAS
» UK, US and Canadian visitors need a passport, but not a visa, for stays of up to three months with at least six months' validity remaining. Citizens of other countries should check with their nearest French embassy or visit the official EU portal http://europa.eu.

» For more information, look up the website of the French tourist office (www.franceguide.com) or French Embassy (www.ambafrance-uk.org or www.consulfrance-newyork.org).

» Carry a photocopy of the relevant pages of your passport, so you can leave the passport in your hotel safe. Keep a note of your passport number in case of loss or theft.

» Passport and visa rules can change at short notice so check before booking your visit.

LONGER STAYS
» UK and other EU citizens wishing to stay longer than three months should apply for a *Carte de Séjour* from the Préfecture de Police. US and Canadian visitors need a *Carte de Séjour* and visa.

» For more information call the French Consulate in your home country (see below).

TRAVEL INSURANCE
» Make sure you have full health and travel insurance.

» EU nationals receive reduced-cost health treatment with a European Health Insurance Card, but full insurance is still advised. For everyone else, full insurance is a necessity. Check your insurer has a 24-hour helpline.

CUSTOMS

FROM ANOTHER EU COUNTRY
Below are the guidelines for the quantity of goods you can bring to France from another EU country, for personal use:

» 800 cigarettes; or	» 110 litres of beer
» 400 cigarillos; or	» 10 litres of spirits
» 200 cigars; or	» 90 litres of wine (of which only 60 litres can be sparkling wine)
» 1kg of tobacco	» 20 litres of fortified wine (such as port or sherry)

FROM A COUNTRY OUTSIDE THE EU
You are entitled to the allowances shown below only if you travel with the goods and do not plan to sell them.

» 200 cigarettes; or	» 2 litres of wine
» 100 cigarillos; or	» 1 litre of spirits or strong liqueurs over 22% volume; or
» 50 cigars; or	» 2 litres of fortified wine, sparkling wine or other liqueurs
» 250g of tobacco	
» 50g of perfume	» Up to €175 of all other goods
» 250cc/ml of eau de toilette	

FRENCH EMBASSIES AND CONSULATES ABROAD

COUNTRY	ADDRESS	WEBSITE
Australia	31 Market Street, St. Martin's Tower, Level 26, Sydney, NSW 2000. Tel (02) 9268 2400	www.ambafrance-au.org
Canada	42 Sussex Drive, Ottawa, Ontario, K1M 2C9. Tel 613/789-1795	www.ambafrance-ca.org
Germany	Parizer Platz 5, 10117 Berlin. Tel 030 590 03 90 00	www.ambafrance-de.org
Ireland	36 Ailesbury Road, Ballsbridge, Dublin 4. Tel 01 277 5000	www.ambafrance-ie.org
Italy	Piazza Farnese 67, 00186 Rome. Tel 06 68 60 11	www.ambafrance-it.org
New Zealand	13th floor, 34–42 Manners Street, Wellington 6142. Tel 644 384 25 55	www.ambafrance-nz.org
South Africa	3rd floor, Standard Bank Building, 191 Jan Smuts Avenue, PO Box 1027, Parklands 2121 Johannesburg. Tel 011 778 56 00	www.consulfrance-jhb.org
Spain	Calle Marqués de la Ensenada 10, 28004 Madrid. Tel 91 700 78 00	www.consulfrance-madrid.org
UK	58 Knightsbridge, London, SW1X 7JT. Tel 020 7073 1000	www.ambafrance-uk.org
USA (Los Angeles)	10390 Santa Monica Boulevard, Suite 410 & 115, Los Angeles, CA 90025. Tel 310/235-3200	www.consulfrance-losangeles.org
USA (New York)	934 Fifth Avenue, New York, NY 10021. Tel 212/606-3600	www.consulfrance-newyork.org

MONEY MATTERS

France is one of 17 European countries that have adopted the euro as their official currency. Euro notes and coins were introduced in January 2002, replacing the franc.

BEFORE YOU GO

» It is advisable to use a mixture of cash, traveller's cheques, ATM/debit cards and credit cards, rather than relying on one means of payment during your trip.

» Check that your credit or debit card can be used to withdraw cash from ATMs in France. Also check what fee will be charged.

» Traveller's cheques are a safer way of bringing in money as you can claim a refund if they are stolen— but commission can be high when you cash them.

CREDIT CARDS

Most restaurants, shops and hotels in Paris will accept credit cards, but some have a minimum spending limit on transactions.

ATMS

The city has plenty of ATMs, with instructions often given in a choice of languages. Most accept MasterCard, Visa and Diners Club. You'll need a four-digit PIN.

BANKS

» Most banks in Paris are open Monday to Friday from 10 to 5, but usually close at noon the day before a public holiday.

» Only banks with change signs change traveller's cheques or foreign currency. You'll need to take your passport.

BUREAUX DE CHANGE

» Bureaux de change have longer opening hours than banks, but exchange rates are invariably worse than major banks.

» You'll find them across the city, including at train stations, airports and some department stores.

» Avoid changing large amounts of traveller's cheques at hotels, where the rates may not be competitive.

LOST/STOLEN CREDIT CARDS

• Before you set off, make a note of the number to ring if your credit card is stolen and keep it separately from the card itself.

WIRING MONEY

» In an emergency money can be wired from your home country, but this can be time-consuming and expensive, as agents charge a fee.

» Money can be wired from bank to bank, taking up to two working days. It can be faster to use Travelex (www.travelex.fr) or Western Union (www.westernunion.com).

» Post offices also wire money (see Post Offices, right).

24-HOUR EXCHANGE SERVICES

» The Champs-Élysées has a 24-hour bureau de change: Bureau de change, Chèquepoint, 150 avenue des Champs-Élysées, 75008. Tel 01 42 56 48 63.

» Roissy-Charles de Gaulle and Orly airports have exchange services, open between 7am and 11.30pm.

REDUCED-PRICE TICKETS

» Students and teachers should contact the International Student Travel Confederation (www.isic.org) in their own country for information about the benefits available.

» Senior citizens may get reductions on transportation and admission to museums by showing a passport.

» For more information about reductions on the entry price for museums and other attractions, see Tickets, ▷ 279.

TAXES

» Non-EU residents can claim a VAT refund (détaxe) of 12 per cent on certain purchases, although you must have spent more than €175 in one shop, at one time.

» Ask the store for the relevant forms, which should be completed and stamped by the trader.

» Present the forms to Customs when you leave France, along with the receipts, and they will be stamped.

» Remember that you may have to show the goods at Customs, so keep them within easy reach.

» Post the forms back to the shop and they will either refund your credit card account or send you a cheque.

» Products exempt from the refund scheme include food and drink, medicine, tobacco, unset gems, works of art and antiques.

» Global Blue (tel +42 1 232 111 111; www.global-blue.com) offers a reimbursement service.

POST OFFICES

» Most post offices have ATMs.

» Cards accepted are listed on each dispenser and instructions are available in English.

» Money can be wired, through Western Union, via most post offices and generally takes only a few minutes to receive.

» International Money Orders can be sent from all post offices (a charge is applied).

» Most larger post offices offer exchange services in various currencies, including United States,

Australian and Canadian dollars and the British pound.

TIPS

» Try to avoid using higher denomination notes when paying taxi drivers and when buying low-cost items in smaller shops.

» Never carry money or credit cards in back pockets, or other places that are easy targets for thieves.

» Keep your spare money and traveller's cheques in your hotel safe until you need them.

TIPPING GUIDE

Restaurants (service included)	Change *
Hotels (service included)	Change *
Cafés (service included)	Change *
Taxis	10 per cent
Tour guides	€2
Porters	€1
Hairdressers	€1–5
Cloakroom attendants	50c
Toilet attendants	Change
Usherettes	50c
* Or more if you are impressed with the level of service	

FOREIGN BANKS

NAME	ADDRESS	TELEPHONE
American Express	11 rue Scribe, 75009	01 47 77 79 28
Bank of Scotland	21 rue Balzac, 75008	01 56 90 71 50
Barclays	24 bis, avenue de l'Opera, 75001	01 44 86 00 00
Citibank	1–5 rue Paul Cézanne, 75008	01 70 75 50 00

EVERYDAY ITEMS AND HOW MUCH THEY COST

A sandwich (take-out)	€2.50–€3.50
Bottle of mineral water (from a shop, 0.5 litres)	€0.75
Cup of coffee (from a café, espresso)	€2–€2.50
(Crème, larger cup with milk)	€2.25–€3.50
Beer (Un demi — half a litre)	€2.50–€3.50
Glass of house wine	€3.50
French national newspaper	€1.20–€1.30
International newspaper	€2.30–€3
Litre of petrol (98-octane unleaded)	€1.48
(diesel)	€1.30
Métro ticket (single)	€1.70
(per ticket if you buy a carnet)	€1.25
Continental breakfast (in bar or café)	€4–€5.50
20 cigarettes (on average)	€5.50

HEALTH

BEFORE YOU GO

» EU citizens receive reduced-cost healthcare in France with the relevant documentation.

» For UK citizens this is the European Health Insurance Card (EHIC; formerly the E111 form). You'll find details of how to obtain one from your nearest post office.

» Even with the EHIC, full health insurance is still strongly advised.

» Full insurance is a must for citizens from non-EU countries.

» Make sure you are up to date with anti-tetanus boosters. Bring any medication you need and pack a first-aid kit. In summer, always bring sun-protection cream.

IF YOU NEED TREATMENT

» The French national health system is complex. Any salaried French citizen who receives treatment by a doctor or public hospital can be reimbursed by up to 70 per cent. The same is true if you are a citizen of an EU member country and have an EHIC. If you are relying on your EHIC, rather than travel insurance, make sure that the doctor you see practises within the French national health service (a conventionné), rather than the private system, otherwise you may face extra

HEALTHY FLYING

• If you are visiting France from the US, Australia or New Zealand you may be concerned about the effect of long-haul flights on your health. The most widely publicized concern is deep vein thrombosis, or DVT. Misleadingly named economy class syndrome, DVT is the forming of a blood clot in the body's deep veins, particularly in the legs. The clot can move around the bloodstream and could be fatal.

• Those most at risk include the elderly, pregnant women and those using the contraceptive pill, smokers and the overweight. If you are at increased risk of DVT see your doctor before departing. Flying increases the likelihood of DVT because passengers are often seated in a cramped position for long periods of time and may become dehydrated.

To minimize risk:

Drink water (not alcohol)

Don't stay immobile for hours at a time

Stretch and exercise your legs periodically

Do wear elastic flight socks, which support veins and reduce the chances of a clot forming

Exercises

1. Ankle rotations	2. Calf stretches	3. Knee lifts
Lift feet off the floor. Draw a circle with the toes, moving one foot clockwise and the other counterclockwise.	Start with heel on the floor and point foot upward as high as you can. Then lift heels high keeping balls of feet on the floor.	Lift leg with knee bent while contracting your thigh muscle. Then straighten leg pressing foot flat to the floor.

Other health hazards for flyers are airborne diseases and bugs spread by the plane's air-conditioning system. These are largely unavoidable but if you have a serious medical condition seek advice from a doctor before flying.

---

charges. In any case, you will have to pay upfront for the consultation and treatment. To reclaim part of these costs, send the feuille de soins (a statement from the doctor) and the relevant EHIC documentation to the Caisse Primaire d'Assurance-Maladie (the state health insurance office) before you leave the country. Call 08 20 90 41 75 or look online at www.amelie.fr to find the nearest office. Attach the labels of any medicine you have to buy.

» If you have to stay overnight in a public hospital, you will have to pay 25 per cent of the treatment costs, as well as a daily charge (forfait journalier). These are not refundable. It is far better to have full health insurance than to rely solely on the EHIC.

» If you are hospitalized while in Paris and have insurance, ask to see the assistante sociale to arrange reimbursement of the costs directly through your insurers.

FINDING A DOCTOR

» If you need to find a doctor (médecin) ask at the local pharmacie (pharmacy) or at your hotel. Appointments are usually made in advance. Emergency house calls (24 hours) can be arranged by calling SOS Médecins (tel 01 47 07 77 77; www.sosmedecins.com).

FINDING A HOSPITAL

» There are plenty of hospitals in Paris—you'll find them listed in the phone book under Hôpitaux. Round-the-clock emergency services are called urgences.

» Private hospitals are a lot more expensive and treatment is not necessarily better. Check you are covered for the costs before receiving treatment.

» For ease of communication, English-speakers may prefer: The American Hospital (63 boulevard Victor Hugo, 92200 Neuilly; tel 01 46 41 25 25;

USEFUL NUMBERS

General emergencies
112

Ambulance (emergencies)
15

Anti-Poison Centre
01 40 05 48 48

FACTS
(Aids advice in English.
Mon–Fri 11–2)
01 44 93 16 69

SOS Dentistes
(24-hour emergency dental service)
01 43 36 36 00

SOS Help
(English crisis information hotline. Daily 3–11)
01 46 21 46 46

SOS Médecins
(24-hour emergency house calls by doctors)
01 47 07 77 77

www.american-hospital.org) or
The Hertford British Hospital (3
rue Barbès, 92300 Levallois-Perret;
tel 01 46 39 22 22; www.british-
hospital.org). Both are private.

TAP WATER

» Tap water in Paris is drinkable,
although you may prefer the taste
of bottled water. In public places,
you may see the sign *eau potable*
(drinking water). Don't drink from
anything marked *eau non potable*.

SUMMER HAZARDS

» The sun can be strong from May
to September. High-factor (SFP) sun
block is recommended.
» There are few biting insects in
Paris, but if you plan to visit the
surrounding region take repellent.

OPTICIANS

» Wearers of glasses and contact
lenses should take their prescription
in case of loss.

DENTAL TREATMENT

» EU citizens can receive reduced-
cost emergency dental treatment
with an EHIC, but insurance is still
advised. The reclaim procedure
is the same as general medical
treatment.
» Other visitors should check their
insurance.
» It's a good idea to have a dental
check-up before you travel.

PHARMACIES

» A pharmacy *(pharmacie)* is
identified by an illuminated green
cross. Most of them are open from
Monday to Saturday 9 to 7 or 8, but
they usually post details on their

OPTICIANS	
Opticiens Krys	40 rue St-Honoré, 75001; tel 01 44 88 98 98; www.krys.com
Optic 2000	92 avenue des Ternes, 75017; tel 01 45 74 47 56; www.optic2000.fr
Lissac Opticien	114 rue de Rivoli, 75001; tel 01 44 88 44 44; www.lissac.com
Alain Afflelou	62 boulevard du Montparnasse, 75006; tel 01 40 49 07 45; www.alainafflelou.com
Optical Center	123–125 rue du Faubourg-St-Martin, 75010; tel 01 42 05 40 40; www.optical-center.com

HOSPITALS WITH EMERGENCY DEPARTMENTS		
NAME	ADDRESS	TELEPHONE
Hôpital Pitié Salpêtrière	47 boulevard de l'Hôpital, 75013	01 42 16 00 00
Hôpital St-Antoine	184 rue du Faubourg-St-Antoine, 75012	01 49 28 20 00
Hôpital Hôtel Dieu	1 place du Parvis Notre-Dame, 75004	01 42 34 82 34
Hôpital Cochin	27 rue du Faubourg-St-Jacques, 75014	01 58 41 41 41
Hôpital Tenon	4 rue de Chine, 75020	01 56 01 70 00

These hospitals are all publicly owned and belong to the Hôpitaux de Paris group (the telephone numbers are those of the emergency departments).

ALTERNATIVE MEDICAL TREATMENT	
Association Française de Chiropratique www.chiropratique.org	1 rue Vergniaud, 75013 tel 01 45 80 15 03
Association Française d'Acupuncture www.acupuncture-france.com	International Council of Medical Acupuncture and Related Techniques. www.icmart.org
Centre de Santé Hahnemann Homoeopathy, Acupuncture, Osteopathy and Herbal Treatment	Naturosanté Website about alternative medical treatments. www.naturosante.com

door of another pharmacy that is
open later (called the *pharmacie
de garde*).
» Pharmacists are highly qualified
and provide first aid, as well as
supplying medication.
» They are not able to dispense
prescriptions from outside the
French health system, so bring any
prescribed drugs you need.
» Some drugs are sold by
prescription, or *ordonnance*, only.
» Pharmacists sell a range of
health-related items, although it

is sometimes less expensive to
go to the supermarket.
» In France, some commonly used
medicines, such as aspirins and
cold remedies, can only be bought
in pharmacies.

ALTERNATIVE MEDICAL TREATMENT

Alternative treatment is available,
although certain types, such as
chiropractics and reflexology, are
not widespread.

LATE-NIGHT PHARMACIES			
NAME	ADDRESS	TELEPHONE	HOURS
Pharmacie les Champs	84 avenue des Champs-Élysées, 75008	01 45 62 02 41	24 hours
Drugstore Champs-Élysées	133 avenue des Champs-Élysées, 75008	01 47 20 39 25	Mon–Fri 8.30am–2am, Sat noon–2am, Sun 10am–2am
Pharmacie Centrale	52 rue du Commerce, 75015	01 45 79 75 01	Daily until midnight
Pharmacie des Arts	106 boulevard du Montparnasse, 75014	01 43 35 44 88	Daily until midnight
Pharmacie Européenne	6 place de Clichy, 75009	01 48 74 65 18	24 hours
Pharmacie British Villamayor	1 rue Auber, 75009	01 42 65 88 29	Mon–Fri 8.30–8.30, Sat 10–8
Grande Pharmacie Daumesnil	6 place Félix-Eboué, 75012	01 43 43 19 03	24 hours

BASICS

ELECTRICITY

» Voltage in France is 220 volts. Sockets take plugs with two round pins. UK equipment will need an adaptor plug, which you can buy at airports and the Eurostar terminal, as well as *droguerie* stores.

» American appliances using 110–120 volts will need an adaptor and a transformer. Dual voltage equipment should need only an adaptor.

LAUNDRY

» There are two options if you need a laundry service—a *laverie automatique* (laundrette) and a *pressing* (dry-cleaners).

» Dry-cleaners are easily found but are more expensive than a laundrette. Some have an economy service, not recommended for your best silk jacket.

TOILETS

» Every café has toilets, although they are for customers only so you'll need to buy at least a drink. Some are coin-operated. Standards range from smelly to pristine, and you'll occasionally come across the old-fashioned squatter-style toilets.

» It's useful to have some tissues

with you, in case there's no paper. In some stores and museums you'll need to tip the attendant before using the toilets so keep some change handy.

» Ask for *les toilettes* rather than *la toilette* (*la toilette* is what you do when you get washed and dressed in the morning). You can also use *WC*, pronounced *vay, say*.

» Coin-operated public toilets can be found all over Paris and are usually well maintained, with automatic flushing and disinfecting.

MEASUREMENTS

» France uses the metric system. Road distances are measured in kilometres, fuel is sold by the litre and food is weighed in grams and kilograms.

SMOKING

» Smoking is banned in all public places.

» Smoking is allowed in some guestrooms in hotels.

CHILDREN

» At first glance, Paris is not a children's city, with its heavy emphasis on art and culture and its manic traffic. But there are plenty of attractions specifically aimed at

younger visitors (▷ 284 and listings in each region) and many adult-focused museums offer children's worksheets and workshops. Entrance to museums is often free to children.

» Squares and parks have slides and sandpits, and river trips are also a popular option. You can catch a puppet show in some of the larger parks (including the Jardin du Luxembourg) on Wednesday, Saturday and Sunday afternoons.

» Restaurants do not generally turn up their noses at the sight of a pushchair (stroller), although it is probably best to aim for family-style bistros where staff are often more helpful. Chain restaurants (such as Bistro Romain and Hippopotamus) usually have a good-value children's menu, as do many other places.

» July and August are good times to try to get special family deals at hotels, as this is when they are less likely to be booked by people on business travel. If you need special facilities, reserve ahead.

» On the Métro and most buses, children under four travel free and children between the ages of four and nine can use half-price tickets. But bear in mind that the crowded trains can be unpleasant for children and that manoeuvring pushchairs (strollers) up and down the countless stairs en route to the platforms is not easy.

» Inter-Service Parents is a free telephone advisory service that provides information (in French only) on babysitting agencies and children's activities, among other things (tel 01 44 93 44 88; www.epe-idf.com; open 9.30–12.30, 1.30–5). Alternatively, you can contact Baby Sitting Services (tel 01 46 21 33 16; www.babysitting services.com).

» If you need baby-changing facilities, try the restrooms in department stores and the larger museums. These are often more hygienic and have areas for babies.

» You can buy baby food and other items in supermarkets and pharmacies.

VISITORS WITH DISABILITIES

» Although Paris is not an ideal city for people with special needs, modern or refurbished hotels (space providing) offer specially adapted facilities. Major museums and sights generally have good access and staff available to assist. Information is available on their websites.

» *Access in Paris* is a comprehensive guidebook. It covers accommodation and access to major sights. See www.accessinparis.org. Another useful website is www.access-able.com.

» Mobile en Ville (tel 06 82 91 72 16; www.mobile-en-ville.asso.fr) provides information for wheelchair users and organizes social events and rides through Paris.

CAR RENTAL

» Driving in Paris is not recommended (▷ 62–63), but you may like to rent a car if you are venturing farther afield. It is a good idea to book in advance, especially if you want an automatic transmission car. Make sure full insurance is included in the package. You can also arrange car rental through some travel agents when you book your travel arrangements.

» Chauffeur-driven cars include Prestige Limousines (31 rue de Neuilly, 92110, Clichy; tel 01 47 30 54 54; www.prestige-limousines.fr).

LOCAL WAYS

» Greetings are often more formal in France, especially when they are written rather than spoken. Always offer to shake hands when you meet someone, and use *vous* rather than *tu* when addressing them.

» It is polite to use *Monsieur*, *Madame* or *Mademoiselle* when speaking to people you don't know, although think carefully about whether to choose *Madame* or *Mademoiselle* for a woman.

» The 'Continental kiss' may seem strange, but it is a common form of greeting among friends. Members of the opposite sex kiss each other once on each cheek, though suburbanites and people from the provinces go through this procedure two or three times.

» Communicating in French is always the best option, even if you can manage only *bonjour*, *s'il vous plaît* and *merci*. The French are very protective about their language and the visitor who speaks loud English is much less welcome than the one who squeaks out *s'il vous plaît*, however poorly pronounced. If you can't understand the French reply, respond with *Parlez-vous anglais?* and hope the answer is *oui*.

» Churches require visitors to wear suitably modest clothes and some prefer you not to wander around during services. Don't take any photos inside without checking it is permitted.

» Waiters should be addressed as *Monsieur, Madame* or *Mademoiselle* when you are trying to attract their attention. Never use *garçon*.

CONVERSION CHART

FROM	TO	MULTIPLY BY
Inches	Centimetres	2.54
Centimetres	Inches	0.3937
Feet	Metres	0.3048
Metres	Feet	3.2810
Yards	Metres	0.9144
Metres	Yards	1.0940
Miles	Kilometres	1.6090
Kilometres	Miles	0.6214
Acres	Hectares	0.4047
Hectares	Acres	2.4710
Gallons	Litres	4.5460
Litres	Gallons	0.2200
Ounces	Grams	28.35
Grams	Ounces	0.0353
Pounds	Grams	453.6
Grams	Pounds	0.0022
Pounds	Kilograms	0.4536
Kilograms	Pounds	2.205
Tons	Tonnes	1.0160
Tonnes	Tons	0.9842

CAR RENTAL COMPANIES INCLUDE

NAME	ADDRESS	TELEPHONE	WEBSITE
Ada	Gare du Nord, 75010	01 44 65 00 10	www.ada.fr
Avis	5 rue Bixio, 75007	0821 230 760	www.avis.fr
Citer	42 cours de Vincennes, 75012	01 44 73 07 41	www.citer.fr
Europcar	Central booking	0825 358 358	www.europcar.fr
Hertz	Central booking	0825 86 18 61	www.hertz.fr
Rent-a-Car	Central Booking	0891 70 02 00	www.rentacar.fr

PLACES OF WORSHIP

Whatever your religion, you should be able to find the appropriate church, temple, mosque or synagogue in Paris, although Catholics obviously get the biggest choice.

Catholic	Every *arrondissement* has at least four or five Catholic churches. There are daily services at Notre-Dame (▷ 124–127) and Sacré-Cœur (▷ 232–235).
Jewish	Synagogue: 10 rue Pavée, 75004; tel 01 42 77 81 51. Métro: St-Paul.
Muslim	Mosquée: place du Puits-de-l'Ermite, 75005; tel 01 45 35 97 33. Métro: Jussieu, Place Monge, Censier-Daubenton.
Protestant	American Cathedral: 23 avenue George V, 75008; tel 01 53 23 84 00. Métro: Alma-Marceau.
	American Church: 65 quai d'Orsay, 75007; tel 01 40 62 05 00. Métro: Invalides.
	Church of Scotland: 17 rue Bayard, 75008; tel 01 48 78 47 94. Métro: Franklin D. Roosevelt.
	St-George's English Church: 7 rue Auguste Vacquerie, 75016; tel 01 47 20 22 51. Métro: Charles de Gaulle-Étoile.
	St-Michael's Church of England: 5 rue d'Aguesseau, 75008; tel 01 47 42 70 88. Métro: Madeleine.
Russian Orthodox	St-Alexandre de la Néva: 12 rue Daru, 75008; tel 01 42 27 37 34. Métro: Courcelles.

FINDING HELP

Most visits to Paris are trouble-free, but make sure you have adequate insurance to cover any health emergencies, thefts or legal costs that may arise. If you do become the victim of crime, it is likely to be at the hands of a pickpocket, so always keep your money and mobile phone safely tucked away.

PERSONAL SECURITY

» Take a note of your traveller's cheque number, as you will need it to make a claim in case of loss.
» Don't keep wallets, purses or mobile phones in the back pockets of trousers, or anywhere else that is easily accessible to thieves. Belt bags can be particular targets as thieves know you are likely to have valuables in them. Keep an eye on your bags in restaurants, bars and on the Métro, and hold shoulder bags close to you, fastener inwards, when you are walking in the streets.
» Thieves like crowded Métro trains, airports, the Gare du Nord station, flea markets and tourist hotspots. Be especially vigilant if someone bumps into you—it may be a ploy to distract you while someone snatches your money.
» If you are the victim of theft, you must report it at the local police station (commissariat) if you want to claim on your insurance. Keep the statement the police give you. You must also contact your credit card company as soon as possible to cancel any stolen cards.
» Paris is no more or less safe for women visitors than any other western European city. Be alert and deal with unwanted attention firmly and politely.
» Keep valuable items in your hotel safe.
» Outside the périphérique, some of Paris's suburbs can be rough.

Unless you are with someone who knows the city well, it is best to stick to central areas.

LOSS OF PASSPORT

» Note your passport number and photocopy the page that carries your details, in case of loss or theft. If you lose it, report it to the police, then contact your embassy.

POLICE

» Each arrondissement has several police stations, including a main one that is open 24 hours where you can report crime. For information on driving licences and residency permits, go to the central Préfecture de Police, on the Île de la Cité.

» The Paris police wear blue uniforms, with dark blue caps. The Seine is under the control of the river police. Demonstrations are watched over by the CRS.

FIRE

The French fire brigade deals with a range of emergencies. They are trained to give first aid.

HEALTH EMERGENCIES
▷ 270–271.

LOST PROPERTY

The Bureau des Objets Trouvés is at 36 rue des Morillons, 75015 (tel 0821 00 25 25 (€0.12 per min); Mon–Thu 8.30–5, Fri 8.30–4.30).

EMBASSIES AND CONSULATES

COUNTRY	ADDRESS	WEBSITE
Australia	4 rue Jean-Rey, 75015; tel 01 40 59 33 00	www.france.embassy.gov.au
Canada	35 avenue Montaigne, 75008; tel 01 44 43 29 00	www.france.gc.ca
Germany	13–15 avenue Franklin Roosevelt, 75008; tel 01 53 83 45 00	www.paris.diplo.de
Ireland	12 avenue Foch, 75116; tel 01 44 17 67 00	www.embassyofireland.fr
Italy	51 rue de Varenne, 75007; tel 01 49 54 03 00	www.ambparigi.esteri.it
Spain	22 avenue Marceau, 75008; tel 01 44 43 18 00	www.maec.es
UK	35 rue du Faubourg-St-Honoré, 75008; tel 01 44 51 31 00	http://ukinfrance.fco.gov.uk
US	2 avenue Gabriel, 75008; tel 01 43 12 22 22	http://france.usembassy.gov

LOCAL POLICE STATIONS

ARRONDISSEMENT	ADDRESS	TELEPHONE
1	place du Marché St-Honoré	01 47 03 60 00
2	18 rue du Croissant	01 44 88 18 00
3	4 rue Ours	01 42 76 13 00
4	27 boulevard Bourdon	01 40 29 22 00
5	4 rue de la Montagne Ste-Geneviève	01 44 41 51 00
6	78 rue Bonaparte	01 40 46 38 30
7	9 rue Fabert	01 44 18 69 07
8	1 avenue du Général Eisenhower	01 53 76 60 00
9	14 bis rue Chauchat	01 44 83 80 80
10	26 rue Louis Blanc	01 53 19 43 10
11	14 pass Charles Dallery	01 53 36 25 00
12	80 avenue Daumesnil	01 44 87 50 12
13	144 boulevard de l'Hôpital	01 40 79 05 05
14	114–116 avenue du Maine	01 53 74 14 06
15	250 rue de Vaugirard	01 53 68 81 00
16	62 avenue Mozart	01 55 74 50 00
17	19 rue Truffaut	01 44 90 37 17
18	79 rue Clignancourt	01 53 41 50 00
19	3 rue Erik Satie	01 55 56 58 00
20	48 avenue Gambetta	01 44 62 48 00

EMERGENCY NUMBERS

General emergency number	112
Ambulance	15
Police	17
Fire	18

COMMUNICATION

TELEPHONES

French numbers All telephone numbers in France have 10 digits. The country is divided into five regional zones, indicated by the first two digits of the phone number (see chart, right). You must dial these two digits, even if you are calling from within the zone.

International calls To call France from the UK dial 00 33, then drop the first zero from the 10 digit number. To call the UK from France, dial 00 44, then drop the first zero from the area code. To call France from the US, dial 011 33, then drop the first zero from the 10 digit number. To call the US from France, dial 00 1, followed by the number.

Call charges For calls within France, peak period is from Monday to Friday 8 to 7. You'll save money if you call outside of this time. Numbers beginning with 08 have special rates. 0800 or 0805 numbers are free. 0810 and 0811 numbers are charged at local rate. Other 08 numbers cost more than national calls—sometimes considerably more. Watch for the prefixes 0893, 0898 and 0899, which are particularly expensive.

» When reserving show tickets by telephone or calling for tourist information, you may be calling a higher-rate number. This is usually indicated by the prefix 089.

PAYPHONES

» Nearly all public payphones in Paris now use a phone card (télécarte) rather than coins. You can buy these (with 50 or 120 units) at post offices, tabacs, newsagents and France Telecom shops. Some phones also accept certain credit cards, although this may make the calls more expensive.

USEFUL TELEPHONE NUMBERS

Directory Enquiries	
National	118 008
International	118 700

» If you are calling one of the emergency numbers, you will not be charged.

» The phones give instructions in various languages—press the flag button to select your choice. If the phone displays the blue bell sign, you can receive incoming calls.

» Public phones in cafés and restaurants use cards, coins or have to be switched on by staff, in which case you pay after the call. They tend to be more expensive than public payphones.

» Check the rates before you use a hotel phone, as calls can be substantially higher than from a public payphone.

MOBILE PHONES

You can usually use your own mobile, but there are a few points to check before leaving:

» Contact your Customer Service department to find out if you have any restrictions on making calls from France.

» Check if you need an access code to listen to your voicemail.

» Make sure the numbers memorized in your directory are in the international format.

» Check the call charges, which can rise dramatically when you use your phone abroad.

» You can choose to rent a mobile phone or SIM card on arrival in Paris but this can be rather an expensive solution. You could try Call'Phone (2 avenue de la Porte de St-Cloud, 75016; tel 01 40 71 72 54; www.callphone.com; also branches in

COUNTRY CODES FROM FRANCE

Australia	00 61
Belgium	00 32
Canada	00 1
Germany	00 49
Ireland	00 353
Italy	00 39
Netherlands	00 31
New Zealand	00 64
Spain	00 34
Sweden	00 46
UK	00 44
US	00 1

PREFIXES

00	International
01	Île-de-France (including Paris)
02	Northwest France
03	Northeast France
04	Southeast France
05	Southwest France
06	Mobile telephone numbers
0800/0805	Toll-free
08	Special-rate numbers

Roissy-Charles de Gaulle and Orly airports).

SENDING A LETTER

» Stamps (timbres) are sold at post offices and tabacs. Letters are posted in yellow mail boxes. Some have two sections: one for mail to Paris and the suburbs (Paris—Banlieue) and the other for national and international mail (autres départements/étranger).

» A letter (lettre) sent abroad from France should take between two and five days to arrive, although it can take longer. Write par avion (by air) on the envelope or postcard.

» For registered post, ask at the post office for the letter to be sent recommandé.

» If you are sending a parcel (colis) abroad your options are prioritaire (priority) or the less costly, but slower, économique (economy).

» Colissimo International is a La Poste service offering delivery in four to eight days (depending on destination) on parcels up to 30kg (66lb).

GUIDE CALL CHARGES

TYPE OF CALL	INITIAL CHARGE	EACH FURTHER MINUTE
Peak, local and national	€0.078 (1 min)	€0.028
Off-peak, local and national	€0.078 (1 min)	€0.014
Calling the UK, off-peak	€0.11	€0.12
Calling the US, off-peak	€0.11	€0.12

POSTAGE RATES FOR LETTER

Within France	€0.60
To Western Europe	€0.77
To Eastern Europe	€0.77
To Africa	€0.89
To America	€0.89
To Asia	€0.89
To Australia	€0.89

POST OFFICES

» Post offices (bureaux de poste) are well signposted. The postal service is known as La Poste.

» Opening hours are generally Monday to Friday from 8 to 7, Saturday from 8 to 12, although some branches may open later.

» Post offices tend to be busiest at lunchtime and in the late afternoon on weekdays.

» Facilities usually include phones, photocopiers, fax (télécopieur) and access to the Minitel directory service. Poste restante services are available, although you will have to pay a fee.

» The post office at 52 rue du Louvre is open 23 hours (7.20am–6.20am). Other central post offices include:

» Paris Archives, 67 rue des Archives, 75003.

» Paris Bastille, 12 rue Castex, 75004.

» Paris Gare de Lyon, 25 boulevard Diderot, 75012.

» Paris Hôtel de Ville, 9 place de l'Hôtel de Ville, 75004.

» Paris Île de la Cité, 1 boulevard du Palais, 75004.

» Paris Musée du Louvre, Passage du Grand Louvre, 75001.

» Paris Pigalle, 47 boulevard de Clichy, 75009.

» Paris St-Germain-des-Prés, 53 rue de Rennes, 75006.

» Paris Sorbonne, 13 rue Cujas, 75005.

LAPTOPS

» Most hotels provide modem points. Charges may apply. You may need a modem plug adaptor.

» TGV trains have a few electrical points where you can plug your laptop in if your battery needs recharging, but you'll need a two-pin continental plug or an adaptor.

INTERNET ACCESS

» Internet access is now fairly widespread in the capital.

» You can connect to the Net in trendy cybercafés.

» Some hotels and libraries have internet terminals.

» Many hotels and public buildings have WiFi access but may charge.

CYBERCAFÉS AND INTERNET VENUES

La Baguenaude	30 rue Grande Truanderie, 75001
	tel 01 40 26 27 74; www.labaguenaude.com
Cybersquare	1 place de la République, 75003
	tel 01 48 87 82 36; www.cybersquare-paris.com
Luxembourg Micro	81 boulevard St-Michel, 76005
	tel 01 46 33 27 98; www.luxembourg-micro.com
Le Meilleur des Mondes	4b rue Michel Chasles
	tel 01 43 46 01 64; www.meilleurdesmondes.com
Milk	20 rue Faubourg St-Antoine, 75012
	tel 01 43 40 03 00; www.milklub.com
Paris-Cy	8 rue de Jouy, 75004
	tel 01 42 71 37 37; www.paris-cy.com

Above The logo of the French postal service

MEDIA

TELEVISION

» France has five non-cable television stations: the nationally owned and operated channels 2 and 3, the privately owned 1 and 6, and the Franco-German ARTE (channel 5). Almost all the shows are in French. There are commercials on all channels except ARTE.

» TF1 has news, recent American and French films, soaps and shows.

» France 2 has news, recent French and foreign films, soaps, shows and documentaries.

» France 3, a regional and national channel, has news, regional shows, documentaries and French films.

» ARTE is a Franco-German channel operating from 7pm every day with shows in French and German. International films are shown in their original language and there are also cultural documentaries.

» M6 shows a lot of low-budget films and past American sitcoms and soaps. There are also some interesting documentaries.

» More than 100 digital channels are on offer either through satellite or cable.

» If the TV listings mention VO *(version originale)*, the show or film will be in the original language, with French subtitles (Channel 3 usually screens a good film in VO every Sunday at around midnight).

» Note that French television channels may not keep to schedule.

» Most hotels have a basic cable service, which is likely to include BBC World and CNN. Cable channels now offer multilingual versions of some shows. Ask at your hotel how to use this option. ARTE usually offers a choice between French and German for its cultural shows.

RADIO

» French radio stations are available mainly on FM wavelengths with a few international stations on LW. Reception in Paris is very good. All FM stations are in French. Stations include:

» Chérie FM: 91.3 FM; French mainstream pop, news, reports.

» France Infos: 105.5 FM; news bulletins every 15 minutes.

» France Musique: 91.7 FM; classical and jazz, concerts, operas.

» NRJ: 100.3 FM; French and international pop, techno, rap, R&B.

» Radio Classique: 101.1 FM; classical music.

» Skyrock: 96 FM; rap, hip-hop, R&B.

» BBC Radio 4: 198 kHz LW; news, current affairs, drama.

» BBC Five Live: 909 kHz MW; news and sport.

» BBC World Service: 198 kHz LW; international news.

NEWSPAPERS AND MAGAZINES

» British newspapers are available at large *kiosques* (news-stands) in tourist areas. *The International Herald Tribune* can be found at almost all news-stands, along with *The Economist, USA Today* and *The Wall Street Journal*.

» *Pariscope* is a popular weekly listings magazine. Its competitors are *L'Officiel du Spectacle*. Both are published on Wednesday. *Time Out* publishes a free quarterly Paris magazine available at English-language bookshops such as WH Smith, where you'll also find *Paris Voice*, a free magazine in English.

» If you're looking for a housing exchange or holiday rental in Paris, pick up a free copy of *FUSAC*, a handy small-ads publication published twice a month.

» *Where*, an English-language listings magazine, is distributed free in hotels.

» Weekly news magazines include *Le Nouvel Observateur, Le Point* and *L'Express*.

» For women's fashions, options include *Elle, Vogue* or *Marie Claire*.

» For celebrity gossip and photos, try *Paris Match, Voici* or *Gala*.

CABLE TV

Depending on what cable option your hotel has, you may have some of the following channels:

BBC Prime	With a mix of BBC shows, old and new
Canal J	With children's shows until 8pm
Canal+	Shows recent films (some in the original language)
Euronews	A European all-news channel
Eurosport or Infosport	For major sporting events
Jimmy	Shows some British and American shows like *Friends* and *NYPD Blue* in English or multilingual versions
LCI	All news in French
MCM	The French version of MTV
MTV	Contemporary music channel
Paris Première	A cultural channel with some films in English
Planète	Nature and science documentaries
RAI Uno	Italian
Téva	A women's channel that runs some English-language shows such as *Sex and the City*
TVE 1	Spanish

NEWSPAPERS

French daily newspapers have clear political leanings.

Le Figaro
Mainstream conservative daily.

L'Humanité
Left wing.

Journal du Dimanche
Sunday newspaper.

Libération
A lively paper, more clearly leftist and youth-focused.

Le Monde
This stately paper, left-of-centre, was until recently known for refusing to run photos.

Le Parisien
This tabloid paper is written at a level of French that makes it fairly easy for non-native readers to understand.

FILMS AND BOOKS

FILMS

» The ultimate Paris atmosphere-steeped film is *Amelie* or *Le Fabuleux Destin d'Amélie Poulain* (2001), although it depicts an idealized vision of Montmartre's charm.

» *La Môme* (English: *La Vie en Rose*) (2007) is a harrowing biopic of Edith Piaf, filmed mostly in the heart of Montmartre.

» *The Da Vinci Code* (2006), starring Tom Hanks, has brought a new stream of visitors to the heart of the capital in search of answers to the mystery.

» For a more realistic view of everyday life today in another Paris district, the Bastille, see *When the Cat's Away* (1997).

» *Before Sunset* (2004) was Richard Linklater's sequel to *Before Sunrise* (1995), with Ethan Hawke and Julie Delpy exploring their feelings for each other in Paris.

» Other films set primarily in Paris include *French Kiss* (1995); Woody Allen's romantic musical *Everybody Says I Love You* (1996); *Prêt-à-Porter (Ready to Wear;* 1994), Robert Altman's acidic look at the city's fashion world; and *Jefferson in Paris* (1995), in which James Ivory depicts Paris just before the Revolution.

» No one has better expressed the romance of the City of Light than Audrey Hepburn in such delightful films as *Sabrina* (1954; remade in 1995 with Julia Ormond) and *Funny Face* (1957). In *Love in the Afternoon* (1957) Hepburn cavorts illicitly with Gary Cooper at the Ritz Hotel; she is paired with Cary Grant in *Charade* (1963), a sophisticated crime comedy.

» For tap dances around Paris monuments, see *An American in Paris* (1951), starring Gene Kelly and Leslie Caron.

BOOKS

» For those who prefer to find their atmosphere on the page, Adam Gopnik's essays in *Paris to the Moon* (2000) provide one American's view of life in the French capital today.

Above *Legendary singer Edith Piaf was portrayed by Marion Cotillard in the 2007 film* La Vie en Rose

» Ernest Hemingway's *A Moveable Feast* (published in 1964) and Gertrude Stein's *The Autobiography of Alice B. Toklas* (1933) describe a more romantic era in the early 20th century, when a young couple could live on $5 a day and an art collector could snap up works by Pablo Picasso and Henri Matisse for a song.

» A less flattering portrait of Paris can be found in *Down and Out in Paris and London* (1933), in which George Orwell describes the horrors of trying to survive in the city in the 1930s without a *sou*.

» The classics are always reliable for a vivid historic vision of Parisian life. Read Victor Hugo's *The Hunchback of Notre-Dame* (1831) or *Les Miserables* (1862), or Charles Dickens' take on the French Revolution in *A Tale of Two Cities* (1859).

» Mystery lovers will get into the atmosphere of the City of Light from George Simenon's *Inspector Maigret* series.

» Dan Brown's *The Da Vinci Code* (2003) featured Paris at the centre of a fictitious 2,000-year-old religious cover-up, a story that has captured the popular imagination all over the world.

OPENING TIMES AND TICKETS

TICKETS

» If you want to see as many museums and other sights as possible, it may be worth buying a Paris Museum Pass (www.parismuseumpass.fr). This gives free entry to around 60 museums and monuments in the city, and another 22 in the rest of the Île-de-France. A two-day pass costs €35, a four-day pass €50 and a six-day pass €65. You can buy them from participating museums, the Paris Tourist Office, major Métro stations and FNAC ticket counters. Note that passes do not cover temporary exhibitions for which there is an additional fee.

» Several of Paris's most important attractions are free on the first Sunday of the month, including the Musée Picasso, the Louvre and the Arc de Triomphe.

» Students with an International Student Identity Card and senior citizens receive reduced-price entry at some museums.

» For information on theatre and concert tickets, ▷ 283.

» For information on Métro, bus and RER tickets, ▷ 52–59.

» Most cinemas offer reduced-price tickets for all on Mondays and on Wednesdays. Seats (on both Monday and Wednesday) usually carry a discount of 20 to 30 per cent. Reductions are available for students on certain days (with a valid International Student Identity Card) and for senior citizens (valid proof of identity required).

» Theatres also offer tickets at special prices subject to varying conditions.

» Most museums are free for under-18s and offer reduced prices to young people aged between 18 and 25. Also, most national museums and monuments offer free entry to citizens of EU member countries aged 18–25. Take your passport as proof of residency and age.

» Season tickets are available for people wishing to visit a particular sight or museum several times during a longer stay in Paris. For details apply individually to each museum or sight.

» Most shows, including drama, opera, concerts and sporting events, can be booked through the FNAC shops (www.fnac.com) for a small fee. Tickets for concerts and sporting events are also available from the Virgin Megastore (www.virginmega.fr) for a small booking fee.

NUIT BLANCHE

Every first Saturday in October from 7pm until dawn there is free access to contemporary exhibitions and events throughout the city. Inaugurated in 2002, Nuit Blanche (Sleepless Night) has become the talk of Paris, now attracting almost two million people. Visit www.paris.fr for more information.

NATIONAL HOLIDAYS

France has 11 national holidays (jours fériés), when Métro, bus and RER services are reduced and banks and many museums and shops close. The most steadfastly respected are 1 January, 1 May, 1 November, 11 November and 25 December. If you're in Paris during a national holiday, it's a good idea to ring ahead to see if the sight you want to visit is open.

1 Jan	New Year's Day
March/April	Easter Monday
1 May	Labour Day
8 May	VE Day
A Thursday in May	Ascension Day
May/June	Whit Monday
14 July	Bastille Day
15 August	Assumption Day
1 November	All Saints' Day
11 November	Remembrance Day
25 December	Christmas Day

OPENING TIMES

Banks	Monday to Friday 10–5.	Smaller branches may close for lunch. Others are open on Saturday but closed Monday. Banks close at noon on the day before a national holiday, as well as on the holiday itself.
Museums	Most national museums close on Tuesday (the Musée d'Orsay is a notable exception, closing on Monday). Municipal museums (including the Musée Carnavalet and the Musée Cognacq-Jay) close on Monday.	Entrance is often free on the first Sunday of the month, although this can lead to uncomfortable crowds. The key museums usually have a late-night opening (nocturne), when there are fewer crowds. If you are trekking to the other side of the city to see one of the smaller museums, ring in advance—opening hours can be idiosyncratic and the renovation craze has not helped.
Nightclubs	Club action starts well after midnight and continues to around 5am.	
Pharmacies	Monday–Saturday 9–7 or 8.	All display a list of local pharmacies that open later and on Sunday.
Post offices	Monday to Friday 8–7, Saturday 8–12.	Some branches open later. Paris Louvre post office at 52 rue du Louvre, 77501 (tel 01 40 28 76 00) is open 23 hours a day (7.20am–6.20am).
Restaurants	Lunch is generally served 12–2 or 2.30 and dinner 7.30–10 or 11.	Most Parisians wait until around 9pm to dine out. Brasseries usually serve food all day. Some restaurants close for the whole of August.
Shops	Monday to Saturday 9–7.	Some boutiques have a later start. Lunchtime closures are rare in the city, although small specialist traders may take a one- or two-hour break. Saturday is the busiest shopping day, while on Sunday most shops remain closed.

TOURIST OFFICES

» Paris's main tourist office, which has now moved to rue des Pyramides (see panel, below), is a handy source of information on anything from sightseeing and accommodation to exhibitions and children's activities. You can also buy the Paris Museum Pass and the Paris Visite bus and Métro pass. There are other branches around the city.

» The regional tourist office, the Comité Régional du Tourisme—Paris Île-de-France, has offices at the arrivals terminals at the airports and Disneyland® Resort Paris. It covers the whole of the Île de France, including Versailles.

» In the summer months there are also tourist information kiosks located at various sites around the city:

Above *The Stravinsky Fountain is just next to Centre Georges Pompidou*

Kiosk Bastille

✉ 4 place de la Bastille, 75011 🕐 Jul–Aug daily 11–7 🚇 Bastille

Kiosk Champs-Élysées

✉ Corner of avenue des Champs-Élysées and avenue Marigny, 75008 🕐 Late May to mid-Oct daily 10–7. Closed 14 Jul and 24 Jul 🚇 Champs-Élysées-Clémenceau

Kiosk Hôtel de Ville

✉ place de l'Hôtel de Ville (rue de Rivoli side), 75001 🕐 Jul, Aug daily 10–6 🚇 Hôtel de Ville

Kiosk Notre-Dame

✉ Parvis de Notre-Dame, 75004 🕐 Late May to mid-Oct daily 10–7 🚇 Cité

TOURIST OFFICES	
Paris Tourist Office	**Maison de la France**
(Paris Convention and Visitors Bureau)	The French Tourist Office.
25–27 rue des Pyramides, 75001	(No public access.)
Tel 0892 683 000 (€0.34 per minute)	www.franceguide.com
Open Daily 9–7 Closed 1 May	**Paris Île-de-France**
Métro: Pyramides	11 rue de Faubourg Poissonière, 75009
www.parisinfo.com	(No public access)
Other branches are at the Gare de Lyon (Mon–Sat 8–6), Gare du Nord (daily 8–6), Anvers (daily 8–6), Porte de Versailles (daily 11–5 during trade fairs) and Gare de l'Est (Mon–Sat 8–7; closed public holidays).	www.nouveau-paris-ile-de-france.fr
	There is also an office at Disneyland Resort Paris (Place François Truffaut; tel 01 60 43 33 33).

FRENCH TOURIST OFFICES

The French Tourist Office has a useful website—www.franceguide.com—but its head office in Paris is not open to the public. Some of its offices abroad are listed below.

Australia	**Ireland**	**UK**
Level 13, 25 Bligh Street, Sydney, NSW 2000; tel (02) 9231 5244; email: info.au@franceguide.com	Contact UK office; email: info.ie@franceguide.com	Lincoln House, 300 High Holborn, London WC1V 7JH; tel 09068 244 123 (60p per min); email: info.uk@franceguide.com
Canada	**Italy**	
1800 avenue McGill College, Suite 1010, Montréal, H3A 3J6; tel (514) 876-9881 or 1 866 313-7262; email: canada@franceguide.com	email: info.it@franceguide.com	**USA (New York)** www.franceguide.com email: info.us@franceguide.com
	Spain Calle Serrano 16, 28001 Madrid; tel 93 302 05 82 email: info.es@franceguide.com	**USA (Los Angeles)** www.franceguide.com email: info.losangeles@franceguide.com
Germany Postfach 100128, D-60001 Frankfurt am Main (No public access); email: info.de@franceguide.com		

USEFUL WEBSITES

www.fodors.com
A comprehensive travel-planning site that lets you research destinations and ask questions of fellow travellers (in English).

www.franceguide.com
You'll find practical advice on everything from arriving in France to buying a property on this site, belonging to the French Tourist Office. There are also features on holidays in other parts of France (in French, English, German, Italian, Spanish, Dutch, Portuguese).

www.parismuseumpass.com
The organization that runs the useful Paris Museum Pass (in French, English).

www.lemonde.fr
Catch up on current events on the site of Le Monde newspaper (in French).

www.meteofrance.com
Up-to-date and detailed weather forecasts for Paris and the rest of France (in French).

www.monuments-nationaux.fr
Learn more about some of Paris's most historic monuments, including the Arc de Triomphe, Panthéon and Notre-Dame, on the Centre des Monuments Nationaux' site (in French, English).

www.pagesjaunes.fr
France's phone directory, online (in French, English).

www.paris.fr
The information on the city council's website ranges from current events to exploring Paris's bicycle ways. There is also news about the running of the city, aimed at residents (in French, English).

www.parisdigest.com
An independent site that guides you to the best the city has to offer, whether you want to sightsee, shop or eat out (in English).

www.parisfranceguide.com
A site aimed at English-speakers living in or visiting Paris, with information ranging from fashion to visiting the dentist (in English).

www.nouveau-paris-ile-de-france.fr
Special offers, plus information on events, hotels, the Métro and the weather, on the site of the Île de France regional tourist office (in French, English, German, Spanish).

www.parisinfo.com
The website of the Paris Tourist Office is packed with information on sights, restaurants, shops, hotels, events and the Métro. It also has useful links to other sites (in French, English).

www.parisvoice.com
An insider's view of Paris, aimed at English-speaking Parisians. Includes book reviews, an entertainment calendar and even an agony aunt advice column (in English).

www.ratp.fr
The site of Paris's Métro and bus operator, with information about getting around (in French, English and German).

www.rmn.fr
Site of the Réunion des Musées Nationaux (in French, English).

www.theAA.com
The Automobile Association website contains a helpful route planner if you are planning excursions farther afield. You can also buy maps of France (in English).

Other websites are listed alongside the relevant sights, or in the On the Move and Practicalities chapters.

KEY SIGHTS QUICK WEBSITE FINDER

SIGHT	WEBSITE	PAGE
Arc de Triomphe	www.monuments-nationaux.fr	186–189
Centre Georges Pompidou	www.centrepompidou.fr	156–161
Conciergerie	www.monuments-nationaux.fr	112–113
Grande Arche	www.grandearche.com	254
Institut du Monde Arabe	www.imarabe.org	116
Les Invalides	www.invalides.org	74–75
Jardin du Luxembourg	www.senat.fr	118–119
Montmartre	www.montmartrenet.com	226–227
La Mosquée	www.la-mosquee.com	117
Musée des Arts Décoratifs	www.ucad.fr	195
Musée Carnavalet	www.carnavalet.paris.fr	164–165
Musée du Louvre	www.louvre.fr	198–203
Musée Marmottan Monet	www.marmottan.com	78–79
Muséum National d'Histoire Naturelle	www.mnhn.fr	121
Musée National du Moyen Âge– Thermes de Cluny	www.musee-moyenage.fr	122–123
Musée d'Orsay	www.musee-orsay.fr	80–83
Musée Picasso	www.musee-picasso.fr	167
Musée Rodin	www.musee-rodin.fr	85
Notre-Dame	www.notredamedeparis.fr	124–127
Opéra Palais Garnier	www.operadeparis.fr	204
Panthéon	www.monuments-nationaux.fr	128
Parc de la Villette	www.villette.com www.cite-sciences.fr and www.cite-musique.fr	230–231
Sacré-Cœur	www.sacre-coeur-montmartre.com	232–235
Sainte-Chapelle	www.monuments-nationaux.fr	132–133
Tour Eiffel	www.tour-eiffel.fr	90–95
Tour Montparnasse	www.tourmontparnasse56.com	89

SHOPPING

There are around 17,000 shops in Paris. When it comes to shopping, Paris has it all: fine department stores, quirky and super-chic boutiques, inexpensive chain stores, big and small flea markets, and everything in-between.

FASHION
Clothing, of course, is the thing to buy in Paris, still the world's fashion capital in spite of serious competition from London, New York and Milan. All the top-name designers have boutiques in the city, concentrated on Faubourg St-Honoré and avenue Montaigne and in St-Germain-des-Prés. For those on a tighter budget, *dépôt-vente* (second-hand) shops sell Madame's (and occasionally Monsieur's) designer cast-offs from last year's collections, often at very reasonable prices. The rue d'Alésia is lined with stock shops selling labels at big discounts.

La Vallée Outlet Shopping Village (3 cour de la Garonne, 77700 Serris, tel 01 60 42 35 00; www.lavalleevillage.com; open Mon–Sat 10–7, Sun 11–7; RER line A4 to Val d'Europe, 45 min from Paris) sells designer clothing at discounts of up to 60 per cent. Designer corners can be found in the three top department stores: the exclusive Left Bank Le Bon Marché and the huge Right Bank stores Galeries Lafayette and Printemps. The BHV department store is less expensive and not as chic. It is famous for its fully stocked DIY basement. Chain stores are concentrated in Forum des Halles and on the Champs-Élysées, rue de Rivoli and boulevard St-Michel, while independent boutiques are clustered in Le Marais and St-Germain-des-Prés, with a scattering of more youthful, offbeat shops along the Canal St-Martin, in Montmartre near Métro Abbesses and on and around rue Oberkampf.

If shoes are your thing, head directly for rue du Cherche-Midi and rue de Grenelle, in the 6th and 7th *arrondissements* respectively, for the top names in shoe designs.

PERFUME
Paris is also perfume capital of the world. All the department stores sell the major names in fragrances and every district has a perfumery.

FOOD
There is plenty of choice for food lovers, from foie gras to fine wine and champagne, in shops such as Hédiard and Fauchon in place de la Madeleine, the Grande Épicerie de Paris next to Le Bon Marché department store, and Lafayette Gourmet in Galeries Lafayette. Many *boulangeries* make their own chocolate (look for the word *chocolatier*) and special chocolate shops abound, but you can also get bars of high-quality chocolate in any supermarket.

ANTIQUES AND BOOKS
For antiques and second-hand bargain hunters, the Marché aux Puces de St-Ouen (▷ 225) is a virtual city of antiques and bric-a-brac, while smaller markets at Porte de Montreuil (open Sat–Sun 7am–8pm) and Porte de Vanves (avenue Georges-Lafenestre; Sat–Sun 7–3; and avenue Marc-Sangnier, 75014; Sat–Sun 7–1) may also offer bargains. Roving flea markets *(brocantes)*, often set up in the streets at weekends, are always fun to browse through. Fine antiques shops are clustered around quai Voltaire and rue de Beaune in the 7th *arrondissement* and in the Louvre des Antiquaires, where some 250 vendors sell their wares, across rue de Rivoli from the museum. For rare books, wander through the 5th and 6th *arrondissements* and along the *quais* of the Seine, lined with *les bouquinistes* (booksellers' stalls).

PRACTICALITIES
Stores are generally open from 9 or 10am to 7 or 7.30pm. Most stores close on Sunday, although many boutiques in the Marais are open on Sunday afternoon. Small boutiques may close on Monday morning and at lunchtime. Most stores accept major credit cards. Always say *bonjour* and *au revoir* to sales staff. If they offer unwanted assistance, say *Je regarde* ('just looking').

ENTERTAINMENT AND NIGHTLIFE

Paris has a long and rich heritage in the performing arts, ranging from the classics through to avant-garde, at venues from small clubs to huge auditoriums. To find out what's on, check magazines such as *Pariscope* and *L'Officiel des Spectacles*. These magazines, published every Wednesday and sold for less than a euro, should help to keep you up to date with the nightlife of Paris and the places to be seen. The action doesn't start until after midnight at most clubs, and usually continues until dawn on Fridays and Saturdays. You'll often have to pay an entrance fee, and dress well to get past the bouncers. If clubbing isn't your scene, there are thousands of bars across the city, ranging from small and friendly to fiery Latino or trendy-chic.

THEATRE

The founding of the Comédie Française (www.comedie-francaise.fr) in 1680 kick-started a national love of the theatre, and Paris now offers a wealth of classical, avant-garde and foreign-language plays. French theatre tends to be rather intellectual—the Comédie Française still concentrates on the classics. Many theatres are closed from mid-July to September.

DANCE

Modern and contemporary dance is an active force within French arts. Leading the way is the Centre Georges Pompidou (▷ 156–161).

CLASSICAL MUSIC

Paris has no world-renowned orchestra, and live classical music has less of a high profile here than in some European capitals. However, several ensembles, such as the Orchestre de Paris (www.orchestredeparis.com), have an annual schedule. Versailles' *Grandes Eaux Musicales* (▷ 262) are also popular. Churches often host reasonably priced classical music concerts—look for posters on the noticeboards.

JAZZ

Paris's plethora of small clubs, including Duc des Lombards (▷ 175), cater for an army of aficionados. Jazz festivals include the Autumn Festival du Jazz, and Paris Jazz in the Bois de Vincennes.

BALLET AND OPERA

The ornate Opéra Palais Garnier (▷ 213) and Opéra Bastille (▷ 175)

lead the field. The Opéra Bastille opened in 1989 and is a striking example of modern architecture. Reserve well in advance.

CINEMAS

The French are renewing their interest in home-grown films, but you should always be able to find an English-language movie if you want to—your best bet is one of the multiplex cinemas. Look for the symbol 'VO' *(version originale)*, which shows that a non-French film is being shown in its original language. For something more Parisian in character, try one of the many art-house cinemas.

CABARET

Paris's world-famous cabaret venues tend to attract tourists rather than locals. Many offer a joint dinner-and-show ticket and you can unload a small fortune on the exorbitantly priced drinks.

BOOKING TICKETS

Most theatre box offices sell tickets to their own performances and will accept phone bookings with payment by credit card. If you are calling from abroad, be aware that box offices often have '089' premium-rate numbers. It may be less expensive to use the venue's general administration number, then ask to be put through to the box office *(bureau de location)*. FNAC stores (www.fnac.com) are ticket agents.

For rock/pop/jazz concerts try Virgin Megastore (www.virginmega.fr), or for multi-venue arts festivals try the tourist office. The Kiosque

Théâtre sells cut-price tickets for the day of the performance for most Paris theatres. There are outlets at 15 place de la Madeleine and at Gare Montparnasse. Matinée performances are often less expensive than evening shows, and tickets for that day's performances (if available) are also sold at a discount.

DRESS CODE

Evening theatre, operatic and orchestral performances require smart but not necessarily formal clothing, although you can dress to the hilt if you want to. For other types of performance, casual clothing is perfectly acceptable.

Opposite *Beneath its huge glass dome, Galeries Lafayette department store displays its amazing selection of wares*
Below *Le Champo cinema in the Latin Quarter shows retrospectives of classics*

SPORTS AND ACTIVITIES

Highlights of the Parisian sporting calendar include the clay-court Roland-Garros International Tennis Grand Slam tournament (late May to early June, ▷ 285), the final leg of the Tour de France bicycle race in July (▷ 285) and the Prix de l'Arc de Triomphe horse race in October. There are also many rugby and soccer international matches. The Paris St-Germain soccer team play at the Parc des Princes, although France's international soccer and rugby matches are held at the Stade de France (tel 01 55 93 00 00; ticketline 0892 700 900; www.stadefrance.fr).

Participatory sports are not high on most people's agenda during a visit to Paris, but if you want to sweat off some calories head to the Bois de Boulogne (▷ 250) and Bois de Vincennes (▷ 251) for bicycling, jogging or boating. There are also gyms and swimming pools dotted around the city. For golf, contact the Fédération Française de Golf (tel 01 41 49 77 00; http://ffg.org). Boules, or *pétanque*, is popular in parks and grassy squares.

HEALTH AND BEAUTY

If you feel like unwinding away from Paris's crowded streets, there are a number of ways you can indulge yourself. Treatments include a seven-hour thalassotherapy (seawater spa therapy) session at Villa Thalgo (▷ 213), massages and mint tea at a hammam (▷ 175) or reflexology and shiatsu at Aquarelle Institute (▷ 99).

CHILDREN'S PARIS

Many of the city's museums and galleries arrange children's activities (often on Wednesday or Saturday) and provide worksheets. Entry is often free to under-18s. Parks such as the Jardin du Luxembourg have a variety of amusements for youngsters, including puppet shows, model yachts and playgrounds. Outside the city limits, there are the popular Disneyland® Resort Paris (▷ 256–257), Parc Astérix and the Le 104 (Cent Quatre)—a centre of creativity and artistic production with a special Maison des Petits for young childen.

FESTIVALS AND EVENTS

For the dates of France's 11 national holidays ▷ 279.

JANUARY

FÊTE DES ROIS
6 January
Epiphany is celebrated with a special almond cake—*galette des rois*.

CHINESE NEW YEAR
Late January/early February
The Chinese New Year is celebrated between the avenue d'Ivry and avenue de Choisy.
☎ Tolbiac, Porte de Choisy

APRIL

MARATHON INTERNATIONAL DE PARIS
First Sunday in April
www.parismarathon.com
Paris's marathon starts on the Champs-Élysées and finishes just behind the Arc de Triomphe.
☎ 01 41 33 15 68 🚇 Charles de Gaulle-Étoile

MAY

FOIRE DE PARIS
www.foiredeparis.fr
Garden, home and leisure are the themes of this fair.
✉ Paris Expo, Porte de Versailles, 75015 ☎ 01 40 68 22 22 🚇 Porte de Versailles

FÊTE DU TRAVAIL
1 May
Labour Day processions wind their way through the streets.

LA NUIT DES MUSÉES
www.nuitdesmusees.culture.fr
Night-time access to the capital's museums from 6pm is free for one night in mid-May.

PRINTEMPS DES RUES
www.leprintempsdesrues.com
A weekend of outdoor events occurs at various locations, with a different theme each year.
☎ 01 47 97 36 06

MAY–JUNE

ROLAND-GARROS
www.rolandgarros.com
The prestigious French Tennis Open lasts two weeks and attracts the world's best players.
✉ Stade Roland Garros, 2 avenue Gordon-Bennett, 75016 ☎ 0826 65 00 00 for tickets or 01 47 43 51 61 for information 🚇 Porte d'Auteuil

JUNE

FÊTE DE LA MUSIQUE
21 June
www.fetedelamusique.culture.fr
Free concerts are held all over the city, featuring everything from classical to techno.
☎ 01 40 03 94 70

JULY

LE CARNAVAL TROPICAL DE PARIS
www.carnavaltropicaldeparis.fr
The colours and sounds of France's Caribbean departments come alive in this parade along the Champs-Élysées during early July.
☎ 066 60 40 73 12

FÊTE NATIONALE
14 July
Fireworks light up the sky and fire station bells sound on 13 July for Bastille Day. These celebrations are followed by a military parade along the Champs-Élysées on 14 July.

TOUR DE FRANCE
www.letour.fr
This famous long-distance bicycle race finishes among the crowds on the Champs-Élysées.
☎ 01 41 33 14 00

JULY–AUGUST

PARIS QUARTIER D'ÉTÉ
www.quartierdete.com
Drama, music and dance performances are held in open

spaces all over the city.
☎ 01 44 94 98 00

PARIS PLAGES
Four weeks from mid-July to mid-August
www.paris.fr
Since its launch in 2002, this is the top event of the Parisian summer when the city turns into a seaside resort. Three areas on the banks of the Seine are transformed into pebble and sand 'beaches' that are open from 8am to midnight.

FESTIVAL DE CINÉMA EN PLEIN AIR
www.villette.com
An open-air film festival.
✉ Parc de la Villette, 75019 ☎ 01 40 03 75 75 🚇 Porte de la Villette, Porte de Pantin

SEPTEMBER–DECEMBER

FESTIVAL D'AUTOMNE
Mid-September to December
www.festival-automne.com
An avant-garde cultural festival, at various venues.
☎ 01 53 45 17 17

OCTOBER

FIAC (FOIRE INTERNATIONAL D'ART CONTEMPORAIN)
Five days in October
www.fiacparis.com
A vast modern-art fair.
✉ Grand Palais du Louvre ☎ 01 47 56 64 21 🚇 Louvre

NUIT BLANCHE
First Saturday of October
Concerts and other events take place in unusual venues across the city through the night.
☎ 39 75 (Mairie de Paris information)

NOVEMBER

BEAUJOLAIS NOUVEAU
Third Thursday in November
Bars spill out into the street as the new Beaujolais arrives.

EATING

Paris is often described as the capital of gastronomy so a meal out has to live up to a big reputation. France claims to have invented haute cuisine, and the standard it sets for the very best restaurants—the Michelin star—is famed throughout the world as the epitome of gastronomic excellence.

Top chefs such as Alain Senderens and Guy Savoy dictate the food fads of tomorrow. Alain Ducasse even has an out-of-town cooking school where you can learn his fusion-food techniques, while the Cordon Bleu school in central Paris teaches the rules of classic cuisine. If your budget isn't up to the crème de la crème of Paris's restaurants, there are hundreds of less expensive choices, from regional French cuisine to North African, Lebanese or Japanese. Be prepared to take time over your meal—good food is a way of life for many Parisians and meals are something to be enjoyed, rather than rushed.

RESTAURANTS

Restaurants have higher prices than brasseries or bistros but will often provide a refined setting, elegant cuisine and a good wine list. For a special treat, look for multi-starred Michelin chefs such as Alain Ducasse and Guy Savoy. Dress smartly and book well in advance. The *menu dégustation*, only found in the finest restaurants, is a prix-fixe menu offering a sample of the finest

dishes accompanied by a selection of appropriate wines.

BRASSERIES AND BISTROS

Brasseries are lively but informal restaurants that open long hours. Some have wonderful 19th-century settings. Popular dishes include *steak-frites* and *choucroute* (sauerkraut). Bistros are often small, family-run restaurants serving traditional cuisine, with a limited choice of wines. A new breed of bistros is now springing up, launched by some of Paris's top chefs as satellite venues to their flagship restaurants.

CAFÉS, BARS AND SALONS DE THÉ

Cafés and bars serve coffee, tea (not particularly recommended in Paris), infusions, soft drinks, alcohol and snacks. Most open from around 9am (some earlier) until well into the evening and many have outdoor seating, perfect for people-watching. *Salons de thé* (tea rooms) open from noon until late-evening and some are in grand settings (such as Muscade, ▷ 215).

CUTTING COSTS

If you are on a budget, have your main meal at lunchtime, when most restaurants serve a *menu du jour*, or daily menu, of two or three courses with a glass of wine for around 50 per cent of the cost in the evening. Most restaurants will offer prix-fixe meals in the evening with three, four or more courses, the best of which is the *menu gastronomique*.

OPENING TIMES

Most restaurants and bistros keep strict serving times. Restaurants open at 12 for lunch service, close at 2.30, then reopen for dinner service at 7.30. Most Parisians take an hour for lunch and either eat in the staff canteen or in a local bistro. The evening meal is the most important meal of the day and is usually taken *en famille* between 8 and 9pm. Restaurants stop taking orders between 10 and 11pm. If you want to eat later, try a brasserie or some of the venues in Les Halles or the Marais area. Some restaurants close at weekends and a number close during August when many Parisians leave the city on holiday.

ETIQUETTE

Most restaurants include service in the price of dishes. This is indicated by *service compris* or *s.c.* If the service is exceptional you can leave a tip. Elegant dressing is part of French life and you should dress up to enjoy the experience that is a top-class French restaurant. While few restaurants have a strict dress code, most Parisians dress well when they dine out. Address staff as *Monsieur* and *Mademoiselle* or *Madame* (if over 25). By law, restaurants and cafés must be no-smoking.

A QUICK GUIDE TO CUISINE IN PARIS
REGIONAL FRENCH

The advantage of dining in Paris is that you can eat the great regional dishes without leaving town. Below is a quick guide to French regional cuisine. For the names of individual dishes, see the Menu Reader, ▷ 288–289. For restaurants serving regional French cuisine, see Restaurants by Cuisine, ▷ 291.

The Mediterranean

The sultry climate of Languedoc-Roussillon and Provence encourages wonderful fresh produce. The staples of dishes *à la provençale* include wild herbs, virgin olive oil and garlic. *Ratatouille*—tomatoes, onions, courgettes (zucchini) and aubergines (eggplants) cooked slowly in garlic and olive oil—epitomizes the cuisine of the region. In days gone by meat was tough (raised on the poor sun-shrivelled grasslands of the upper hills) and cooked slowly in casseroles such as daubes or *estouffades* to bring out the taste. The most famous is cassoulet, a slow-cooked dish of sausages and duck or goose with haricot beans.

The Pyrenees and the southwest

The cuisine of the southwest offers some of the quintessential French luxury foods—truffles (a fungus), cèpes (a form of mushroom) and foie gras (goose or duck liver). Unlike in the southeast, goose fat is the base of most dishes, the most famed of which is *confit d'oie* (preserved goose cooked in its own fat). Seasonal crops of walnuts and prunes are particularly prized, as is air-dried ham from Bayonne. Some of France's finest wines come from the southwest region, including the *grand crus* of Bordeaux. Cognac produces the most exquisite of French brandies.

Brittany and Normandy

Brittany still looks to the sea for its culinary inspiration with excellent oysters, shellfish and fresh fish. The dish *lobster à l'Armoricaine* was invented in the Côtes-d'Armor. Lambs raised on the salt flats of the coastal plains around the Baie du Mont-St-Michel and the Cotentin Peninsula are said to have a hint of salt in their meat. Normandy's cuisine concentrates on two main products—pork and apples. Every morsel of the pig is used—even the intestines are transformed into delicious *andouilles* (sausages). Apples don't form the accompaniment to pork but are turned into excellent cider and calvados (apple brandy). Pancakes are the predominant desserts of the region and Normandy produces one of the country's finest cheeses, Camembert.

Alsace-Lorraine

Alsace-Lorraine, in the northeast, has bounced between France and Germany for centuries and dishes like *choucroute* (pickled cabbage with sausage, smoked ham and pork) or *cervelas* (sausage) salad are popular, accompanied by wines such as Riesling and Gewürztraminer. Quiche Lorraine was invented here. Munster is a soft fermented cheese from the Vosges mountains, often with added cumin.

Jura and the Alps

Until recently these mountain areas had to be self-sufficient in winter and prepared foods accordingly. They still have an excellent reputation for *charcuterie* (dried and prepared meats) and jams. Gratin and fondues are traditional dishes.

Burgundy and the northern Rhône

Praised by the French as the birthplace of cuisine during the Middle Ages, Burgundy matches its top-notch wines with sublime dishes such as *boeuf bourguignon* (beef in red wine), *coq au vin* (male chicken in red wine sauce) and delicious *escargots* (snails).

VEGETARIAN

Traditional French dishes are usually meat or fish based, but some restaurants specialize in non-meat dishes (▷ 291).

WORLD

Paris has a vast selection of restaurants serving non-French cuisine, ranging from Italian and Belgian to Japanese, Chinese and Thai. North African dishes are popular and couscous restaurants can be found in every *quartier*. Couscous is wheat grain (coarse semolina) steamed over broth and then heaped in a moist, buttery pile and topped with fresh vegetable stew. This comes with your choice of meat—the best bet is usually *brochettes d'agneau* (lamb kebabs) or *méchoui* (roast lamb). The other mainstay of Moroccan, Algerian and Tunisian cuisine is the *tagine*. Baked in a clay dish, *tagine* is a meat stew (lamb or chicken) with added olives, almonds, prunes and preserved lemons. You can find Chinese restaurants all over the city, especially in Chinatown in the 13th *arrondissement*. For kosher restaurants, try Le Marais.

HAUTE CUISINE

Haute cuisine is top-quality cooking practised by chefs such as Guy Savoy and Alain Ducasse. In recent years it has been influenced by nouvelle cuisine, leading to generally lighter dishes.

Opposite *Dine beneath the glass dome at Brasserie Printemps in Printemps store*

THE MEDITERRANEAN

...à la languedocienne: with tomatoes, aubergines (eggplant), cèpes (a type of mushroom) and garlic.

...à la niçoise: with olive oil, garlic, tomatoes, onion and herbs, plus olives, capers, anchovies and tarragon.

...à la provençale: with olive oil, garlic, tomatoes, onions and herbs.

Bouillabaisse: fish stew served with *aioli* (garlic mayonnaise) or *rouille* (chilli and garlic mayonnaise).

Brandade de morue: paste of salt cod, milk, garlic and olive oil.

Cargolade: stew of snails in wine.

Cassoulet: a thick stew of haricot beans and garlic with duck or goose and pork sausage.

Daube: meat stewed in wine.

Foie gras à la toulousaine: goose liver in pastry.

Pistou: sauce comprising ground garlic, basil and cheese bound with olive oil.

Ratatouille: tomatoes, onions, courgettes (zucchini) and aubergines (eggplants) slow-cooked in garlic and olive oil.

Salade niçoise: tomatoes, French beans, anchovies, olives, peppers and boiled eggs.

Soupe de poisson: a soup of puréed mixed fish.

THE PYRENEES AND THE SOUTHWEST

...à la basquaise: meat served with Bayonne ham, cèpes and potatoes.

...à la bordelaise: with red wine sauce accompanied by mixed vegetables.

...à la landaise: dishes cooked in goose fat with garlic.

...à la périgourdine: accompanied by a truffle or foie gras sauce, or stuffed with truffles or foie gras.

Confit de canard: pieces of duck that are salted, cooked and then preserved in their own fat.

Foie gras: the enlarged liver of maize-fed geese or ducks, cooked and served either whole or in slices hot or cold.

Lièvre à la royale: hare boned and stuffed with bacon cooked in wine and served with a truffle sauce.

Magret de canard: boned duck breast, grilled or fried.

BRITTANY, NORMANDY AND THE LOIRE

Agneau de prés-salés: lamb from animals raised on the salt marshes.

Beurre blanc: butter whipped with white wine vinegar and shallots.

Châteaubriand: a thick cut of tenderloin steak for two people with shallot, herb and white wine sauce.

Coquille St-Jacques: scallop served hot in its shell in a cream sauce topped with melted cheese or toasted breadcrumbs.

Cotriade: fish stew.

Crêpes and galettes: pancakes with either sweet or non-sweet fillings.

Homard à l'armoricaine: lobster served flambéed in a cream and wine sauce.

Moules marinières: mussels in a white wine, shallot and parsley sauce.

Noisette de porc aux pruneaux: loin of pork cooked with prunes.

Plat (assiette or plateau) de fruits de mer: seafood platter consisting of mixed crayfish *(langouste)*, oysters *(huîtres)*, prawns/shrimps *(crevettes)*, mussels *(moules)*, crab *(crabes)* and whelks *(bulots)*, served on ice.

Sauce normande: made with cider and cream.

Tarte tatin: upside-down apple tart.

THE NORTH AND ALSACE-LORRAINE

Bäeckeoffe: mixed meat cooked in wine with potatoes and onions.

Carbonnade flamande: beef slow-cooked in beer and spices.

Chou rouge à flamande: red cabbage cooked with apples in vinegar and sugar.

Choucroute garnie: pickled cabbage cooked in wine with pork, sausage and smoked ham, served with boiled potatoes.

Jambon en croûte: ham in a pastry case.

Quiche Lorraine: egg custard tart with bacon, onions and herbs.

Salade de cervelas: cold sausage in vinaigrette sauce.

Waterzooi: a soup originating from Belgium, made of a vegetable and cream stew, with either chicken or freshwater fish.

BURGUNDY AND THE NORTHERN RHÔNE

Andouille: tripe and pork sausage served cold.

Andouillette: tripe and pork sausage served hot, usually grilled.

Boeuf bourguignon: beef slow cooked with onions and mushrooms in red wine.

Boudin: black pudding/blood sausage.

Coq au vin: male chicken with mushrooms and onions stewed in red wine (traditionally Chambertin).

Escargots à la bourguignonne: snails in garlic and parsley butter.

Jambon persillé: ham and parsley in jelly served cold in slices.

Pommes à la lyonnaise: fried sliced potatoes and onions.

Poulet de Bresse: chicken from Bourg en Bresse (considered the best in France).

Poulet (or jau) au sang: chicken in a blood-thickened sauce.

Quenelles de brochet: individual fish mousses with cream sauce.

Saladier à la lyonnaise: cooked sheep's feet and pig's trotters, ox tongue and calf's head served with vinaigrette dressing.

Opposite *La Crémaillère 1900 is a classic French brasserie on place du Tertre, Montmartre*

JURA AND THE ALPS

Diots: pork sausages.

Fondue: two different types: *au fromage*, bread cubes dipped in molten cheese mixed with wine (and sometimes kirsch); or *bourguignonne*: meat cubes cooked in oil, then dipped into sauces.

Gratin dauphinois: sliced potatoes baked in milk with nutmeg.

Gratin savoyard: sliced potatoes with cheese cooked in stock.

CORSICA

Aziminu: a type of *bouillabaisse* (see The Mediterranean).

Brocciu: a sheep's cheese found only on Corsica.

Fiadone: cheesecake with lemon.

Fritelles de brocciu: fried doughnuts of cheese and chestnut flour.

Oursins: sea urchins, a local delicacy.

Piverunta: lamb stew with bell peppers.

Raffia: a skewer of roasted lamb offal.

Sanglier: wild or semi-wild pig (wild boar).

Tianu di fave: pork stew with haricot beans.

SAUCES

…à la meunière: a method of serving fish, fried and served with butter, lemon juice and parsley.

Béarnaise: egg yolk, vinegar, butter, white wine, shallots and tarragon.

Béchamel: a classic sauce of flour, butter and milk. Often a base of other sauces such as mornay, with cheese.

Chasseur: hunter's style, cooked with wine, mushrooms, shallots and herbs.

Demi-glace: brown sauce of stock with sherry or Madeira wine.

Diane: cream and pepper sauce.

HOW TO ORDER STEAK

The French taste is for meat to be lightly cooked. Lamb will automatically come rare (unless you demand otherwise). If you order steak, you will be asked how you would like it cooked. The options are as follows:

Bleu: blue, the rarest steak, served warm on the outside but uncooked and cool in the middle.

Saignant: bloody, or rare, the steak is cooked until it starts to bleed and is warm in the middle.

Above *A typical menu of a restaurant serving traditional French cuisine*

À point: literally 'at the point'. The meat is cooked until it just stops bleeding. Many restaurants serve steak *à point* with some blood in the middle. Those who want a warm pink middle but no visible blood could try asking for steak *plus à point*. It's not an official term, but good restaurants should oblige.

Bien cuit: 'well cooked', served with only a narrow pink middle. If you want no pink to remain, ask for it *bien bien cuit*, although your waiter may not be able to hide his disdain!

Auteuil
L'Auberge du Mouton Blanc

Bastille
Le Bar à Soupes
Bistrot l'Oulette
Bistrot du Peintre
Bofinger
Chez Paul
Les Grandes Marches
Le Train Bleu

Champs-Élysées
6 New York
L'Alsace
L'Appart
Guy Savoy
Market
Pierre Gagnaire
Spoon
Villa Spicy

Champ de Mars
Jules Verne
Le Violon d'Ingres

Concorde
Maxim's

Grands Boulevards
Brasserie Flo
Le Grand Café
Pomze

Grenelle
L'Ami Jean

Les Halles
Ambassade d'Auvergne
Au Pied de Cochon
Joe Allen Restaurant
Le Pharamond

Île St-Louis
Nos Ancêtres Les Gaulois

Invalides
L'Affriolé
L'Arpège
La Ferme St-Simon
La Fontaine de Mars
Thoumieux

Latin Quarter
Bouillon Racine
Le Reminet
La Tour d'Argent

La Truffière

Louvre/Palais Royal
Café Marly
Le Grand Colbert
Muscade
Spring

Montmartre
Au Pied du Sacré-Cœur
Au Virage Lepic
Aux Cadet de Gascogne
La Bonne Franquette
Bistro Poulbot
Chamarré Montmartre
La Crémaillère 1900
Georgette
Le Moulin de la Galette
L'Oriental
Pétrelle
La Poutre
Le Restaurant
Rose Bakery
La Table d'Eugene

Montparnasse
Le Ciel de Paris
La Coupole

République
Chez Jenny
Chez Prune

St-Germain-des-Prés
Alcazar
Au Relais Louis XIII
Coffee Parisien
Le Comptoir
Jacques Cagna
Le Petit St-Benoît
Le Procope
Ze Kitchen Galerie

Ternes
Hiramatsu

Trocadéro
Fakhr El Dine
Le Marée Passy
Paul Chere

Left *Joe Allen Restaurant is a convenient stop in Les Halles*

American
Coffee Parisien
Joe Allen Restaurant

Belgian
Bouillon Racine

French—Bistro
L'Affriolé
Au Pied du Sacré-Cœur
Au Virage Lepic
Bistro Poulbot
Bistrot l'Oulette
Bistrot du Peintre
La Bonne Franquette
Chez Paul
Chez Prune
La Fontaine du Mars
Georgette
Paul Chere
Le Petit St-Benoît
Pétrelle
La Poutre
Le Reminet
Spring
La Table d'Eugene
Le Violon d'Ingres

French—Brasserie
Bofinger
Brasserie Flo
Café Marly
La Coupole
La Crémaillère 1900
Le Grand Café
Le Grand Colbert
Le Moulin de la Galette
Nos Ancêtres Les Gaulois
Le Train Bleu

French—Elegant
L'Arpège
Au Relais Louis XIII
Le Ciel de Paris
Les Grandes Marches
Guy Savoy
Hiramatsu
Jacques Cagna
Jules Verne
Maxim's
Muscade
Pierre Gagnaire
Le Procope
La Tour d'Argent
La Truffière

Above *Classic French cuisine is served at Le Train Bleu at the Gare de Lyon*

French—Regional
L'Alsace
Ambassade d'Auvergne
L'Ami Jean
L'Appart
L'Auberge du Mouton Blanc
Au Pied de Cochon
Aux Cadet de Gascogne
Chez Jenny
La Ferme St-Simon
Le Pharamond
Thoumieux

Fusion
6 New York
Chamarré Montmartre
Market
Spoon
Ze Kitchen Galerie

Lebanese
Fakhr El Dine

North African
L'Oriental

Pan-Asian
Villa Spicy

Seafood
La Marée Passy

Tea Rooms
Muscade

Trendy
Alcazar
L'Appart
Le Comptoir
Market
Pomze
Spoon

Vegetarian
Le Bar à Soupes
Rose Bakery

Paris has the whole range of accommodation options, whether you're looking for sumptuous luxury at the world-famous Ritz, a comfortable 3-star hotel in the Latin Quarter or a low-cost hostel. The city's hotels have had a (sometimes deserved) reputation for being dated and pokey, but recent years many have seen a complete overhaul. Small designer boutique-hotels have popped up in the once-inexpensive Marais district and up river to the west, and some of the classic hotels have added health spas so guests can indulge in some welcome post-sightseeing pampering.

LUXURY
At the top of the spectrum are the luxury hotels, some of them straight out of another era. Their prices on a one-off basis are high, but some give discounts through travel agents so it is worth asking back home before your trip.

ON A BUDGET
Paris is one of the rare European capitals where you can find a pleasant, affordable place to stay in a central part of the city. Prices often drop in July and August, when there are few business trips, and rise in May, June, September and October—the trade fair months. Hotel websites often include special offers and reductions, so compare before booking.

Check whether the room price includes breakfast as it is often extra. It is usually cheaper to buy your croissant and coffee in a local café rather than at the hotel.

If you are bringing or renting a car, ask whether parking is available and how much it costs. Parking on the street can be expensive and is usually frustrating.

Chain hotels on the outskirts can be less expensive, although they lack Parisian character. You'll also have to spend time taking the Métro or RER into the heart of the city.

WHICH DISTRICT?
Every district in Paris has its good and bad points and choosing which *quartier* to stay in depends on your priorities. The 8th *arrondissement* (the Champs-Élysées, avenue George V, avenue Montaigne and Faubourg St-Honoré) has a high concentration of luxury and 4-star hotels and is handy if you want to shop for designer labels. You can also find luxury in the 1st *arrondissement* (Tuileries, Louvre, place Vendôme), although the side streets here have

2- and 3-star hotels. Farther north, the 9th *arrondissement* (Opéra, Grands Boulevards, Faubourg Montmartre) is packed with hotels, many of them 2-star. Across the river, St-Germain-des-Prés and the Latin Quarter are less business-focused than their Right Bank counterparts and closer to the atmosphere of *vieux* Paris. There are plenty of 2- and 3-star hotels, as well as restaurants and cafés. Here, you are well placed for visiting the Île de la Cité. If you choose to stay in less central areas, check how close you are to a Métro or RER station.

The Staying by Area box on the opposite page lists the hotels according to area, to help you find a hotel in the part of the city where you want to be.

Above *If cost is no consideration, the Ritz hotel on place Vendôme offers impeccable service in a luxurious setting*

ALTERNATIVES TO HOTELS

Of course, you don't have to stay in a hotel. For tips on other types of accommodation, see below.

PRICES

Prices given for the hotels in each region are for two people sharing a double room for one night, unless otherwise stated.

TIPS ON STAYING IN PARIS

» The Paris Tourist Office (tel 01 49 52 42 63; www.parisinfo.com) has information on places to stay.

You can reserve rooms if you visit in person.

» To rent an apartment, options include the UK-based Apartment Service (tel 020 8944 1444 from the UK; 011 44 20 8944 1444 from the US; www.apartmentservice.com); Home Rental Service at 120 avenue des Champs-Élysées, 75008 (tel 01 42 25 65 40; www. homerental. fr); and Paris Lodging at 25 rue Lacépède, 75005 (tel 01 43 36 71 69; http://fr.apartem.com).

» For bed-and-breakfast accommodation with host families

you could try France Lodge at 2 rue Meissonier, 75017 (tel 01 56 33 85 80; www.francelodge.fr). Apartments are also available (tel 01 56 33 85 85).

» Some farms in the Île de France have converted barns into holiday homes with kitchens, providing a base for taking the RER trains into the city and for exploring the countryside around Paris.

STAYING BY AREA

The hotels are listed alphabetically (excluding Le or La) in each region. Here they are listed by area.

Arc de Triomphe
Hôtel Élysées Céramic
Hôtel Splendid Étoile

Bastille
Auberge Internationale des Jeunes
Corail Hôtel

Champs Élysées
Hôtel Astrid
Hôtel du Bois
Hôtel Franklin Roosevelt
InterContinental Paris Avenue
    Marceau
Hôtel Residence Foch
Hôtel Tilsitt

Concorde
Hôtel Costes

Gare du Nord
Hôtel Kube

Île St-Louis
Hôtel des Deux Îles

Invalides
Grand Hôtel Lévêque
Hôtel 7 Eiffel
Hôtel de L'Avre
Hôtel la Bourdonnais
Hôtel Duc de St-Simon
Hôtel a l'Eiffel Rive
    Gauche
Hôtel Latour-Maubourg
Hôtel Lenox St-Germain
Hôtel de Londres Eiffel
Hôtel Saint-Dominique

Hôtel Valadon Colors
Relais Bosquet

Latin Quarter
Familia Hôtel
Hôtel Claude Bernard
Hôtel des Grandes Écoles
Relais St-Jacques
Les Rives de Notre-Dame

Louvre/Palais Royal
Hôtel Washington Opéra

Le Marais
Bourg Tibourg
Castex Hôtel
Hôtel Bellevue et du Chariot d'Or
Hôtel Murano
Hôtel du Petit Moulin
Hôtel St-Merry
Hôtel St-Paul Le Marais
Hôtel Saintonge
Les Jardins du Marais
Pavillon de la Reine

Montmartre
Hôtel Damrémont
Hôtel Eldorado
Hôtel Ermitage
Hôtel Particulier
Ibis Hôtel Sacré-Cœur
Mercure Montmartre
Premium Hôtel Montmartre
Roma Sacré-Cœur

Montparnasse
L'Atelier Saint Germain
Hôtel Delambre

Opéra
Hôtel Lautrec Opéra
Hôtel Queen Mary
Hôtel de Vendôme
Ritz

Passy
Hameau de Passy
Hôtel Square

Pigalle
Chat Noir Design Hôtel
Hôtel Amour
Villa Royale

République
Auberge de Jeunesse Jules Ferry

St-Germain-des-Prés
Grand Hôtel des Balcons
L'Hôtel
Hôtel de l'Abbaye St-Germain
Hôtel Atlantis St-Germain-des-Prés
Hôtel du Globe
Hôtel Madison
Hôtel La Perle

Tuileries
Le Meurice

Outside the Périphérique
Auberge de Jeunesse Cité des
    Sciences (beyond Porte de Pantin
    to the northeast)
Auberge de Jeunesse Clichy
    (beyond Porte de Clichy to the
    north)

Even if you're far from fluent, it is always a good idea to try to speak a few words of French while in Paris. The words and phrases on the following pages should help you with the basics, from ordering a meal to dealing with emergencies.

CONVERSATION

What is the time?
Quelle heure est-il?

When do you open/close?

I don't speak French.
Je ne parle pas Français

Do you speak English?
Parlez-vous anglais?

I don't understand.
Je ne comprends pas.

Please repeat that.
Pouvez-vous répéter (s'il vous plaît)?

Please speak more slowly.
Pouvez-vous parler plus lentement?

What does this mean?
Qu'est-ce que ça veut dire?

Write that down for me please.
Pouvez-vous me l'écrire, s'il vous plaît?

Please spell that.
Pouvez-vous me l'épeler, s'il vous plaît?

I'll look that up (in the dictionary).
Je vais le chercher (dans le dictionnaire).

My name is...
Je m'appelle...

What's your name?
Comment vous appelez-vous?

This is my wife/husband.
Voici ma femme/mon mari.

This is my daughter/son.
Voici ma fille/mon fils.

This is my friend.
Voici mon ami(e).

Hello, pleased to meet you.
Bonjour, enchanté(e).

I'm from...
Je viens de...

I'm on holiday (vacation).
Je suis en vacances.

I live in...
J'habite à...

Where do you live?
Où habitez-vous?

Good morning.
Bonjour.

Good evening.
Bonsoir.

Goodnight.
Bonne nuit.

Goodbye.
Au revoir.

See you later.
A plus tard.

How much is that?
C'est combien?

May I/Can I?
Est-ce que je peux?

I don't know.
Je ne sais pas.

You're welcome.
Je vous en prie.

How are you?
Comment allez-vous?

I'm sorry.
Je suis désolé(e).

Excuse me.
Excusez-moi.

That's all right/no problem.
De rien.

USEFUL WORDS

Yes
Oui

No
Non

There
Là-bas

Here
Ici

Where
Où

Who
Qui

When
Quand

Why
Pourquoi

How
Comment

Later
Plus tard

Now
Maintenant

Open
Ouvert

Closed
Fermé

Please
S'il vous plaît

Thank you
Merci

SHOPPING

Could you help me, please?
(Est-ce que) vous pourriez m'aider, s'il vous plaît?

How much is this?
C'est combien?/Ça coûte combien?

I'm looking for...
Je cherche...

When does the shop open/ close?
A quelle heure ouvre/ferme le magasin?

I'm just looking, thank you.
Je regarde, merci.

This isn't what I want.
Ce n'est pas ce que je veux.

This is the right size.
C'est la bonne taille.

Do you have anything less expensive/smaller/larger?
(Est-ce que) vous avez quelque chose de moins cher/plus petit/plus grand?

I'll take this.
Je prends ceci.

Do you have a bag for this, please?
(Est-ce que) je peux avoir un sac, s'il vous plaît?

Do you accept credit cards?
(Est-ce que) vous acceptez les cartes de crédit?

I'd like...grams please.
Je voudrais...grammes, s'il vous plaît.

I'd like a kilo of...
Je voudrais un kilo de...

What does this contain?
Quels sont les ingrédients?/Qu'est-ce qu'il y a dedans?

I'd like...slices of that.
J'en voudrais...tranches.

Bakery
Boulangerie

Bookshop
Librairie

Chemist/Pharmacy
Pharmacie

Supermarket
Supermarché

Market
Marché

Sale
Soldes

NUMBERS

1	un
2	deux
3	trois
4	quatre
5	cinq
6	six
7	sept
8	huit
9	neuf
10	dix
11	onze
12	douze
13	treize
14	quatorze
15	quinze
16	seize
17	dix-sept
18	dix-huit
19	dix-neuf
20	vingt
21	vingt et un
30	trente
40	quarante
50	cinquante
60	soixante
70	soixante-dix
80	quatre-vingts
90	quatre-vingt-dix
100	cent
1000	mille

POST AND TELEPHONES

Where is the nearest post office/ mail box?
Où se trouve la poste/la boîte aux lettres la plus proche?

How much is the postage to...?
A combien faut-il affranchir pour...?

I'd like to send this by air mail/ registered mail.
Je voudrais envoyer ceci par avion/ en recommandé.

Can you direct me to a public phone?
Pouvez-vous m'indiquer la cabine téléphonique la plus proche?

What is the number for directory enquiries?
Quel est le numéro pour les renseignements?

Where can I find a telephone directory?
Où est-ce que je peux trouver un annuaire?

Where can I buy a phone card?
Où est-ce que je peux acheter une télécarte?

Please put me through to...
Pouvez-vous me passer..., s'il vous plaît?

Can I dial direct to...?
(Est-ce que) je peux appeler directement en...?

Do I need to dial 0 first?
(Est-ce qu')il faut composer le zéro (d'abord)?

What is the charge per minute?
Quel est le tarif à la minute?

Have there been any calls for me?
(Est-ce que) j'ai eu des appels téléphoniques?

Hello, this is...
Allô, c'est...(à l'appareil)

Who is speaking please...?
Qui est à l'appareil, s'il vous plaît?

I would like to speak to...
Je voudrais parler à...

DAYS, MONTHS, HOLIDAYS, TIMES

Monday	lundi
Tuesday	mardi
Wednesday	mercredi
Thursday	jeudi
Friday	vendredi
Saturday	samedi
Sunday	dimanche

January	janvier
February	février
March	mars
April	avril
May	mai
June	juin
July	juillet
August	août
September	septembre
October	octobre
November	novembre
December	décembre
spring	printemps
summer	été
autumn	automne
winter	hiver
Easter	Pâques
Christmas	Noël
morning	matin
afternoon	après-midi
evening	soir
night	nuit
today	aujourd'hui
yesterday	hier
tomorrow	demain
day	le jour
month	le mois
year	l'année

HOTELS

Do you have a room?
(Est-ce que) vous avez une chambre?

I have a reservation for...nights.
J'ai réservé pour...nuits.

How much each night?
C'est combien par nuit?

Double room.
Une chambre pour deux personnes/ double.

Twin room.
Une chambre à deux lits/avec lits jumeaux.

Single room.
Une chambre à un lit/pour une personne.

With bath/shower/lavatory.
Avec salle de bain/douche/WC.

Is the room air-conditioned/ heated?
(Est-ce que) la chambre est climatisée/chauffée?

Is breakfast/lunch/dinner included in the cost?
(Est-ce que) le petit déjeuner/le déjeuner/le dîner est compris dans le prix?

Is there an elevator in the hotel?
(Est-ce qu')il y a un ascenseur à l'hôtel?

Is room service available?
(Est-ce qu')il y a le service en chambre?

When do you serve breakfast?
À quelle heure servez-vous le petit déjeuner?

May I have breakfast in my room?
(Est-ce que) je peux prendre le petit déjeuner dans ma chambre?

Do you serve evening meals?
(Est-ce que) vous servez le repas du soir/le dîner?

I need an alarm call at...
Je voudrais être réveillé(e) à... heures.

I'd like an extra blanket/pillow.
Je voudrais une couverture/un oreiller supplémentaire, s'il vous plaît.

May I have my room key?
(Est-ce que) je peux avoir la clé de ma chambre?

Will you look after my luggage until I leave?
Pouvez-vous garder mes bagages jusqu'à mon départ?

Is there parking?
(Est-ce qu')il y a un parking?

Where can I park my car?
Où est-ce que je peux garer ma voiture?

Do you have babysitters?
(Est-ce que) vous avez un service de babysitting/garde d'enfants?

When are the sheets changed?
Quand changez-vous les draps?

The room is too hot/cold.
Il fait trop chaud/froid dans la chambre.

Could I have another room?
(Est-ce que) je pourrais avoir une autre chambre?

I am leaving this morning.
Je pars ce matin.

What time should we leave our room?
A quelle heure devons-nous libérer la chambre?

Can I pay my bill?
(Est-ce que) je peux régler ma note, s'il vous plaît?

May I see the room?
(Est-ce que) je peux voir la chambre?

Thank you for your hospitality.
Merci pour votre hospitalité.

Swimming pool.
Piscine.

No smoking.
Non fumeur.

Sea view.
Vue sur la mer.

GETTING AROUND

Where is the information desk?
Où est le bureau des renseignements?

Where is the timetable?
Où sont les horaires?

Does this train/bus go to...?
Ce train/bus va à...?

Do you have a Métro/bus map?
Avez-vous un plan du Métro/des lignes de bus?

Please can I have a single/return ticket to...?
Je voudrais un aller simple/un aller-retour pour..., s'il vous plaît.

I'd like to rent a car.
Je voudrais louer une voiture.

Where are we?
Où sommes-nous?

I'm lost.
Je me suis perdu(e).

Is this the way to...?
C'est bien par ici pour aller à...?

I am in a hurry.
Je suis pressé(e).

Where can I find a taxi?
Où est-ce que je peux trouver un taxi?

How much is the journey?
Combien coûte la course?

Go straight on.
Allez tout droit.

Turn left.
Tournez à gauche.

Turn right.
Tournez à droite.

Cross over.
Traversez.

Traffic lights.
Les feux.

Intersection.
Carrefour.

Corner.
Coin.

No parking.
Interdiction de stationner.

Train/bus/Métro station.
La gare SNCF/routière/la station de Métro.

Do you sell travel cards?
Avez-vous des cartes d'abonnement?

Do I need to get off here?
(Est-ce qu')il faut que je descende ici?

Where can I buy a ticket?
Où est-ce que je peux acheter un billet/ticket?

Where can I reserve a seat?
Où est-ce que je peux réserver une place?

Is this seat free?
(Est-ce que) cette place est libre?

MONEY

Is there a bank/currency exchange office nearby?
(Est-ce qu')il y a une banque/un bureau de change près d'ici?

Can I cash this here?
(Est-ce que) je peux encaisser ça ici?

I'd like to change sterling/dollars into euros.
Je voudrais changer des livres sterling/dollars en euros.

Can I use my credit card to withdraw cash?
(Est-ce que) je peux utiliser ma carte de crédit pour retirer de l'argent?

What is the exchange rate today?
Quel est le taux de change aujourd'hui?

COLOURS

brown	marron/brun
black	noir(e)
red	rouge
blue	bleu(e)
green	vert(e)
yellow	jaune

RESTAURANTS

I'd like to reserve a table for... people at...
Je voudrais réserver une table pour...personnes à...heures, s'il vous plaît.

A table for..., please.
Une table pour..., s'il vous plaît.
We have/haven't booked.
Nous avons/n'avons pas réservé.
What time does the restaurant open?
A quelle heure ouvre le restaurant?
We'd like to wait for a table.
Nous aimerions attendre qu'une table se libère.
Could we sit there?
(Est-ce que) nous pouvons nous asseoir ici?
Is this table taken?
(Est-ce que) cette table est libre?
Are there tables outside?
(Est-ce qu')il y a des tables dehors/à la terrasse?
Where are the toilets?
Où sont les toilettes?
Could you warm this up for me?
(Est-ce que) vous pouvez me faire réchauffer ceci/ça, s'il vous plaît?
Do you have nappy-changing facilities?
(Est-ce qu')il y a une pièce pour changer les bébés?
We'd like something to drink.
Nous voudrions quelque chose à boire.
Could we see the menu/ wine list?
(Est-ce que) nous pouvons voir le menu/la carte des vins, s'il vous plaît?
Is there a dish of the day?
(Est-ce qu') il y a un plat du jour?
What do you recommend?
Qu'est-ce que vous nous conseillez?
This is not what I ordered.
Ce n'est pas ce que j'ai commandé.
I can't eat wheat/sugar/salt/pork/ beef/dairy.
Je ne peux pas manger de blé/ sucre/sel/porc/bœuf/produits laitiers.
I am a vegetarian.
Je suis végétarien(ne).
I'd like...
Je voudrais...
Could we have some more bread?
(Est-ce que) vous pouvez nous apporter un peu plus de pain, s'il vous plaît?

How much is this dish?
Combien coûte ce plat?
Is service included?
(Est-ce que) le service est compris?
Could we have some salt and pepper?
(Est-ce que) vous pouvez nous apporter du sel et du poivre, s'il vous plaît?
May I have an ashtray?
(Est-ce que) je peux avoir un cendrier, s'il vous plaît?
Could I have bottled still/ sparkling water?
(Est-ce que) je peux avoir une bouteille d'eau minérale/gazeuse, s'il vous plaît?
The meat is too rare/ overcooked.
La viande est trop saignante/trop cuite.
The food is cold.
La nourriture est froide.
Can I have the bill, please?
(Est-ce que) je peux avoir l'addition, s'il vous plaît?
The bill is not right.
Il y a une erreur sur l'addition.
We didn't order this.
Nous n'avons pas commandé ça.
I'd like to speak to the manager, please.
Je voudrais parler au directeur, s'il vous plaît.
The food was excellent.
La nourriture était excellente.

FOOD AND DRINK

Breakfast	Petit déjeuner
Lunch	Déjeuner
Dinner	Dîner
Coffee	Café
Tea	Thé
Orange juice	Jus d'orange
Apple juice	Jus de pomme
Milk	Lait
Beer	Bière
Red wine	Vin rouge
White wine	Vin blanc
Bread roll	Petit pain
Bread	Pain
Sugar	Sucre
Wine list	Carte/liste des vins
Main course	Le plat principal
Dessert	Dessert
Salt/pepper	Sel/poivre

Cheese	Fromage
Knife/fork/spoon	Couteau/fourchette/cuillère
Soups	Soupes/potages
Vegetable soup	Soupe de légumes
Chicken soup	Soupe au poulet
Lentil soup	Soupe aux lentilles
Mushroom soup	Soupe aux champignons
Sandwiches	Sandwichs
Ham sandwich	Sandwich au jambon
Dish of the day	Plat du jour
Fish dishes	Les poissons
Prawns	Crevettes roses/bouquet
Oysters	Huîtres
Salmon	Saumon
Haddock	Églefin
Squid	Calmar
Meat dishes	Viandes
Roast chicken	Poulet rôti
Casserole	Plat en cocotte
Roast lamb	Gigot
Mixed cold meat	L'assiette de charcuterie
Potatoes	Pommes de terre
Cauliflower	Chou-fleur
Green beans	Haricots verts
Peas	Petits pois
Carrots	Carottes
Spinach	Épinards
Onions	Oignons
Lettuce	Laitue
Cucumber	Concombre
Tomatoes	Tomates
Fruit	Les fruits
Apples	Pommes
Strawberries	Fraises
Peaches	Pêches
Pears	Poires
Fruit tart	Tarte aux fruits
Pastry	Pâtisserie
Chocolate cake	Gâteau au chocolat
Cream	Crème
Ice cream	Glace
Chocolate mousse	Mousse au chocolat

TOURIST INFORMATION

Where is the tourist information office, please?
Où se trouve l'office de tourisme, s'il vous plaît?
Do you have a city map?
Avez-vous un plan de la ville?

Where is the museum?
Où est le musée?

Can you give me some information about...?
Pouvez-vous me donner des renseignements sur...?

What are the main places of interest here?
Quels sont les principaux sites touristiques ici?

Could you point them out on the map please?
Pouvez-vous me les indiquer sur la carte, s'il vous plaît?

What sights/hotels/restaurants can you recommend?
Quels sites/hôtels/restaurants nous recommandez-vous?

We are staying here for a day.
Nous sommes ici pour une journée.

I am interested in...
Je suis intéressé(e) par...

Does the guide speak English?
(Est-ce qu')il y a un guide qui parle anglais?

Do you have any suggested walks?
Avez-vous des suggestions de promenades?

Are there guided tours?
(Est-ce qu')il y a des visites guidées?

Are there organized excursions?
(Est-ce qu')il y a des excursions organisées?

Can we make reservations here?
(Est-ce que) nous pouvons réserver ici?

What time does it open/close?
Ça ouvre/ferme à quelle heure?

What is the admission price?
Quel est le prix d'entrée?

Is there a discount for senior citizens/students?
(Est-ce qu')il y a des réductions pour les personnes âgées/les étudiants?

Do you have a brochure in English?
Avez-vous un dépliant en anglais?

What's on at the cinema?
Qu'est-ce qu'il y a au cinéma?

Where can I find a good nightclub?
Où est-ce que je peux trouver une bonne boîte de nuit?

Do you have a schedule for the theatre/opera?
(Est-ce que) vous avez un programme de théâtre/d'opéra?

Should we dress smartly (fancily)?
(Est-ce qu')il faut mettre une tenue de soirée?

What time does the show start?
A quelle heure commence le spectacle?

How do I reserve a seat?
Comment fait-on pour réserver une place?

Could you reserve tickets for me?
Pouvez-vous me réserver des billets?

ILLNESS

I don't feel well.
Je ne me sens pas bien.

Could you call a doctor?
(Est-ce que) vous pouvez appeler un médecin/un docteur, s'il vous plaît?

Is there a doctor/pharmacist on duty?
(Est-ce qu')il y a un médecin/docteur/une pharmacie de garde?

I feel sick.
J'ai envie de vomir.

I need to see a doctor.
Il faut que je voie un médecin/docteur.

I need to see a dentist.
Il faut que je voie un dentiste.

I have a headache.
J'ai mal à la tête.

I've been stung by a wasp/bee.
J'ai été piqué(e) par une guêpe/abeille.

EMERGENCIES

Please direct me to the hospital.
(Est-ce que) vous pouvez m'indiquer le chemin pour aller à l'hôpital, s'il vous plaît?

I have a heart condition.
J'ai un problème cardiaque.

I am diabetic.
Je suis diabétique.

I'm asthmatic.
Je suis asmathique.

I'm on a special diet.
Je fais un régime spécial.

I am on medication.
Je prends des médicaments.

I have left my medicine at home.
J'ai laissé mes médicaments chez moi.

I need to make an emergency appointment.
Je dois prendre rendez-vous d'urgence.

I have bad toothache.
J'ai mal aux dents.

I don't want an injection.
Je ne veux pas de piqûre.

Help!
Au secours!

I have lost my passport/wallet/purse/handbag.
J'ai perdu mon passeport/portefeuille/porte-monnaie/sac à main.

I have had an accident.
J'ai eu un accident.

My car has been stolen.
On m'a volé ma voiture.

I have been robbed.
J'ai été volé(e).

SHOPPING

Butcher	Boucherie
Dairy	Laiterie
Department store	Grand magasin
Drugstore	Droguerie
Dry cleaner	Pressing
Fishmonger	Poissonnerie
Grocery shop	L'Épicerie
Laundry	Blanchisserie
News-stand	Kiosque
Pastry shop	Pâtisserie
Pork butcher	Charcuterie
Sweet shop	Confiserie
Tobacconist	Tabac

IN AND AROUND TOWN

Bridge	Pont
Castle	Château
Church	Église
Exhibition	Exposition
Museum	Musée
Open	Ouvert
Closed	Fermé
Ticket	Billet
Free	Gratuit
Reduced price	Tarif réduit

ACTIVITIES

Hire a bicycle
Louer un vélo

Do a cookery course
Faire un cours de cuisine

Hiking
La randonéé
Horse-riding
Monter à cheval (equitation)
Fishing
La pêche
Jogging
Le jogging
Go sailing/sufing
Faire la voile/le surf
Go skiing
Faire du ski
Watch/play football
Regarder le foot/jouer au foot
Go swimming
Faire la natation
Do some reading (in a library)
Faire la lecture (dans une bibliothèque)
Play tennis
Jouer au tennis
Watch television
Regarder la télé

AT THE AIRPORT

Airport
Aéroport
Airline
Compagnie aérienne
Aeroplane
Avion
Terminal
Aérogare
To land
Atterrir
Arrivals
Arrivées
Luggage
Bagages
Luggage claim
Livraison des bagages
Carry-on luggage
Bagages à main
Luggage trolley (cart)
Chariot
Checked-in luggage
Bagages enregistrés
Passport
Passeport
Visa
Visa
Customs
Douane
To declare
Déclarer
Departures
Départs

Buy a ticket
Acheter un billet
Make a reservation
Faire une réservation
One-way ticket
Billet simple
Plane ticket
Billet d'avion
Return (round trip) ticket
Billet aller-retour
Check-in
L'enregistrement
Economy class
Classe touriste
First class
Première classe
Stopover
Escale
Check in luggage
Enregistrer les bagages
Boarding pass
Carte d'embarquement
Security check
Contrôle de sécurité
Duty-free
Boutique hors taxes
Flight
Vol
Gate
Porte
Early
En avance
Late
En retard
Shuttle bus
Navette
To board
Embarquer
Take off
Décoller
Passenger
Passager
Pilot
Pilote
Steward
Steward
Stewardess
Hôtesse de l'air

DRIVING

Car	Voiture
Motorway (highway)	Autoroute
Bicycle	Vélo (bicyclette)
Motorbike	Une moto
To move (traffic)	Circuler
Driver	Conducteur
To drive	Conduire

To overtake	Doubler
Traffic jam	Embouteillage
To the right	À droite
To the left	À gauche
Straight ahead	Tout droit
Motorway toll road	Autoroute à péage
Red light	Feu rouge
Green light	Feu vert
On the way	En route
To park	Stationner
To turn	Tourner
To cross	Traverser
To fill it up (fuel)	Faire le plein
Fuel	Essence
Unleaded fuel	Essence sans plomb
Diesel	Diesel
To break down	Être/tomber en panne
Indicator	Clignotant
Brake lights	Feux de stop
Headlights	Phares
Accelerator	Accélérateur (champignon)
Brakes	Freins
Windscreen wipers	Essuie-glaces
Windscreen	Pare-brise
Steering wheel	Volant

CAR HIRE

I'd like to rent a car.
Je voudrais louer une voiture.
I'd like an automatic car.
Je voudrais une voiture avec transmission automatique.
I'd like a compact car.
Je voudrais une voiture compacte.
I'd like a mid-range car.
Je voudrais une voiture intermédiaire.
I'd like a large car.
Je voudrais une voiture luxe.
I'd like a convertible car.
Je voudrais une voiture décapotable.
I'd like a 4x4 car.
Je voudrais un quatre quatre.
Is insurance included?
L'assurance est-elle comprise?
Can I return it to Nice/Lyon?
Puis-je la rendre a Nice/Lyon?
I'd like a road map.
Je voudrais une carte.
I'd like a street map.
Je voudrais un plan.

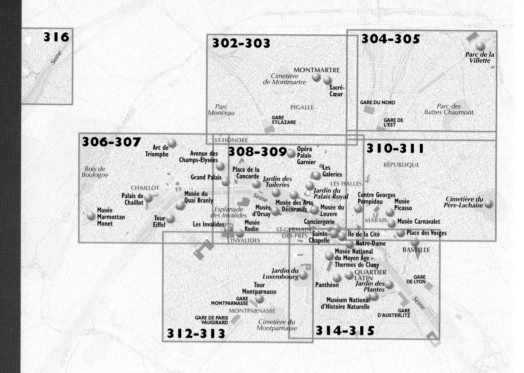

316

302-303

MONTMARTRE
Cimetière
de Montmartre
Sacré-
Cœur

Parc
Monceau
PIGALLE
GARE
ST-LAZARE

304-305

Parc de la
Villette

GARE DU NORD

GARE DE
L'EST

Parc des
Buttes Chaumont

ST-HONORÉ

306-307

Arc de
Triomphe

Avenue des
Champs-Elysées

Bois de
Boulogne

Place de la
Concorde

308-309

Opéra
Palais
Garnier

Les
Galeries

RÉPUBLIQUE

310-311

Grand Palais
Jardin des
Tuileries

LES HALLES

CHAILLOT

Musée du
Quai Branly

Jardin du
Palais Royal

Centre Georges
Pompidou

Musée
Picasso

Cimetière du
Père-Lachaise

Palais de
Chaillot

Musée des Arts
Décoratifs

Musée
d'Orsay

Musée du
Louvre

Musée
Marmottan
Monet

Tour
Eiffel

Esplanade
des Invalides

Musée
Rodin

MARAIS

Musée Carnavalet

Les Invalides

Conciergerie

Place des Vosges

ST-GERMAINS-
DES-PRÈS

Sainte-
Chapelle

Île de la Cité

Notre-Dame

INVALIDES

Musée National
du Moyen Âge -
Thermes de Cluny

BASTILLE

312-313

Jardin du
Luxembourg

QUARTIER
LATIN

Panthéon

Jardin des
Plantes

GARE
DE LYON

Tour
Montparnasse

GARE
MONTPARNASSE

Muséum National
d'Histoire Naturelle

GARE
D'AUSTERLITZ

MONTPARNASSE

GARE DE PARIS
VAUGIRARD

Cimetière du
Montparnasse

314-315

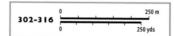

302-316

| 0 | 250 m |
| 0 | 250 yds |

▬	Motorway	🔵	Recommended sight
▬	Main through road	⬛	Building of interest
▬	Secondary road	⬛	Park or garden
—	Other road	▬	Railway station
- - -	Road in tunnel	🇮	Tourist information centre
═══	Minor/Restricted road	●	Métro station
═════	Footpath	🅿	Car parking

MAPS

Map references for the sights refer to the individual locator maps within the regional chapters. For example, the Tour Eiffel has the reference ✚ 70 G7, indicating the locator map page number (70) and the grid square in which the Tour Eiffel sits (G7). These same grid references can also be used to locate the sights in this section. For example, Tour Eiffel appears again in grid square G7 within the atlas, on page 307.

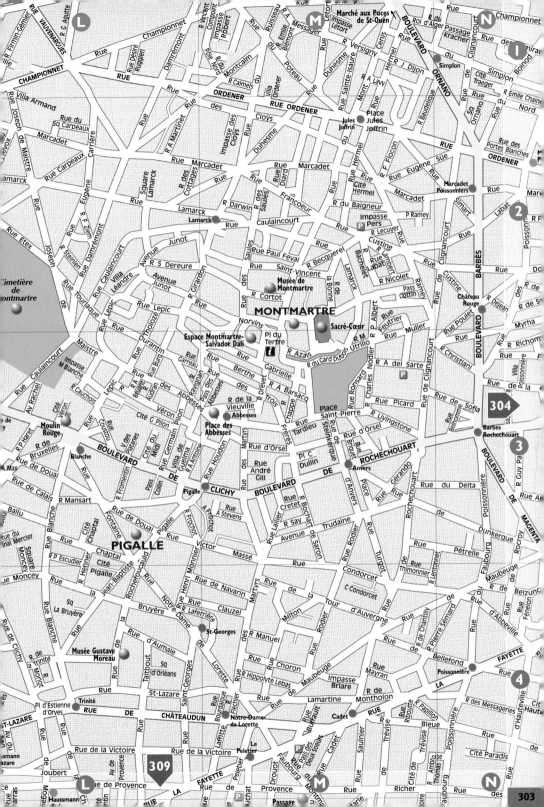

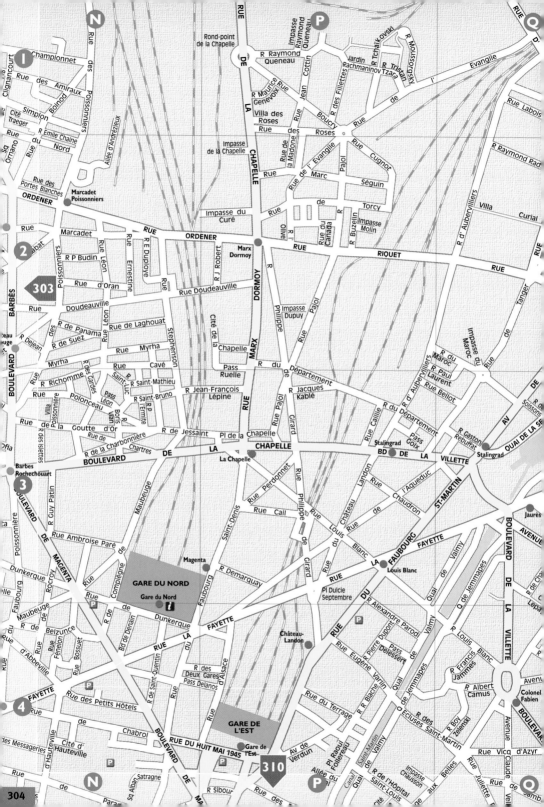

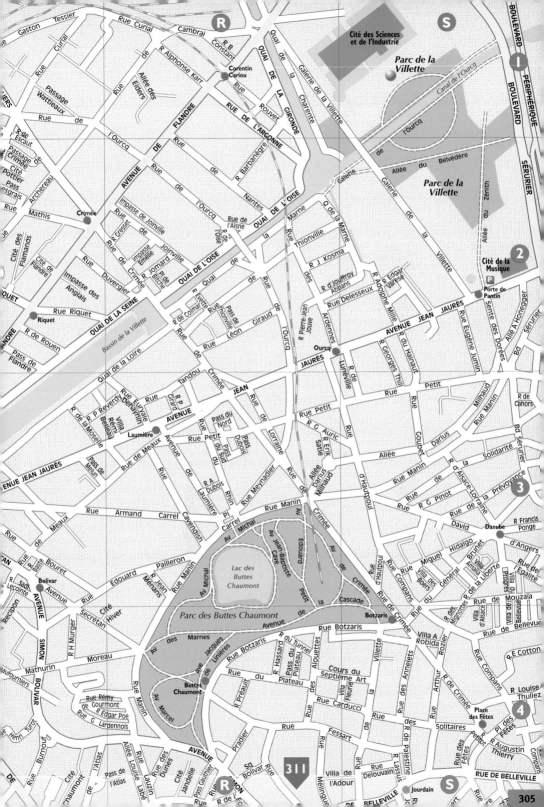

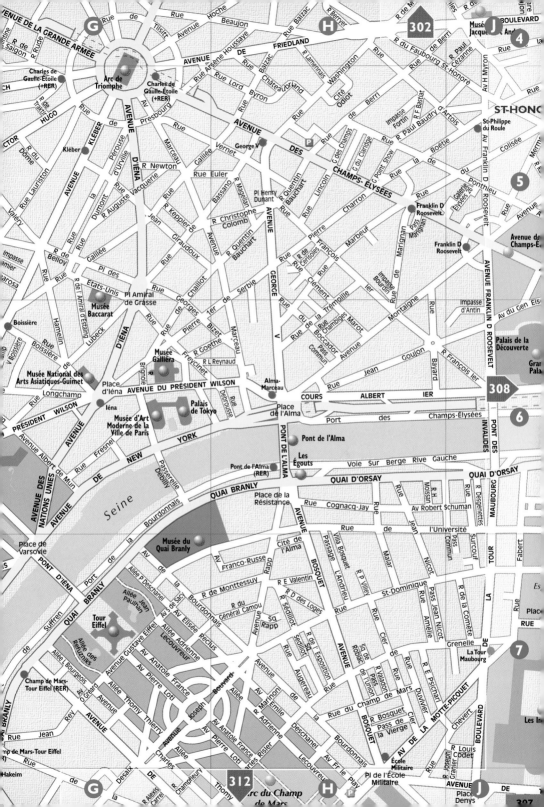

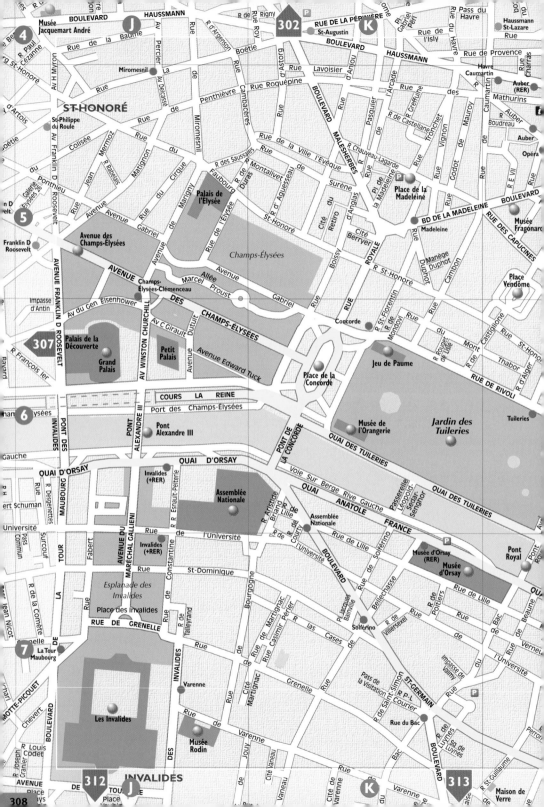

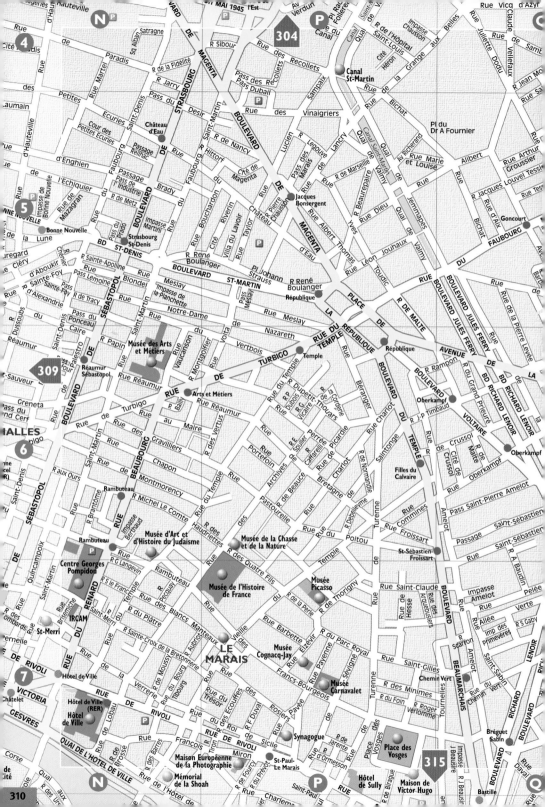

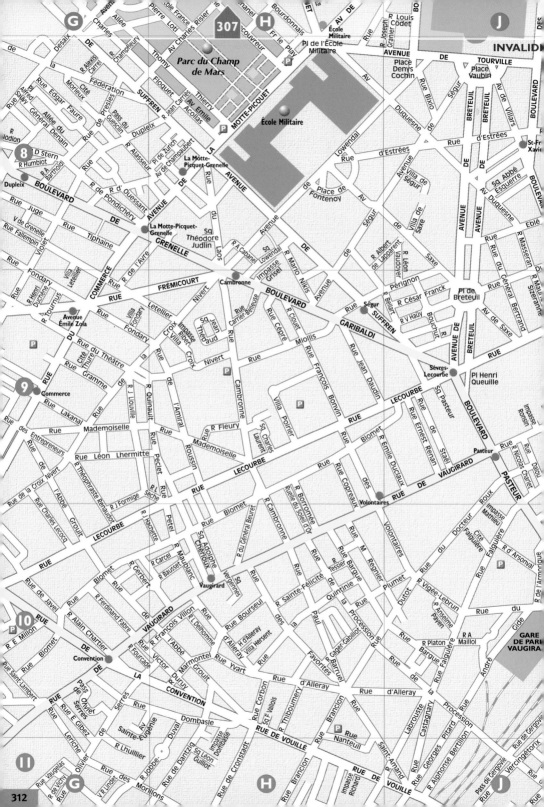

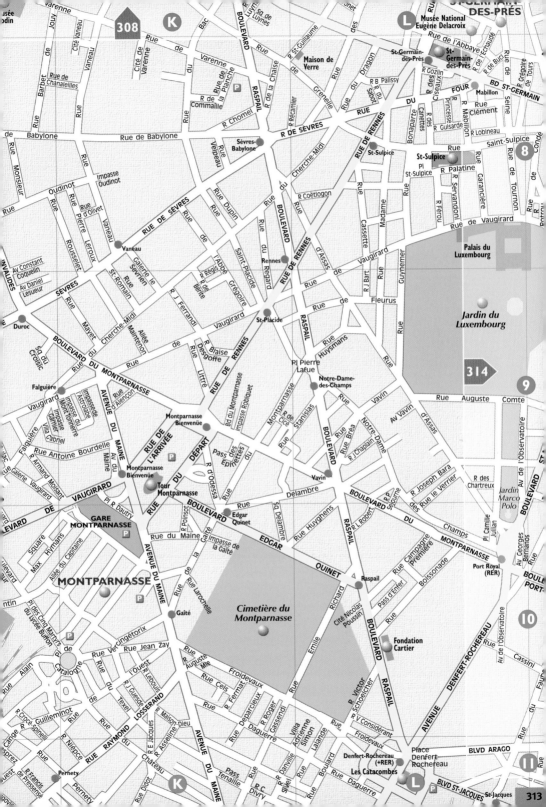

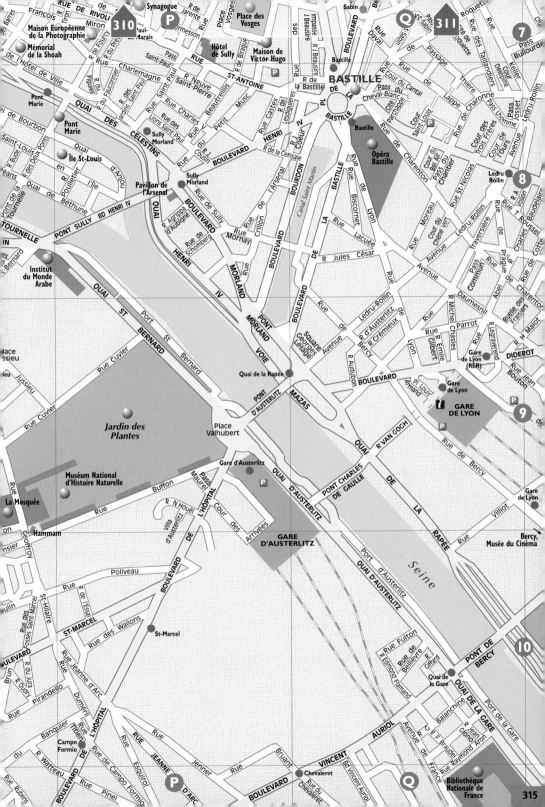

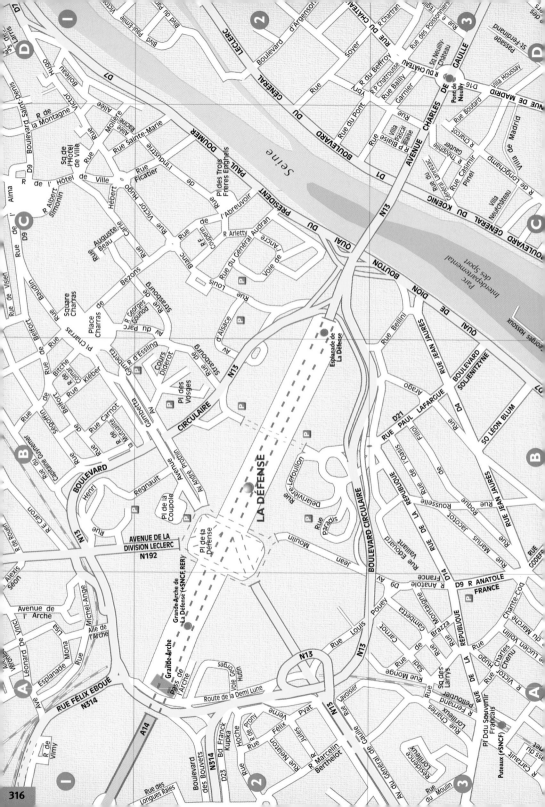

MAPS | INDEX

MAPS INDEX

PICTURES

The Automobile Association would like to thank the following photographers, companies and picture libraries for their assistance in the preparation of this book.

Abbreviations for the picture credits are as follows:

(t) top;
(b) bottom;
(l) left;
(r) right;
(AA) AA World Travel Library.

4 AA/K Blackwell;
5 AA/K Blackwell;
6 AA/K Blackwell;
7 AA/K Blackwell;
8 AA/J Tims;
9l AA/K Blackwell;
9r AA/K Blackwell;
10 AA/K Blackwell;
11 AA/K Blackwell;
12 AA/K Blackwell;
13t AA/K Blackwell;
13b AA/K Blackwell;
14 AA/K Blackwell;
15l AA/C Sawyer;
15r Steve Wood/Rex Features;
16 AA/K Blackwell;
17t Illustrated London News;
17b AA/T Souter;
18 AA/J Tims;
19t AA/C Sawyer;
19b AA/K Blackwell;
20 AA/T Souter;
21t AA/B Rieger;
21b AA/T Souter;
22 AA/K Paterson;
23l AA/T Souter;
23r AA/C Sawyer;
24 AA/K Blackwell;
25 AA/K Blackwell;
26 AA/K Blackwell;
27t Mary Evans Picture Library;
27b AA;
28 AA/J Tims;
29l AA/K Blackwell;
29r Mary Evans Picture Library;
30 Photolibrary Group;
31t Eric Feferberg/AFP/Getty Images;
31b Mary Evans Picture Library;
32 Chateau de Versailles, France/Peter Willi/ The Bridgeman Art Library;
33t AA/M Jourdan;
33b AA/M Jourdan;
34 Chateau de Versailles, France/Lauros/ Giraudon/The Bridgeman Art Library;
35t Château de Champs-sur-Marne, France/ Lauros/Giraudon/The Bridgeman Art Library;
35b Bibliothèque Historique de la Ville de

Paris, Paris, France/Archives Charmet/The Bridgeman Art Library;
36 Mary Evans Picture Library;
37l AA/P Kenward;
37r Mary Evans Picture Library;
38 AA/K Blackwell;
39t AA/K Blackwell;
39b AA;
40 AA/K Blackwell;
41t Mary Evans Picture Library;
41b Mary Evans Picture Library/Mary Evans ILN Pictures;
42 AA/K Blackwell;
43t AFP/Getty Images;
43b AA/K Blackwell;
44l Photolibrary Group;
44r Thomas Coex/AFP/Getty Images;
45 AA/K Blackwell;
46 AA/C Sawyer;
48 AA/K Blackwell;
49 AA/C Sawyer;
50 Photolibrary Group;
51 AA/C Sawyer;
52 AA/K Blackwell;
53 AA/C Sawyer;
55 AA/T Souter;
60 AA/K Paterson;
61 AA/M Jourdan;
62 AA/K Paterson;
64 AA/K Blackwell;
67 AA/K Blackwell;
68 AA/K Blackwell;
72 AA/K Blackwell;
73 AA/C Sawyer;
74 AA/K Paterson;
75 AA/K Paterson;
76 AA/K Blackwell;
77 AA/K Blackwell;
78 Musée Marmottan, Paris, France/ Giraudon/The Bridgeman Art Library;
79 Musée Marmottan, Paris, France/ Giraudon/The Bridgeman Art Library;
80 AA/K Blackwell;
81l AA/K Blackwell;
81r AA/K Blackwell;
82 AA/K Blackwell;
84 AA/K Blackwell;

85 AA/K Blackwell;
86 AA/K Blackwell;
87 AA/K Blackwell;
88 AA/B Rieger;
89 AA/K Blackwell;
90 AA/T Souter;
91 AA/M Jourdan;
92l AA/B Rieger;
92r AA/K Blackwell;
93 AA/K Blackwell;
94 AA/M Jourdan;
95 AA/K Blackwell;
96 AA/K Blackwell;
98 AA/K Blackwell;
100 AA/C Sawyer;
102 AA/K Blackwell;
106 AA/K Blackwell;
110 AA/K Blackwell;
111 AA/K Blackwell;
112 AA/T Souter;
113 AA/K Blackwell;
114 AA/C Sawyer;
115 AA/C Sawyer;
116 AA/M Jourdan;
117 AA/K Blackwell;
118 AA/K Blackwell;
119l AA/K Blackwell;
119r AA/K Blackwell;
120t AA/T Souter;
120b AA/M Jourdan;
121 C Harrison;
122 AA/K Paterson;
123 AA/C Sawyer;
124 AA/P Enticknap;
125 AA/K Blackwell;
126 AA/C Sawyer;
128 AA/M Jourdan;
129 AA/K Paterson;
130 AA/K Blackwell;
131l AA/C Sawyer;
131r AA/M Jourdan;
132 AA/J Tims;
134 AA/K Blackwell;
135 AA/M Jourdan;
136 AA/K Blackwell;
137 AA/K Blackwell;
138 AA/K Blackwell;

139 AA/K Blackwell;
140 AA/K Blackwell;
142 AA/C Sawyer;
144 AA/K Blackwell;
148 AA/K Blackwell;
152 AA/K Blackwell;
153 AA/K Blackwell;
154 AA/K Blackwell;
155 AA/K Blackwell;
156 AA/T Souter;
157 AA/K Blackwell;
158 AA/K Blackwell;
159l AA/M Jourdan;
159r AA/K Blackwell;
160 AA/W Voysey;
161 AA/K Blackwell;
162 AA/K Blackwell;
163 AA/K Blackwell;
164 AA/K Blackwell;
165l AA/M Jourdan;
165r AA/K Paterson;
166 AA/K Blackwell;
167 Photolibrary Group;
168 AA/K Blackwell;
169 AA/K Blackwell;
170 AA/M Jourdan;
171 AA/K Blackwell;
172 AA/K Blackwell;
174 AA/C Sawyer;
176 AA/B Rieger;
178 AA/C Sawyer;
182 AA/K Paterson;
186 AA/K Blackwell;
187 AA/K Blackwell;
188l AA/K Blackwell;
188r AA/M Jourdan;
190 AA/K Blackwell;
191 AA/J Tims;
192 AA/K Blackwell;
193 K Glendenning;
194 AA/K Blackwell;
195 AA/K Blackwell;
196 AA/C Sawyer;
197 AA/K Blackwell;
198 AA/M Jourdan;
200 Louvre, Paris, France/The Bridgeman Art Library;
201 AA/M Jourdan;
202l AA/M Jourdan;
202r Louvre, Paris, France/Giraudon/The Bridgeman Art Library;
203 AA/P Enticknap;
204 AA/K Blackwell;
205 AA/K Blackwell;

206 AA/M Jourdan;
207 AA/K Blackwell;
208 AA/K Blackwell;
209 AA/M Jourdan;
210 AA/K Blackwell;
212 AA/K Blackwell;
214 AA/K Blackwell;
216 AA/K Blackwell;
220 AA/K Blackwell;
224 AA/M Jourdan;
225 AA/K Blackwell;
226 AA/K Blackwell;
227l AA/K Blackwell;
227r AA/K Blackwell;
228 AA/C Sawyer;
229 AA/K Blackwell;
230 AA/M Jourdan;
232 AA/B Rieger;
233 AA/K Blackwell;
234 AA/K Blackwell;
235l AA/J Tims;
235r AA/K Paterson;
236 AA/M Jourdan;
237 AA/M Jourdan;
238 AA/M Jourdan;
240 AA/K Blackwell;
242 AA/K Blackwell;
246 AA/K Blackwell;
250 AA/K Blackwell;
251 AA/K Blackwell;
252 AA/D Noble;
253 Michael Jenner/Robert Harding;
254 AA/K Blackwell;
255 AA/K Blackwell;
256 © Disney;
257 © Disney;
258 AA/M Jourdan;
259 AA/M Jourdan;
260 AA/K Blackwell;
261 AA/M Jourdan;
262t AA/M Jourdan;
262b AA/M Jourdan;
264 AA/K Blackwell;
265 AA/K Blackwell;
266 AA/K Blackwell;
267 AA/K Blackwell;
272 AA/K Blackwell;
276 AA/K Blackwell;
278 © PicHouse/Everett/Rex Features;
280 Eddie Linssen/Alamy;
282 AA/K Blackwell;
283 AA/K Blackwell;
284 AA/K Blackwell;
286 AA/K Blackwell;

289t AA/K Blackwell;
289b AA/K Blackwell;
290 AA/C Sawyer;
291 AA/K Blackwell;
292 AA/K Blackwell;
301 AA/K Blackwell.

CREDITS

Series editor
Sheila Hawkins

Project editor
Strange Editorial Services

Design
Liz Baldin at Bookwork Creative Associates Ltd

Cover design
Chie Ushio

Picture research
Elizabeth Allen

Image retouching and repro
Sarah Montgomery

Mapping
Maps produced by the Mapping Services Department of AA Publishing

Text updated by Lindsay Bennett

Indexer
Marie Lorimer

Production
Lorraine Taylor

See It Paris
ISBN 978-0-87637-137-4
Fifth Edition

Published in the United States by Fodor's Travel and simultaneously in Canada by Random House of Canada Limited, Toronto.
Published in the United Kingdom by AA Publishing.
Fodor's is a registered trademark of Random House, Inc., and Fodor's See It is a trademark of Random House, Inc.
Fodor's Travel is a division of Random House, Inc.

Color separation by AA Digital Department
Printed and bound by Leo Paper Products, China
10 9 8 7 6 5 4 3 2

Special Sales: This book is available for special discounts for bulk purchases for sales promotions or premiums. Special editions, including personalized covers, excerpts of existing books, and corporate imprints, can be created in large quantities for special needs.
For more information, write to Special Markets/Premium Sales, 1745 Broadway, MD 6-2, New York, NY 10019
or e-mail specialmarkets@randomhouse.com
Important Note: Time inevitably brings changes, so always confirm prices, travel facts, and other perishable information when it matters. Although Fodor's cannot accept responsibility for errors, you can use this guide in the confidence that we have taken every care to ensure its accuracy.

A05121
Maps in this title produced from cartographic data © Tele Atlas N.V. 2005 Tele Atlas
© IGN France
Transport map © Communicarta Ltd, UK
Weather chart statistics supplied by Weatherbase © Copyright 2003 Canty and Associates, LLC

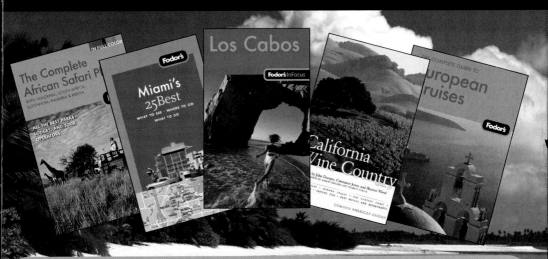